THE GOSPEL AS SOCIAL REVOLUTION

The Role of the Church in the Transformation of Society

Timothy Black

Reach Africa, Inc

ISBN-13: 9798673811665
ISBN-10: 1477123456

Cover design by: Art Painter
Library of Congress Control Number: 2018675309
Printed in the United States of America

TABLE OF CONTENTS

LIST OF TABLES, FIGURES AND DIAGRAMS

SUMMARY

ACKNOWLEDGEMENTS

CHAPTER ONE

1 Introduction
2 Setting the Stage
3 Outlining the Approach
4 Theological Framework

CHAPTER TWO

1 Introduction
2 Defining the Movement
3 Rise of the Movement
    3.1 Early beginnings

    3.2 The Reformation

4 Shaping the Movement
    4.1 Puritans

    4.2 Evangelical Revival and The Great Awakening

    4.3 The 'Great Reversal'

5 Examining the Movement
    5.1 Polarisation of the movement

    5.2 Focus of the movement

6 Conclusion

CHAPTER THREE

1 Introduction
2 Biblical Definition of Poverty
    2.1 Inherent value

    2.2 Relationship through covenant

    2.3 Ownership of land

2.4 Moral responsibility

3 God's Intervention on Behalf of 'the poor'
   3.1 God's provision for 'the poor'

   3.2 Scriptural warnings concerning 'the poor'

   3.3 New Testament provisions for 'the poor'

   3.4 Summary

4 Poverty and Poverty Alleviation Defined
   4.1 Definition of poverty

   4.2 Definition of poverty alleviation

   4.3 Multi-dimensional perspective

   4.4 Narrowing the focus

   4.4 Shifts in emphasis

   4.5 Summary

5 Conclusion

CHAPTER FOUR

<u>1 Introduction</u>
   1.1 Defining Socio-rhetorical analysis

   1.2 Defining the interpretive process

2 Inner Texture of James 2.1-13
   2.1 James 2.1-13 as a rhetorical unit

3 Intertexture of James 2.1-13
   3.1 Introduction

   3.2 The holiness code: James 2.8 (Lev. 19.18)

   3.3 Acts of partiality: James 2.9 (Lev. 19.15)

   3.4 Structure of the argument (James 2.8-11)

   3.4 Unity of the law (James 2.10)

   3.5 Application of the Decalogue (James 2.11)

   3.6 Application of the Holiness Code and Decalogue

   3.7 Conclusion of the elaboration (James 2.12-13)

   3.8 A saying of Jesus (James 2.5)

4 The Social and Cultural Texture of James 2.1-13
   4.1 Establishing the rhetorical situation of James 2.1-13

5 Inner Texture of James 2:14-26
    5.1 Introduction
    5.2 James 2.14-26 as a rhetorical unit

6 Intertexture of James 2.14-26
    6.1 Introduction
    6.2 The *Shema:* James 2.19
    6.3 Faith and action: James 2.21-25
    6.4 Friend of God: James 2.23b
    6.5 Faith and hospitality: James 2.25

7 The Social and Cultural Texture of James 2.14-26
    7.1 Establishing the rhetorical situation of James 2.14-26
    7.2 The cultural script of honour and shame
    7.3 The social nature of the rhetoric in the unit
    7.4 The cultural nature of the rhetoric of the unit

8 Conclusion
CHAPTER FIVE

1 Introduction
2 Developments in Practical Theology and Missiology
    2.1 Philosophical foundations
    2.2 Praxis-focused orientation
    2.3 Rise of existentialism
    2.4 Transition to postmodernism

3 Practical theology as a discipline
    3.1 Practical reasoning: Browning's model
    3.2 'Christopraxis': Anderson's model

4 Practical Theology as an Emerging Methodology
    4.1 Methodology of active mission
    4.2 Strategy for contextual relevance
    4.3 Practical theology requires mission focus

5 Conclusion
CHAPTER SIX

1 Introduction

2 The Historical Precedent for Activism

  2.1 Introduction

  2.2 Early examples of 'activism'

  2.3 Scriptural precedent

  2.4 Warnings from Scripture

  2.5 Emphasis on justice

  2.6 Examples of generosity

  2.7 Evangelical dualism

  2.8 Shift in approach

  2.9 Call to mission

  2.10 Conclusion

3 Socio-rhetorical Interpretive Results from James 2

  3.1 Introduction

  3.2 Inner textual results of James 2.1-26

  3.3 Intertextual results of James 2.1-26

  3.4 The social and cultural texture of James 2.1-26

4 Definition of Poverty and Need

  4.1 Introduction

  4.2 Defining poverty

  4.3 Defining a process

5 Theological Model in Context

  5.1 Introduction

  5.2 Engagement as Christopraxis

  5.3 The South African context

  5.4 Relational apartheid

  5.5 Model of repentance

  5.6 Understanding context

  5.7 Understanding mission

  5.8 Implementation

  5.9 Transformational mission

6 Conclusion

CHAPTER SEVEN

1 Introduction

2 The Continuing Crisis
    2.1 Carnegie 1 & 2

    2.2   The Kairos Document and Evangelical Witness in South Africa

    2.3 Move to the margins

3 Discipleship for Social Responsibility
    3.1 Spiritual formation

4 Developing an Approach for Mission
    4.1 Defining the framework of the engagement

    4.2 Defining the character of the engagement

    4.2 Orientation to community

5 Proposing a Model for Mission
    5.1 Constructing the model

    5.2 Mapping the process

    5.3 The literature search

    5.4 Institutional mapping

    5.5 Sample business interviews

    5.6 Community needs assessment

    5.7 Analysing the results

    5.7 Application

    5.8 Summary

6 Conclusion

REFERENCE LIST

LIST OF TABLES, FIGURES AND DIAGRAMS

Tables

Table 3.1
Max-Neef's Matrix of needs/satisfiers   115

Table 7.1
Outline of the Zanokhanyo training course   371

Figures

Figure 3.1
List of Needs (Human Scale Development)   112

Figure 7.1
Business organisational qualities—Business IQ   352

Figure 7.2
Social IQ and EQ—2008   353

Figure 7.3
Community resources: satisfaction levels—2008 358

Figure 7.4
Felt needs of the Langa community—2004   362

Figure 7.5
The P-Index felt needs of Langa—2004   366

Figure 7.6
Types of social bonding in Langa—2008   368

SUMMARY

The purpose of this research is to contribute to the discussion regarding the role that the fight against poverty should play in the mission of the evangelical movement. It will consider evangelical history and trace the changes that occurred to evangelical focus that separated the proclamation of the gospel from holistic mission that cared for the poor.

The Epistle of James Chapter 2 will be examined according to socio-rhetorical interpretive techniques to see how the structure of the arguments remains a force that should be just as impactful now as it was then in defining appropriate, faith-motivated living. Faith that is not evidently displayed through corresponding works is not living faith.

Dualism is a significant theme. The division between faith and life, public and private, physical and spiritual was evident in the early church as will be seen in the faith/works discussion of James 2. Dualism remains a significant impediment for the evangelical movement and individual Christ followers that constrains a biblically holistic understanding of mission and ministry. What results is a shadow of the gospel that may not even, according to James, represent true faith.

ACKNOWLEDGEMENTS

The author wishes to express his appreciation to the following persons and organisations that have helped to make this thesis possible.

The Zanokhanyo Network/Common Good teams—you are on the forefront of what it means to live the gospel for the glory of Christ on behalf of the poor. Your friendship and sacrifice have challenged me in ways that you will never know.

Dr. Godfrey Harold—our journey together began with an Honours degree many years ago. Your love for the Scriptures is infectious and I appreciate your enthusiasm for theology. Thanks for reading many pages written by my hand over the years and critiquing my work in a way that encourages me to keep going. You always have a book or article that is just the thing to move my research along.

Dr. Attie van Niekerk—Your insightful comments during this research have been most welcomed. If my writing has any merit it has been helped along by your careful analysis of my work. Thank you for taking the time to help bring structure to what often seems like chaos.

James and William Black—you became men and moved overseas during the course of this project. May you find pleasure in God as you serve others. It is still great to be your Dad and I am looking forward to spending more time with you and Mackenzie...

Leslie—You are a great gift! Thanks for applying your significant editing skill to this work and for giving me the encouragement to finish. You remain the best researcher in the family and I am a fortunate man to be your husband. 'If the rests as good as the last has been, here's hail to the rest of the road...'

Soli Deo Gloria

Tim Black
Cape Town 2020

CHAPTER ONE
THE GOSPEL AS SOCIAL REVOLUTION: THE ROLE OF THE CHURCH IN THE TRANSFORMATION OF SOCIETY

1 Introduction

This book has been born out of the sense of helplessness that I faced as a youth pastor at a local church in Cape Town. We were running a sewing course to try to teach women in a local township community how to provide for themselves and their families by learning a skill. For all of our efforts over the 6 week course, the women who successfully finished did not own sewing machines and were not able to turn their new skill into any sort of income stream. We were mis-guided when we thought that this course was even a partial answer to the scourge of unemployment. We meant well, but were confronted by the reality of our good intentions being thwarted by the poverty machine. There were lots of reasons for why these women were in poverty in the first place and we naively assumed we could solve their problems with a crash course on the basics of sewing. We had a lot to learn.

But this desire to learn carried us on a journey that continues to this day to find solutions to the entrenched poverty that still maintains a tight grip on the people of South Africa. We have learned a great deal through research, through trial and error and through careful listening. And we have seen God use these feeble efforts to move through a simple programme that helps people—thousands of people—find hope and healing and meaningful employment during a time when the percentage of people out of work is reported by the government at over 30.1%[1].

We did know a few things that remain true. First, God cares about people in poverty. We knew that we somehow needed to do something because it just didn't seem right that people were living in shacks packed tightly together without running water or toilets. These people were our neighbours, living just a few kilometers away from our nice, leafy suburb. We had running water and toilets along with solid roofs that weren't like to be in danger of blowing off during a severe rainy day in the middle of a Cape winter storm.

Secondly, we knew that since God cared about people in poverty, we should as well. The more we studied the Scriptures the more evidence began to stack up that the powerless—those trapped in poverty for a myriad of reasons—had a champion in God and should have one in His people. And Jesus, the 'in the flesh' example of what God is like, was quite pointed in his reference to people, particularly religious people, who failed to care for those in need. 'White-washed tombs' and 'hypocrites' were just a few of the more common phrases Jesus used for the religious leaders who didn't take him or his teachings seriously.

And finally, we knew that Christians had gotten confused about these first two things and had largely abandoned the proper care for those in need as part of their gospel mandate. Jesus is asked by a Pharisee what the greatest commandment is. Jesus' response is simple, yet incredibly profound: 'Love God, love your neighbor as you love yourself. Everything depends upon this' (Mt 22.34-40). At times it seems as if the Church, Jesus' bride in waiting, has become pre-occupied with other things so that the thing that seems so closely connected to God's heart—loving our neighbours—has become an activity on the fringe of what it means to be a Christ-follower.

So, in light of what we now know, what is the way forward? The purpose of this book is to encourage Christ followers, Jesus' bride, to rightly engage poverty as a gospel mandate. The call to love our neighbours has a modifier. We are to love 'as we love ourselves'. This calls us into relational living that is costly—it spends our privilege, it spends our resources, it spends our gifts and abilities—all for the glory of Jesus.

2 Setting the Stage

In Luke 16:19-31, Jesus tells a parable about a rich man and a poor man living in a non-descript community that could describe any other community in places around the globe where the rich and the poor are in close proximity, sharing nearby spaces. The poor man, Lazarus, is laying at the gate of the rich man. He is covered with sores. He is hungry, 'longing to eat what fell from the rich man's table.' As he lays at the gate, dogs lick his flesh.

The rich man is described as being 'dressed in purple and fine linen and liv(ing) in luxury every day.' Although Lazarus is apparently known to the rich man, he is likely no more than a nuisance, similar to the beggars who stand on street corners at intersections around the world looking for small change or bits of food.

Both men die.

In a significant reversal, the rich man ends up tormented in hell, while Lazarus is carried by angels to Abraham's side. The rich man calls out to Abraham for help in soothing his agony, but Abraham responds, 'Son, remember that in your lifetime you received your good things while Lazarus received bad things, but now he is comforted here and you are in agony' (Luke 16.27).

From a purely literary point of view, this seems like poetic justice; the calloused rich man gets what he deserves. But this parable leaves us with an uneasy feeling. Are the rich punished for being rich and the poor rewarded for simply being poor? What if the rich man worked hard for what he had? We don't have enough information to know for sure as Jesus doesn't really resolve the scene: Abraham refuses to be drawn into a rescue effort for the rich man's family even with significant pleading. Although there might be a back story, we don't know what that story is or what the rich man did to Lazarus that merited this radical reversal. We don't know that he did anything. We only know what he didn't do, which might be the point. It is not said that the rich man oppressed Lazarus, but that he callously failed to engage the poor man sitting at his gate.

Every day we move around the cities in our world taking no notice of the Lazarus sitting at our gate. We become so used to the sights associated with poverty that we no longer really see them. They have faded into the scenery, part of a permanent back drop in our international landscape.

If there is anything that the story helps us see, it is that we live as beings in community. As humans we are on a journey together at some level: we inhabit similar spaces and share similar experiences. We have human solidarity and share common contexts. We all suffer the issues that are present in our communities, whether they be environmental issues, traffic problems, power cuts, natural disasters, inflation or political inaction or instability. Whether we care to admit it or not, one person's deprivation has consequences that impact us all. So it may not only be what we have done to others that is important to consider, but of equal importance is what we fail to do in the face of someone else's need when we have the ability to engage.

This book seeks to contribute to the discussion identifying the role that poverty alleviation should play as an expression of the mission of the evangelical movement in its presentation of the 'gospel.' It will consider historical changes in mission methodology, some reasons behind these changes and the need for the restoration of a holistic, biblically-focused approach to ministry and evangelism. A socio-rhetorical interpretation of the New Testament book of James Chapter 2 will be used as a guide for the discussion. The results should be a theologically appropriate development model for the evangelical movement that is faithful to Scripture and centred on good development practices to engage the issues around poverty and poverty alleviation in local South African communities.

3 Outlining the Approach

The evangelical[2] movement is firmly rooted in the Protestant tradition. The Reformation, especially in its Calvinistic expressions, displayed a fresh and vibrant demonstration of Christianity in its relationship to the world. The fundamental structures of that world were viewed through a new lens and 'sentenced to be reformed' (Smith 2009:248). Wherever Calvin's teachings were embraced, the preaching of the gospel brought transformation to society. Those who inherited and espoused these traditions were instrumental in spreading a message that was intent upon bringing a thorough reformation of culture that impacted the structures of human society as well as the persons living within them. This was the soil from which the evangelical movement emerged in the 18th century, but slid into decline to be eclipsed by a form of dualism at some point late in the 19th century. It has not yet fully recovered.

Issues around dualism in its various forms are a major theme of this research. The division between faith and life, public and private, physical and spiritual continues to prevent the evangelical movement and individual Christ followers from a holistic understanding of mission and ministry.

In order to be faithful to Scripture, the modern evangelical movement must return to a historical interpretation of the gospel and the mission of the church. James 2 helps to legitimise this statement, particularly when examined in a socio-rhetorical context with a view to demonstrating appropriate Christian discipleship. J. Andrew Kirk succinctly defines this objective:

> The battle is not so much for the biblical gospel. The struggle is to discover how personal evangelism, social involvement, personal integrity, growth in the knowledge of God and in Christian fellowship can all be related together as indispensable parts of a total Christian witness (1985:16).

One must act out what one speaks: 'Christian rhetoric without tangible acts of love is hypocrisy' (Greer & Smith 2009:47).

4 Theological Framework

The epistemological basis for this research is located firmly within the evangelical tradition in an effort to thoroughly engage the evangelical movement in its theological praxis, particularly as it relates to activities around poverty alleviation. Although there are other empirical approaches available, the goal of this research is to bring change to current evangelical praxis which, if it is to occur at all, is more likely through influence exerted from within its own paradigm.

There will be two interdependent models enlisted to provide structure for this research: a socio-rhetorical model devised by Vernon Robbins for interpreting the James 2 text and a compelling practical theology model offered by Don Browning and modified by Ray Anderson to guide evangelical praxis. These models will together serve to focus the evangelical community by defining contextual biblical responsibility and behaviour.

Evangelicals have often used an interpretive framework based upon a historical-grammatical approach for determining meaning. The task of the interpreter is identified by A. Berkely

Mickelson as '. . . find(ing) out the meaning of a statement (command, question) for the author and for the hearers and readers, and thereupon to transmit the meaning to modern readers' (Mickelson in Padilla 2009:193). This action results in a static interpretation that, according to C. Rene Padilla, does not go far enough. He is rightly looking to take the biblical message from its original context and produce the same impact in modern hearers as was intended for the original audience. The text illuminates the contemporary situation and, at the same time, the contemporary situation illuminates the text. This is a

> hermeneutical cycle which would make it possible for the contemporary readers or hearers to perceive present-day reality from a biblical perspective, even as the original readers and hearers could perceive their own reality from the perspective of a worldview rooted in revelation (Padilla 2009:194).

This hermeneutical cycle makes it possible for an interpreter to articulate a theology which is both faithful to biblical revelation and relevant to one's context at the same time.

Socio-rhetorical interpretation is a useful tool to achieve the goals identified by Padilla. Vernon Robbin's socio-rhetorical interpretive model invites a detailed examination of the text while moving interactively into the world of the people who wrote the texts and into one's present world. Robbin's model examines both the overt and covert elements of persuasive communication while integrating a sociological study of the underlying beliefs, values and convictions found in the texts one reads and in the communities in which one lives. Language usage and lifestyle are assimilated in a way that brings, 'literary criticism, social-scientific criticism, rhetorical criticism, postmodern criticism, and theological criticism together into an integrated approach to interpretation' (Robbins 1996:2). Socio-rhetorical interpretation will help one properly exegete the text of James 2 by bringing, 'skills we use on a daily basis into an environment of interpretation that is both intricately sensitive to detail and perceptively attentive to large fields of meanings in the world in which we live' (Robbins 1996:2). The result of this interpretation provides one with a hermeneutical theology from which correct evangelical praxis can be determined.

Attention to a hermeneutical theology will guide one's practical theology. Ray Anderson states that '(p)resent interpretation of Scripture must be as faithful to the eschatological reality and authority of Christ as to scriptural reality and authority' (Anderson 2001:37). Anderson cites Don Browning's model of practical theology to illustrate a process which Browning calls 'practical reason,' . . . 'integrating theory and practice in an ongoing process of action and reflection' (Anderson 2001:26). In Browning's model, the theological task is placed at the centre of the social context where the theologian and the church mediate the gospel of Christ. Critical to this mediation is action-reflection prompted by incidents that ask how the gospel of Christ answers the questions 'What then shall we do?' and 'How then should we live?' John Swinton calls this the crux of practical theology, serving as a 'critical reflection on the actions of the church in light of the gospel and Christian tradition' (Swinton in Anderson 2001:26).

While affirming Browning's model as a framework for postmodern thought, Anderson reorients Browning's theological model by changing its focus. Anderson suggests the model lacks a '. . . christological concentration at the core and a trinitarian theology at the foundation' (Anderson 2001:29). Anderson exchanges 'experience' at the centre of Browning's model with 'Christopraxis' which he defines as 'the continuing ministry of Christ through the power and presence of the Holy Spirit' (Anderson 2001:29). This is a useful revision which will be explored in detail in Chapter 5.

CHAPTER TWO

THE RISE AND FALL OF GOSPEL ENGAGEMENT WITHIN THE EVANGELICAL MOVEMENT

'The church is the church only when it exists for others. The church must share in the secular problems of ordinary human life, not dominating, but helping and serving' (Bonhoeffer 1971:382).

1 Introduction

Christianity has been plagued for over a century by a dichotomy in its praxis. Liberals have reduced the mission of God to social action and evangelicals, in response, have defined it as making individual converts through a proclamation of the 'gospel.' Grant and Hughes (2009: Intro) call this a 'case, common in the history of theology, of a bad argument being countered by an equally bad one.' Although there was never a complete polarization between evangelism and social action, there was enough suspicion generated between the two camps that social action was damned by many evangelicals for its ties to liberalism and proselytizing evangelism shunned by liberals for its association to fundamental evangelicalism.

The beginning stages and development of any movement will likely contain what may appear to be false starts and difficult to discern progress as things begin to take shape and stabilise. This chapter will define and describe the historical development of the evangelical movement from the Reformation to the present day, charting its progress and growth. It will also highlight the motives inherent within evangelicalism that have defined its character historically. These motives often resulted in behaviour that clearly demonstrated a calling through conviction. As some of these motives changed, the movement lost much of its dynamism and transformative impact. Much of this change is still being felt today as the movement seeks to recover what was lost.

Key leaders had a tremendous impact throughout this process as the evangelical movement formed. Major developments along the way played a significant role in the current composition and emphases of the modern evangelical movement. Some of these major developments will be explored to establish the trends that resulted. Overall, the evangelical movement is complicated, meaning that volumes could be written, and have been written, to chart the characteristics of the movement and its global impact. This chapter merely scratches the surface to provide background for a basic understanding of the growth of evangelicalism that contributes to its current shape and focus.

Finally, some significant issues plague modern evangelicalism. The way that these matters developed will be explored in a way that highlights the differences that have emerged between the evangelicalism of the 16th century and what has arisen in the late 19th to early 21st centuries. Cultural narrow-mindedness and shallow social perspectives converged to produce what John Oliver of Malone College has termed 'A Failure of Evangelical Conscience.'[3] The result was that evangelical Christianity rather consistently opposed or simply ignored cultural currents that demanded social justice and civil rights. The full significance of this 'failure' has yet to be fully understood, but it would appear that the evangelical movement has missed a great opportunity for a powerful movement of the gospel. It may still have time to recover its mandate if it wishes to do so.

2 Defining the Movement

'Evangelicalism' is not and has never been, at least according to Mark Noll, an 'ism' like other Christian-isms—as in Catholicism, Presbyterianism, and Anglicanism. Rather it is made up of 'shifting movements, temporary alliances, and the lengthened shadows of individuals' (Noll 1994:8). Therefore, discussions around the evangelical movement tend to describe the way things are as well as personal attempts to provide some order to describe a multifaceted, complex set of urges and organisations.

The word *evangelical* has carried several different senses throughout church history, but almost all relate in some way to its etymological meaning of 'good news.' *Euangelion* (εὐαγγέλιον) is the Greek noun from which evangelical is transliterated. It is regularly employed by the New Testament writers to signify 'glad tidings—the good news, the gospel—of Jesus who appeared on earth as the Son of God to accomplish God's plan of salvation for needy humans' (Noll 2003:16). 'Evangelical' religion has always been 'gospel' religion with a specific focus on salvation brought through Jesus Christ.

The term 'evangelical' was already in use during the English Middle Ages describing, for example, the message about salvation in Jesus or to refer to the four Gospels (Matthew, Mark, Luke, John) which describe the life, death, and resurrection of Jesus. Moreover, in addition to these uses, medieval students of Scripture often referred to the Old Testament book of Isaiah as 'the evangelical prophet' based upon its prophetic reference to the life and work of Christ (Noll 2003:16).

'Evangelical' began to take on meanings specifically associated with the Protestant Reformation during the sixteenth century. Martin Luther proclaimed an 'evangelical' account of salvation in Christ in contradiction to what he considered the scandalous teachings of the Roman Church. In this way, 'evangelical' rapidly assumed 'a critical cast, since it was posing a contrast between faithful adherence to the gospel message of the New Testament and Catholic perversions of that message' (Noll 2003:16). In the midst of conflict, the positive and negative connotations of 'evangelical' quickly multiplied. Noll (2003:17) highlights these uses:

- It stood for justification by faith instead of trust in human works as the path to salvation;
- It defended the sole sufficiency of Christ for salvation instead of the human (and often corrupted) mediations of the church;
- It looked to the once-for-all triumph of Christ's death on the cross instead of the repetition of Christ's sacrifice in the Catholic mass;
- It found final authority in the Bible as read by believers in general instead of what the Catholic Church said the Bible had to mean; and
- It embraced the priesthood of all Christian believers instead of inappropriate reliance on a class of priests ordained by the church.

These differences were so marked that the term 'evangelical' became virtually synonymous with 'Protestant' (Noll 2003:17).

However, it is necessary to refine the definition further. Timothy George defines evangelicals in *Christianity Today*—often considered by many to be *the* authority on evangelicalism[4]-- as the 'worldwide family of Bible-believing Christians committed to sharing with everyone the transforming good news of new life in Jesus Christ, an utterly free gift that comes through faith alone in the crucified and risen Savior' (George 1999:62).

Although this definition is a very basic starting point, there has been little consensus achieved among those who have tried to describe the evangelical movement. Part of the challenge that anyone faces in seeking to define the movement more specifically lies in the evangelical movement's great diversity. Global Evangelicalism is immense, with men and women on every continent describing themselves as evangelical while comprising varied economic groupings, political philosophies, and denominational affiliations. The majority are Protestant, but even among Protestants, there is an incredibly diverse denominational mosaic.

However, the consensus in most academic quarters has emerged around the most oft-used general definition of the term 'evangelical' by British historian David Bebbington (1989:2). He has identified four qualities that have been special marks of Evangelical religion:

> Conversionism, the belief that lives need to be changed; activism, the expression of the gospel in effort; Biblicism, a particular regard for the Bible; and what may be called crucicentrism, a stress on the sacrifice of Christ on the cross. Together they form a quadrilateral of priorities that is the basis of Evangelicalism.

According to Larsen (2008:28), these four pillars have 'no rival anywhere near as influential or popular and are unlikely to be replaced by an alternative structure any time soon.'

However, these compulsions have never brought about a cohesive or easily definable movement. Shifts over time change the tenets that would identify the evangelical nature of a group or organisation so that institutions considered 'evangelical' at one time may not be labelled the same later. However, there have continued to be denominations and local congregations that have served as organised manifestations of the evangelical movement since it was first recognised as a movement.

3 Rise of the Movement

3.1 Early beginnings

Evangelicalism, when seen in the wider perspective of church history, is best, as some insist, understood as a revival movement within orthodox Christianity. It has a theological centre shaped by the

'trinitarian and Christological consensus of the
early church, the formal and material principles of
the Reformation, the missionary movement that
grew out of the Great Awakening and the new
movements of the Spirit that indicate "surprising
works of God" are still happening in the world
today' (George 2008:15).

This view of evangelical history, often referred to as *gospel
successionism* is clearly touted by evangelical theologian J.I.
Packer as,

'the Christianity, both convictional and behavioural,
which we inherit from the New Testament via the
Reformers, the Puritans, and the revival and missionary leaders of the eighteenth and nineteenth centuries....the heritage, I mean, which includes Athanasius
and Augustine, Martin Luther and John Calvin, Richard Hooker (demonstrably an evangelical) and John
Owen, Jonathan Edwards, George Whitefield and John
Wesley, Charles Spurgeon and John Charles Ryle, Robert Aitken and William Booth, the great Presbyterian
theologians of Scotland and North America, the spirituality of the English Puritans and the East African revival, and much, much more (Packer 1978:2).

One can also see traces of this successionist view evidenced
early on through leaders in the era of the Reformation. Melanchthon eulogised Luther at his death by placing him in the
line of gospel succession:

After the apostles comes a long line, inferior, indeed,
but distinguished by the divine attestations: Polycarp, Irenaeus, Gregory of Neocaesaria, Basil, Augustin,
Prosper, Maximus, Hugo, Bernard, Tauler and others.
And although these later times have been less fruit-
ful, yet God has always preserved a remnant; and that
a more splendid light of the gospel has been kindled
by the voice of Luther cannot be denied[5] (Stewart
2001:1).

Under this normative understanding, evangelical Christianity was defined as the 'biblical, doctrinal and experiential Christianity, ... the "faith once delivered to the saints" (Stewart 2001:2) in an 'unbroken tradition of biblical, gospel-based Christianity, reaching back in time through the eighteenth century revival, the Puritans, the Reformers, the Lollards and other dissenters, and then right back to New Testament Christianity' (James [s.a]:1).

David Bebbington would disagree, and it is important to engage with his argument.[6] He acknowledges elements of truth in the notion that there has been a constant witness to biblical truth through the two millennia since the time of Christ. However, he argues that the evidence points to a more subtle evangelical history around a movement that has 'altered enormously over time in response to the changing assumptions of Western civilisation' (Bebbington 1989:19).

For Bebbington to demonstrate that modern evangelicalism appeared as a new phenomenon in the eighteenth century, he needs to establish certain features of the movement as distinctively different. The trademarks he settles upon are found within his definition and are characteristically evangelical preoccupations: conversion, the cross, the Bible and activism. Bebbington acknowledges that three of these characteristics were not particularly new: 'conversionism, Biblicism and crucicentrism had been as much a part of Puritanism as they were of Methodism' (Bebbington 1989:35). What was the most distinguishing difference in the evangelical movement was 'its new dynamism or expansive energy for mission and service: its *activism*' (Hindmarsh 2008:328).

But it seems as if activism, claimed as missing by Bebbington, does exist, although maybe not with the same fervour and energy as witnessed during the Great Awakening. Bebbington (1989:10) defines 'activism' by referring to a remark by Jonathan Edwards: 'Persons after their own conversion have commonly expressed an exceeding great desire for the conversion of others. Some have thought that they should be willing to die for the conversion of any soul . . . ' (Edwards 1736:348). This passion for bringing the Gospel to others was certainly a hallmark of 18th- century evangelicalism and fits the definition of 'activism.'

Bebbington further broadens 'activism' so that it can also describe high energy exerted in general religious activity. He points out the transformation exhibited in the role of a minister of religion, noting that '. . . the evangelical clergy as a body is indefatigable in ministerial duties' instead of simply going about their daily activities like a member of the landed gentry (Bebbington 1989:11). He writes further that this 'activism' spilled over into, 'efforts in such causes as public health, . . . Wilberforce's campaign against the slave trade and Nonconformist political crusades around 1900 . . . ,' all seen as representative of newfound evangelical fervour (Bebbington 1989:12).

It seems, according to this more general definition used by Bebbington, that one could use 'activism' to describe not only evangelistic or mission activities but any passionate energy exerted in religious activity as a response to faith. This would mean that 'activism' is the 'playing out of these doctrines (Bebbington's Quadrilateral) practically, as evident in, but not limited to, evangelism and missions' (Sweeney & Withrow 2008:284). Noll (2003:19) also weighs in, calling activism the 'dedication of all believers, including laypeople, to lives of service for God . . . .' Therefore, if there is sufficient evidence to trace the line of evangelicalism according to the definition espoused by Bebbington—all four elements of the definition—one would be able to assert that the evangelical movement predates the 1730s, contrary to Bebbington's argument. The development and nature of the Reformation and its principal actors will be explored as a guide to this discussion.

3.2 The Reformation

3.2.1 Social and political influences

Luther and Calvin are normally touted as principle movers in the Reformation. However, the movement actually had its foundation in the work of 'a wider network of theologians, professors, and students operating through associated universities and academies' as well as the convergent aspects of the social, political and economic landscape that were relevant to the movement's success (Hunter 2010:66).

This combination of influences merged to form a tapestry that set the stage for the leadership that appeared. The Holy Roman Empire was without political or administratively consolidated leadership while most of central Europe was comprised of hundreds of autonomous, self-governing principalities and organisations. Political rivalries and dynastic conflicts marked the entire region, pitting the landed nobility against one another in their constant efforts to expand their powers. Concurrently, there existed a growing discontent among the common people due to the inequities of power and wealth and the onerous duties that resulted. They yearned for new social freedoms that seemed unobtainable. Moreover, adding to these internal tensions were threats from the expanding Ottoman Empire in the East and tenuous relations with France and England. It was these preoccupations and other distractions that kept the Imperial authority from 'attending to the challenge of the new reformers' when the Reformation presented itself (Hunter 2010:65).

Other factors were equally important. The late medieval economy was facing changes. International commerce expanded dramatically during the 16th-century and the primary beneficiaries of this growing wealth, particularly in central and northern Europe, were a class of merchants, entrepreneurs, financiers, and others scattered throughout an array of cities and towns located along its key trading routes. Concentrations of wealth and power were controlled by fewer members of the nobility and landed aristocracy. 'The increasing prosperity and self-sufficiency of the towns and cities gave birth to a new and alternative commercial elite that were not only independent of the concentrated power of the church and its defenders, but who were eager to protect their growing political and, ipso facto, religious autonomy' (Hunter 2010:65). The Reformation was significantly enabled by the political autonomy of these towns and cities and their increasing wealth.

3.2.2 Leadership and focus

This social and political context paved the way for the emergence and expansion of the movement and the growing influence of the early reformers. At its heart, the Reformation was an intellectual and moral revolution that originated within the theological faculty of a German university. Late medieval theology and religious practice were challenged by its bibliocentric focus. At the foundation of this revolution was the fact that the leading reformers were all exceptional scholars. 'In addition to the Bible, they had mastery over the ideas, logic, language, and texts of classical thought and medieval scholasticism' (Hunter 2010:66). And, as one will see, they could also be considered early evangelicals.

i Martin Luther

Martin Luther, according to Cameron MacKenzie (2008:171), was an evangelical who believed that the Reformation was a 'return to the teachings of Paul and the New Testament.' Although he was certainly born from the Catholic tradition, what was new about his faith and the movement he initiated was his understanding of the gospel. 'Evangelical' (German evangelisch; Latin evangelicus), therefore, is a term Luther employed positively to describe true Christianity' (MacKenzie 2008:171)[7]. Very early it was associated with the Reformation as a whole, although the reference to the label does not mean that 'evangelical' as defined since would necessarily have anything in common with Luther, although there are significant continuities between the beliefs of the Reformer and later evangelicals that would place them within the evangelical movement. After all, George Whitefield and Jonathan Edwards found fundamental agreement with sixteenth century Protestants (MacKenzie 2008:173)[8].

However, even though there are significant differences between Luther and those who would come later, those differences should not obscure what were clearly evangelical characteristics of Luther's faith. Foundational to his understanding of Christianity were the following:

> (1) an exclusively biblical basis for the truths of Christianity (*Biblicism*); (2) the centrality of justification by grace through faith in the atoning work of Christ (*crucicentrism, conversionism*); (3) the need to oppose those errors in the church that militate against the truth of the gospel; (4) the agreement of this faith with the beliefs of the true church through the ages; and (5) the necessity of good works as the fruit of faith (*activism*) (MacKenzie 2008:173 (*emphases added*)).

Although these characteristics are not precisely the same as the four qualities defined by David Bebbington, one can see enough overlap in this list to justify employing an 'evangelical' label to Martin Luther. In statements that he intended as general descriptions of what it means to be Christian, Luther expressed an evangelical faith that was based upon Scripture as its foundation, Christ-centred and active in love. Luther's faith had, at its heart, basic convictions about the grace of God, the sinfulness of humanity, the ransom for sin, and offer of salvation by Jesus Christ for all who believe. These are considered benchmarks of the evangelical movement.

Compared to later evangelicals, Luther's activism was quite conservative. However, Luther makes it clear that saving faith and good works are two separate, but necessary things.

Such faith, renewal and forgiveness of sins are followed by good works. What is still sinful or imperfect in them will not be counted as sin or defect, for Christ's sake . . . . Therefore, we cannot boast of many merits and works, if they are viewed apart from grace and mercy. (see Althaus in MacKenzie 2008:195 ftnt.).

'Activism' is the element of the evangelical quadrilateral that Bebbington believes is missing before the 18th century. However, Luther exhibits 'activism' by his conviction that correct theology includes care for those in poverty as an outworking of faith. The Reformation was concerned early on with the relationship of theology to poverty.[9] Luther bases his theological position upon the conviction that salvation is not the process or goal of life, but rather its premise. The repentant sinner is freely accepted by the mercy of God without ethical or religious prerequisites. Luther defines his understanding of Christianity by the doctrine of justification by faith. This doctrine is the foundation for Christian activity in the world and leads to charity towards one's neighbour. 'Such faith, through the working of the Holy Spirit, and by which we are reckoned and have become righteous and holy, performs good works through us, namely love toward the neighbour, prayer to God, and the suffering of persecution' (MacKenzie 2008:195).

Luther's emphasis on the Word also relativized all human constructions, freeing them from ideology by re-orienting them as service to one's neighbour. This thinking fit squarely within the meaning of 'activism'. The gospel is thus proclaimed 'with hand and mouth.'[10] Therefore, it's hard to rationalise the plight of the poor as a particular form of 'blessedness' as was taught by the medieval church since there is no salvific benefit in being poor *or* in giving alms. This concept alone gave the reformers a new theological foundation for their work in poverty relief and reforming social policy. They had 'de-ideologized the medieval approach to the poor which had obscured the problem of poverty' (Lindberg 1981:46).

The Reformation is traditionally dated from the posting of

the Ninety-Five Theses of 1517 and by 1519 Luther had raised the connection between theology and social concern in his writings against the brotherhoods. These associations had been originally intended for works of charity but through the proliferation of masses and the accumulation of good works they had degenerated into egocentric means of obtaining salvation. He states his guidelines as follows:

> If men desire to obtain a brotherhood, they should gather provisions and feed and serve a tableful or two of poor people for the sake of God. . . Or they should gather money into a common treasury, each craft for itself. Then in cases of hardship, needy and fellow workmen might be helped to get started, and be lent money, or a young couple of the same craft might be fitted out respectably from this common treasury.[11]

These guidelines were the seed for the institutionalisation of relief for the poor and the reform of social welfare that was expressed in the Wittenberg city ordinances of 1520, 1521, and 1522. The Wittenberg Order, issued by the City Council on 24 January 1522, established a Common Chest for 'poor relief, low interest loans provided for workers and artisans, and the subsidy of education and training for children of the poor' (Lindberg 1981:47).

In summary, the new theology of the Reformers inaugurated a radical transformation in social policy and programme and brought revolution to the Church. This transformation was 'activism' at its finest. These new forms of social welfare quickly spread throughout Germany with the Wittenberg Order serving as the model for the movement. Luther was rightly convinced that the fundamental human rights of equality, freedom, and brotherly love found their basis in the Christian faith so that, despite many difficulties, the early Reformation development of poverty relief proceeded to implement this vision requiring care and concern for 'personal dignity and (the) public alleviation of suffering' (Lindberg

1981:48).

ii John Calvin

In similar and somewhat more obvious fashion, John Calvin demonstrated attributes through his writing and ministry that offer clear evidence that would also define him as an 'evangelical.' This section shall review the four 'isms' of Bebbington's definition through evidence seen in Calvin's life and ministry. Although the elements are sometimes merged, they are nevertheless clearly visible. 'Activism,' perceived as care and concern for the poor, serves to place Calvin firmly alongside Luther within the evangelical movement.

The centrality of Scripture was at the forefront of Calvin's thinking. 'He is paramount among the Reformers in emphasising the principle of *sola scriptura* in the faith of the church' (Helm 2008:202). He focuses his efforts in a constant polemic against the practices of the Roman Catholic Church, accusing the Church of 'obscuring the Word of God with her traditions and of nullifying its effect in practice' (Helm 2008:202). Calvin's commentaries bear witness to the focused way in which he displayed the tapestry of Scripture to those embracing the Reformed movement.

Scripture is critical for enabling one to understand God and oneself more clearly, manifesting intrinsic evidence of its God-breathed authenticity:

> Let this then stand as a fixed point, that those whom the Spirit has inwardly taught rest firmly upon Scripture, and that Scripture is self-authenticated, and that it is not right for it to be made to depend upon demonstration of reasoning, for it is by the Spirit's witness that it gains in our minds the certainty that it merits (Calvin 1997: vii, section v).

For Calvin, Scripture is not to be speculated over, but to be understood and applied, being both necessary and sufficient for faith and life.

Like Luther, Calvin considered his conversion the pivotal event in his life. In his preface to his *Commentary on the Psalms* he compares himself to the psalmist David when he writes:

> And first, since I was too obstinately devoted to the superstitions of Popery to be easily extricated from so proud an abyss of mire, God by a sudden conversion subdued and brought my mind to a teachable frame, which was more hardened in such matters than might have been expected from one at my early period of life. Having thus received some taste and knowledge of true godliness, I was immediately inflamed with so intense a desire to make progress therein, that although I did not altogether leave off other studies, I yet pursued them with less ardour (Calvin & Anderson 2010: Preface p. xi).

Calvin seems quite clearly to endorse the possibility of an instantaneous conversion, leading to the recognition of an important truth: sin has brought spiritual death. As no one can raise himself to life, supernatural regeneration is required. So it is important to stress for Calvin the 'distinction between the inception of new life (regeneration in a narrow sense) and the conscious expression of the effects of this in repentance, faith and love (a conversion experience)' (Helm 2008:203).

Central to Calvin's understanding of theology is the person and work of Christ.

> It was his task to swallow up death. Who but the Life could do this? It was his task to conquer sin. Who but very Righteousness could do this? It was his task to rout the powers of world and air. Who but a power higher than world and air could do this? Now where does life or righteousness, or lordship and authority of heaven lie but with God alone? Therefore our most merciful God, when he willed that we be redeemed, made himself our Redeemer in the person of his only-begotten Son (Calvin 1997: II.xii.ii).

Calvin had a principal role in the development of two fundamental areas of Christology: first, the threefold work of Christ as prophet, priest, and king and secondly, the twofold grace of justification and sanctification that proceeds from our union with him. It is our union with Christ that is central to Calvin's understanding of the link between justification, sanctification, and the sacraments.

'By baptism, we are united with Christ in his death and resurrection. By faithful partaking of the Lord's Supper, our union with Christ is confirmed with visible signs as Christ comes to us by his Spirit' (Helm 2008:205). The heart of Calvin's theology was Christ, and the cross was the centre of his understanding of Christ's work.

Calvin did not see himself in a narrow sense as a missionary or evangelist. However, his writings express the need for conversion and the need for the proclamation of . . . 'the goodness of God to every nation' (Commentary on Isa 12:5). He had compassion for the lost condition of people which he claimed should also drive all Christians to witness. He declared in a sermon on Deuteronomy 33,

> if we have any kindness in us, seeing that we see men go to destruction until God has got them under his obedience: ought we not to be moved with pity, to draw the silly souls out of hell, and to bring them into the way of salvation? (Calvin in Helm 2008:206 ftnt. 20).

Calvin remarked further that a Christian who is not involved in witness is actually denying faith:

> [T]he godly will be filled with such an ardent desire to spread the doctrines of religion, that everyone not satisfied with his own calling and his personal knowledge will desire to draw others along with him. And indeed nothing could be more inconsistent with the nature of faith than that deadness which would lead a man to disregard his brethren, and to keep the light of

knowledge choked up within his own breast (Calvin's Commentary on Is. 2.3).[12]

Calvin's concern for the church was not only focused on France, but he sought reformation of the church 'in such places as Scotland, and England, Spain and Poland, Hungary and the Netherlands' (Helm 2008:207). His ideas about the expansion and all-inclusive nature of God's kingdom—especially in reference to the calling of the Gentiles—arise from his careful attention to the Scriptures. He desired to see Christ worshipped not only at home but around the world.

Calvin's writings provide ample evidence that he exhibited the necessary elements required by Bebbington to qualify him as an 'early evangelical.' A section of a prayer that he prayed following a sermon he gave just before he died brings together the evidence that such a claim is so:

> Since you desire all men to acknowledge you as Saviour of the world, through the redemption by our Lord Jesus Christ, may those who do not know him, being in darkness and captive to ignorance and error —may they by the light of your Holy Spirit and the preaching of your gospel, be led into the way of salvation, which is to know you, the only true God, and Jesus Christ whom you have sent (Calvin's Sermons on the Beatitudes in Helm 2008:208 ftnt.).

It is also important to note the social vision of John Calvin, who has been described as a 'constructive revolutionary' (Smith 2009:247). A detailed study of his sermons in Geneva suggest that his focus was on the practical necessity of glorifying God now—not waiting for another world and happiness there. One can imagine the likely reaction of the merchants of Geneva wishing to separate their economic activities from biblical ethics upon hearing this message:

> There would be those who would rather that the wheat spoil in the granary so that it will be eaten by vermin, so that it can be sold when there is want (for

they only wish to starve the poor people) . . . See the wheat collected; how well our Lord has poured out his grace and his benediction so that the poor world would be nourished. But the speculator will gather it in granaries and lock it up securely, till finally the cry of famine is heard and that's no longer possible. What will happen? It will be spoiled and rotten. How true it is that our Lord is mocked by those who want to have much profit . . . . These people entomb the grace of God, as if they warred against his bounty and against the paternal love which he displays toward everyone (Graham in Smith 2009:247 see ftnt.).

Calvin's teaching is clearly prophetic. It emphasizes a concern for social justice, serving to illustrate that the Reformation introduced a fresh vision of Christianity as it related to society in which the fundamental structures of that world were 'held up to judgement' and 'sentenced to be reformed' (Wolterstorff 1983:3). Wolterstorff continues by identifying this vision as 'world-transformative Christianity' in contrast to what he calls 'avertive' forms of religion. These 'avertive' forms motivate a desire to escape from what are seen to be the 'inferior realms of the social and political worlds, in order to cultivate spiritual purity and "attain closer contact with a reality outside oneself which is higher, better, more real"' (Wolterstorff in Smith 2009:248).

4 Shaping the Movement

Wherever Calvin's teaching was embraced, this world-transformative vision of the whole world renewed by the preaching of the gospel was experienced. This vision was clearly visible in Scotland where the Reformation put down deeper roots among ordinary people than anywhere else in Europe save for Switzerland. John Knox and his colleagues took hold of Calvin's utopian vision, demonstrating the transformation that the gospel could bring to a quickly changing world that was experiencing extensive social and cultural upheaval. They set about broad-scale transformation by designing a system of education that included placing a schoolmaster in every town, radically changing the universities and introducing legislation which 'curbed the power of oppressive landlords and proposed practical measures to relieve poverty' (Smith 2009:248). One can argue that the Calvinist desire to reform human society was reinforced eschatologically through the hope that the triumph of the gospel would bring far-reaching social transformation. This desire can be traced to Calvin himself as he exhorted Christians to 'hope boldly' in the confidence that, despite opposition, Christ would one day 'surpass our opinion and our hope' (Murray in Smith 2009:251).

Luther, Calvin and their allies redefined Western Christianity and 'inaugurated a new theological tradition, evangelical Protestantism, founded on the supreme authority of Scripture and centred on intense preoccupation with salvation through faith in Christ's atoning sacrifice' (Coffey 2008:272). The early Reformers' basic theological convictions were defended and elaborated in what is recorded by Philip Schaff as 'the Creeds of the Evangelical Churches' (Schaff 1878: Chapter 5). Eighteenth-century evangelicals operated within this evangelical Protestant tradition, defending the core of its creeds. Essentially, evangelicalism was theologically derivative which, to a remarkable degree, continues to be the case.

This was the framework from which the evangelical movement emerged in the eighteenth century. The nature and direction of Western Civilisation were challenged and transformed by the Reformation, ushering in a series of other movements that were not alternative directions but expansions with the same social vision as the Reformation.

4.1 Puritans

The English Puritan movement caught this same vision of socially transformative Christianity, continuing within the earlier framework of the Reformers. Brian Cosby ([s.a.]:307) proposes the following working definition of 'Puritanism':

> A 'Puritan' was one who, politically, reacted against the *via media* of the Elizabethan Settlement in favour of a more thorough reformation in England; who, socially, promoted evangelism, catechism, and spiritual nourishment through the preaching and teaching of the Bible; who, theologically, held the views of Luther's doctrine of faith (*sola fide*), Calvin's doctrine of grace (*sola gratia),* and the Reformers' doctrine of Scripture (*sola scriptura*); and who, devotionally, strove for personal holiness, a practical faith, communion with God, and the glory of God in all things.

In *A Quest for Godliness*, James I. Packer (1990:329) defines the Puritans as:

> Englishmen who embraced whole-heartedly a version of Christianity that paraded a particular blend of biblicist, pietist, churchly and worldly concerns. Puritanism, was essentially a movement for church reform, pastoral renewal and evangelism, and spiritual revival.

Others acknowledge this same view. Carl Trueman (in Coffey 2008: 266) insists that all four elements of Bebbington's evangelical quadrilateral are 'rooted in the Reformation,' noticeably present within Puritanism. Puritans were seen at the vanguard of the movement to evangelise modern England and spread the gospel of evangelical Protestantism. J.I. Packer (1990:46) contends that English Puritanism in both its Tudor and Stuart phases was primarily a movement set on national evangelisation and personal revival. He writes that by the middle of the 17th century, 'a work of grace was in progress in England every whit as potent and deep as its counterpart a century later.' In fact, cultural markers indicated Puritan 'activism': A play titled *Bartholomew Fair* staged in 1614 contained a Puritan character named 'Zeal-of-the-Land-Busy' (Coffey 2008:266). There appears to be a strong connection between Puritanism and evangelicalism.

Historians acknowledge this continuity. David Bebbington emphasises this relationship between Puritans like Richard Baxter and evangelicals like Philip Doddridge and George Whitefield, suggesting that 'in many respects Evangelical religion prolonged existing lines of development.' 'Even Methodism,' he continues, 'had roots in the Puritan tradition . . . inherit(ing) a substantial legacy from the Puritans' (Bebbington 1989:34-35).

Mark Noll affirms an even greater emphasis on the Puritan roots of evangelicalism:

> The Puritan movement featured many themes that eighteenth-century evangelicals would later promote as well, especially intense preaching about the need for a saving Christ and calculated opposition to the merely formal religion that Puritans saw infecting the Church of England (Noll 2003:53).

Additionally, Puritans promoted 'grace-centred Protestantism that would rise again in the evangelical revival'. Even though 'aggressive heart religion' was widely denounced through its association with the Puritan Revolution, key leaders like Richard Baxter, Joseph Alleine, John Bunyan, Cotton Mather, Thomas Boston and Isaac Watts kept alive 'the traditions of experiential Calvinism' with its 'evangelical emphases.' Their books were eagerly read by evangelicals so that when the revival of the 1730s came the news about it was quickly spread across the English-speaking world by a well-established network of Calvinist divines (Noll 2003:56).

However, while noting continuities between the Puritans and evangelicalism, Noll and Bebbington are also keen to identify what they believe to be key differences. Noll argues that 'even as it pushed towards a more personal and more internal practice of the Christian faith, Puritanism still remained a traditional religion of traditional European Christendom' (Noll

2003:54). He illustrates this in the following ways.

First, they retained 'the ideal of a comprehensive, unified society' promoting 'coercive plans for the comprehensive reform of society' while holding 'state-church assumptions.' Evangelicals, by contrast, 'endorsed a profound shift from concern with godly order to godly fellowship, from religious uniformity to toleration, and from communalism to voluntarism' (Noll 2003:50-56).

Second, Noll implies that Puritans were 'doctrinal precisionists, committed to high standards of doctrinal orthodoxy' such as those set out in the Westminster Confession. In contrast, evangelicals were shaped by the shift 'from Christian faith defined as correct doctrine towards Christian faith defined as correct living.' Spiritual fellowship was not impeded by theological differences (Noll 2001b:13).

Third, Noll claims that 'where Puritanism retained an exalted role for the clergy and great respect for formal learning, evangelicals since the eighteenth century have been powered by lay initiative and . . . wary of formal scholarship' (Noll 2001b:13-14).

Bebbington, in similar manner, also cites differences between the Puritans and the Evangelical movement, indicating three significant ways he believes this is so. First, there was stimulus given to this new evangelical movement by an alternative High Church tradition called *Ecclesia Anglicana*. This 'primitive Christianity' appealed chiefly to young men so that these 'religious societies soon became the vehicle for spreading this primitive Christianity throughout the land' (Bebbington 1989:36). Members devoted themselves to 'self-examination, directed prayer, monthly communion, fasting and the quest for holiness' (Bebbington 1989:36). Prison visitation, caring for the sick and offering help for the poor formed a regular part of the traditional discipline of the religious societies.

Bebbington records the second symptom of this discontinuity with the 'assimilation of influences from Continental Protestantism' (Bebbington 1989:38). The Wesley's were decisively influenced by Luther, but it was Lutherans living and working around them that had greater sway upon their lives and ministry. Protestants were often under attack—Protestants in Salzburg were expelled by Austrian troops and sought refuge elsewhere. It was alongside a group of these refugees that John Wesley sailed to Georgia. Wesley consulted a group of their ministers trained at Halle about their convictions. This was the centre of the Lutheran movement most impacting evangelical origins: Pietism. A manifesto written for the movement urged the need for 'repentance, the new birth, putting faith into practice and close fellowship among true believers' (Bebbington 1989:39). Pietism's influence on Lutheranism modelled much of what Whitefield and Wesley were to undertake in the English-speaking world.

Finally, a decisive impact for Bebbington on the further emergence of evangelicalism at this later time was the reorganisation of the Moravians under the guidance of Count Nicholas von Zinzendorf, a man who had been impacted by Pietism but now identifying wholly with the Moravians. Under Zinzendorf's leadership, Moravians became a dynamic missionary force, spreading the message that true religion must not be a matter of speculation, but of experience. Forgiveness is made available by the Lamb of God, to be accepted personally for the forgiveness of sins. Emphasis on the cross, faith, forgiveness of sins and assurance of salvation led to intense devotion to Christ. Wesley himself was deeply influenced by the Moravians, actually serving as a member of a predominantly Moravian Fellowship for two years after his missionary trip to Georgia. 'Evangelicalism learned much from the Moravians' (Bebbington 1989:40).

Mission activity was key. It was unusual to find a Protestant leader encouraging the spread of the gospel beyond existing Christendom in the sixteenth and seventeenth centuries.

Protestant missionary activity was rare in comparison to the Roman Catholic initiatives. The Scriptural impulse to 'Go' at the end of Matthew's gospel was thought to apply only to the early church. This scandal was recognised by Cotton Mather, a leading Puritan of the New World, who regretted that 'so little had been done by the churches of the Reformation to spread the faith' (Benz in Bebbington 1989:41).

Noll and Bebbington are both considered excellent historians, but it seems quite likely that they each exaggerate the differences between seventeenth-century Puritanism and eighteenth-century evangelicalism, resulting in an overall failure to appreciate Puritanism's 'dynamism and diversity' (Coffey 2008:255). There were powerful counter-currents within Puritanism that appear to have been overlooked. Moreover, if one considers the three features of modern evangelicalism highlighted by Noll, all three apply to Puritanism as well. First, Puritanism (like evangelicalism) was 'an extraordinarily complex phenomenon . . . diverse, flexible, adaptable and multiform' (Collinson in Coffey 2008:264). It is important to note that the Presbyterian, Congregationalist, Baptist and Quaker movements all sprang from Puritanism, not evangelicalism. Second, Puritanism, like evangelicalism, was 'profoundly affected by its popular character.' Puritanism was associated by Monarchs and bishops with the "dreaded spectre of popularity; Puritanism formed a popular religious culture in its own right; and Puritan radicals were purveyors of a populist, anti-intellectual style of charismatic 'enthusiasm'" (Coffey 2008:264). Third, 'innovative but informal networks of communication . . . sustained the transnational character' of Puritanism as much as evangelicalism, giving it 'much of its distinctive shape.' By the middle of the seventeenth century, evangelical Protestants have established networks of communication across the Atlantic (Bremer in Coffey 2008:264).

The evangelical composition of the movement is also observable in its socially transformative nature, following on from its Reformation attributes. Nicholas Wolterstorff quotes a sermon preached by Thomas Case before the House of Commons in 1641:

> Reformation must be universal ... reform all places, all persons and callings; reform the benches of judgement, the inferior magistrates ... Reform the universities, reform the cities, reform the countries, reform inferior schools of learning, reform the Sabbath, reform the ordinances, the worship of God. ... You have more work to do than I can speak ... Every plant which my heavenly father hath not planted shall be rooted up (Wolterstorff 1983:8-9).

This is a much different world from that of the Middle Ages in which social structures were treated as immoveable and permanent. This is revolutionary: the structures of human society, not merely the 'persons who exist within these structures,' must be changed so that they are brought in line with the will of a 'just and holy and gracious God' (Wolterstorff 1983:8-9).

There are certainly differences of degree, and one could argue that evangelicalism was *more* diverse than Puritanism. However, the continuities are as striking as are the discontinuities. Hans Küng argues in his major work on the history of Christianity, movements like Puritanism, Pietism, evangelical revivalism, and fundamentalism can all be placed within the 'Protestant evangelical paradigm of the Reformation' alongside traditional Lutheran and Reformed religion (Küng in Coffey 2008:271). He continues that in the Evangelical Revival,

> the characteristic concerns of the Reformation stand at the centre: justification by faith and the rebirth of the new person in the spirit of Christ. Here a fundamental role is played on the one hand by being overwhelmed with God's grace and on the other by the

believing trust of sinful men and women (in Coffey 2008:271).

But doctrinal truth was not the only characteristic of evangelicalism. Revivalist fervour was also critical. Whitefield, Edwards, and the Wesley's were quite clear that their work entailed a 'revival, awakening, or quickening of a well-established religious tradition that had grown somewhat drowsy' (Coffey 2008:272). That awakening was about putting fire back into Protestant hearts. Whitefield's *Journal* is filled with references to blazing hearts, melted souls, tearful faces, liberty of spirit, enlargement of the heart, inward feelings, and experimental religion—not the language of the Enlightenment; it is the language of Puritanism. There was no doubt in the minds of Anglican critics of evangelicalism that this was a return of Puritan zeal. William Warburton complained of 'the old Puritan fanaticism revived under the new name of Methodism' (Wood in Coffey 2008:273).

Evangelicalism, as it began to emerge as a movement, 'always involved more than the revival of religion, but from the beginnings, both revivals and the longing for revival were always critical' (Noll 2003:76). This fed on its origins in Puritanism, paving the way for what came to be called 'The Great Awakening.'

4.2 Evangelical Revival and The Great Awakening

George Whitefield, Jonathan Edwards and the Wesley brothers —John and Charles—attracted most of the attention from historians, for good reason. However, they were hardly alone in this effort as they were participants in a fairly vibrant 'transatlantic network of relationships committed to the renewal of Christian faith' (Hunter 2010:70).

The leadership of these movements in Britain and the American colonies had varied backgrounds, although those who were most prominent were largely from well-established families of the merchant and professional classes. They were the products of excellent education received at elite universities. For example, John and Charles Wesley, George Whitefield, John Gambold, John Clayton, James Hervey, Benjamin Ingham, and Thomas Brougham were all Oxford-trained; John Erskine and Thomas Gillespie were educated at Edinburgh; Jonathan Edwards, David Brainerd, Jonathan Parsons, Samuel Hopkins, and Joseph Bellamy were trained at Yale; and Thomas Prince Sr., Benjamin Colman, Josiah Smith, and Ebenezer Pemberton were educated at Harvard. They formed an alternative elite as part of the dominant Christian tradition, hailing from 'communities of English non-conformists, Scottish Presbyterians, and New England Puritans' (Hunter 2010:71). Interestingly, evidence indicates that these evangelical pastors were connected to each other and had an awareness of each other's activities.

However, the public upsurge of awakening that became known as the Evangelical Revival in Britain and the Great Awakening in America did not materialise out of thin air. When the revivals came, they were formed by the direct influence of three earlier Christian movements: 'an international Calvinist network in which English Puritanism occupied a central position, the pietist revival from the European continent and a High-Church Anglican tradition of rigorous spirituality and innovative organization' (Noll 2003:50). These specific movements were a reflection of the great religious changes that were inaugurated with the Reformation.

These changes grew out of groundwork traced to the late seventeenth and early eighteenth centuries. Anglican missionaries were well established throughout the colonies from the Society for the Propagation of the Gospel in Foreign Parts by the 1730s. They were actively 'supporting missionaries, providing libraries, and setting up charity schools' (Hunter 2010:71). These societies, along with others, not only helped to prepare people for revival but contributed to the revival that already existed in northern New England and parts of

Wales, Scotland, and England. Although at this point it had not effectively permeated regions or denominations, there was a shared mission across colonial America and Great Britain carrying the common Evangelical message of spiritual new birth through grace.

Local events had rippling effects that transformed widely separated phenomena into an interconnected movement. The first of these took place in Northhampton, Massachusetts in the fall of 1734 born out of the religious seriousness of the town's youth following the untimely death of two well-regarded young people. Jonathan Edwards was the local pastor of the town church and a sermon series that he preached on the theme 'Justification by Faith Alone' received tremendous response. Edwards (1736:348) writes:

> All seemed to be seized with a deep concern about their eternal salvation; all the talk in all companies, and upon occasions was upon the things of religion, and no other talk was anywhere relished; and scarcely a single person in the whole town was left unconcerned about the great things of the eternal world.... (N)o one family that I know of, and scarcely a person, has been exempt.

By March of 1735 other towns in Hampshire County were experiencing this turn to vibrant, all-consuming faith. News quickly circulated about the hundreds that were 'brought to a lively sense of the excellency of Jesus Christ and his sufficiency and willingness to save sinners, and to be much weaned in their affections from the world' (Edwards 1736:348). Altogether, about twenty-five communities throughout western Massachusetts and central Connecticut experienced the stir of revival that had touched off in Northampton. Although the intensity of the revival began to decline in the spring of 1735, in general it was more 'widely spread, more intense and more out of the control of the ministers' (Noll 2003:78).

However, with the Spring of 1735 came life-changing experiences for other young men that were unknown to the larger world. Scotland, Wales, and England also saw an explosion of concern for the gospel to be taken to the unconverted. Along with Edwards came Ebenezer and Ralph Erskine in Scotland, Howell Harris in Wales and George Whitefield in England, all of whom preceded the Wesley brothers in the evangelical awakening (Shelley 2008:332).

England was an unlikely place for a nationwide revival of passionate faith. The wealthy and well-educated of the Enlightenment had pushed religion from the centre of life to its outside edges. The order of the day was focused around moderation for everything. Church historian Bruce Shelley (2008:332) captures this mood quite accurately: 'Ministers blandly ignored the traditional Christian doctrine of man's sinfulness. Instead, men approached God with gentle awe and cheerfulness.' John Tillotson, Archbishop of Canterbury, vigorously denounced what he termed to be 'religious enthusiasm.' They should, instead, express 'proper behaviour'... by... 'reform(ing) their conduct; they should be generous, humane and tolerant, and avoid bigotry and fanaticism' (Shelley 2008:333). Structures organised around every area of life were strict, especially for the churches. Local Anglican rectors were expected to be in complete control of all spiritual activity within their parishes. The population was guided by the partnership of the Anglican Church and the British state, which meant that all preaching was to take place on Sundays in churches. Anything contrary to this was considered 'incendiary and fanatical' (Noll 2001a:223). Out of doors preaching was virtually unheard of so that if it did occur, it was considered seditious.

4.2.1 John Wesley

Such thinking was ignorant of the general conditions of the English Society. Britain's labouring population was crammed into dank housing on narrow, filthy streets. In Bristol, as in much of Britain, society's safety net had failed. Riots had already broken out protesting squalid living conditions, something that would regularly be repeated throughout the eighteenth century. Moreover, churches were failing to keep up with the population or provide for its spiritual needs. Society was ripe for massive change.

John Wesley, Oxford graduate and Anglican clergyman, stepped into this void. He describes what took place on 2 April 1739 in his journal:

> At four in the afternoon I submitted to be more vile, and proclaimed in the highways the glad tidings of salvation, speaking from a little eminence in a ground adjoining to the city, to about three thousand people. The scripture on which I spoke was this (is it possible any one should be ignorant that it is fulfilled in every true minister of Christ?), 'The Spirit of the Lord is upon Me, because He hath anointed Me to preach the gospel to the poor. He hath sent Me to heal the broken-hearted; to preach deliverance to the captives, and recovery of sight to the blind; to set at liberty them that are bruised, to proclaim the acceptable year of the Lord' (Wesley 1903:66).

John Wesley was willing to break the religious structures that had defined his well-disciplined life to bring a message of salvation and hope to people who had never heard it before. This was a momentous step. Wesley was content to ignore parish boundaries for the sake of winning souls. He justified open-air preaching by its effectiveness in 'attracting large numbers, inducing conviction of sin and bringing about conversions' (Bebbington 1989:65). This was one evidence of the pragmatic temper of John Wesley and the Evangelical movement. Other Evangelicals were similarly engaged so that even when planning church buildings, the focus was on function: it was to be designed for preaching. The church building was to 'be cheap and there were to be no obstacles to a clear vision such as pillars' (Bebbington 1989:65).

4.2.2 George Whitefield

George Whitefield was a major catalyst for this broad transatlantic movement. He extensively travelled throughout England and Wales along with seven trips to the colonies and fourteen to Scotland. He was a central figure in a vast network that included 'hundreds of ministers, evangelists, financial backers, printers, and ordinary laypeople' (Hunter 2010:71). However, his personal and regular correspondence with the main revival figures in Britain and America may have been his most significant contribution to the Awakening. Often his writing was practical—circulating devotional material, recommending good books, collecting funds for missionary work. Other communication was more strategic; discussion would centre upon theological matters, the nature of piety and the practice of revivalism so that even though these letters seemed personal in nature they were actually intended for public consumption.

The evangelical movement that was defined by the Great Awakening emerged as a form of Christianity that constituted 'a remarkable example of religion as a powerful agent for political and social change' (Smith 2009:250). Although this claim is demonstrated in a variety of ways, it can be seen clearly in a popular poem of William Cowper, friend and colleague of John Newton, as he critiques the city of London based on profound insight into the sources of the wealth being paraded within the city and the price being exacted for this development on the other side of the world. Cowper (1835:247-48) writes:

It is not seemly, nor of good report,
That she is slack in discipline; more prompt
To avenge than to prevent the breach of law;
That she is rigid in denouncing death
On petty robbers, and indulges life
And liberty, and ofttimes honour too,
To peculators of the public gold;

That thieves at home must hang, but he that puts
Into his overgorged and bloated purse
The wealth of Indian provinces, escapes.

Cowper's poem manages to 'critique the bias of the criminal justice system, defend the rights of the poor and oppressed, and expose the hypocrisy and rapacious greed of capitalists who had begun the plunder of lands and peoples on the other side of the globe' (Smith 2009:250).

4.2.3 William Wilberforce

Cowper's thinking was not isolated. The general headquarters for evangelical crusades in London was a small town 3 miles from the city called 'Clapham.' The village was the country residence of a group of wealthy and fervent evangelicals who sought to practice 'saintliness in daily life and to live with eternity in view' (Shelley 2008:366). A host of causes were birthed in this quiet little town: 'The Church Missionary Society (1799), the British and Foreign Bible Society (1804), The Society for Bettering the Condition of the Poor (1796), The Society for the Reformation of Prison Discipline' as well as many others (Shelley 2008:367). However, the leading cause attended by this group was the abolition of the slave trade, led by William Wilberforce. Wilberforce, a member of Parliament, made his first speech on the trafficking of slaves in the House of Commons in 1789. Through the tireless effort of Wilberforce and his evangelical Clapham colleagues, they reached victory in 1807 when the slave trade was abolished. The Emancipation Act, which freed the slaves in the sprawling British Empire, came on 25 July 1833, just four days before Wilberforce's death (Shelley 2008:369).

4.2.4 Other evangelical leaders

Other evangelicals around the European continent were motivated by their faith to engage with poverty and other social issues, following in the footsteps of the Reformers and Puritans. Johann Wichern, known as the 'father of the Inner Mission,' was strongly influenced by the religious quickening in Germany marked by its strong mission movement. He began visiting the impoverished homes of some of his Sunday school students, which stirred him to concern for home mission in addition to foreign mission. Wichern began what he called a 'ragged school' for the care and education of neglected children in a poverty-stricken area of Hamburg in 1833. Fifteen years later he presented a gripping speech to a large meeting of the German Evangelical Church, proclaiming that 'love no less than faith is the Church's indispensable mark' (Lindberg 1981:49). The Church committed itself to public service, enacting practical programmes of aid to the poor through special education, hospitals, orphanages, prison reform and other ministries that grew from Wichern's influence in the following decades (Lindberg 1981:49).

Throughout Europe at this time there were religious revival movements which inspired social concerns for people trapped in poverty caused by factors related to the Industrial Age. British Methodists 'laboured at adult education, schooling for children, reform of prisons, abolition of slavery and aid to alcoholics. The YMCA (1844), YWCA (1855), and the Salvation Army (1865) were just a few of the many charitable institutions and organisations created to relieve the harmful effects of industrialism' (Lindberg 1981:49). Many evangelicals felt righteous anger expressed as outrage concerning the structural injustices that condemned millions of people to impoverishment in a society that claimed to be Christian in character. Thomas Guthrie of Edinburgh, identified as 'the friend of the poor and oppressed' on a statue in his honour, claimed that the urban poor were doubly deprived of justice since the squalor in which they lived forced them to seek any means possible for survival. They were convicted of crimes traced to the heartlessness and greed of respectable society. Guthrie, in exasperation, warned of the possibility of insurrection and revolution, urging the upper classes to realise that their interests were inextricably intertwined with those of the poor. God has decreed that 'those who neglect the interests of others shall themselves suffer in the end' (Smith 2009:258).

William Booth carried on in the evangelical passion of John Wesley, although he departed from Wesleyan Methodism because of its departure from its founder's world transformative faith. Like Wesley, he pursued his passion for evangelism and continued to use language suggesting that the 'salvation of souls' was always a high priority in his urban mission. However, as many other urban evangelists from both the United States and Europe came to realise, there were many other mitigating factors working against a positive response to the gospel when it was proclaimed to the poor. Booth asks what hope can there be for the 'bastard of a harlot, born in a brothel, suckled on gin, and familiar from earliest infancy with all the bestialities of debauch, violated before she is twelve, and driven onto the streets by her mother?' (Booth 1890:37). He concludes that such a poor woman has little chance in this life, nor in the next! Being surrounded by these overwhelming social needs led Booth and his companions to recognise that evangelism could not be separated from social action.

Norris Magnusson (in Smith 2009:261) explains how they came to this realisation:

> Entering the slums in pursuit of the evangelism that remained their chief concern, they gained there an almost unparalleled knowledge of the conditions in which the poor had to live. Encountering that kind of need, they responded with energy and growing sympathy and indignation. The extensive first-hand experience of rescue workers in the slums taught them both the worth of the poor and the heaviness of the environmental pressures that weighed upon them. It taught them also that society bulwarked the prosperous and oppressed the helpless.

Booth (1890) writes what comes to be one of the key texts to describe evangelical social theology during the last decade of the nineteenth century. He confesses that the sight of helpless and vulnerable people being trampled by 'beasts in human shape' has led him to doubt God's existence. In a particularly bold section, he indicts the owners of firms which 'reduce sweating to a fine art,' defraud workers of rightful wages, steal from widows and orphans, and then dismiss criticism of their actions by making professions 'of public spirit and philanthropy.' Booth states a devastating verdict upon them: '. . . these men are nowadays sent to parliament to make laws for the people. The old prophets sent them to hell—but we have changed all that. They send their victims to hell, and are rewarded by all that wealth can do to make their lives comfortable' (Booth 1890:11).

It is significant to note that evangelicals were truly non-conformists in every sense of the word—whether they were in the United States, Britain, or on the European continent or whether they were Anglicans, Lutherans, or members of non-established churches. 'Official' churches were largely indifferent to the predicament of the poor in their countries or the devastating effect of colonial policies on the residents of Europe's overseas colonies. The plight of the poor galvanised those impacted by the Awakenings so that they were moved to compassion by the 'degrading conditions in slums and prisons, in coal-mining districts, on the American frontier, in West Indian plantations, and elsewhere' (Bosch 2011:287). Those within the evangelical movement held together the dual elements of evangelism and social involvement that was their 'mission.' William Booth once famously described these as 'Siamese twins—to kill one is to slay them both' (Davies-Kildea 2012:2). It was inconceivable that these activities could be separated—evangelising the poor without engaging their social circumstances would be considered morally questionable, especially if one was making a long-term commitment to the people in a community. Conversely, to provide only for the external symptoms of poverty and need without addressing the personal, spiritual conditions that often exacerbated such suffering was unthinkable.

William Booth describes the evolution of his thinking in this regard:

> As time wore on, the earthly miseries connected with the condition of the people began to force themselves more particularly on my notice . . . . (A)s I came to look more closely into things . . . I discovered that the miseries from which I sought to save man in the next world were substantially the same as those from which I everywhere found him suffering in this. . . . I saw that when the Bible said 'He that believeth shall be saved,' it meant not only saved from the miseries of the future world, but from the miseries of this also. That it came with the promise of salvation here and now; from hell and sin and vice and crime and idleness and extravagance, and consequently very largely from poverty and disease, and the majority of kindred woes (Booth in Davies-Kildea 2012:3).

William Booth is not alone in this thinking. The successors of other evangelical traditions point to a time when coming to faith meant joining the anti-slavery, temperance or women's suffrage movements. Eighteenth and nineteenth-century evangelicalism was activist in its ideals. Social action was seen as a logical consequence of individual conversion. Charles Finney, a somewhat controversial revivalist, unleashed a mighty impulse toward social reform as was demonstrated by his work and the way he understood the gospel. He believed that the call to a renewed Christianity 'incorporated the implicit demand that true conversion evidence itself in good works and a commitment to the welfare of others' (Dayton 1976:17). For Finney, to be converted was to forsake one's interests for the sake of the needs of others. He facilitated this by setting up a series of 'benevolent societies' for every conceivable philanthropy and social concern. Finney's converts immersed themselves into this work (Dayton 1976:18).[13]

4.3 The 'Great Reversal'

The period surrounding the U.S. Civil War marks a major point of transition in evangelical social concern. According to historian Timothy Smith,[14] the church connected evangelism with social responsibility for most of its history. However, that changed for the evangelical church between the years 1865-1930 due to at least three major factors: premillennialism, individualism, and a reaction to the social gospel (Goheen 1992:2).

4.3.1 Major factors

i Premillennialism

The majority of the protestant church was postmillennial in the middle of the nineteenth century. In 1859 an influential theological quarterly confidently asserted that postmillennialism was the 'commonly received doctrine' among American Protestants.[15] It dominated the religious press, the leading seminaries, most of the Protestant Clergy and was ingrained in the contemporary mind. However, by the early twentieth century, it had largely vanished—Lewis Sperry Chafer claimed in 1936 that it was 'without living voice' (Moorhead 1984:61). This eschatological shift had a significant impact on the social concern in the evangelical church. Timothy Weber (in Goheen 1992:2) summarises this situation:

> Though not all premillennialists accepted the extreme position on the futility of reform activities, one must finally conclude that premillennialism generally broke the spirit of social concern which had played such a prominent role in earlier evangelicalism. Its hopeless view of the present order left little room for

God or for themselves to work in it. The world and the present age belonged to Satan, and lasting reform was impossible until Jesus returned to destroy Satan's power and set up the perfect kingdom. Consequently, though there were significant exceptions, premillennialists turned their backs on the movements to change social institutions. In time, the social conscience of an important part of American Evangelicalism atrophied and ceased to function. In that regard, at least, premillennialism broke faith with the evangelical spirit which it had fought so hard to preserve.

This change in eschatological interpretation dramatically affected the evangelical church's understanding and practice of mission so that social concern had largely vanished from the concern of the evangelical church.

There are a number of reasons that brought this about. First, premillennialism stressed the future consummation of the kingdom, sometimes almost exclusively. The current stage of the kingdom was inconsequential, necessitating no further care or concern on the part of believers for the state of the world or the social conditions of those living within it.

Second, premillennialists took a pessimistic view of the world and its systems. Earthly matters would grow progressively worse to culminate finally in cataclysmic tribulation. This philosophy of history yielded expected results: why rearrange the deck chairs on the sinking Titanic? Any social action contemplated by the evangelical church lost any sense of urgency in its mission. It had 'learnt to tolerate corruption and injustice, to expect and even welcome them as signs of Christ's imminent return' (Bosch 2011:290).

Third, sin was viewed by late nineteenth and early twentieth-century premillennialists as only personal in nature without structural foundations. Moreover, if sin is personal and private, then salvation is also personal. D L Moody stressed personal sins like dancing, drunkenness, and disregard of the

Sabbath, among other things, which required a personal salvation. He identifies his position clearly:

> I look at this world as a wrecked vessel. God has given me a lifeboat, and said to me, 'Moody, save all you can. God will come in judgment and burn up this world.... The world is getting darker and darker; its ruin is coming nearer and nearer. If you have any friends on this wreck unsaved, you had better lose no time in getting them off' (Weber in Goheen 1992:2).

Motivation centred on the personal salvation of souls without concern for physical circumstances since they were only temporal.

Finally, when premillennialists viewed the kingdom of God as present, they viewed it as inward. The kingdom of God is to be found within you. The kingdom of God in Jesus' ministry was 'purely religious, supernatural, future oriented, predominantly spiritual and inward . . . (without) political, national or earthly design' (Bosch 2011:279). There was no appeal to people to 'abandon most of the standards of respectable American middle-class way of life. It was to these standards, in fact, that people were to be converted' (Marsden in Bosch 2011:325). Premillennialist churches and agencies were run in the same manner as efficient businesses. No one noticed any incongruence in advocating 'withdrawal from the world while at the same time managing the church as if it were a secular organisation' (Bosch 2011:326).

The shift from postmillennialism to premillennialism along with its accompanying pessimism and individualism uncoupled social responsibility from the mission of the evangelical church in the early twentieth-century. David Bosch (2011:325) summarises:

> As revivalism and evangelicalism slowly adopted premillennialism, the emphasis shifted away from the social involvement to exclusively verbal evangelism. In the course of time virtually 'all progressive social

concern, whether political or private, became suspect among revivalist evangelicals and was relegated to a very minor role' . . . . By the 1920s the 'Great Reversal' . . . had been completed; the evangelicals' interest in social concerns had, for all practical purposes, been obliterated.

ii Individualism

The first reason for this shift in social concern was theological —a change to a premillennialist view of eschatology and history. But the second reason was the individualistic view of humanity that was dominant in discussions regarding sin and salvation. Revivalist evangelists ignored structural evil by reducing sin to personal vices, describing salvation as getting off a sinking ship onto a lifeboat, one person at a time. Therefore, when some expressed a desire to engage in social issues, they were interested only in attempting relief efforts with little concern for addressing any of the structural origins of the problem. John Stott (1992:353) describes this position: 'To ignore the dehumanising evils of society, while preaching the humanizing influence of salvation, is to be guilty of an inner contradiction which misrepresents God and distorts the gospel.'

iii Reaction to the social gospel

The Social Gospel grew out of a secularised postmillennialism in the nineteenth- century. The commitment to social reform that was a corollary of evangelicalism was lost in the process. Richard Lovelace (1981:4) comments as follows:

> In the late 19th century, under the deforming impact of dispensational pessimism and liberal optimism, the broad river of classical evangelicalism divided into a delta, with shallower streams emphasizing ecumenism and social renewal on the left and confessional orthodoxy and evangelism on the right.

Mainline churches gradually abandoned the broad scope of

classical postmillennialism and no longer regarded history as an antithesis between the kingdom of God and the kingdom of darkness.

The social gospel movement was characterised by secular thinking undergirded by the following basic concepts:

1. **Progress** was now considered an intrinsic process brought about by human programmes and effort, not the powerful working of the gospel by the movement of God's Spirit.

2. **History** was moving ahead toward a golden age with sin defined as ignorance and identified with the structures of society which were in the process of being addressed.

3. **Salvation** meant reforming society through education and developmental programmes, bolstered by an optimistic view of history inherited from the Enlightenment. It was anchored entirely in this world, leaning upon human initiatives to usher in the kingdom of God, depending entirely upon human efforts for success.

4. The **kingdom of God** was a present reality offering continuity between creation and redemption. The old earth is being renewed and transformed (Goheen 1992: 3). It involved, 'no discontinuities, no crises, no tragedies or sacrifices, no loss of all things, no cross and resurrection' (Niebuhr 1959:191). An indulgent God admitted 'souls' to his 'heaven' on the recommendation of his kind son (Niebuhr 1959:135). Christ the redeemer became, 'Jesus the benevolent and wise teacher, or the spiritual genius in whom the religious capacities of humankind were fully developed' (Bosch 2011:329).

5 Examining the Movement

Many evangelicals during the early 20th century did not share the convictions or optimism of the social gospel adherents and reacted strongly against the theological liberalism that was seeping into the churches of Europe and America. Feeling like they had their backs against the wall, they became preoccupied with the defence and proclamation of the gospel since no one else appeared to be upholding historic, biblical Christianity. They were also disillusioned and pessimistic following World War 1 due to their exposure to human evil and suffering. Earlier social programmes had failed so that all attempts at reform were considered useless. Historic Reformed Christianity moved into retreat (Stott 1985: 25). Until well into the 1960s, 'social involvement remained under the cloud of suspicion it had attracted in the 1920s' (Bebbington 1989:264).

5.1 Polarisation of the movement

5.1.1 Theological separation

Secularised postmillennial social gospel theology and premillennial evangelical theology became sharply polarised. Evangelicals reacted to the imbalance that was created by giving up their social conscience, viewing social concern with suspicion at best and, at worst, as a complete betrayal of the gospel. Instead of social and corporate concern, evangelicals concerned themselves almost exclusively with the salvation of the individual, emphasising the soul over the body and stressing heaven, eternity and the future over life here and now. In America, this polarisation encouraged the emergence of an aggressive fundamentalism, while in Britain it tended more towards retreat and a 'personal holiness movement' (Smith 1998:77). Not until the 1940s did a number of American evangelicals begin taking a stand against the anti-intellectualism and separatism of fundamentalism. Among these was Carl F. H. Henry.

i Challenge from history

Henry (1947:44-45) challenged evangelicals to return to their historical roots and once again take seriously the social responsibilities of the church. He writes:

> Whereas once the redemptive gospel was a world changing message, now it has narrowed to a world-resisting message . . . . Fundamentalism in revolting against the Social Gospel seemed also to revolt against the Christian social imperative . . . . It does not challenge the injustices of the totalitarianism, the secularism of modern education, the evils of racial hatred, the wrongs of current management relations, and inadequate bases of international dealings.

Henry and Billy Graham joined in organising the first of what was to become a series of influential and formative conferences culminating in the Lausanne movement. Though originally conceived as a challenge to the World Council of Churches' emphasis on social concerns rather than personal conversion, the prominent and recurring theme of Lausanne 1974 was on the relationship between evangelism and social problems due to the provocative plenary addresses given by Samuel Escobar and René Padilla. Padilla spoke on 'Evangelism and the World,' reminding participants that 'evangelism cannot be reduced to the verbal communication of doctrinal content, with no reference to specific forms of man's involvement in the world' while condemning the too-common identification of Christianity with the 'American way of life' (Padilla in Clawson 2012:795). A few days later, Escobar made a strong statement in favour of integral mission, affirming that evangelism and social action were 'inseparable' (Escobar in Clawson 2012:795). These addresses had a huge impact at the Congress and were credited with 'causing a significant shift in Christian thinking' (Clawson 2012:795)

The final form of the Lausanne Covenant included not just one sentence of social concerns as originally intended by some of the more conservative conveners, but an entire section on 'Christian Social Responsibility.' It stated that while 'reconciliation with man is not reconciliation with God, nor is social action evangelism, nor is political liberation salvation, nevertheless we affirm that evangelism and socio-political involvement are both part of our Christian duty . . . the salvation we claim should be transforming us in the totality of our personal and social responsibilities' (Douglas in Clawson 2012:796). John Stott (1984:9) described it as a 'recovery of our temporarily mislaid social conscience.' It is clear that the influence of Lausanne 74 provided the global evangelical movement with greater awareness of the need for an integral approach to both evangelism and social justice.

The direct impact of the Lausanne Movement also helped to legitimise social ministries and progressive political activism within the broader evangelical community. With well-known evangelical leaders like Billy Graham and John Stott assigning their approval to statements on Christian Social Responsibility and Radical Discipleship, these concepts 'entered the mainstream of evangelical dialogue and became acceptable evangelical theologies not just for Latin Americans, but North American evangelicals as well' (Clawson 2012:797).

ii Further polarisation

However, despite mainstream acceptance of this new thinking, the New Christian Right overshadowed the influence of the Lausanne Movement. There was a secular conservative backlash to the radical social reforms of the 1960s and 70s that was marked by a resurgence of conservative social and theological values within the evangelical movement. Emerging evangelical leaders such as James Dobson, Pat Robertson, and Jerry Falwell showed a willingness to engage with socio-political issues, but mainly around sexual morality, abortion or other conservative political matters that impacted 'family values.' Additionally, they controlled powerful media outlets that enabled them to sway large conservative audiences and exercise political clout. The concerns around poverty and economic justice which had motivated evangelicals concerned with integral mission were 'either neglected by the Christian Right, or, more commonly, seen as part of the liberal agenda that in their view was to blame for the moral and spiritual decline of American society' (Clawson 2012:797). Throughout the last two decades of the twentieth century, in both perception and reality, North American evangelicalism became defined by the conservative politics of the Christian Right. This coincided with the increased fragmentation among the members of the evangelical left. By the late 1990s, some of these leaders were lamenting an apparent disconnect between the more moderate, socially concerned mission organisations and colleges and the broader, more socially conservative general evangelical faith community. (Clawson 2012:797).

5.2 Focus of the movement

But the struggle for a return to evangelical roots continued along lines relating to mission. Integral mission, according to René Padilla, is 'the concrete expression of a commitment to Jesus Christ as Lord of the totality of life and of all creation' (Padilla in Clawson 2012:792). There is no real distinction between serving 'spiritual' needs and serving 'physical' needs because Jesus is considered Lord over all of creation and every sphere of life. Thus, the mission of the church cannot simply be condensed to making religious converts but must embrace action on behalf of the poor and in the service of social justice.

This definition of mission fits with the approach given by Kritzinger, Meiring and Saayman (1994) in their book 'On being witnesses.' They list the goal of mission as a threefold formula: 'They should serve to manifest the glory and greatness of God's grace; they should plant churches; and they should call people to conversion' (1994:36). For the authors, these elements should not be considered in a narrow or one-sided way, but 'can only be pursued in a holistic way' (Kritzinger *et al.* 1994:39). In saying this, they refer to the comprehensive approach of Hoekendijk, which states, 'The intense universality of salvation and the radical application of Christ's kingship over the whole of life demand that we address people in their total environment' (Hoekendijk in Kritzinger *et al.* 1994:36). Hoekendijk's approach encompasses *kerygma* [proclamation], *diakonia* [ministry of service], *koinonia* [communion or fellowship], and they add a fourth dimension *leitourgia*, [the public worship service of God].

The goals of planting churches and calling people to conversion—two of the three goals of mission—are characteristic elements of the missionary era and would be quite normal activities for evangelical congregations. In a dualistic framework where spiritual activities remain separate from the physical, these activities are housed comfortably within a private, religious context 'with little reference to the public world – with, of course, exceptions, such as the South African church's involvement in the struggle for and against apartheid' (van Niekerk 2014a:2).

Kritzinger *et al.* instead emphasise a 'holistic approach' to mission—addressing 'people in their total environment'—to engage the 'privatised' gospel, '. . . a Christian spirituality of inwardness' followed by many as the predominant practice of faith (see Jenson in van Niekerk 2014a:2). This holistic approach forces one out of dualism into the reality and fullness of God's Kingdom.

This understanding of mission is validated by Christopher Wright, who believes that mission 'flows from the heart of God.' In his book titled, *'The mission of God,'* Wright (2006:22) observes that *'the whole Bible is itself a "missional phenomenon."'* The Bible gives us the

> story of God's mission through God's people in their
> engagement with God's world for the sake of the

whole of God's creation... and with its center, focus, climax and completion in Jesus Christ. Mission is not just one of a list of things that the Bible happens to talk about, only a bit more urgently than some. Mission is... "What it's all about."

Forgiveness of our personal sins sits within this framework. However, this is not the 'whole gospel.' The church can 'reduce the gospel,' but

the Bible itself will reduce our tendency to reduce the gospel to a solution to our individual sin problem and a swipe card for heaven's door, and replace that reductionist impression with a message that has to do with the cosmic reign of God in Christ that will ultimately eradicate all evil from God's universe (and solve our individual sin problem too, of course) (Wright 2010:31).

However, neither of these approaches confronts the division between what is considered private religion and public life nearly as strongly as Lesslie Newbigin. He writes that in the Roman world of the 1st century, private religion '. . . dedicated to the pursuit of a purely personal and spiritual salvation for its members . . . flourished as vigorously . . . as it does in North America today' (Newbigin 1986:99). Toleration existed because it did not challenge the political order. 'The early church refused such protection because it could not accept relegation to a private sphere of purely inward and personal religion' (van Niekerk 2014a:2). It presented itself as a '. . . public assembly to which God is calling all men everywhere without distinction. This made a collision with the imperial power inevitable – as inevitable as the cross' (Newbigin 1986:99-100).

5.2.1 Emerging integral mission

When the 1989 Lausanne Congress was held in Manilla, Philippines, many non-Westerners perceived a deliberate move on the part of its North American organisers to move the focus away from integral mission back towards the primacy of evangelism over social engagement. Over a decade later, progressive evangelicals Tom and Christine Sine would remark that 'an integrated approach to mission has been losing ground in recent years . . . as a number of evangelicals in the United States have embraced a view of social responsibility shaped by the religious and political right that largely ignores social justice issues' (Sine & Sine 2003:73).

However, despite the signs of marginalisation and decline, the ideas of integral mission have remained a steady influence within the evangelical movement. Key locations within the evangelical community, such as seminaries and liberal arts colleges, have become centres of influence over the past few decades. Additionally, rapid globalisation has contributed to an increased awareness of the state of the world through the rapidly expanding global electronic hardwiring of the planet into an electronic nervous system. Global events no longer happen in a remote corner of the earth but are instead broadcast instantly through social networking sites that impact how we see ourselves and how we see others. Borders are melting. Distance is diminishing. We can 'experience' the desperate needs around us through our interconnected global village.

What this has meant is that the evangelical community is deeply fragmented. Even though the Lausanne movement and follow-up conferences have been in evangelical consciousness for nearly forty years, 'the majority of American pastors have not heard of the Lausanne Covenant, let alone any of the follow-up consultations on an integrated approach to missions' (Sine & Sine 2003:73). There remains an intense debate among evangelical leaders in the United States who are clearly aware of the continuing international dialog on integral mission. But along with this has come a noticeable shift in concern towards the environment and the poor along with other progressive social concerns evidenced in two watershed documents released by the National Association of Evangelicals. First, in 2005: *For the Health of the Nation: An Evangelical Call to Civic Responsibility,* favouring, 'effective governmental programs and structural changes' that would lead to a just economy, fairer trade and foreign policies focused on reducing global poverty, supporting human rights and religious liberty, encouraging Christians to engage in practical peacemaking, strongly endorsing environmental stewardship and calling for governments to restrain the use of military force. This was followed in 2008 by the 'Evangelical Manifesto: A Declaration of Evangelical Identity and Public Commitment,' which was signed by over seventy prominent leaders calling for the 'expansion of our concerns beyond single-issue politics, such as abortion and marriage, and a fuller recognition of the comprehensive causes and concerns of the Gospel,' such as poverty, violence, racism and pandemic diseases (Clawson 2012:799).

Additionally, integral mission has received more attention by prominent evangelical leaders that have had global audiences from across the theological spectrum. Pastors such as Tim Keller at Redeemer Presbyterian in New York City, Bill Hybels, former Pastor at Willow Creek Church in the suburbs of Chicago, and Rick Warren at Saddleback Community Church in Orange County, California were a few of the American pastors that came out solidly in favour of active engagement with poverty alleviation initiatives as a movement of the gospel. Other writers such as Jim Wallis (*God's Politics*), Ron Sider (*Rich Christians in an Age of Hunger*), Richard Stearns (*Hole in the Gospel*) and Timothy Chester (Micah Network) have been embraced by evangelicals encouraged by these authors and others to engage practices of social justice and lifestyles of radical discipleship.

5.2.2 Current context

However, it's hard to measure whether this increased popularity of integral mission and its activities has yielded much in the way of community transformation as the gospel moves evangelicals toward service.

Lausanne 2010 held in Cape Town, South Africa, took place 'to strengthen, inspire and equip the Church for world evangelization in our generation, and to exhort Christians in their duty to engage in issues of public and social concern' (Padilla 2011:87).

Padilla expressed concern in a number of areas, especially around the dichotomy that influences a large segment of evangelicalism, especially in the West, between evangelism and social responsibility. The wording of the Lausanne mission statement reflects this dichotomy in that it intends to 'strengthen, inspire and equip the Church for world evangelization' but only 'exhort Christians' in their duty to engage with social issues. He argues that the *primary* mission of the church is 'world evangelization conceived in terms of the oral delivery of the Gospel, while engagement on matters of public concern—the good works through which Christians fulfil their vocation as "light of the world" to the glory of God (Matt. 5:14-16)—are a *secondary* duty for which Christians do not need to be strengthened, inspired, or equipped but only exhorted' (Padillia 2011:87). It appears that the focus, later emphasised in a plenary session dedicated to *a strategy for the evangelization of the world in the generation* reflected a numbers-based approach to evangelism typical of the 'market mentality that characterizes a sector of evangelicalism in the United States' (Padilla 2011:87).

This means that the primacy of evangelism remains the oral delivery of the gospel—certainly critical in reaching the world for Christ, but only part of the 'good news.' Unfortunately, there seems to be little change in emphasis that would reflect a variation from Lausanne's corporate position in 1974, even though much headway had been accomplished in the intervening years around evangelical thinking about the importance of social responsibility in the presentation of the gospel.

So, much of the nature of early twentieth century evangelicalism still prevails, particularly among rank and file evangelicals. There has been a useful shift in theological understanding so that social concern is at least considered as part of the evangelical church's mission. However, the struggle remains around how to relate social responsibility to the verbal proclamation of the gospel in the mission of the church, particularly in its local form.

In South Africa, there is a broad consensus growing among churches of diverse backgrounds that 'the church should be involved with those who suffer, people who are poor, oppressed, HIV patients, vulnerable children, gender issues, combatting crime and corruption, the destruction of the ecology – to work towards a healthy and sustainable society, beginning in the local community' (van Niekerk 2014a:4). The question of how this should be accomplished requires the application of resources from varied disciplines to meet the complexity of the problem in a local South African context. This question will be explored further in Chapter 7 by examining a church-based approach for empowering unemployed people.

6 Conclusion

This chapter has traced the history of the Evangelical movement from the Reformation into our current context. David Bebbington's (1989:2) definition listing conversionism, crucicentrism, Biblicism and activism as necessary elements to define an evangelical provides a well-respected and accurate guideline for assessment. Although Bebbington only follows the movement from the 1730s with the Great Awakening, others provide the details to trace evangelicalism much further back in history.

Historically, the evangelical movement always contained a

concern for the social needs of others as a key element in a holistic understanding of the gospel. Leaders previously highlighted were concerned about others in a way that indicated a more thorough understanding of the gospel that went beyond the proclamation of a message. They were deeply concerned about man and society and saw their mandate as transformative agents on a mission as followers of Jesus. The structural change that they brought to society was evident in many ways as demonstrated by the abolishment of the slave trade and engagement with the structures of industrial civilisation. Their mark can still be felt as the gospel moved through nations and impacted societies.

However, due to many factors and a significant change in theological focus, the evangelical movement lost its world transformative engagement and retreated into a survivalist mentality that abandoned its desire to engage with many of the serious social needs around them. The 'Great Reversal' was instrumental in curbing social involvement, functioning as a protectionist stance against the social gospel movement while accepting and promoting a premillennialist theology that envisaged a world that would become increasingly worse to usher in the return of Christ, and therefore should not be engaged.

Recently, the evangelical movement has shown some signs of change as a result of global evangelical conferences and movements identifying the necessity of an integral approach to evangelism and mission. Significant steps have been taken to outline a way forward that would engage the desperate needs in society with a holistic movement of the gospel. These measures have been met with limited success and participation. Although the tide seems to be slightly turning, there is a long journey necessary to return the evangelical movement to its historical roots as a transformative agent that engages the overwhelming needs of society with the gospel.

Chapter 3 will discuss poverty as it is defined by society and through Scripture. It will also consider a research approach that will provide the structure for a holistic developmental intervention based upon basic human needs.

CHAPTER THREE

DEFINITION OF POVERTY AND POVERTY ALLEVIATION WITHIN A DEVELOPMENTAL FRAMEWORK

Poverty is pain; it feels like a disease. It attacks a person not only materially but also morally. It eats away one's dignity and drives one into total despair.
(A poor woman, Moldova 1997)

1 Introduction

In the previous chapter, the discussion traced the development of the Evangelical movement. Historical evidence shows that, from its earliest days, there was care for the needs of the poor as an important focus and part of its gospel mandate. This was prominent from the Reformation until the end of the nineteenth century. The questions to now consider are around whether the need for such engagement with poverty is still necessary and then, if so, whether the Evangelical community still bears responsibility to carry out such engagement as a mandate of the gospel.

It is important to start this section with a few definitions. Economist Adam Smith proposed a conceptual definition of poverty over two hundred years ago, categorising a person in poverty as one missing 'not only the commodities which are indispensably necessary for the support of life, but whatever the custom of the country renders it indecent for creditable people, even of the lowest order, to be without'[16] (Smith 1776, Book 5, Chapter 2, Article 4).This definition has provided a general framework used to define poverty for hundreds of years. The human condition(s) which might classify one as being 'in poverty' have complicated interpretations based on multiple factors considering available resources, contextual standards, and public perceptions that take into consideration what a particular society would determine as unjust—an 'unacceptable' standard of living.

Such a framework is helpful for this study. This chapter will look at poverty from different vantage points. First, poverty will be examined from a Biblical perspective. It will consider intended human flourishing and covenant and how that guides our description of poverty and the way forward. Poverty is a series of broken relationships and Scripture addresses this in light of who God is and what He desires for creation. Community is a crucial part this discussion.

Poverty will then be viewed through the eyes of those living in poverty around the world. This is a people-centred approach that details the depth of poverty as much more than simply a lack of income. Those living in poverty know what this feels like as they live with the physical and psychological challenges of brokenness at many levels in the day to day struggle to merely survive.

People-centred poverty requires a people-centred approach that can fight against those things that steal *shalom*. A people-centred approach that can be used to help one frame an intervention to alleviate poverty is Human Scale Development as described by Manfred Max-Neef. The term 'poverty' is not generally helpful in that it is not detailed enough. Instead, poverty, as seen from an overall perspective in Human Scale Development, is comprised of 'poverties' that can be individually engaged. This approach will be described in detail. At the conclusion of this chapter, it is hoped that one will have a sense of the way forward for the evangelical movement in a way that is faithful to Scripture and unites communities into a movement seeking *shalom* as a mission imperative.

Interventions to fight poverty can be structured by churches in mission, bringing hope and healing to local South African communities.

2 Biblical Definition of Poverty

This section explores the biblical perspective regarding poverty and its alleviation, including God's expectations for his followers as they related to the poor in their midst. The Hebrew Scriptures contain many passages describing the poor and the requirements placed upon Israel concerning provision for the poor and those groups in society normally impoverished.[17] There are serious ramifications for failing to engage properly.

In similar fashion the New Testament, beginning with the teachings of Jesus, encourages special care for the poor as a requirement for followers of Christ. Jesus qualifies 'loving your neighbour' by relating it to the way that one loves oneself. Moreover, the Early Church, in following this example, offers a model for poverty alleviation that is challenging to consider in its scope and in the way that it impacted the 1st Century world. The gospel rapidly spread by demonstration through meeting the needs of others.

2.1 Inherent value

To understand poverty, one must understand the framework defining creation. This framework starts with God, who is inherently relational, existing as three-in-one from all eternity. All human beings are also relational and endowed with value and dignity based upon their unique design that springs from humanity's creation in God's image. This is a critical motivation that forms the basis defining care for all people, especially those considered by worldly status as being less valuable than others.

> Then God said, 'Let us make man in our image, after our likeness. And let them have dominion over the fish of the sea and over the birds of the heavens

and over the livestock and over all the earth and over every creeping thing that creeps on the earth.' So God created man in his own image, in the image of God he created him; male and female he created them (Gen. 1.26-27).

God is concerned for the man and woman He created, a concern founded upon mankind's special created status as image-bearers of God. This unique status gives humans intrinsic value. Human beings, therefore, as the 'image bearers' of God innately deserve respect and dignity. All people are on equal footing regardless of financial standing, status or power. Those in poverty are no less the 'image bearers' of God than are those who are prosperous.

Because man is relational by nature, humans flourish when these relationships (with God, self, others, and the rest of creation) are functioning properly. These relationships are described by Steve Corbett and Brian Fikkert (2009) as follows:

- Relationship with God: This is the primary relationship, with all others flowing from this one. Human beings, according to the Westminster Shorter Catechism, are created to 'glorify God and to enjoy him forever.' This is one's 'calling,' the purpose for which mankind was created. 'When we do this, we experience the presence of God as our heavenly Father and live in a joyful, intimate relationship with Him as His children' (2009:57-58).

- Relationship with Self: As people are created in the image of God, one has inherent worth and dignity with a high calling to reflect God's being.

- Relationship with Others: God created us to live in loving relationship with one another.

- Relationship with Creation: Mankind is called to be a steward for what God has created. He is the owner. God called humans to 'interact with creation, to make possibilities into realities, and to be able

to sustain ourselves via the fruits of our stewardship' (2009:58).

Since mankind is a relational being, poverty is what results
when 'relationships do not work, are not just, are not for life,
and are not harmonious or enjoyable. Poverty is the absence
of shalom in all its meanings.[18] (Myers1999:86). This has ramifications that impact everything and will be discussed in
greater detail later in this chapter and in Chapters 6 and 7.

As God's image bearers, no one is insignificant, and no one
is worthless. Life has meaning and importance because God's
imprint is upon one's humanity. Given this fact, Duane Elmer
states, 'we must see others as God sees them, treat them as he
would and name them as he names them' (2006:63). Therefore, on this basis, all people should be treated with the respect and dignity that God has given them; God's image is pro-
faned when people are either mistreated or considered as less
valuable than others. 'One cannot honor God and at the same
time treat another person in a manipulative, dehumanizing,
disrespectful way' (Elmer 2006:63).

2.2 Relationship through covenant

Even though all humanity has special significance brought
about through the process of creation, Israel is singled out by
God for special relationship. One realises through the Scriptural narrative Israel's ethical and redemptive significance
when God calls and nurtures Israel into existence through
Abraham. The Hebrew Scriptures are not merely given as a
collection of moral teachings to enable individual Hebrews
'to lead privately upright lives before God' (Wright 2004:51),
although this is not to deny that there is an individual component in moral choices and behaviour. Instead, the individual
is addressed as part of a communal gathering to ensure the
moral and spiritual health of the whole community. Christopher Wright (2004:51) provides insight here:

God's purpose ... (was) to create a new community of

people who in their social life would embody those qualities of righteousness, peace, justice and love that reflect God's own character and were God's original purpose for humanity.

This insight is a significant framework for one's understanding of Scripture. There is relevance to the 'social angle' preempting the question of what the passage is saying **to me**. Instead, the passage must be studied within its social context in the Hebrew Scriptures, asking how this passage contributes to one's understanding of the social and ethical life of Israel. How does this text shape that society? The follow-up question might then be what it might have to say within the existing community of God's people and then its impact on human society in general. Walter Brueggeman (1980:1098-99) focuses this discussion with a challenge to constantly consider the covenantal nature of ancient Hebrew faith for both the Church and the world:

> We may re-articulate our covenantal hope for the world. So long as this subversive paradigm [covenant] is kept to God and church, we are safe enough. Its character of surprise and threat becomes clear when the covenant is related to the world beyond the believing community. The covenantal paradigm affirms that the world we serve and for which we care is a world yet to be liberated. A theology of covenanting is not worth the effort unless it leads to energy and courage for mission . . . The three belong together: a *God* who makes covenant by making a move toward the partner (Hos. 2:14, 18-20); a *community* that practices covenant by the new forms of Torah, knowledge and forgiveness (Jer. 31:31-34); and a *world* yet to be transformed to covenanting, by the dismantling of imperial reality (Is. 42:6-7; 49:6).

The critical challenge that remains upon closer examination is this: How must one behave and what kind of person must one be to stay consistent with this vision of God and his purposes? Moreover, the Church, as the expression of the new Israel, is to reflect these qualities of God's character—his righteousness, justice, peace, and love—both within and outside of the covenant community. They were, and we are, a distinctive people called to mission reflecting the character of God.

This unique experience was intended to display powerful lessons. Israel was to learn two (at least) important things: 'who really was God (YHWH, the LORD), and how they were now to live (in obedience)' (Wright 2004:53). There were both theological and ethical implications for them resulting from their unique history.

> [35]To you it was shown, that you might know that the LORD is God; there is no other besides him (Deut. 4.35). [39]Know therefore today, and lay it to your heart, that the LORD is God in heaven above and earth beneath; there is no other. [40]Therefore you shall keep his statutes and his commandments, which I command you today, that it may go well with you and with your children after you, and that you may prolong your days in the land that the LORD your God is giving you for all time (Deut. 4.39,40).

It was essential for Israel to know the nature and identity of the God with Whom they were now in covenant. With this understanding, they would know how to live in such a way as to attract the attention of the nations around them, 'namely, in responsive and grateful obedience to his will and ways' (Wright 2004:53). Wright summarises the richness of this relationship as follows:

> First, Israel has had a *unique experience* of God's revelation and redemption. As a result of this, secondly, they now have a *unique knowledge* of the identity of the LORD as God. That in turn means, thirdly, that they now have a *unique responsibility* to live in the midst of the nations in a manner that reflects in their own behaviour the ethical character of the LORD as expressed in the commands he has given them for their own good (Wright 2004:53).

The failure to grasp fully the uniqueness of this relationship carried consequences.

With this in mind, it is now possible to move into a more well-defined and focused understanding of this covenantal relationship through specific examples concerning the poor and God's protective care. There are economic principles at play here around land and possessions. God claims ultimate ownership: 'The land shall not be sold in perpetuity, for the land is mine. For you are strangers and sojourners with me' (Lev. 25.23). This has clear ramifications that bear upon all of life in community as God's people.

Consideration will then be given to the teachings of Jesus who consummates covenant with God in himself, claiming that, 'Whoever has seen me has seen the Father' (Jn. 14.9). The consequences of this statement bring to life ultimate covenant society lived out through a people who display God's heart for true community as followers of Jesus to a world that is in pain. However, as long as this subversive paradigm is kept to God and the church, 'we are safe enough.' Brueggemann (1980:1098) continues:

> The covenantal paradigm affirms that the world which we serve, and for which we care, is a world yet to be liberated. . . (which) leads to energy and courage for mission. . . . (T)he world is intended by God to be a community that covenants, that distributes its produce equally, that values all its members, and that brings the strong and the weak together in common work and common joy. . . . And the mission of the believing community is to articulate, anticipate and practice that transformation which is sure to come.

This is the challenging model of covenant offered by the Early Church to the evangelical movement for the alleviation of poverty. Mission in this context seeks to transform impoverished communities to ultimately reflect the covenantal community which is to come, impacting life in all of its aspects.

2.3 Ownership of land

This impact is seen in the economic foundation of Israel as a covenant community regarding ownership. The land was given to Israel within the context of covenant, outlining the context of the gift and its reciprocal commitments. The land was an outward display of God's faithfulness to Israel and Israel's covenantal relationship with God. Israel was dependent upon God, which was good because God is dependable. And one way that he displayed his dependability was by providing the gift of land as he had promised:

> And you shall make response before the Lord your God, 'A wandering Aramean was my father. And he went down into Egypt and sojourned there, few in number, and there he became a nation, great, mighty, and populous. [6] And the Egyptians treated us harshly and humiliated us and laid on us hard labor. [7] Then we cried to the Lord, the God of our fathers, and the Lord heard our voice and saw our affliction, our toil, and our oppression. [8] And the Lord brought us out of Egypt with a mighty hand and an outstretched arm, with great deeds of terror, with signs and wonders. [9] And he brought us into this place and gave us this land, a land flowing with milk and honey. [10] And behold, now I bring the first of the fruit of the ground, which you, O Lord, have given me.' And you shall set it down before the Lord your God and worship before the Lord your God (Deut. 26.5–10 (ESV).

But the land still belonged to the LORD. He retained the ultimate title of ownership. 'The land shall not be sold in perpetuity, for the land is mine. For you are strangers and sojourners with me' (Lev. 25.23). The Israelites' relationship to God as described in this verse is quite interesting. The Hebrew term *gērîm wĕtôšābîm* referred to a class of people within Israelite society who did not own any land since they had been either descendants of the old Canaanite population or were immigrant workers (Wright 2006:292). This group of people was totally dependent on the Israelite household within which they were residing. As long as the host Israelite household was economically viable and remained on their land, these dependents had a measure of security.

The LORD places himself as the landowner while the Israelites, as indicated throughout Scripture, are his dependent tenants. As long as they remained in covenant with the LORD, they were secure. But if they rebelled against his rule, there would be consequences; they could forfeit his protection and would risk becoming landless aliens again. So, although the Israelites possessed the land, the LORD owns the land which means that the, '. . . Israelites were accountable to their divine landlord for proper treatment of what was ultimately his property' (Wright 2004:94).

This relationship generated a wide range of responsibilities for the Israelites to follow. It also meant that no one could simply do what he or she liked with this property. Wright (2004:95) classifies these responsibilities under three broad headings: 'responsibility directly to God; responsibility to one's family; responsibility to one's neighbours.' He outlines these responsibilities in greater detail as follows:

> Responsibility to God for the land included such things as tithes and first fruits of the harvest, other harvest laws, and the sabbatical legislation as it affected the land—the fallow year, the release of debt-pledges and the jubilee year. Responsibility to the family included the fundamental law of inalienability; that is, that land was not to be bought and sold commercially but preserved within a kinship framework. This principle was then buttressed by other kinship responsibilities that related directly or indirectly to land—redemption procedures, inheritance rules and levirate marriage. Responsibility towards one's neighbours included a host of

civil laws and charitable exhortations concerning damage or negligence to property, safety precautions, respect for integrity of boundaries, generosity in leaving harvest gleanings, fair treatment of employees and, indeed, of working animals (Wright 2004:95).

What this means, then, is that there is nothing that an Israelite can do with the land that is outside of God's jurisdiction: It is God's land and is always ultimately under his control.

This is the backdrop to help bring clarity to the regulations surrounding the land in the Old Testament. However, it does not just relate to the land. The foundation for economic life in Israel was to be based upon accountability to God for not only the land and the things that he provides, but also for each other, meaning that no one has exclusive claim over anything. Any individual claim over anything is countered by the fact that both the resources and the power to use them are gifts from God: 'You may say to yourself, "My power and the strength of my hands have produced this wealth for me." But remember the LORD your God, for it is he who gives you the ability to produce wealth' (Deut. 8.17-18). We are accountable to God for the wealth he has enabled us to produce and how we use it. According to Wright (2004:166), this is a moral responsibility requiring justice, compassion and generosity. It continues to reflect the uniqueness of God's people as they represent his character to the world around them.

2.4 Moral responsibility

Justice is a key component. Rolf Knierim (1995) details the importance of justice in Scripture:

The concern for justice pervades the entire Old Testament. It is found in the historical, legal, prophetic, and wisdom literature, and in the Psalms as well. It is found throughout the entire history of the Old Testament literature. . . . The evidence shows that the concern for justice was one, if not the central, factor by which ancient Israel's multifaceted societal life was united throughout its historical changes... No sphere of Israel's life was exempt from concern for justice, and the LORD was known to be at work in all its spheres.

God is clear about his feelings for justice: 'For I, the LORD, love justice' (Is. 61.8). Justice is a key component to the proper ordering of society, so much so that when justice is trampled upon, the foundations of civil society begin to crumble. For Wright (2004:253), the Hebrew Scriptures are clear about this: 'If justice perished, the foundations of the whole cosmic order would disintegrate, because justice is fundamental to the very nature of the LORD, the Creator of the universe and to the core of God's government of history.'

For Israel, justice is not an abstract concept. Instead, it is essentially theological, rooted in the nature of God. It flows from his activities in history and is demanded of those in covenant with him. Ultimately, it will be wholly established on earth as a key element of his fully realised kingdom.

There is a wide range of Scripture declaring that the LORD is a God of justice. This is foundational to any discussion on poverty as it establishes the motivation for God's demanding justice as a core characteristic of his people. Psalm 33.5 is instrumental in defining the nature of God: 'The LORD loves righteousness and justice; the earth is full of his unfailing love.' But the phrasing here—'righteousness and justice'—denotes, 'a single complex idea expressed through the use of two words' (Wright 2004:255). These two words in Hebrew are important to know.

   1. The first is the root צדק (ṣdq). The denominative verb is צָדֵק (ṣādēq) found as well in three parent noun forms as follows:
   a. צֶדֶק (ṣedeq) justice, rightness,
   b. צְדָקָה (ṣĕdāqâ) justice, righteousness, and
   c. צַדִּיק (ṣaddîq) just, lawful, righteous.

The root meaning is probably 'straight'; something fixed and fully what it should be or something by which other things are measured. It is the act of doing what is required according to a fixed standard, conforming to what is right or expected according to the nature of the situation or the demands of the relationship.

These words are all highly relational. Hemchand Gossai (1993) includes a section on them in his definition of the term relationship.

> In order for an individual to be *ṣaddîq* [righteous], it means that of necessity he or she must exist and live in a manner which allows him or her to respond correctly to the values of the relationship [which may include relationships of spouse, parent, judge, worker, friend, etc.] . . . In essence then *ṣdq* [*ṣādēq*] is not simply an objective norm which is present within society, and which must be kept, but rather it is a concept which derives its meaning from the relationship in which it finds itself. So we are able to say that right judging, right governing, right worshipping and gracious activity are all covenantal and righteous, despite their diversity.

In its first appearance in Scripture, *ṣĕdāqâ* is a relationship word. Abraham shows a strange willingness to trust in Yahweh's word with what appears to be little evidence for doing so from the previous three chapters of Genesis. Moreover, Yahweh counts this as *ṣĕdāqâ* (Gen. 15.6). 'This is not legal fiction whereby he is treated as if he had lived by the norms of right living when he had not. Rather, it is Yahweh's declaration that such trust counts as *ṣĕdāqâ*' (Goldingay [s.a.]:3). Believing God's outrageous promises expresses such loyalty and trust that God approves of Abraham.

    2. The second word is the root שָׁפַט (*šāpaṭ*) meaning to judge or govern, dealing with judicial activity at every level. It has three derivatives as follows:

שֶׁפֶט (*šepeṭ*) *judgment.*
שְׁפוֹט (*šĕpôṭ*) *judgment.*
מִשְׁפָּט (*mišpāṭ*) *justice, ordinance.*[19]

In the broadest sense, *šāpaṭ* means,

> 'to put things right, to intervene in a situation that is wrong, oppressive or out of control and to 'fix' it. This may include confronting wrongdoers, on the one hand, and, on the other hand, vindicating and delivering those who have been wronged. Such action is not confined to a court of law, but may take place in other ways; for example through battle. That is why the figures in the book of Judges have that name. They 'judged' Israel by putting things right—militarily, religiously, legally—with Samuel being the model of all three' (Wright 2004:257).

The derived noun, *mišpāṭ*, can describe the whole process of litigation or the final rendering of a decision. It can also mean legal ordinance based on case law or past precedence or can include one's legal right. However, *mišpāṭ* can also refer to a wider sense of justice brought about through action. It is, 'what needs to be done in a given situation if people and circumstances are to be restored to conformity with *ṣedeq/ṣĕdāqâ*. *Mišpāṭ* is a collective set of actions—something you do' (Wright 2006:366). 'Justice as an appeal for a response means *taking upon oneself the cause of those who are weak in their own defense* [cf. Is. 58.6; Job 29.16; Jer. 21.12]' (Mott 1993:79).

The two words *ṣĕdāqâ* and *mišpāṭ* are paired, as is often the case, to form a comprehensive phrase as in Psalm 33.5, 'The LORD loves righteousness and justice; the earth is full of his unfailing love.' The closest English expression to the Hebrew phrase would likely be 'social justice,' although that phrase might still be too abstract for the intended meaning of the pair of Hebrew words. These Hebrew words are concrete nouns, unlike the more abstract English nouns normally used for translation, meaning that, 'they are actual things that you do, not concepts that you reflect upon' (Wright 2004:257). '"Just judgment" is a better equivalent, though the "judgment" is not confined to judicial decisions' (Goldingay [s.a.]:3). Goldingay's additional insight here is helpful:

> Together mishpat (mišpāṭ) and sedaqah (ṣĕdāqâ) thus form a powerful combination. They point to an exercise of authority that has a certain relational and social commitment and to a certain relational and social vision that expresses itself in decisive action. While they operate in the court, they also operate in government and in community relationships. Neither refers directly either to "justice" or to "righteousness" (Goldingay [s.a.]:3).

The pairing of these words resulting in the meaning "just judgment" recognises that the exercise of such an authoritative judgment is intended to restore community harmony, not just right an individual wrong. Psalm 33 provides an understanding of the LORD that is set firmly within the historical context of his relationship with Israel. He is celebrated as the creator, redeemer, judge, and saviour. Justice, as a concept, is set firmly within this understanding so that they knew what it meant to say that the LORD loved justice.

All of Israel's economic activities were to be completely saturated by justice. Simple honesty in the marketplace is a fundamental principle of economic justice:

> [13] Do not have two differing weights in your bag— one heavy, one light. [14] Do not have two differing measures in your house—one large, one small. [15] You must have accurate and honest weights and measures, so that you may live long in the land the Lord your God is giving you. [16] For the Lord your God detests anyone who does these things, anyone who deals dishonestly (Deut. 25.13–16 NIV84).

This justice extends to all who are employed in one's economic activities, requiring prompt payment of wages due for the poor one employs to avoid sin, regardless of whether this person is an Israelite or foreigner (Deut. 24.14).

However, biblical justice goes further. It requires compassion for those who are vulnerable, meaning that the wealth that comes as a result of one's economic activity must be held and used with an overarching goal of compassion. It is a covenantal duty that is commanded even though it is ultimately a matter of the heart and emotions. What is important is not whether one feels compassion, but whether one acts with compassion. Compassion is to pervade all of one's activities so that generosity is the result:

> [7] If there is a poor man among your brothers in any of the towns of the land that the Lord your God is giving you, do not be hardhearted or tightfisted toward your poor brother. [8] Rather be openhanded and freely lend him whatever he needs. [9] Be careful not to harbor this wicked thought: "The seventh year, the year for canceling debts, is near," so that you do not show ill will toward your needy brother and give him nothing. He may then appeal to the Lord against you, and you will be found guilty of sin. [10] Give generously to him and do so without a grudging heart; then because of this the Lord your God will bless you in all your work and in everything you put your hand to. [11] There will always be poor people in the land. Therefore, I command you to be openhanded toward your brothers and toward the poor and needy in your land (Deut. 15.7–11 NIV84).

This generosity springs from a heart grateful for the generosity of God, which the Israelite is to reflect: 'Supply him liberally from your flock, your threshing floor and your winepress. Give to him as the Lord your God has blessed you' (Deut. 15.14 NIV84).

This is a crucial consideration that, when fully developed,

brings clarity to some of Jesus' teachings around care for one's neighbour and the framework for New Testament theology as witnessed in the life of the Early Church. Although one might argue that much of the Hebrew Scriptures no longer bear on those outside of the Israelite community, Craig Blomberg (1999:32) insists instead that 'Every command [from the Old Testament] reflects principles at some level that are binding on Christians.' This applies even to parts of the Hebrew Scriptures that are now fulfilled in Christ as one sees, for example, that the principle of offering God sacrifices remains in force, though it has been changed in practice by Christ's work. Acceptable sacrifice, now, is the presentation of one's body as a 'living sacrifice' (Rom. 12.1-2) while one is to be content with what one has because God is always present (Heb.13.5).

3 God's Intervention on Behalf of 'the poor'

God has intervened at various times throughout human history to liberate the poor and oppressed.[20] This is seen early in Scripture as He moves to free the Children of Israel from slavery in Egypt. God's appearance to Moses from within a burning bush was the tangible reminder that God was at work to bring about an end to the suffering and injustice experienced by the Children of Israel at the hand of the Egyptians.

> Then the Lord said, 'I have surely seen the affliction of my people who are in Egypt and have heard their cry because of their taskmasters. I know their sufferings, and I have come down to deliver them out of the hand of the Egyptians' (Exodus 3.7-8a).

Although the liberation of slaves was not God's only purpose in the Exodus,[21] it was at the heart of His design (Sider 1997:43).

The introduction God uses for the Ten Commandments begins in this same revolutionary theme: 'I am the Lord your God, who brought you out of the land of Egypt, out of the house of slavery' (Deut. 5.6). God desires to be known as the Liberator of the Oppressed by His people. One misses the intent of this significant event in the lives of the people of God unless one recognizes that at this pivotal point in history, the 'Lord of the universe was at work correcting oppression and liberating the poor' (Sider 1997:44).

It also appears that God's behavior toward the poor can mirrors his commitment to them. Sugirtharajah (in Howitt & Morphew [sa]:47) details these passages:

> God has a concern for the poor. He listens to them (Psalm 69:33; 34:6; Isaiah 41:17). He delivers the needy when he cries (Psalm 72:12), setting him on high, far from affliction (Psalm 107:41). He gives to the poor (Psalm 112:9; 132:15), raising them up from the dust (1 Samuel 1:8; Psalm 113:7), and is their refuge and protector (Isaiah 3:13-15; 24:4 ff; 25:4; Zephaniah 3:12; Psalm 14:6). He consoles and comforts them (Isaiah 49:13), and is the helper of the fatherless (Psalm 10:13).

God upholds the poor. He administrates justice for them (Deut. 10.18; Job 36.6; Ps. 10.17; 25.9; 72.4; 82.3; 140.12), delivering them in their affliction (Job 36.15; Ps. 35.10; 72.12; 76.9; 82.3; Jer. 20.13) and defending the widow, the fatherless, and the stranger (Ex. 22.21-24; Deut. 10.17-19; Ps. 68.5; 69.5; 82.3). God saves the needy from the sword (Job 5.15) and pleads their cause (Is. 51.22).

God also demands a similar concern from his people (Ex. 22.21-24; Lev. 19.10; Deut. 15.1-11; 24.14; Is. 58.1-12; Jer. 7.5-7; Ezek. 16.49; Zech. 7.10), and from their king (Is. 11.4; Jer. 22.16; Ps. 22.1-4). Moreover, through the prophets he zealously denounces every form of oppression (Amos 2.6-8; 4.1-3; 6.4-8; Micah 2.1-3; Is. 3.13-15; 10.1-4; Jer. 22.13f; Ezek. 34.1-24).

God's concern for the poor is so far-reaching that he goes beyond pleading their cause to actually identifying himself with them. 'He who oppresses the poor insults his

Maker' (Prov. 14.31), while to be 'kind to the poor' is to 'lend to God' (Prov. 19.17). He sees them as 'his people' (Is. 3.15), extending himself to punish those who harm them (Job 22.9; Ps. 109.16; Is. 1.23-24; 3.13-15; Jer. 5.28-29; 22.3, 15-19; Ezek. 16.48-50; 22.7, 14-15, 29-31; Amos 2.6; 4.1-3; 5.12-16; 8.4-8; Mal. 3.5) and blessing those who are good to them (Job 29.11-17; 42.12-16; Ps. 41.1; Prov. 14.21; 17.5; 19.17; 29.14; Jer. 7.6-7, 22.3).

3.1 God's provision for 'the poor'

God proactively instituted a number of principles or laws in Scripture to prevent class distinctions and poverty from arising and gaining a foothold in society. In the relatively egalitarian society of small farmers as would be found in ancient Israel, families would possess enough resources to earn a living that would have been regarded as sufficient and acceptable, not minimal. Although not every family would have the same income, each family would have equal economic opportunity, thereby enabling them to earn an income that would meet their basic needs while also allow them to be respected members of their communities. Land ownership helped each extended family to acquire the necessities to obtain a decent livelihood through responsible work (Sider 1997:68).

3.1.1 Old Testament prescriptive laws

To help safeguard this opportunity for sufficient provision, God instituted laws to ensure that any economic disadvantages that arose would be abated through the year of Jubilee and the sabbatical year. In similar fashion, other prescriptive laws were put in place to enable those who were poor to still have ways to provide for themselves.

i Year of Jubilee

Through the year of Jubilee (Lev. 25.8-55), God desired to achieve a revolution in Israelite society every 50 years. Its purpose was to avoid extremes of wealth and poverty among his people, in most instances providing for restoration of prior economic status through redistributive measures.

Essential points of the law were as follows:

- Freedom for all slaves and debtors (Lev. 25.40-41). A parallel is seen in Israel's flight from Egypt depicted in the Exodus (Lev. 25.38).

- Restitution of each clan's patrimony—a type of agrarian reform accompanied by the redistribution of wealth.

And you shall consecrate the fiftieth year, and proclaim liberty throughout the land to all its inhabitants. It shall be a jubilee for you, when each of you shall return to his property and each of you shall return to his clan (Lev. 25.10).

This helps remind the nation of Israel of the conquests of Canaan and the equitable distribution of land as described in Joshua.

- Rest for the land, allowing it to lie fallow (Lev. 25.11).

All of these provisions of the law related to freedom (for debtors, slaves, property, and even the land). Ezekiel referred to this time as 'the year of liberty' (Ezek. 46.17). The Jubilee was a physical reminder that helped Israel re-experience the events recorded in Exodus and Joshua.

The theological basis for this controversial command was that all of their possessions, including the land as has been previously mentioned, actually belonged to God and were merely on loan. Therefore, instead of being *owners*, they were meant to function as good *stewards* (Blomberg in Howitt & Morphew [sa]). 'Land will not be sold in perpetuity, for the land is mine. For you are strangers and sojourners with me' (Lev. 25.23).

Before and after the year of jubilee, the land could be bought or sold. However, the buyer did not actually buy the land so much as he purchased a certain number of harvests. 'If the years are many, you shall increase the price, and if the years are few, you shall reduce the price, for it is the number of the crops that he is selling to you' (Lev. 25.16). However, the selling of harvests came with a caveat: the sale must be fair. 'You shall not wrong one another, but you shall fear your God; for I am the LORD your God' (Lev. 25.17).

The year of jubilee created a structure that automatically impacted everyone. It also allowed for self-help and self-development so that, once the land was returned, the poor person could once again provide for his own living (Sider 1997:72).

ii Year of sabbatical

The Jewish seventh year of sabbatical was, in effect, a religiously mandated fallow year for all fields.

> For six years you shall sow your land and gather in its yield, but the seventh year you shall let it rest and lie fallow, that the poor of your people may eat; and what they leave the beasts of the field may eat. You shall do likewise with your vineyard, and with your olive orchard (Ex. 23.10-11).

It is believed that the purpose for this was two-fold:

- Environmental: By not planting in the seventh year the land could be restored with the nutrients that would normally be removed during normal farming activities.

- Concern for the poor: God was ensuring that the poorest of the poor would be able to eat (Sider 1997:71).

Israelite slaves also received their freedom every seventh year (Deut. 15.12-18), as poverty would sometimes force Israelites into indentured servitude to pay off debts or to simply keep from starving (Lev. 25.39-40). However, God decreed that slavery was not to be permanent and that, when it ended, the master was to share his produce generously with the slave:

> And when you let him go free, you shall not let him go empty-handed. You shall furnish him liberally out of your flock, out of your threshing floor, and out of your winepress. As the LORD your God has blessed you, you shall give to him (Deut. 15.13-14).

Finally, the sabbatical position on loans was the most radical of all (Deut. 15.1-6). God decreed that every seven years all debts had to be cancelled (Deut. 15.1), even adding that people were not allowed to refuse loans in the sixth year simply because the money would be lost in twelve months (Deut. 15.9). In the same manner as with the year of jubilee, the sabbatical year was brought about to ensure justice, not charity, providing the relief of debts to prevent a widening gap between those who had capital and those without productive resources. Deuteronomy 15 was both 'an idealistic statement of God's demand and also a realistic reference to Israel's sinful performance' (Sider 1997:71). God knew that poverty would remain, hence the statement, 'Since there will never cease to be some in need on the earth, I therefore command you ...' (Deut. 15.11a). However, this did not imply that he would allow everyone to go on with his or her lives and their businesses in total ignorance of the poor. Instead, his instituted law meant that those with means were expected to, '... open wide your hand to your brother, to the needy and to the poor in your land' (Deuteronomy 15.11b). There is evidence indicating that the sabbatical year was only practiced occasionally, which is one of the reasons suggested for God's punishment of Israel by exile in Babylon (Lev. 26.34-35; 2 Chron. 36.20-21).

3.1.2 Old Testament protective laws

i Protective laws on tithing and gleaning

There were additional laws established which, if practiced,

would aid specific groups such as the Levite, the poor, the sojourner, the widow, and the orphan. One such law required the laying aside of one tenth of all farm produce as a tithe:

> At the end of every three years you shall bring out all the tithe of your produce in the same year and lay it up within your towns. And the Levite, because he has no portion or inheritance with you, and the sojourner, the fatherless, and the widow, who are within your towns, shall come and eat and be filled, that the Lord your God may bless you in all the work of your hands that you do (Deut. 14.28-29).

Another law, the law of gleaning, decreed that farmers should leave portions of their harvest untouched so that the poor could go and glean there:

> When you reap the harvest of your land, you shall not reap your field right up to its edge, neither shall
>
> you gather the gleanings after your harvest. And you shall not strip your vineyard bare, neither shall you gather the fallen grapes of your vineyard. You shall leave them for the poor and for the sojourner: I am the Lord your God (Lev. 19.9-10).

Likewise, farmers were instructed not to collect forgotten sheaves left in the field, olive tree boughs were not to be 'gone over again,' and vineyards were not to be gleaned after grape collection (Deut. 24.18-31).

ii Additional laws and commands regarding the poor

Further protective and provisional measures concerning the 'general poor' appear in the following categories:

- Significant emphasis was placed upon ensuring justice for the poor. The Israelites were to guard against perverting the judgment of the poor in disputes (Ex. 23.6), showing partiality (Ex. 23.3), taking bribes (Deut. 10.17), making use of dishonest scales, weights, ephah, and hin (Lev. 19.36), oppressing the afflicted (Prov. 22.22), and committing violence

(Jer. 22.3). Instead, they were to learn 'to do good; seek justice, correct oppression; bring justice to the fatherless, plead the widow's cause' (Is. 1.17).

- The area of money lending also provided care for the poor. The Israelites were prohibited from charging interest on loans (Ex. 22.25) or keeping a person's pledge overnight (Ex. 24.12). Furthermore, collectors of the poor man's pledge were not allowed to enter the houses of those who owed them. They were to stand outside and wait while the man of the house went inside to collect the pledge, thereby ensuring that adequate respect and dignity for the poor would be upheld (Deut. 24.10-11).

- Special conditions were laid down for the ritual cleansing of 'poor' lepers who were healed to reduce the amount of the usual fee.

But if he is poor and cannot afford so much, then he shall take one male lamb for a guilt offering to be waved, to make atonement for him, and a tenth of an ephah of fine flour mixed with oil for a grain offering, and a log of oil; also two turtledoves or two pigeons, whichever he can afford. (Lev. 14.21-22a).

- The payment of wages to the poor carried additional requirements, mandating that a worker who was poor and needy was to be paid his or her wages each day before the sun went down (Deut. 24.13).

3.2 Scriptural warnings concerning 'the poor'

In addition to the numerous laws, commands, and principles found in Scripture, there are also a number of warnings given for those who would abuse or ignore the poor. These warnings include the following:

3.2.1 **Curses.** Since the poor were a class of people who could fall prey to various forms of abuse more readily than others, a promise and a warning with consequences were issued to prevent this from happening. 'He who gives to the poor will lack nothing, but he who closes his eyes to them receives many curses' (Prov. 28.27).

3.2.2 **Reproach.** In the section in Proverbs dealing with the Wisdom of Solomon, the Israelites are warned that when the poor are oppressed it 'insults his Maker' (Prov. 14.31). Those who oppress the poor to increase their wealth are also guaranteed that 'they will only come to poverty' (Prov. 22.16).

3.2.3 **Cut-off.** Those who shut their ears to the cry of the poor will be cut off from the Lord. 'Whoever closes his ear to the cry of the poor will himself call out and not be answered' (Prov. 21.13).

3.2.4 **Death.** Ezekiel, in the section dealing with the refutation of a false proverb, warns those who oppress the poor and needy of grave consequences:

> He oppresses the poor and needy. He commits robbery. He does not return what he took in pledge. He looks to the idols. He does detestable things. He lends at usury and takes excessive interest. Will such a man live? He will not! Because he has done all these detestable things, he will surely be put to death and his blood will be on his own head (Ezek. 18.12-13 NIV).

3.2.5 Judgment. God's passion for justice would be a two-edged sword. The middle of the 8th century B.C.E. was a time of economic prosperity and political success unknown since the time of Solomon. However, in the midst of this prosperity, God sent the prophet Amos to announce the unpopular news that God would soon destroy the Northern Kingdom. Amos saw first-hand the terrible oppression of the poor as the rich 'trample the head of the poor into the dust of the earth' (Amos 2.7). The extravagant lifestyle of the rich was built upon the backs of the poor, even to the extent that they bribed judges and turned the needy aside from the gate of the city (Amos 5.11-12). The prophet's messages of warning were clear. Israel's disobedience was described as a gross failure along two areas: idolatry and mistreatment of the poor (Sider 1997:69). The failure of Israel to heed these warnings resulted in Israel's destruction and captivity within a few short years after Amos had spoken.

3.3 New Testament provisions for 'the poor'

First-century Christians affirmed Old Testament teachings by their behavior as they responded to the physical needs evident around them, especially those needs seen in the Early Church communities. This followed the lead of Jesus as he identified his mission to his mostly Jewish audience.

3.3.1 The Incarnation

Christians believe that God revealed himself in Jesus of Nazareth. Therefore, to have a better understanding of God's activity in the world and to know what true Christian praxis and commitment demands, it is important to comprehend how Jesus defined his mission. In Luke 4.18-19, Jesus does this by quoting the prophet Isaiah:

> The Spirit of the Lord is upon me, because he has anointed me to proclaim good news to the poor. He has sent me to proclaim liberty to the captives and recovering of sight to the blind, to set at liberty those who are oppressed, to proclaim the year of the Lord's favour (Luke 4.18-19).

After reading these words, Jesus informed his audience that he was the fulfilment of this Scripture,[22] accurately portraying the past and present human situation. (Howitt & Morphew [sa]). Jesus' words are examined more closely in the following section.

i The poor

Jesus focused much of his attention on the poor, a group that dominated the Palestinian population at that time.[23] He was poor himself as described in the following ways:

- He was born in a stable,
- Jesus' family was poor, [24]
- Jesus was a refugee, [25]
- He was an immigrant in the land of Galilee, [26]
- He humbly submitted Himself to John the Baptist's baptism,[27]
- Jesus warned a potential disciple of the type of life-style to expect by saying that He had no home. [28]

When Jesus addressed the poor, he did so from a position of equality, not superiority. He was familiar with poverty, suffering, hunger, mourning and ostracism. The Apostle Paul summarises Jesus incarnation as follows: 'For you know the grace of our Lord Jesus Christ, that though he was rich, yet for your sake he became poor, so that you by his poverty might become rich' (2 Cor. 8.9).

ii The captives

In 1st century Palestine, the poor and oppressed were trapped with no way of improving their situation, much the same as it in many third world countries today. Many prisoners were not murderers, rapists or other violent criminals, as they would have been executed for their crimes. In 1st century Palestine, most prisoners were imprisoned because they could not afford to pay back their debtors[29] (Westermann in Howitt & Morphew [sa]:53 footnote). This would imply, then, that when Jesus was referring to the 'captives and prisoners,' he was not referring to two separate groups, but to one: *the poor*, imprisoned because of their debt and poverty (Howitt & Morphew [sa]:53).

iii The blind

Jesus included 'the blind' in the same categories as the poor and the captives, suggesting that he thought of them as part of the same needy group. It is interesting that poverty appears in the context as a related circumstance in six of the seven instances that Luke mentions the blind.[30]

iv The oppressed

Jesus described the poverty stricken as *oppressed*. As previously noted, *oppression* and *injustice* appear to be some of the root causes of poverty in the Bible. The Hebrew Scriptures use twenty verbal roots that show up more than five hundred times describing *oppression* (Howitt & Morphew [sa]:53).

In the face of this, Jesus offers Himself as the solution to the suffering and disillusionment of those in poverty in the following ways:

v The bringer of 'good news'

Jesus went about proclaiming the 'good news.' This was a radical message, one that had a revolutionary impact on society. 'The actual "good news" which he came to proclaim was that the Kingdom of God had arrived, ushered in through his ministry by announcement and demonstration, and through his death and resurrection. It is important to note that it was aimed at the poor' (Howitt & Morphew [sa]:54).

vi The proclaimer of freedom

An essential element in the coming of the Kingdom of God is the liberation of the oppressed: 'He has sent me to proclaim liberty to the captives, and recovering of sight to the blind, to set at liberty those who are oppressed' (Lk. 4.18).
According to Hanks,

> The church has often fallen into the trap of legitimizing the oppression that the established order maintains. Many Christians wish to preach a gospel of socio-political freedom to the poor, whereas others want to offer forgiveness of sins to the rich. Jesus, however, did not offer us the alternative of spreading two gospels. His gospel is one of freedom

97

for the poor, which is bad news for the rich unless they genuinely repent, identify with the poor and share their goods with them (Howitt & Morphew [sa]:54).

Such radical action has practical ramifications that upend existing social conventions. It is easier to maintain oppression than to do the hard work that freedom requires.

vii Recoverer of sight to the blind

Jesus' mission statement also included providing 'recovery of sight to the blind' (Lk. 4.18). John the Baptiser tested Jesus' authenticity as the Messiah by sending his disciples to Jesus with questions about his identity. Jesus responded to their questions by saying:

> Go and tell John what you have seen and heard: the blind receive their sight, the lame walk, lepers are cleansed, the deaf hear, the dead are raised up, and the poor have good news preached to them (Lk. 7.22).

Jesus' response has to do with what he is accomplishing through his work, which in turn identifies him as the Messiah. Events are happening through his activities that go way beyond the claim to a title.

viii Proclaimer of the year of the Lord's favour

This may be the most dramatic part of Jesus' mission statement, referring to the year of Jubilee (Lev. 25) discussed earlier in this chapter. As previously mentioned, the Jubilee was implemented to prevent massive economic disparity between the rich and the poor and, had Israel followed this law, it would have prevented many of the extremes of wealth and poverty that occurred in society.

But according to Hanks (in Howitt & Morphew [sa]), Jesus taught his disciples to practice Jubilee in the following ways:

- Not by sowing, reaping or harvesting, but by living by faith, always trusting that God will provide for one's needs. (Mt. 6.25-26, 31-33; Lk. 12.29-31).

- By remitting all debts (Mt. 5.40-42; Lk. 6.33; Lk. 12.30-33, 16.1-15).
- By redistributing wealth (Lk. 11.42, 12.30-33; Acts 2.44-45, 4.32-37).

3.3.2 Early church community

1st century Christians endorsed the Old Testament teachings by signs that economic relationships in the new community of Jesus' followers had radically changed. There was wide-scale sharing in the earliest Christian church:

> Now the full number of those who believed were of one heart and soul, and no one said that any of the things that belonged to him was of his own, but they had everything in common (Acts 4.32).

i Generosity

There is ample evidence that the early church continued the pattern of generous sharing practiced by Jesus (Acts 2.43-47; 4.32-37; 5.1-11; 6.1-7). Luke records in Acts 2.44, immediately after noting that three thousand were converted at Pentecost, that 'all who believed were together and had all things in common.' Physical needs in the new communities of Christ followers were met by the generous sharing of all resources, which included personal property being freely sold to aid the needy within the fellowship (Acts 4.36-37; 5.3-4).

God's desire that the obedience of Israel would result in the elimination of poverty within society (Deut. 15.4) only reached fulfillment in the early church community. They ate meals together with 'glad and generous hearts' (Acts 2.46b) and experienced unity, being of 'one heart and soul' (Acts 4.32). This was a new community defined by the visible transformation of their lives, including their views on personal possessions (Sider 1997:77). The impact of this transformation was striking: their number was growing dramatically

(Acts 2.47b) and 'with great power the apostles gave their testimony to the resurrection of the Lord Jesus ...' (Acts 4.33).

They organised administrative systems to ensure that economic needs were met justly. As mentioned earlier in this chapter, it appears that the Jerusalem church included a significant number of Hellenists—Greek-speaking Jews or possibly Greeks that had converted to Judaism. Somehow, the Hebrew-speaking majority had overlooked the needs of the Hellenist widows. When this injustice was made known to the apostles, they responded by choosing seven Spirit-filled men to look after the minority group, with all seven being members of the group that had suffered the discrimination. Actions like this resulted in 'the number of disciples (multiplying) greatly in Jerusalem' (Acts 6.7) (Sider 1997:78).

It is important to note that The Early Church did not insist on economic equality or abolish private ownership. Peter confirms this when he reminds Ananias that he was under no obligation to either sell his property or donate the proceeds from the sale to the church (Acts 5.4). Sharing was not compulsory, but could be offered voluntarily. Genuine love and care for others in the community were the motivations for sharing personal possessions. Some, in fact, did not offer everything. John Mark's mother, for example, retained her house (Acts 12.12) and additional passages indicate that others retained their possessions as well.

ii Love

A deep caring for one another in the Early Christian community is at the essence of their faith. Their love for God manifested in their love for others. It was not superficial since regularly and repeatedly, '... they sold their possessions and goods and distributed them to all, as any had need' (Acts 2.45). If the need was greater than the available funding, they simply sold property. The needs of fellow members of the faith community became the deciding factors, not individual financial security or property rights. 'For the earliest Christians, one-ness in Christ meant sweeping liability for and availability to the other members of Christ's body' (Sider 1997:79).

However, followers of Christ must not let their generosity end with other Christians. Jesus' teaching not only permits but requires his followers to extend care for the poor and oppressed outside of the faith. The story of the Good Samaritan teaches that anyone in need is to be considered one's neighbour (Lk. 10.29-37). Matthew 5.43-45 is even more explicit:

> You have heard that it was said, 'You shall love your neighbour and hate your enemy.' But I say to you, Love your enemies and pray for those who persecute you, so that you may be sons of your Father who is in heaven. For he makes his sun rise on the evil and on the good, and sends rain on the just and on the unjust.

Jesus restrains his followers from being concerned only for their neighbours who would normally be members of their own ethnic or religious group. Instead, he encourages his followers to imitate God, who does good to everyone.

However, the command actually goes much deeper. In Matthew 22.35-40, a lawyer asked Jesus a question to test him. He queries, 'Teacher, which is the great commandment in the Law?' The reply of Jesus is stunning, particularly if one gives serious consideration to its full ramifications:

> And he said to him, 'You shall love the Lord your God with all your heart and with all your soul and with all your mind. This is the great and first commandment. And a second is like it: You shall love your neighbour as yourself. On these two commandments depend all the Law and the Prophets' (Mt. 22.37-40).

It is correctly understood that the Great Commandment tells humanity to love God. This injunction of Jesus would not surprise his first-century hearers, nor would it shock those of the 21st century. What is striking, however, is the level of care that is expected toward 'one's neighbours.' Jesus tells this lawyer that he must love his neighbour in the same way and with the same intensity that he loves himself. Although it would be seen as normal to love oneself, what Jesus adds here is that as one wishes to be loved, one must love one's neighbour. This means that as a man naturally wants the best for himself, so he must equally desire the best for his neighbour. John Piper (1996:283) describes it this way:

> He (Jesus) commands, 'As you love yourself, so love your neighbour.' Which means: As you long for food when you are hungry, so long to feed your neighbour when he is hungry. As you long for nice clothes for yourself, so long for nice clothes for your neighbour. As you desire to have a comfortable place to live, so desire a comfortable place to live for your neighbour. As you seek to be safe and secure from calamity and violence, so seek safety and security for your neighbour.

The ramifications are quite radical. 'In other words, make the measure of your self-seeking the measure of your self-giving' (Piper 1996:283).

iii Responsibility

The general theme that runs through this Chapter and appears as a common refrain throughout Scripture is this: God's desire is for his people to live together in community in such a way that all families would have the ability to earn a decent living and that those who are not able to care for themselves would still have provision. God discloses his attitude toward the weak and what he correspondingly expects of the strong, thereby forming the principle that is the basis for the Old Testament provisions for Jubilee, the sabbatical year, tithing, and gleaning.

The New Testament presupposes this theme and emphasises

it. Paul associates the Old Testament requirement for justice with Christian responsibility for the poor (2 Cor. 9.9-10). Jesus, in his ethical teaching and practice, stands in the tradition of the prophets; an understanding of Jesus or New Testament ethics is not possible unless seen through that connection.

> Woe to you, scribes and Pharisees, hypocrites! For you tithe mint and dill and cumin, and have neglected the weightier matters of the law: justice and mercy and faithfulness. These you ought to have done, without neglecting the others (Mt. 23.23).

Two aspects of this passage are worth noting:

- Jesus carries on the prophetic attack against all forms of piety that leave out social justice.

- He clearly indicates the place of the Old Testament teachings about justice, reflecting the highest level of Old Testament ethics essential to his new order (Mott 1982:77).

The obligation to do justice makes followers of Jesus responsible for the state of society in a comprehensive way. 'Wherever there is basic human need, we (Christians) are (obligated) to help to the extent of our ability and opportunity' (Mott 1982:77). 'Do not hold back good from those who are entitled to it, when you possess the power to do it' (Prov. 3.27), sums up this teaching and indicates how to relate it to a variety of circumstances, including 'not only our personal resources but also our class position and political opportunities' (Mott 1982:77). Walter Brueggemann (1980:1098) provides insight:

> The faithful community knows something about the world, hopes something for the world, and expects something of the world. What it knows and hopes and expects is that the world is to be transformed.... And that, perhaps, is the most important

and most subversive thing the church can now do: to refuse to give up on the world and its promised transformation.

3.4 Summary

All humankind has been created by God with intrinsic value. All are created as equals, meaning that no one person has more or less value than any other. The Hebrew Scriptures contain many passages describing the poor and the requirements placed upon Israel concerning provision for the poor and for those groups in society normally impoverished because of this God ordained status. Although poverty was present in a Jewish community, the goal according to Scripture, was for it to be temporary and for needs to be met by members of the local community who were to help restore one back to 'wholeness.' Freedom was to be restored, land was to be restored, and communities were to be made whole. There were serious ramifications promised for those failing to properly discharge these duties.

In similar fashion and in line with the Hebrew Scriptures, the New Testament, beginning with the teachings of Jesus, encourages special care for the poor as a requirement for followers of Christ. Jesus qualifies 'loving your neighbour' by relating it to the way that one loves oneself. Moreover, the Early Church, in following this example, offers a model for poverty alleviation that is challenging to consider in its scope and in the way that it impacted the 1st Century world. The gospel rapidly spread through what became a missional movement on display as the Church met the needs of others.

4 Poverty and Poverty Alleviation Defined

4.1 Definition of poverty

As one looks around the global landscape, it is obvious that poverty continues to have a significant impact on 21st century society, with many factors that contribute to the overall picture that describes poverty. It can be defined in a narrow sense or more broadly. Leibbrandt, Woolard and Bhorat (2001:42) define poverty in a narrow sense using income as the standard: 'the inability [of an individual or household] to attain a minimal standard of living, with standard of living being measured in terms of consumption or income levels.' On the other hand, Kalie Pauw and Liberty Mncube give a broader definition by stating that poverty 'might consist of a variety of components, including household income/consumption, human capabilities, access to public services, employment and asset ownership' (2007:3). Poverty can be defined in ranges 'representing a state of bare survival, to embracing access to resources that would enable a person to participate fully in their broader society' (Studies in Poverty and Inequality 2007:10).

To restate the definition of Bryant Myers (1999:86) from the first section of this chapter, 'poverty is the result of relationships that do not work, that are not just, that are not for life, that are not harmonious or enjoyable. Poverty is the absence of shalom in all its meanings.' This introduction of non-income measures for defining poverty helps to provide a more complete assessment of poverty in its different dimensions. This returns the discussion to determining what one considers as 'unacceptable' as proposed by Adam Smith. By identifying what is unacceptable, a society clearly speaks about how it would like things to be, thereby taking the discussion beyond merely using income thresholds to define poverty to deciding the minimum standards for what it should be like and feel like to live in one's community.

4.2 Definition of poverty alleviation

Poverty alleviation, then, is not just providing the necessary income that will bring people out of poverty. That is an approach to poverty from a dualistic frame of reference that only speaks to one part of the problem. An income approach on its own may fit a poverty relief concept but will not have longer term benefits.[31] By contrast, longer-term poverty alleviation is an approach that seeks to bring people to a sense of wholeness, able to fully participate as equal members in society. It is seeking to impact poverty in a way that engages all of the effects of poverty on a person or community. Moreover, at some level, it is bringing about justice. This fits the United Nations Development Reports [UNDR] view that poverty is the 'denial of opportunities and choices most basic to human development to lead a long, healthy, creative life and to enjoy a decent standard of living, freedom, dignity, self-esteem and respect from others' (StatsSA 2000:54). This view is a multi-dimensional perspective that sees the lack of sufficient income as only one element in the total picture defining poverty.

4.3 Multi-dimensional perspective

A multi-dimensional view is helpful. It provides a comprehensive platform from which to engage poverty, helping on to gain an understanding of poverty by hearing how it is experienced from people living in impoverished communities. The World Bank researchers used an inductive approach to uncover the overall scope of poverty as it impacts the poor who describe poverty from their personal experiences (1999:26).

There were five main findings listed in the study gathered from these 'poverty experts' who were asked the basic question: what is poverty? First, numerous factors converge to make poverty a complex, multidimensional phenomenon. There is never one single cause, but 'many interlocking factors (that) cluster in poor people's experiences and definitions of poverty' (World Bank 1999:27). For example, in the Mindanao region of the Philippines, women said, '"we boil bananas for our children if food is not available. In some cases, when the Department of Agriculture distributes corn seeds, we cook these seeds instead of planting them.' Ironically, they borrow money to acquire these seeds. The cycle of poverty continues as they are unable to pay for these loans" (World Bank 1999:27).

Second, as expected, it was found that poverty is often described as the lack of what is necessary for physical well-being — mainly food, but also housing, land, and other assets. Poverty is the absence of multiple resources leading to physical scarcity. It is described in interviews as follows:

- Your hunger is never satiated; your thirst is never quenched; you can never sleep until you are no longer tired. —Senegal 1995

- It's the cost of living, low salaries, and lack of jobs. And it's also not having medicine, food and clothes. —Brazil 1995

- When I leave for school in the mornings I don't have any breakfast. At noon there is no lunch, in the evening I get a little supper, and that is not enough. So when I see another child eating, I watch him, and if he doesn't give me something I think I'm going to die of hunger. —A 10-year-old child, Gabon 1997 (World Bank 1999:29).

Third, poor people's definitions reveal important psychological aspects of poverty. They are keenly aware of their lack of voice, power, and independence, which subject them to exploitation and exposes them to rudeness, humiliation, and inhumane treatment by both private and public government agents from whom they seek help. They feel the pain brought about by their unavoidable violation of societal norms and their inability to maintain cultural identity by participating in traditions, festivals, and rituals. They are unable to participate fully in their community, leading to a failure of social relations. Although poverty is material in nature, psychological impacts are caused through 'distress at being unable to feed one's children, insecurity from not knowing where the next meal will come from, and shame by having to go without foods that have strong symbolic value' (World Bank 1999:31). Additionally, parents frequently relate that they deal with food insecurity by going hungry so that they will not have to see their children starve.

Other stories are as equally distressing: The decision to abandon babies to increase the likelihood that the baby or the family will survive is a severe reality. In Tbilisi, Georgia, there have been increasing reports of babies abandoned at maternity wards as well as of mothers selling children to raise support for the remaining children. One respondent heard that a woman sold her child for $500 to support her family, while another witnessed a young woman near Tbilisi's central train station trying to sell her child, telling passers-by, "The child will die of hunger — take him even if you don't pay" (World Bank 1999:36).

Fourth, the absence of basic infrastructure — particularly roads, transport, water, and health facilities — emerged as a critical need. Poor transportation infrastructure compounds problems around obtaining service provisions such as health care and education. While literacy is viewed as important, schooling receives mixed reviews, as it is often considered irrelevant in the lives of poor people. One example is particularly disturbing:

> Take the death of this small boy this morning, for example. The boy died of measles. We all know he could have been cured at the hospital. But the parents had no money and so the boy died a slow and painful death, not of measles, but out of poverty. — A man from Ghana (World Bank 1999:36).

Finally, poor people focus on assets rather than income and link their lack of physical, human, social, and environmental assets to their vulnerability and exposure to risk. Two Vietnamese men respond as follows:

- In my family if anyone becomes seriously ill, we know that we will lose him because we do not even have enough money for food so we cannot buy medicine. —Vietnam 1999

- Livestock are part of the yearly household reserves. If they get a disease and die we have nothing to support us in between harvests. —Vietnam 1999 (World Bank 1999:40).

This description of poverty described by those trapped within it provides a disturbing picture of the scope of the overall scope and impact of poverty.

One will notice a few things from these descriptions that are useful for considering a way forward for the evangelical movement and the church. First, although there are similarities in the form that poverty takes around the world, poverty is experienced differently and therefore manifests differently in geographically diverse communities. Communities will need to be carefully assessed before attempting initiatives in a way that listens carefully to what they are experiencing. Second, although income deprivation is a significant factor contributing to the challenges associated with poverty, there are significant psychological aspects of poverty revealed in these experiences that will need to be holistically addressed within communities.

The World Bank Report revealed a substantial breakdown in relationships across all areas of community life for most of the respondents in their study. Poverty goes beyond income measurements to the unfulfilled desire for *shalom*—peaceful, just relationships in a holistic framework. The Report showed in stark brutality examples of 'relationships that do not work, that are not just, that are not for life, that are not harmonious or enjoyable . . . the absence of *shalom*' (ital. added) as defined by Bryant Myers (1999:86).

Poverty has been described as complex and multidimensional, with people living in deficit, living without assets, with psychological damage and feelings of powerlessness. Each of these short testimonies from people in poverty adds to the definition, painting a bleak picture of how being in poverty is experienced. Poverty is a deeply personal. One who views poverty from the outside sees what one's 'world view and education, and training allow us to see. We need to be aware of this and work hard at seeing *all* there is to see' (Myers 1999:81).

However, due to the complexity of poverty, it is unlikely that there will ever be a comprehensive theory of poverty as there is always more that can be seen and heard and experienced. One must work to see all that there is to see in the fight against poverty, trying hard to be as holistic in one's approach as possible for the sake of those in poverty.

4.4 Narrowing the focus

It seems useful, at this point, to return to a quote from Walter Brueggemann (1980:1098) in his reference to a faithful community:

> The faithful community knows something about the world, hopes something for the world, and expects something of the world. What it knows and hopes and expects is that the world is to be transformed.... And that, perhaps, is the most important and most subversive thing the church can now do: to refuse to give up on the world and its promised transformation.

The task of God's people is rooted in the mission of Christ. As was previously mentioned, Jesus preached the good news of the kingdom of God in word and deed and now calls the church to do the same. His example draws his followers into mission, as they 'refuse to give up on the world and its promised transformation.'

The efforts taken to define poverty are not merely to be seen as an academic exercise, for the way poverty is defined plays a significant role in determining what solutions should be used to engage it. This is the step that takes one beyond a dualistic mentality that identifies poverty purely from a physical perspective referring to a lack of income, moving instead into a holistic engagement that fights poverty by dealing with it physically, emotionally and spiritually. This approach engages more than the symptoms but instead looks for the root causes.

4.4 Shifts in emphasis

Understanding the root causes of poverty is useful since this understanding will determine how one responds. Hearing the cries of poor people and feeling their sense of powerlessness and shame shapes one's understanding of development and the correct ways to engage poverty holistically. If one misunderstands what causes the symptom(s), the cure will either be wholly ineffective or will likely cause serious side effects. This moves beyond seeing poverty as only an inability to meet physical needs versus the failure to meet social/psychological needs as well.

In the stories told by poor people, details tend to describe the lack of material things in far more psychological terms, such as shame, powerlessness, inferiority, and hopelessness. If one tries to engage poverty at the material level, it will not go nearly far enough to be an adequate approach. Therefore, solutions to eliminate poverty must go beyond the material as well.

4.4.1 People matter

For Manfred Max-Neef (2005:8), it is important to construct systems to fight poverty 'as if people matter.' As an economist, he realises shortcomings inherent within the field, particularly as related to efforts aimed at alleviating poverty. He writes (2005:8-9):

> Economics, as it is still being taught in the Universities, is presumed to be a *value-free science*. In fact, the argument runs that the "intromission" of values distorts the economic process. This being so, it should not be surprising that, for example, efforts to overcome poverty tend to fail systematically. Contrary to such naïve assumptions, it should instead be obvious that if ethical principles and values that should conform a society oriented towards the common good are not made explicit, no policies coherent with the challenge can successfully be designed.

Max-Neef's insights are a helpful reflection of what the World Bank Researchers have also found to be true. The complexity of poverty makes a 'one size fits all' approach seem ludicrous, meaning that one should not be surprised at the utter failure of an economic approach that is 'values free.' People are not only **rational**, but are also **relational** (emphasis added). The failure to consider them in this way will fatally flaw any proposed intervention aimed at poverty. Therefore, the approach must be one of 'transdisciplinarity.' Transdisciplinarity, as Max-Neef (2005:10) argues, 'recognises as simultaneous modes of reasoning the rational and the relational . . . represent(ing) a clear challenge to the binary and lineal logic of Aristotelian tradition.' The complexities and chaos of the world in its contemporary context will not be solved by simplistic answers. 'Our relation with a complex world and a complex Nature requires complex thought' (Max-Neef 2005:14). Unless transdisciplinary approaches can be used, it will not be possible 'to find solutions to situations such as poverty, unemployment and sustainability' (Max-Neef 2005:14).

Max-Neef's model ties in well with the holistic understanding of poverty being comprised of broken relationships, relationships that 'are fragmented, dysfunctional or oppressive'[32] (Myers 1999:86). Poverty is also a complex, multilayered problem. To find a solution that will alleviate or eliminate poverty requires that one use multifaceted tools; the tools of 'anthropology, sociology, social psychology, spiritual discernment, and theology, all nicely integrated' (Myers 1999:86).

4.2.2 Human Scale Development

This integration is critical. The causes that trap people in poverty are rooted in complexity, evidenced by the fact that, 'we are rarely analysing a specific problem but instead a web of complex issues that cannot be resolved through the application of conventional policies founded upon reductionist disciplines' (Max-Neef 1991:15). For Max-Neef, one should not speak of *poverty* but of *poverties.* For him, any fundamental human need that is not adequately satisfied reveals a human poverty. This understanding requires that for development policy to be effective, it must go beyond conventional economic rationale and be applied to the person as a whole. Needs can be expressed, 'as deprivation and as potential' ... so that if one can understand '(t)he relations ... between needs and their satisfiers ... it (is) possible to develop a philosophy and a policy for development which are genuinely humanistic' (Max-Neef 1991:22). This approach appears quite useful for one engaging with poverty in a South African context.

i Needs-based approach

Max-Neef suggests nine fundamental, non-hierarchical needs as a framework by which one must interpret and address the widespread poverty facing humanity in the 21st Century. He poses three postulates as an outline of this structure:

1. Development is about people, not about objects.
2. Fundamental human needs are finite.
3. Fundamental human needs are universal across time and space (Max-Neef 1991:16, 18).

ii People-centric focus

Max-Neef provides useful insight here in defining the concept of poverty from a people-centric focus. The first postulate serves as an indirect criticism of conventional strategies that define poverty and, ultimately, poverty alleviation solely through the *quantitative* growth of systems as indicated by indices and statistical measurement. This was shown earlier. Max-Neef argues that, since it is *people* who find themselves trapped in poverty, measuring poverty must focus on the *qualitative* growth of *people*. Development must result in improving the situation of real individuals and actual conditions. 'The best development process will be that which allows the greatest improvement in people's quality of life' (Max-Neef 1991:16).

This improved 'quality of life' is what is being pursued through Human Scale Development and the matrix of needs and satisfiers. Max-Neef (1991:16) explains that improving the 'quality of life' means improving the 'possibilities people have to adequately satisfy their fundamental human needs.' This improvement results in development or the alleviation of poverty.

Max-Neef's theory contains a list of needs. This leads to his second postulate that *fundamental human needs are finite*. He lists nine basic needs which he describes as axiological: *affection, creation, freedom, identity, idleness, participation, protection, subsistence and understanding.* In addition to these axiological needs there are four *existential* needs, those of *being, having, doing and interacting.* The third postulate adds an additional qualifier to the needs by arguing that these fundamental human needs are *universal across both space and time.* Max-Neef would say that the needs have been and will be effectual without time limitations and have been experienced by all people groups across all continents.

For Max-Neef, the list of needs according to Human Scale Development is complete--no other fundamental needs exist outside of it. However, he does leave room for transcendence, an experience of reality apart from rationality: 'The belief in parallel worlds is something that I myself have allegoric- ally referred to as, "There is a world in which you have to see in order to believe, and there is another world in which you have to believe in order to see" . . . . (W)hat appears to be increasingly evident is that we can no longer assume that there is just one reality, fully describable and understandable in terms of pure reason' (Max-Neef 2005:12). This 'second reality' leaves room in Max-Neef's methodology for the need for God. Without this understanding, one could argue that there is no opportunity for true holistic development. Yamini Narayan (2013:138), writing in *Sustainable Development,* also recognises the need for a transcendent role in sustainable de- velopmental practices: 'Values, or the application of spiritual principles, have been the missing ingredient in most past ap- proaches to sustainable development . . . . The exciting thing about addressing sustainability at the level of values is the potential to create self-generating human systems building a more sustainable and thus ever-advancing civilization.'

Also, the list must be understood as a non-hierarchical, fully integrated system within which there is lots of interaction. The need for subsistence alone takes precedence. Otherwise, the list is considered completely flat with each need being equally important.

There are nine *axiological* needs: affection, creation, freedom, identity, participation, protection, subsistence, idleness and understanding and four *existential* needs: being, having, doing, interacting. The four existential needs can be understood as the needs by which the axiological needs are realised. For example, the need for protection is experienced at the four existential levels: through being, having, doing, and interact- ing. One needs to be protected, to have protection, to do ac- tivities that lead to protection, and to be able to interact in a safe place. This same example has application to all nine of the axiological needs.

iii Small is the way forward

Human Scale Development suggests that the best approach to meeting these needs is at the 'human scale.' Small groups, termed 'micro-organisations,' are the focus for development, thereby changing the role of macro-organisations such as government to one of visible support for micro-organisations. Development is about creating self-reliance in the individual which sustains the improvement of communities through meeting the nine needs. For Max-Neef (1982:167), small is the critical way forward:

> (P)robably what we need instead of a theory, is a purpose. A purpose that allows for people's full participation, through multi-level action processes, starting at grass-root levels and stretching from the village to the global order. A purpose in the spirit of the Third System Project, which states that 'starting from the base of society, each unit should be able to initiate its own course of action and solve all the problems it is able to solve. This is the essence of self-reliance and self-management. Problems beyond the reach and perspective of primary communities would be solved by larger units according to the nature of the task and in such a manner as to ensure the participation of those concerned, as well as the accountability of those exercising power.

iv Approach is transdisciplinary

This serves as a challenge to mainstream economic theory by moving the focus solely from economics to society in general. Poverty is not primarily to be engaged from a top-down approach at the macro level, although there remains an important role for government and others in this process. Instead, the successful engagement of poverty begins with people in the community through a transdisciplinary approach. Max-Neef (2005:14) writes, 'only in so far as transdiscipline can penetrate and transform the economistic vision of the world, can we aspire to find solutions to situations such as poverty, unemployment and sustainability.' Disciplines are inter-related, making it necessary to construct theory and conduct research in a new way.

This is an important insight. Due to the complexity of the concept of poverty, Human Scale Development is valuable as it can be applied across all ranges of society, irrespective of income, education and cultural standing. For example, a wealthy man who is robbed at gunpoint lives with a poverty: his need for protection is not being satisfied. There is a grammatical shift here as well—he *has* a poverty rather than lives *in* poverty. This subtle difference yields profound implications as it gives the concept of poverty a specific meaning. Poverty is no longer a vague term defining one's state of being. It is simply the lack of a specific need, such as protection or affection or whatever other stated combination is lacking from the list of human needs. And because it is more narrowly defined, it should also be easier to specifically address as one must simply put *satisfiers* in place to ensure that the specific need is met. According to Max-Neef, once the need is met then that poverty will be effectively eliminated.

v *Poverty generates pathologies*

There is an additional dimension to Max-Neef's interpret-ation of poverty. He writes that 'poverties are not only poverties. Much more than that, *each poverty generates patholo-gies*. This is the crux of our discourse' (Max-Neef 1991:19). This concept is a central component of Human Scale Develop-ment. Clarke (1993:17) explains by way of summary:

> If fundamental needs are not met over an extended period of time, or are met by false satisfiers, then poverty in one form or another will result. If unmet needs are not understood and acted upon, a com-plex and persistent sickness will take hold of society, a *pathology* which can only be addressed by radical

117

changes and the combined effort of many influences and experts.

vi Needs met by satisfiers

Human needs can be met by 'satisfiers.' For Max-Neef (1991:17), a 'satisfier may contribute simultaneously to the satisfaction of different needs, or, conversely, a need may require various satisfiers in order to be met.' The relationship, therefore, between satisfiers and needs is not static. While needs remain within a fixed list, satisfiers will vary across time and space, with Max-Neef (1991:18) going so far as to suggest that 'one of the aspects that define a culture is its choice of satisfiers.'

Additionally, needs can be fulfilled at different levels, with varying intensities and within three contexts:
    (a) With regard to oneself (*Eigenwelt*);
    (b) With regard to the social group (*Mitwelt*);
    (c) With regard to the environment (*Umwelt*); (Max-Neef 1991:18).

The quality and intensity of the levels and the contexts will depend on time, place and circumstances. In the following Table (3.1), Max-Neef describes the existential categories as:
   • Being—attributes (personal or collective) that are expressed as nouns
   • Having—institutions, norms and mechanisms, tools (not in a material sense), laws, etc. that can be expressed in one or more words
   • Doing—actions (personal or collective), that can be expressed as verbs
   • Interacting—locations and milieus (as times and spaces) (Max-Neef 1991:32-33).

Needs according to existential categories. Needs according to axiological categories	Being	Having	Doing	Interacting
Subsistence	Physical health, mental health, equilibrium, sense of	Food, shelter, work	Feed, procreate, rest, work	Living environment, social setting

	humour, adaptability			
Protection	Care, adaptability, autonomy, equilibrium, solidarity	Insurance systems, savings, social security, health systems, rights, family work	Cooperate, prevent, plan, take care of, help	Living space, social environment, dwelling
Affection	Self-esteem, solidarity, respect, tolerance, generosity, receptiveness, passion, determination, sensuality, sense of humour	Friendships, family, partnerships, relationship with nature	Make love, caress, express emotions, share, take care of, cultivate, appreciate	Privacy, intimacy, home, space of togetherness
Understanding	Critical conscience, receptiveness, curiosity, astonishment, discipline, intuition, rationality	Literature, teachers, method of educational policies, communication policies	Investigate, study, experiment, educate, analyse, mediate	Settings of formative interaction, universities, academies, groups, communities, family
Participation	Adaptability, receptiveness, solidarity, willingness, determination, dedication, respect, passion, sense of humour	Rights, responsibilities, duties, privileges, work	Become Affiliated, cooperate, propose, share, dissent, obey, interact, agree on, express opinions	Settings of participative interaction, parties, associations, churches, communities, neighbourhoods, family
Idleness	Curiosity, receptiveness, imagination, recklessness, sense of humour, tranquility, sensuality	Games, spectacles, clubs, parties, peace of mind	Daydream, brood, dream, recall old times, give way to fantasies, remember, relax, have fun, play	Privacy, intimacy, spaces of closeness, free time, surroundings, landscapes
Creation	Passion, determination, intuition, imagination, boldness, rationality, autonomy	Abilities, skills, method, work	Work, invent, build, design, compose, interpret	Productive and feedback settings, workshops, cultural groups, audiences, spaces for expression, temporal freedom
Identity	Sense of belonging, consistency, differentiation, self-esteem, assertiveness	Symbols, language, religion, habits, customs, reference groups, sexuality, values, norms, historical memory, work	Commit oneself, integrate oneself, confront, decide on, get to know oneself, recognise oneself, actualise oneself	Societal rhythms, everyday settings, settings to which one belongs, maturation stages
Freedom	Autonomy, self-esteem, determination, passion, assertiveness, open mindedness, boldness, rebelliousness, tolerance	Equal rights	Dissent, choose different from, run risks, develop awareness, commit oneself, disobey	Temporal/spatial plasticity

Table 3.1 Matrix of needs/satisfiers (see Max-Neef 1991:32-33).

Each need is satisfied in accordance with the existential category listed above. The list is complete in itself, according to Max-Neef, and must be understood as an integrated system, meaning that within the list exists significant interaction. Whereas Maslow's well-known list of needs is hierarchical, for Max-Neef, as has been previously mentioned, the list is completely flat, giving each need equal value except for subsistence.

Also, there is a list of 'satisfiers' for all of the needs that may or may not be useful in actually meeting the need appropriately. Max-Neef identifies five types of satisfiers as follows:

1. **Destroyers or violators**-this type of satisfier not only fails to meet the need but it also negatively affects the satisfaction of other needs. This satisfier is often forced upon people by those with power.

2. **Pseudo-satisfiers**-these are elements that 'generate a false sense of satisfaction of a given need' (Max-

Neef 1991:31). Although they do not have the same aggressiveness as the destroyer or violator, they may, after a period of time, impair the satisfaction of the need. They are generally induced 'through propaganda, advertising or other means of persuasion' (Max-Neef 1991:31).

3. **Inhibiting Satisfiers**-these are those that generally oversatisfy a given need which curtails the possibility of satisfying other needs. They have often originated in 'deep-rooted customs, habits and rituals' (Max-Neef 1991:34).

4. **Singular satisfiers**-these are those that satisfy one particular need in isolation, a trait common in the history of development interventions. Their effect on other needs is neutral, which makes them insufficient.

5. **Synergic Satisfiers**-These satisfiers are the most desirable and effective. Max-Neef (1991:34) writes that they

> . . . are those that satisfy a given need, simultaneously stimulating and contributing to the fulfilment of other needs. They share the attribute of being anti-authoritarian in the sense that they constitute a reversal of predominant values, such as competition and coerciveness.

This final type of satisfier enables the meeting of many of the needs concurrently without negatively impacting the meeting of other needs. Synergic satisfiers are beneficial and can play a significant role in poverty alleviation initiatives.

Max-Neef draws a distinction between what he calls *exogenous* and *endogenous* satisfiers. He argues that the first four satisfiers are 'exogenous to civil society as they are usually imposed, induced, ritualized or institutionalized' (Max-Neef 1991:34). They are forced upon the community from the top down by those in power. Alternatively, the endogenous satisfiers are initiated from the grassroots level where there is ownership, participation and a greater likelihood of successful poverty alleviation.

One more important element to mention in Human Scale Development is the role of economic goods. Goods, understood as economic objects, are a *means* for the satisfaction of needs, not the satisfiers themselves. Thus, although poverty alleviation can occur at some level as needs are satisfied through the use of economic goods, the goods themselves are not necessarily synergic satisfiers as they may only aim to satisfy one need. To truly satisfy a need as a synergic satisfier would require the simultaneous satisfaction of other needs in a contributing way.

4.2.3 Human Scale Development and micro-organisations

The methodology behind Human Scale development has to do with its emphasis on size, particularly on the necessity of smallness. Human Scale, by definition, includes the family, the group, the community and community structures, and the local context, what Max-Neef would term the 'invisible world.' He is against the notion that poverty alleviation is achieved by large-scale external actors. Instead, poverty alleviation is 'a matter of drastic redistribution of power through the organization of horizontal communal integration. It is a matter of passing from destructive giantism to creative smallness' (1982: 55).

He writes further that
> . . . since my concern is with the people of the invisible sectors that account for more than half of the world's population, I no longer believe in 'national solutions' or 'national styles.' I do not even believe in 'national identities'. I do not believe-to put it in a nutshell-in any form of giantism. Hence, as a barefoot economist, I believe in local action and in small dimensions. It is only in such environments that human creativity and meaningful identities can truly surface and flourish. So what next? My reply is this: if national systems have learned to circumvent the poor, it is the turn of the poor to learn how to cir-

cumvent the national systems. (Max-Neef 1982:117).

Development is about people, not about large-scale economic programmes. Large systems, such as conventional government, struggle to make an impact in poverty alleviation, but they do have a significant role to play in the overall engagement. The interface between the macro and micro players is complex, but critical. It requires 'organic articulation' that frees the informal sectors of impoverished society from relationships of dependency. This must take place in a context of thoughtful care. These groups of micro players are not viewed as the sole medium for transformation, but must be strategically highlighted since mainstream development theory tends to ignore what would be termed the 'invisible world.' For effective development to take place, this world must be recognised and engaged. 'Everything that can be done at local levels, is what should be done at local levels' (Max-Neef 1982:117). For Human Scale Development to succeed, it is imperative that diversity, as it exists in all forms, is respected and nourished, including social, economic, political, and religious. This aspect of development practice will bring clarity to the discussion of the role of the local church in activities around poverty alleviation to be found in Chapters 6 and 7.

4.5 Summary

If the ultimate goal of poverty alleviation is to improve the lives of people, then the application of Human Scale Development methodology into situations of poverty would appear to be useful. Needs are met at the human scale level with self-reliance acting as the sustainable medium by which this process takes place. However, instead of independence being the overall goal, it is rather about interdependence. The interdependence of micro-organisations in the invisible world is at the crux of Max-Neef's thesis around poverty alleviation. It is a conscious move towards maximising participation by encouraging networking at the human scale. It improves the quality of life by changing the way that people see themselves, thereby allowing the freedom for greater capacity and potential. New possibilities are created and expanded. For Max-Neef, as the focus on 'local' becomes valuable, then self-confidence increases. (Max-Neef 1991:65).

Human Scale Development 'offers suggestions, while remaining open to further elaboration' (1991: xii). Max-Neef states that

> The proposal we have developed is not a model. It is an open option which is justified only to the extent that we understand it, internalize it and implement it through a praxis that is in itself a process in constant motion (1991:12)

The flexibility within this approach is of great benefit. It speaks to the concerns about its applicability outside of Max-Neef's South American context[33]. As a 'process in motion,' it is able to find application from the South American to the South African context and hypothetically to anywhere else. This theory can be applied by anyone and designed according to one's socio-economic context. As a people-centred approach, it has strengths found in maximising inclusion through active participation, thereby allowing local ownership of the development processes. This focus on 'smallness' places development potential within the reach of any community in poverty. Community groups, and particularly churches, can play a significant role as change agents within their local context.

5 Conclusion

The biblical record of teaching and practice that relates to the community of faith's responsibility to those in need is clear. The Bible details God's desire for transformed economic relationships among his people, beginning in the Hebrew Scriptures to guide Israel and led by example through Jesus and the Early Church. It is essential that contemporary followers of Jesus implement these Scriptural principles that it claims are its mandate in the communities where followers of Jesus exist.

Scripture offers two important clues about the nature of the economic justice that God demands from his people. First, God desires that all individuals have the opportunity to earn a modest living and be dignified members of the community. This statement seems clear from the Old Testament laws that protected people from permanent poverty, God's role as the protector and defender of the poor, Jesus' pronounced mission, in part, as 'bringing good news to the poor' and the generosity directed toward those in need by the Early Church community. Significant focus exists within the Scriptures calling God's people to take an active role in engaging poverty.

Second, God desires that those unable to work be provided for out of the generosity of those who can work. The remarkable growth of the early Christian community is a testimony to the power of such practical ministry.

Jesus' ministry incorporated Old Testament guidelines while also opening up the impact of generous living to those outside the structures of the community of faith, instructing his followers to not only help to meet the needs of 'family,' but that one's reach should be broad enough to include anyone in need. He fulfilled Scripture by demonstrating what living by faith with generosity toward others was intended to be. As a result, the kindness of the Early Church Christians grabbed the attention of 1st century communities and had a powerful evangelistic impact. When Scriptural principles transformed economic relationships among God's people and then describe God's blessing on his people as they implement his commands, there exists a functional model that is applicable for modern day faith communities.

There are many definitions offered to describe poverty. The lack of sufficient income is simply one element in this complex picture. Instead, what is more comprehensive is to consider poverty as a series of broken relationships or unmet 'needs'. The interviews conducted by the World Bank give a face to poverty, describing not only the physical challenges but also detailing the psychological scarring that takes place. The process undertaken to alleviate poverty in a community must be multidisciplinary so that the significant challenges that define the complexity of poverty can be adequately engaged. It must include the views of those living in poverty to be contextual. Whatever can be done locally is what should be done locally.

However, defining poverty is only the beginning of the process necessary to bring about change. Poverty alleviation requires a long-term, focused approach with the desired goal to bring people in society to a sense of equilibrium, both in income levels useful to sustaining productive life and in developmental opportunities. It is about bringing true *shalom* to a local community. Since poverty is more than just a lack of sufficient income, holistically focused community development that addresses the root causes of poverty is essential for effective poverty alleviation to take place.

The next discussion will consider an interpretive examination of James 2 as the author of the Epistle describes a life of faith and the lifestyle that should be in evidence by one making such a claim.

CHAPTER FOUR

INTERPRETING JAMES 2 TO DEFINE 'REAL' FAITH

1 Introduction

J.H. Ropes wrote of James at the beginning of the twentieth century as follows: 'As in the diatribes, there is a general controlling motive in the discussion, but no firm and logically disposed structure giving a strict unity to the whole, and no trace of the conventional arrangement recommended by the elegant rhetoricians' (1916:14). Ropes assessment must be challenged. The underlying premise of this investigation is two-fold: First, it is believed that James 2 is framed according to a standard elaboration pattern for argumentation commonly used by the Greco-Roman rhetoricians that employs structure and purpose to communicate meaning. Corresponding action is required. Second, it is important to recognise that the correct interpretation of this passage, or any passage of Scripture, carries an authority which defines faith and practice.

The Epistle of James is considered an early Christian letter (1:1).[34] According to early epistolary theory, it is 'a substitute for oral communication and could function . . . as a speech' (Aune 1987:158). From a rhetorical perspective, James is intentional discourse: it has a 'message to convey,' seeking to 'persuade an audience to believe it [the message] or to believe it more profoundly' (Kennedy 1984:3).

This study of the Epistle of James is an exercise in rhetorical criticism, which is

> that mode of internal criticism which considers the
> interactions between the work, the author, and the
> audience. As such it is interested in the *product,* the
> *process,* and the *effect,* of linguistic activity, whether
> of the imaginative kind or the utilitarian kind ... it
> regards the work not so much as an object of con-
> templation but as an artistically structured instru-
> ment for communication. It is more interested in a
> literary work for what it *does* than for what it *is* (Cor-
> bett 1969: xxii).

Therefore, what the text does in the hearer or what it intends
to do is of critical importance. The goal is influence.

This functional approach to discourse belongs most predominantly to rhetoric. Stanley Stowers (1986:15) expresses a
view that is characteristic of rhetoric when he says that New
Testament letters should be thought of more, 'in terms of the
actions that the people performed by means of them' rather
than as 'the communication of information.' The inherent social nature of rhetorical analysis makes it a useful tool for exploring the intended social function of the discourse since it
encompasses 'all speech and all aspects of all speech (e.g. as
social discourse, a means of societal formation, and a focus
on the social and cultural contexts of the speaker/writer and
audience)' (Gowler 2010:194). Language, seen as an inherently
social activity, was formed by the speaker to accomplish a
particular purpose.

This is important insight for a study of the book of James.
Rhetorical analysis can help one to discover both the overt
and latent intent in James' rhetoric and to understand how
this is communicated to its audience. These findings can then
be proposed to modern readers of James with application to
current cultural settings and contexts. What results should
be a dynamic understanding of the letter of James for modern
hearers that feels the author's call to them with the same im-

pact and intensity as was felt by hearers in the first century C.E.

The author of the Epistle is intending to evoke a social response in the thinking and behaviour of his hearers. The letter offers clues to the social environment in which it is spoken, underlining the importance of being able to transfer such understanding to one's current context. Rhetorical tradition defines rhetorical discourse as being situationally or contextually specific: it 'comes into being *in* the situation, to *affect* the situation, and to *alter* the situation' through language (Bryant 1973: 36). Rhetorical discourse is inherently social discourse intended to produce social effects. It helps to generate and strengthen personal, social and cultural values and is an 'interpersonal response to pre-existent or emerging conditions; it is the use of language in an avowedly social mission' (Bryant 1973: 32).

It is this 'social mission' for which the letter of James can serve as a useful guide for the church. It is a deliberative discourse that intends, '. . . to persuade an audience to think and act in ways that have significant social consequence . . . that concerns the conflict between the rich and the poor, a social issue that is pivotal in the discourse of the epistle' (Wachob 2000: 23).

This is an important consideration, certainly as one considers the weight of authority carried into a social context through these rhetorical strategies. Paul writes in I Thessalonians 2:13 that, 'When you received the word of God, which you heard from us, you accepted it not as the word of humans, but as it actually is—the word of God.' Paul equates the message he proclaimed to the Thessalonians with the 'word of God.' This is very different from mere human speech, or even mere human words about God. Instead, this is, 'divine speech which changes human lives' (Witherington 2009a:5). It is seen as something living and active, 'which is at work in you who believe.' This fits perfectly; the goal of rhetorical discourse is to bring about an intentional change in behaviour.

1.1 Defining Socio-rhetorical analysis

Into this rhetorical environment emerged 'socio-rhetorical analysis.' This grouping of rhetorical criticism and social-scientific criticism under the banner socio-rhetorical criticism traces its roots to a 1975 article by Vernon K. Robbins entitled 'By Land and By Sea: The We-Passages and Ancient Sea Voyages.'[35] It is an exegetical approach to literature that 'focuses on values, convictions, and beliefs both in the texts we read and in the world in which we live' (Robbins 1996a:1). Socio-rhetorical analysis involves detailed attention to the text itself while moving interactively between the author of the text and one's current context, integrating the ways people use language with the ways they live in the world. Robbins explains the nature of texts as a 'rich tapestry' that, when explored from different angles, shows the different, '. . . textures of meanings, convictions, values, emotions, and actions' (Gowler 2010:195). Socio-rhetorical analysis is useful in bringing, 'literary criticism, social-scientific criticism, rhetorical criticism, postmodern criticism, and theological criticism together into an integrated approach to interpretation' (Robbins 1996a:2). According to Robbins, when these approaches are used interactively, practices of interpretation are brought together that often are separated from one another. The result enables the interpreter to bring multiple textures of the text into view through five different angles that explore the textures within texts: inner texture, intertexture, social and cultural texture, ideological texture and sacred texture[36] (Robbins 1996a:3).

Behaviour is influenced by social customs and traditions. Understanding the society to which one seeks to bring influence is critical in this process. By examining the NT while gleaning the insights one can learn from studying ancient social history, including the oral nature of ancient cultures, and from studying classical Greco-Roman and Jewish rhetoric, one should gain a solid background that serves as a basis for interpretation. This process anchors the text in a historical context. However, New Testament texts are not, 'simply historical, theological or linguistic treatises. Rather, their written discourse is a highly interactive environment' (Robbins 1996b:13).

Interpretation is then revealed in what is primarily a historical discipline, not a hermeneutical one. This means that 'the NT should in the first place be analyzed on the basis of the social and literary realia that actually existed in the first century A.D. (C.E) and on the basis of the sorts of rhetoric that were actually practiced in the first century A.D.(C.E.)' (Witherington 2009b:2). Witherington further explains:

> By this I mean that the proper place to begin when studying NT texts, *in a historical manner*, is to ask a very traditional and historical question: What did this or that author mean to say by writing, or having written, these words? One should begin by respecting the texts as we have them and the historical authors who encoded meaning into these texts in various ways. One should assume that the more one knows about the various ancient contexts, including the social and rhetorical contexts, in which these texts were written, the more one will properly understand them. There can be no talk of the "autonomy of texts" or bandying about of the mythical mantra "all we have is texts" or even of "meaning being largely in the eye of the beholder" if one wants to approach the NT in a truly historical manner (Witherington 2009b:2).

Although Witherington's analysis has its critics[37], his insight is helpful. Thorough knowledge regarding the use of rhetoric in the NT helps one to eliminate many of the theological, ethical, and practical misinterpretations that are possible during an examination of the text.

These 'textures within texts,' therefore, must be considered within a historical context. This means that the Scriptures, and for the purposes of this research chapter 2 of the Epistle of James, should be examined on the basis of the social and literary settings that existed in the first century C.E. as were experienced by its recipients while considering the rhetorical strategies that were being practiced. If one wants to develop a *historical* understanding of what the "authors" of the NT were doing using the art of persuasion and what *their* social worlds were like, then one must carefully apply the tools at one's disposal while remaining faithful to the text. James D. G. Dunn (2003:114) provides useful insight:

> ... the "autonomy" of the text is ... (an) illusion. For the text will always be read in context, whether the historical context of the text, or of its later editions, or the contemporary context of the reader. The text is not like a free-floating balloon to be pulled to earth every so often, its message read, and then released back again into the atmosphere, as though that were its natural setting. As text it was always earth-bound from the first. The reality is that the less attention given to the text's own context, the more likely the text is to be abused by the hermeneutical process.

1.2 Defining the interpretive process

This chapter will consider James 2 through a socio-rhetorical analysis. The socio-rhetorical textures of inner texture, intertexture and social and cultural texture will be featured. These angles are being explored as the most relevant socio-rhetorical textures for the purposes of this study. Underlying this research is a presupposition that 'words themselves work in complex ways to communicate meanings that we only partially understand' (Robbins 1996a:4). It is hoped that this structure may be useful to help fill any such possible gaps.

James 2 shall be broken into two rhetorical units, James 2.1-13 and James 2.14-26, utilising basic elements of socio-rhetorical criticism as a structure to facilitate interpretation.

2 Inner Texture of James 2.1-13

Inner texture is referred to by Robbins as 'getting inside a text' by studying 'features in the language of the text itself,' thereby referring to the patterns and strategies employed by the author to facilitate communication (Robbins 1996a: 7). One explores inner texture by engaging the structure of the text through an examination of the rhetorical strategy in use by the speaker. For William Brosend (2004:16), by examining a text through inner texture is to,

> '. . . experience and appreciate the power of the text to create a world, to create meaning, to persuade, dissuade, and cajole, without reference to other texts, textual history, socio-historical and cultural-anthropological insights, etc. Just the author and the reader, with the text as mode of communication.'

The study of inner texture brings the interpreter as deeply as possible into the inner workings of the text, considering and appreciating its structure and shape without relying on anything outside the text itself.

2.1 James 2.1-13 as a rhetorical unit

[1] My brothers, show no partiality as you hold the faith in our Lord Jesus Christ, the Lord of glory. [2] For if a man wearing a gold ring and fine clothing comes into your assembly, and a poor man in shabby clothing also comes in, [3] and if you pay attention to the one who wears the fine clothing and say, "You sit here in a good place," while you say to the poor man, "You stand over there," or, "Sit down at my feet," [4] have you not then made distinctions among yourselves and become judges with evil thoughts? [5] Listen, my beloved brothers, has not God chosen those who are poor in the world to be rich in faith and

heirs of the kingdom, which he has promised to those who love him? [6] But you have dishonored the poor man. Are not the rich the ones who oppress you, and the ones who drag you into court? [7] Are they not the ones who blaspheme the honorable name by which you were called? [8] If you really fulfill the royal law according to the Scripture, "You shall love your neighbor as yourself," you are doing well. [9] But if you show partiality, you are committing sin and are convicted by the law as transgressors. [10] For whoever keeps the whole law but fails in one point has become accountable for all of it. [11] For he who said, "Do not commit adultery," also said, "Do not murder." If you do not commit adultery but do murder, you have become a transgressor of the law. [12] So speak and so act as those who are to be judged under the law of liberty. [13] For judgment is without mercy to one who has shown no mercy. Mercy triumphs over judgment (ESV).

James 2.1-13 is recognised by nearly all recent commentators as a clearly defined rhetorical unit. Wachob (2000:59) explains:

> It has a definite beginning, an admonition that states the theme of the unit (2.1); a middle, in which the theme is elaborated (2.2-11); and a conclusion, or summarising exhortation (2.12-13).

For Martin Dibelius (1976:124-25) the unit exhibits the characteristics of a 'treatise' where 'ideas are grouped together,' 'closely connected' and 'centred around one theme' while stylistically, the unit reflects features that are found in a diatribe or a sermon. Its content refers to the theme of the 'faith of our glorious Lord Jesus Christ' and 'respect of persons,' which is seen in the conflicting relations between the poor and rich (Dibelius 1976:48).

The significance of James 2.1-13 may be summarised as follows: First, it provides unity and coherence to the letter as a whole. Second, it is one of the best sources for understanding the style and thought of the author. Third, this unit stands alone in the core units of James as the treatise in which the author addresses the particular issue that seems, at least according to Dibelius, to concern him the most: 'the *piety of the Poor*, and the accompanying opposition to the rich and to the world' (Dibelius1976:48).

There is unity in the chapter, both in its semantics and rhetoric. This unity operates as an argument that illustrates the degree to which James relies on rhetorical conventions to organise and present his themes. It is worth considering the background here. Witherington (2007:449) explains:

> Since James can presuppose a Jewish Christian audience whose world of discourse and thought already includes many of the themes, ideas, and imperatives he will use, what was needed was not apologetical arguments that start from ground zero with formal proofs and presume no commonality with the audience or polemics that assume an adversarial situation, but rather elaboration of common themes, ideas, stories, wisdom sayings, analogies, Scriptures and the like.

This pattern of elaboration was not invented by James. He follows the rhetorical literature of the period.[38] This common rhetorical pattern was used extensively before, during and after the writing of James.

2.1.1 Deliberative rhetoric

It is also important to note that throughout this unit James uses deliberative rhetoric to persuade his readers to transform their behaviour or to prevent what might become acts of showing partiality, neglecting acts of charity or otherwise ignoring the standards required of those claiming to have 'faith.' The development of an argument or speech was taught in both the *progymnasmata*[39] and rhetorical handbooks in a programme of study that dealt with the inner unity and organisation of the speech, 'along with the inner logic, structure, and function of its elements' (Mack & Robbins 1989: 2). The standard outline of a speech would consist of 4 parts; an introduction (προοίμιον, *exordium*), a statement of facts (διήγησις, *narratio*), the argumentation (πίστις, *confirmatio*), and a conclusion (ἐπίλογος, *peroratio*) (Mack 1990:41). Although this conventional outline was modelled on the judicial[40] speech, 'it was easily accommodated to the requirements of the deliberative speech' (Mack 1990:42). This pattern served as a basic guide for progymnasmatic or rhetorical composition and will provide the basis for constructing an outline of this passage.

i The theme (propositio)

James 2.1-13 begins with a theme rather than a chreia. A pattern useful for elaborating a 'theme' and for developing a 'complete argument' can be found in the *Rhetorica ad Herennium* (4.43.56-44.56; 2.18.28; 2.29.46).[41]

James 2.1-13 conforms closely to this pattern, elaborating the themes of rich and poor and being doers of the word as introduced in 1.9-11, 22-7. The imperative to 'hold the faith of Jesus Christ without partiality' represents the *propositio*— the proposition to be defended. A central tenet of Judaism and Christianity is that God's justice is impartial and human justice should be as well. This is followed by the *ratio*, here composed as a rhetorical question that expects an assenting response: 'for if a man wearing a gold ring and fine clothing comes into your assembly, and a poor man in shabby clothes also comes in, and if you pay attention to the one who wears the fine clothing . . . , have you not then made distinctions among yourselves and become judges with evil thoughts?' The purpose of the *ratio*, according to the *Rhetorica ad Herennium*, is to establish the underlying basis of the proposition. It is a 'brief explanation' that is 'subjoined' to the theme that provides its 'causal basis' and establishes its truth (2.18.28; cf. 4.53.57). It does so here using the conclusion that those who act with partiality are corrupt judges, considered as being contrary to God. This establishes what is known in rhetorical theory as the *stasis*, the central issue that motivates a particular case. The assertion that the hearers act as evil judges suggests that the *stasis* involves deliberations around both what is just and what is honourable. In fact, the argument in verses 5-11 deals with issues of honour first and then those of legality.

ii The proof (confirmatio)

The proof (*confirmatio*) begins with three rhetorical questions in verse 5, each anticipating an affirmative response and each designed to expose the foolishness of favouring the rich. The first and third arguments concern 'the honourable,' thereby responding to the issue of honour raised in the *ratio* (Wachob 2000:179); the second argument invokes 'the practicable,' another deliberative topic. The first question (vv. 5-6a) characterises an argument from the contrary: it recognises God's choice in making the poor rich 'in faith' and installing them as 'heirs of the kingdom.' This act of installation associates the poor with the honour of the divine king, thereby creating a glaring contrast with the behaviour of those being addressed by James (ὑμεῖς δέ) who dishonoured the poor in their attempts to honour the rich.

The second question (v. 6b) recalls the line of argument from the Hebrew Scriptures of the rich oppressing the poor,[42] but in doing so shifts from aorist tense to present tense, thereby drawing attention to the current practices of the rich. Kloppenborg (1999:761) explains:

> The appeal, in rhetorical terms, is to what is practicable (ῥάδια πραχθῆναι)[43] or advantageous (τὸ συμφέρον) and their opposites. The positioning of verse 6b after verses 5-6a, coupled with the shift in tenses, has the effect of situating the current oppression by the rich between God's *past* choice (ἐξελέξατο) and promise of inheritance (ἐπηγγείλατο), on the one hand, and the as of yet unrealized effects of that promise on the other. This

juxtaposition draws attention to the impracticability of the addressees' behaviour, which collides with the obvious trajectory implicit in God's choices and promises. The final rhetorical question (v 7) returns to the topic of honour and dishonour by adducing the dishonouring of an 'honourable name' (τὸ καλὸν ὄνομα). The use of the aorist passive of ἐπικαλέω in the qualifying phrase (τὸ ἐπικληθὲν ἐφ ὑμᾶς) indicates that God is the source of the new name.[44] Thus it is God's honour that is affronted in the act of blasphemy.

This is a serious charge. Once made, James then shifts to an argument from written law.[45] The point of departure is a claim to which his audience would find agreement; they should live in accordance with the 'Royal Law' (verse 8), a reference to Leviticus 19.18. The selection of this text is appropriate: '... it had achieved the status of a summary of the Law in some sectors of second Temple Judaism and in the Jesus tradition' . . . with . . . 'the context of Leviticus 19 contain(ing) a direct prohibition of partiality that employs the Septuagintalism, πρόσωπον λαμβάνειν' (Kloppenborg 1999:762). Showing partiality is now linked specifically to the 'royal law,' which is expressed in Scripture as 'you shall love your neighbour as you love yourself' (Lev. 19.18; also Mk. 12.31; Lk. 10.27, in answer to a question about inheriting eternal life; Rom. 13.9; Gal 5.14). Showing partiality to the rich and dishonouring the poor do not simply indicate a display of bad manners, but are instead violations of the law as summarised (by Jesus) in the command to love one's neighbour. James then hammers home his point: the violation of one law makes one liable for the entire law. Although this statement has credibility as a Stoic maxim,[46] there is sufficient parallel within all branches of Judaism.[47] James is like Jesus (Mt. 5.21ff.; Mk. 10.19ff.) and Paul (Rom. 13.9ff.) when he turns to the Decalogue for his examples, speaking of adultery and murder in the order found in the Septuagint. 'The "One who said," that is, God, spoke both commandments (all commandments are understood), making no distinction between them or between those who violate one as opposed to another' (Brosend 2004:60). The unity of the Law is assured by the unity of the Lawgiver.

Even though the argument has moved to legal considerations, honour is still considered part of the appeal. This is seen at the end of 2.8, 'if you fulfil the royal law . . . you are acting nobly' (καλῶς ποιεῖτε). James is treating obedience to the Law as a matter of faithful allegiance to one in authority. Honour comes through the faithful execution of a superior's commands, while disobedience is considered dishonourable.

iii The conclusion (conclusio)

This argument is concluded (*conclusio*) in verses 12-13. The *conclusio* has a twofold function: to summarise the argument and to make a final appeal to one's emotions.[48] For Wachob (2000:105), the reference to speaking and acting in verse 12 recalls the fact that προσωπολημψίαι in verses 2.2-4, 2.6a; 2.9 refers to both activities 'and recapitulates the admonition in James 2.1.' The final appeal invokes the superiority of mercy over judgment: the failure to act mercifully brings judgment without mercy. James invites his hearers to consider the consequences of their actions and adjust their behaviour accordingly.

3 Intertexture of James 2.1-13

3.1 Introduction

This section will examine the intertexture of James 2.1-13. Intertextual analysis is a useful exercise because it takes seriously the view that, 'all language is a social possession and bases itself on the notion that all texts are constructed on the foundations of antecedent texts' (Halliday in Wachob 2000:114). Intertexture concerns 'a text's configuration of phenomena that lie outside the text' . . . so that the . . . 'text's configuration of phenomena in the world takes on a richer, thicker quality' (Robbins 1996a:3). It not only brings attention to the way a speaker appears to re-activate existing texts, but it also joins with the view that a text serves as 'both the transmission and maintenance of culture'[49] The text is a 'network of traces'[50] allowing previous voices to speak, aiding one's ability to shape the persuasive influence and power of the arguments. James skillfully uses such references to his advantage in formulating his units in chapter 2.

The discussion here of the intertexture of James 2.1-13 is a limited one with the focus on identifying intertextual allusions in this passage that play a significant role in James' persuasive argument. A useful model for this discussion is to continue the outline found for training students in the *progymnasmata* while also bearing in mind insights from modern literary and rhetorical studies that may be useful. According to the *progymnasmata* and ancient rhetorical handbooks, students 'were taught to elaborate a given theme by first introducing it in the most appealing manner possible' (Wachob 2000:116). To argue effectively, students learned to colour the language of their proposals with as much conventionally accepted material as possible. A proposal would be more readily acceptable to an audience through this appeal to precedent. The rhetorical goal was clear: 'to transfer the audience's adherence from commonly accepted social thought and behaviour to the particular thoughts and actions proposed by the rhetor in elaborating the theme' (Wachob 2000:116). Intertextual references would buttress both the rhetorical form and content of the argument.

In chapter 2 of the letter of James, there are six fairly specific references to earlier texts, each directly signalling an intertextual reference.[51] Four of these are found in the first unit of Chapter 2 (James 2.8, 2.9, 2.11 [two]). The intertextual references in James 2.23 and 25 will be considered later in this chapter. Some general allusions to passages will also be considered during the discussion.

3.2 The holiness code: James 2.8 (Lev. 19.18)

The first significant use of an intertextual formula in James 2 occurs in verse 8. It is marked specifically as an intertextual reference by the phrase κατα την γραφήν, 'according to the scripture.' This is an unusual marker, found only in James in the New Testament.[52] The marker refers to the Scripture known as the love commandment found in the LXX in Leviticus 19.18: ἀγαπήσεις τὸν πλησίον ὡς σεαυτόν. Wachob (2000:117) explains:

> When it occurs in James 2.8 as the first statement of a four-part argument from judgment based on the written law, the intertextual reference functions as a proposition from an authoritative text, 'a true assessment' based on ancient testimony in the written law.

This supports the theme from the analysis of inner texture in 2.1-13 that shows 'acts of partiality' as being incompatible with the 'faith of our glorious Lord Jesus Christ.' It also alludes to Leviticus 19.15 (ESV), which would seem in context with James' argument: 'You shall do no injustice in court. You shall not be partial to the poor or defer to the great, but in righteousness shall you judge your neighbour.'

3.2.1 Represent God through right behaviour

A careful investigation of the respective contexts of the 'love commandment intertext' indicates the following: First, the passage in Leviticus 19.18 is speech attributed to the LORD as an example for Moses as to what he should tell the people of Israel (Lev. 19.1-2). They are to behave in a manner that reflects the LORD since they are His representatives. The repeated phrase 'I am the LORD your God (or I am the LORD)' (Lev. 19.3, 4, 10, 11, 14, 16, 18, 25, 28, 30, 31, 32, 34, 36, 37) was to remind them of this special relationship using holiness as the mark of the covenant.

Leviticus connects the whole corpus of the holiness code with the covenant established between God and Israel at Sinai (Lev. 1.1; 8-9; 27.34); thus the holiness code and the Decalogue together define the relationship between God and Israel in the Torah (Wachob 2000:117-18).

There is a behavioural expectation through this relationship between God and his people. This expectation is framed by the assertion 'You shall keep my statutes' (Lev. 19.19) and the conclusion 'You shall keep *all* my statutes' (Lev. 19.37). The bridge between these two expectations is verse 18:

> 'You shall not take vengeance or bear a grudge against the sons of your own people, but you shall love your neighbor as yourself: I am the Lord' (ESV).

This bridge requires love to neighbours who are relatives, 'sons of your own people.' By the end of Leviticus 19, the behavioural expectation for holiness in God's sight is love to one's neighbour regardless of kinship:

> [33] 'When a stranger sojourns with you in your land, you shall not do him wrong. [34] You shall treat the stranger who sojourns with you as the native among you, and you shall love him as yourself, for you were strangers in the land of Egypt: I am the Lord your God' (Lev. 19.33-34).

This section is closed by what functions as a summation of the entire chapter:

> [37] 'And you shall observe *all* my statutes and *all* my rules, and do them: I am the Lord (Lev. 19.37 italics mine).[53]

Israel, in relationship with a holy God, was expected to display behaviour that would reflect that special relationship. This behaviour was defined by the holiness code, which reached so far as to define holiness in the realm of human relations as love—the love of neighbours without regard to kinship. One **must** love without prejudice according to Leviticus 19.18 and 19.33-34 to verify that one is in right relationship with God. Moreover, there is sufficient evidence to suggest the use of Leviticus 19.18 and 19.33-34 as a summary of the whole law.[54] The failure to love in this way was significant.

James 2.8, in reference to these passages in Leviticus, appears to be appropriating the expectations in this way. A direct comparison reveals that James 2.8 '. . . exploits seven of the twenty-four words in Leviticus 19.18. . . ,' reciting a clause verbatim . . . 'as a subordinate clause of direct discourse in the form of a maxim' (Wachob 2000:120). The word γραφήν marks this passage as an authoritative text. This means that James 2.8 is an "abbreviation" (συστέλλειν) of Leviticus 19.18; the Jamesian reference to the love commandment is properly a rhetorical "recitation" (ἀπαγγελία) of an ancient authority,[55] identified as such since the letter of James originates from what is referred to as a "traditional rhetorical culture," in which, 'oral and written speech interact closely with one another' (Robbins 1991:155). Within such a culture, the "repetition of words and phrases in a written document regularly is the result of 'recitation composition' rather than 'copying'" (Robbins 1991:146). Therefore, when reciting antecedent texts, the rhetorical form allowed as much or as little verbatim reproduction as one deemed necessary. Ancient authors 'continually recast material by adding to it, subtracting from it, rearranging it, and rewording it' (Robbins 1991:164). The focus was on persuasive communication. Therefore, James' use of Leviticus 19.18 can be appropriately labelled as a recitation performance.

3.2.2 Represent the teachings of Jesus

It is important at this point to further underpin James' authoritative framework. His arguments echo the teachings of Jesus. Moreover, it is probable that the author of James assumes that he is faithfully representing the words and actions of Jesus through the context of an argument that is addressed to Christian Jews while clearly highlighting the 'faith of our glorious Lord Jesus Christ' (2.1). 'It is hard to believe that judgments connecting the poor, the promised kingdom, the royal law and the love-commandment could have been heard without thinking of Jesus' words and deeds' (Wachob 2000:122). This reference to Jesus' faith in 2.1 serves as a 'global allusion' that would evoke the whole of what James perceives to be Jesus' beliefs, sayings, and activities.[56] There is an inherent connection between holding Jesus' faith and fulfilling the whole law. In the same manner, the rhetoric in this unit asserts that the love commandment—which Jesus and his servant James both appropriate as a summary of the whole law—is transgressed when one shows partiality.

3.3 Acts of partiality: James 2.9 (Lev. 19.15)

Since James 2.8 features a verbatim match to one clause in Leviticus 19.18, some scholars believe that the language in James 2.9 is also a reference to the author's dependence upon the 'holiness code' in Leviticus. Leviticus 19.15 refers to partiality:

> οὐ ποιήσετε ἄδικον ἐν κρίσει· οὐ λήμψῃ πρόσωπον πτωχοῦ οὐδὲ θαυμάσεις πρόσωπον δυνάστου, ἐν δικαιοσύνῃ κρινεῖς πλησίον σου.

> You shall not render an unjust judgment; you shall not be partial to the poor or defer to the great: with justice you shall judge your neighbour (NSRV).

All 'acts of partiality,' according to this passage, are considered to be unjust.

Additionally, there are specific indicators to identify the general dependence of James 2.9 on Leviticus 19.15, which are as follows:

1. The compound verb προσωπολημπτεῖτε, 'to

143

show partiality, or favouritism,' reflects the sense of λήμψη πρόσωπον (Lev.19:15), the LXX translation of the Hebrew *naw.saw*, 'to favour, to be partial.'[57]

2. Leviticus 19.15 uses the contrasting terms πτωχός (πτωχοῦ) and δυνάστης (δυνάστου), while James' contrast between πτωχός and πλούσιος echoes a corresponding concern for justice in social relations between the poor and the powerful. (Bammel, TDNT VI: 888).

There are some who would argue that the allusion in James 2.9 seems only a tenuous link to Leviticus 19.15. Not only is there no citation formula, but there is also no verbatim correspondence to the passage. However, the lack of these indicators does not disprove the hypothesis that James 2.9 draws on Leviticus 19.15. Instead, what seems likely is that the author is alluding to Leviticus 19.15. James 2.9 is a good example of 'recitation composition' that rearranges and rewords the antecedent text. It appears that the author has reformulated the language of Leviticus 19.15 in James 2.9, thereby developing a rhetorical judgment that suits the purposes of his argument. This follows Theon of Alexandria's encouragement to his rhetorical students that they learn how to recite not only 'in the same words' but 'in other words as well' (Hock and O'Neil 1986:95 in Robbins 1996a:42). There is ample evidence of material referring to antecedent texts that display little verbatim language.[58]

3.4 Structure of the argument (James 2.8-11)

The composition of the argument here is fairly clear. In James 2.8, the author is addressing a behaviour that is opposite of loving one's neighbour as oneself. In agreement with Leviticus 19, the love commandment and the prohibition against partiality are single precepts in the whole law. But James takes Leviticus 19.18 further by following Jesus' teaching that ascribes the love commandment as a summary of the whole law. Furthermore, James 2.9 appears to be a strategic recasting of the reference to 'acts of partiality' (Lev. 19.15) as a premise in an enthymeme, thereby indicating the beginning of a new argument. The rhetoric in James reconfigures the prohibition against 'acts of partiality' in Lev. 19.15 while agreeing that 'acts of partiality' are 'unjust judgments.' This is significant. The author has taken a precept from written law which functions as a summary of the whole law (Lev. 19.15) and has constructed a rhetorical judgment. Therefore, actions of partiality in Lev. 19.15 are effectively interpreted by our author as the opposite of loving one's neighbour as oneself. According to Wachob (2000:125), 'the Levitical partiality-prohibition is recontextualized and strategically transformed in James' rhetoric; now "acts of partiality," as ἁμαρτία ("sin"), are a failure to fulfil the whole law (James 2.9-11).'

James 2.10 and 11 are the final elements in a four-part argument (James 2.8-11) from judgment based upon the written law. This section also contains unambiguous intertextual references to the social codes, the conventions of thought, and the literature of the milieu that would assist the author in formulating his argument.

The summary of this 4 part argument is as follows:

1. Result/Theme based upon Authoritative Testimony: 2.8

If you really fulfill the royal law according to the Scripture, "You shall love your neighbor as yourself," you are doing well. (ESV)

2. Result/Argument from the Contrary: 2.9

But if you show partiality, you are committing sin and are convicted by the law as transgressors. (ESV)

3. Rule/Rationale: 2.10

For whoever keeps the whole law but fails in one point has become accountable for all of it. (ESV)

4. Case/Confirmation of Rationale with Authoritative Testimony: 2.11

For he who said, "Do not commit adultery," also said, "Do not murder." (ESV)

Conditional Result:

If you do not commit adultery but do murder, you have become a transgressor of the law (= you have become guilty of the whole law) (ESV) (Lightstone 2002:215).

3.4 Unity of the law (James 2.10)

The intertextual rationale introduced in James 2.10 is interesting. James, in asserting that one becomes guilty of the whole law when failing in any one point, is following a well-known hermeneutical rule that the law in all its parts is one law.[59] For James, the integrity of the law is derived from the presupposition that there is one God, one law-giver who is calling His people to holy behaviour in response to His holiness. Lev.19 makes this clear in the many references to God that require the holiness of his people. 'And the Lord spoke to Moses, saying, "Speak to all the congregation of the people of Israel and say to them, You shall be holy, for I the Lord your God am holy'" (Lev. 19.1–2 (ESV)). The inability to keep all of the laws in their entirety was the failure to live up to the standards imposed by God.

This concept of the 'oneness of God's law' in James 2.10 is analogous to the Stoic notion of the solidarity of the virtues (and vices): whoever has one, has all of them.[60] Augustine, (*Epistula 167 ad Hieronymum 4*), has combined this passage with this Stoic concept: 'whoever has one virtue has all of them, and whoever does not have a particular one has none. If this is true, then the statement [in James] is confirmed.' Christianity presupposes universal sinfulness. Augustine apparently feels the contradiction between his Christianity and this Stoic notion that would include the statement put forward by James. According to Dibelius, Augustine is right in paralleling the Stoic concept with that of James 2.10, even though they had nothing to do with each other originally (Dibelius 1976:146). It seems apparent that James 2.10 was influenced by Judaism, making it unlikely that Stoic philosophy was the determining influence for James.

3.5 Application of the Decalogue (James 2.11)

Verse 11 plainly signals an intertextual reference: The citation formulas (ὁ εἰπών, εἶπεν καί) introduce two commandments from the Decalogue, showing that this passage is also a judgment based upon the written law. Additionally, while the rhetorical recitation in James 2.8 carefully excerpts and abbreviates Leviticus 19.18, the text here is not considered verbatim recitation.

The commandments cited are prohibitions against adultery and murder:

> οὐ μοιχεύσεις (LXX Ex. 20.13; Deut. 5.17). You shall not commit adultery (Ex. 20.14; Deut. 5.18) (ESV).

> οὐ φονεύσεις (LXX Ex. 20.13; Deut. 5:18). You shall not murder (20:13; Deut. 5.17) (ESV).

The listed order here of the commandments needs explanation. James 2.11 presents these two commandments in an order that diverges from the Masoretic Text. There the commandments against murder and adultery are listed as the sixth and seventh commandments respectively, which is also the sequence found in other portions of the New Testament and by Josephus (see Mk. 10.19, which varies in the manu-script tradition; Mt. 19.18, 5.21,27; and Josephus *Antiquities* iii.91)[61]. James reverses this arrangement, thereby agreeing with the LXX, some manuscripts of the Masoretic Text, and the writings of Philo, Luke and Paul (Wachob 2000:128).

In explaining the form and order of the commandments in James 2.11, 'some scholars have suggested that the author is simply following a written source other than the LXX or Masoretic Text, or that he is perhaps simply re-iterating com-mon oral church-teaching' (Laws 1980:114). These sugges-tions, however, are based on the notion that James' reference to previous texts is mainly,

> scribal reproduction(s), which, 'consisted of mak-ing copies of extant texts, transcribing messages and letters from dictation, and reproducing stock documents like receipts. A person received train-ing in these skills during the elementary and gram-matical phases of education (Robbins 1991:161).

Wachob would instead assert to the contrary, which seems warranted according to earlier discussions, that James' use of previous texts here and elsewhere are not 'scribal reproduc-tions' but are instead 'progymnastic compositions.' Robbins (1991:161) goes on to explain that this kind of composition, 'in contrast to scribal reproduction, consisted of writing traditional materials clearly and persuasively rather than in the oral or written form it came to the writer.' He further recommends that "the phrase 'progymnastic rhetoric' refers to the phenomenon and the term 'progymnastic compos-ition' relates to the writing activities associated with [the Progymnasmata] . . . . The full spectrum of progymnastic composition is outlined and discussed in those 'Elementary Exercises'" (Robbins 1991:161). What is important to under-stand, therefore, is that whatever sources the author of James may be using, he is 'reciting' the words of the law in the form he chooses. As has been seen earlier in this passage, when

James wants to recite an intertextual resource verbatim, he has done so.[62] This also means that when it suits his rhetorical purposes, he will adapt or thoroughly reformulate a text to achieve his intended outcome.

3.6 Application of the Holiness Code and Decalogue

Additionally, it is important to note that James 2.8 and 11 bring together in one discourse commandments from both the Holiness Code and the Decalogue. This is the tradition within which James has been trained. However, within the structure of James 2.1-13, commandments from the written law are endorsed and included under a reference to 'Jesus faith' (2.1). These written commandments function as supporting proofs for the theme of 2.1 within the rhetorical construction.

It is also important to note that the Decalogue commandments operate as the minor premise in an epicheirema produced by verses 2.10 and 11. This serves to confirm the hermeneutical principle in verse 10, the justification for judgment based on the written law. Certain facts are clear: 2.11 acts as the final statement in the four-part argument based on the law (2.8-11) and is the final proof in the confirmation (2.5-11).

> Namely, just as the violation of the law by committing adultery or murder (2.11) is a failure to fulfil the whole law as summarized in the love-commandment (2.8), even so acts of partiality, whether within the community (2.2-4, 6a) or outside it (2.6b-7), are sinful acts that render one guilty of the whole law (2.9-10). As transgressions of God's law, acts of partiality are therefore incompatible with Jesus' faith – that is what Jesus believed, said, and did – and should be avoided (2.1) (Wachob 2000:130).

The structure of James' argument, deftly woven, leads to an

unavoidable conclusion.

3.7 Conclusion of the elaboration (James 2.12-13)

There are other intertextual references in the conclusion of the elaboration in verses 12 -13. One of these is the reference to the law as νόμου ἐλευθερίας ('the law of liberty (freedom),' 2.12). This is the second and final time that James mentions the law in this way. This appearance is used here in the same sense as in 1.25 (ESV) where it includes the modifier describing it as the 'perfect law, the law of liberty.' In considering the use with which James has made of that Jewish legal principle, one can assume that the author is applying the same principle and understanding to this passage as well.

There is no precise linguistic parallel for 'the law of liberty' (freedom), although it would likely, 'echo conventional understandings in the culture' which might not necessarily be easily identifiable to a modern audience (Wachob 2000:130). However, it is believed that these phrases, including the 'royal law' (2.8), are '. . . Jamesian epithets for "the whole law" (2.10), the law of God's kingdom (2.8; cf. 2.5)' (Wachob 2000:130). The law is 'perfect' and 'whole' because it comes from God, a common understanding throughout the Hebrew Scriptures and Jewish thought.[63] Moreover, this is a familiar theme in Hellenistic philosophical beliefs as well, suggesting that James is also making innovative applications from the broader culture. Philo (*Mos.* 2.14) writes regarding the Law of Moses that it remains, 'firm, unshaken, immovable, stamped as it were, with the seals of nature herself.'

In a closer inspection of the intertexture of James 2.13, the themes of 'judgment' and 'mercy' are regularly expressed throughout conventional Jewish thought and literature. James acknowledges these themes in accordance with general Jewish understanding:

> For judgment is without mercy to one who has shown no mercy. Mercy triumphs over judgment

(2.13 ESV).

J.H. Ropes (1916:201) confirms this common Jewish understanding in Jer. *Baba* q. viii, 10, 'Every time that thou art merciful, God will be merciful to thee; and if thou art not merciful, God will not show mercy to thee.' This reference is very similar to the text in James 2.13. Betz (1985b:133) correctly sums up the evidence:

> for all branches of Judaism the exercise of mercy was one of the preeminent religious and social duties. This duty was based on the belief that God is a God of mercy. Early Christian theology continued this tradition in a variety of ways.

The widely accepted view is that James draws on Jewish tradition here rather than a saying of Jesus, although Jesus' Sermon on the Mount clearly states this same theme.[64]

James 2.12-13 forms an epicheirema, a logical deduction, which produces an excellent rhetorical summation for the elaboration in 2.1-11. Moreover, although it stands on its own as an entirely logical argument, it also provides a useful transition to the subsequent elaboration in 2.14-26 by summarising the preceding argument as a call for a specific kind of behaviour toward a poor neighbour. The concluding statement argues that those who hold the 'faith of the Lord Jesus' are not to unjustly judge their poor neighbours by showing partiality to the wealthy. Instead, they are to love the poor as they love themselves by showing them mercy.

Thus far, the analysis of the intertexture of James 2.1-13 has focused on preceding texts from the LXX that are interspersed with and coloured by contextual ideas and values from within the culture from which the text originates. Moreover, as the inner textual analysis of the passage has shown, the whole passage is a 'thoroughly logical progymnastic elaboration' which is also reflected throughout its intertexture (Wachob 2000:134).

3.8 A saying of Jesus (James 2.5)

The logic and content of James 2.1-13 reveal that the inter-personal activities of the audience are measured with relation to Jesus' faith, God's activities, God's law and judgment under God's law. How one behaves in word and deed toward one's poor neighbour is of great importance carrying significant consequence. Wachob (2000:135) writes, 'the logic of the rhetoric subsumes the references to God's action, law and judgment under a reference to Jesus' faith and argues that holding Jesus' faith and fulfilling God's law are counterparts.'

This theme is supported by the language in James 2.5 that, intertextually speaking, resonates with language from a well-known saying of Jesus,[65] although commentators are quick to note that the text does not specifically quote Jesus. Nevertheless, in James there are, 'certain sayings that reflect a widespread terminological, material, and religio-historical appropriation of a tradition of Jesus' sayings, (with) the prevailing conclusion among scholars. . . (being) that the text definitely alludes to sayings that in other literature are directly attributed to Jesus' (Dibelius 1976:28-29). Other evidence is supportive of this.[66]

However, possibly the clearest indication that James is referring to a saying of Jesus relates to the text in James 2.5 that 'the kingdom' is promised to 'the poor.' Although it is true that the Hebrew Scriptures and Jewish literature reflect the notion that God has a special concern and care for the poor, there '. . . are no references in the OT, Intertestamental literature, or the Talmud specifically saying that God is giving the kingdom to the poor,' . . . rightly concluding that this 'makes it unlikely that a Jewish source rather than a saying of Jesus was in James' mind' (Deppe 1990:90). He continues:

> Additional support for the presence of a saying of Jesus lies in the fact that the word 'kingdom' is not Jamesian vocabulary; James 2.5 is the only occur-

rence of this term in the epistle. Certainly the employment of a term particularly associated with the preaching of Jesus is evidence that James is alluding to the same saying quoted in Mt. 5.3 and Lk. 6.20. This is confirmed by the fact that even critical exegetes like Dibelius and Laws admit the probability that James is consciously referring to a logion previously spoken by Jesus. (Deppe 1990:91)

The Epistle of James does not necessarily reflect a knowledge of the canonical Gospels but of the traditions and/or the sources of the Gospels, and 'it is quite possible that some of these sayings and injunctions were known to James as sayings of Jesus' (Koester 1990:75). However, if this text is truly a saying of Jesus, a question naturally arises: Why is it not directly attributed to Jesus by the author of James?

There are a few likely reasons, the chief one being that James 2.5 has a specific function to play within this particular discourse. Other intertextual references[67] attributed to Jesus share two key terms that link them to James 2.5: οἱ πτωχοί and ἡ Βασιλεία. All five of these texts produce a sentence that features the same basic theme—God's kingdom is promised to the poor—and all but the passage in James are attributed to Jesus. Such sayings are a particular kind of reminiscence and may be variously attributed.[68] In fact, it is the attribution of a saying that can be the means of rhetorical proof, certainly when the saying is attributed to a person who carries authority (Robbins 1988:4). The attributed saying necessarily says something about the person to whom it is attributed, revealing particular information about

aspects of life, thought, and action in a mode which integrates attitudes, values, and concepts with personal, social, and cultural realities. The people featured in chreiai become authoritative spokesmen regarding positive and negative truths about life. These 'authorities' transmit social, cultural, religious, and philosophical heritage into later historical epochs (Robbins 1988:4).

Consequently, the sayings of Jesus in Matthew 5.3, Luke 6.20b, *The* Gospel *of Thom*as, 54 and *The Epistle of Polycarp to the Phil-ippians*, 2.3 all reflect Jesus' attitudes and actions toward the poor, whereas James 2.5 speaks about God's attitude and actions toward the poor as well as about the author to whom the text is attributed. In all of these texts the focal point of the message concerns 'the poor' and 'God's kingdom.' Wachob (2000:150) explains:

> the language of Jesus is here reformulated into a statement about God, and it is marked by, sub-sumed under and intimately connected to Jesus' faith . . . . The rhetoric of James 2.5 depends upon that connection.

If James is using the reference to Jesus' faith as a way to bring to mind what Jesus himself believed, said, and did, then James, by his implication, is attempting to show that his argument is perfectly in step with Jesus' faith and teaching. It is also re-flective of God's activities on behalf of the poor.

This implication confirms what the prescript to the letter presupposes, that the author is arguing by inference that there is a complete consonance of will and purpose between God and Jesus with James identifying himself as a spokes-man based upon the δοῦλος metaphor (James 1.1).[69] It is also reasonable to suggest that the author assumes that the Heb-rew Christians he is addressing knew this saying of Jesus (at least in some general sense) that he references in James 2.5. If this is true, the allusion James is using is an effective tool to render his argument more acceptable and authoritative.

The form of this passage suggests that James 2.5 is a pro-gymnastic composition since the author appears to have re-structured a saying of Jesus in the same way as he recited the essence of Leviticus 19.15 in James 2.9. Wachob (2000:151) concludes that whether James, activates an antecedent text from the LXX, as in James 2.8,9, and 11, or a religious and social convention within the culture (2.10), or a well-known saying of Jesus (2.5), he uses as much or as little verbatim performance as suits his purpose.

Therefore, James 2.5 is not scribal performance, but a progymnastic construct. It reveals the presence of rhetorical recitation in this saying of Jesus.

Before turning to the social and cultural texture of James 2.1-13, it is important to mention a few additional specific intertextual features of James 2.5. Thus far, the intertexture of James 2.1-13 concerning the law, judgment and what God (and Jesus) said and did is noticeably more similar to Matthew 5.3 than to the other intertextual references of Luke 6.20, the *Gospel of Thomas* 54 and Polycarp's *Philippians* 2.3. There is a strong intertextual link not only in terminology between Matthew 5.3 and James 2.5, but also in 'their reasoning, their focus, and their rhetorical and theological functions' (Wachob 2000:152). The construction of James 2.5 seems to mean that whatever God's reason for choosing the poor, the promise of the kingdom should not be seen as a reward for their earthly poverty. The 'in spirit' qualifier of 'the poor' in Matthew 5.3 is similar to the qualification in James 2.5 that 'the poor' chosen by God are to be 'rich in faith.' In effect, the 'voice' of the speaker in Matthew 5.3 is echoed anew in the voice of James.

4 The Social and Cultural Texture of James 2.1-13

Several presuppositions must again be mentioned to begin this section: First, it is a foundational understanding that rhetoric is social discourse with the intention of evoking a social response in the thinking and/or behaviour of the audience to which it is addressed. With this in mind, the Epistle of James was written within its culture as a social product functioning as a social tool. The letter is rhetorical discourse engaging interpersonal relations to influence them. James has a social function by design. It is always 'pragmatic discourse ... not existing for itself.... To the contrary, rhetorical discourse is generated to change reality and is fundamentally a socially motivated mode of action' (Wachob 2000:154).

The language used in rhetorical discourse is a social possession intrinsically related to its rhetorical context. Since that context is a social context, the language employed in the rhetorical discourse has a texture that provides evidence detailing the social setting or the placement of the thought processes behind or within the discourse. Thus, to probe the social implications of the situation within the discourse of this unit in James should provide 'significant clues both to the social location of its thought and also to its intended social function within its argumentative situation' (Wachob 2000:155). Social context interprets language while language illustrates social context.

Second, analysis and interpretation of the common social and cultural topics in a text may take an interpreter beyond personal presuppositions into the alien social and cultural world of the text. When this happens, the social and cultural texture of the text attains more clarity. Meaning emerges through contextual comprehension. The rhetorical unit does not exist in a social and cultural vacuum, nor can the discourse be understood accurately without a contextual social and cultural framework. Wachob (2000:155) contends:

> Thus, to get inside the discourse of James 2.1-13, to probe the social implication of the situation it evokes, should provide significant clues both to the social location of its thought and also to its intended social function within its argumentative situation

These clues can help one understand the socio-rhetorical purpose of that saying, providing the interpretive structure for application into the modern contextual milieu in a way that reflects the author's rhetorical intention.

4.1 Establishing the rhetorical situation of James 2.1-13

To accurately probe the social and cultural implications of James 2.1-13, it is necessary to establish the rhetorical situation, 'the questions, stasis, and the species of its rhetoric' (Wachob 2000:155). The theme in this unit, primarily related to the conflict between 'poor and rich,' will be explored in light of certain cultural codes or writings that permeated the social context from which James originates. This section will identify some of the social dynamics inherent within the language of the unit to bring greater comprehension to those engaging with the text.

The concept of the rhetorical situation that is used in this study follows the pattern outlined by Lloyd Bitzer (1968). He (1968:6) defines 'rhetorical situation' as:

> a complex of persons, events, objects, and relations presenting an actual or potential exigence which can be completely or partially removed if discourse, introduced into the situation, can so constrain human decision or action as to bring about the significant modification of the exigence.

For Bitzer, the rhetorical situation has three essential components. First is the *'exigence,'* defined as a problem or 'imperfection marked by urgency; it is a defect, an obstacle, something waiting to be done, a thing which is other than it should be' (Bitzer 1968:6). It identifies the audience to be addressed and the change to be effected. While there may be a number of exigencies within a given context, some of them may not be rhetorical. Bitzer (1968:7) identifies the difference: 'An exigence is rhetorical when it is capable of positive modification and when positive modification requires discourse and can be assisted by discourse.'

Second, rhetorical discourse requires an *audience* which, 'must be distinguished from a body of mere hearers or readers:

properly speaking, a rhetorical audience consists only of those persons who are capable of being influenced by discourse and of being mediators of change' (Bitzer 1968:8).

In addition to *exigence* and *audience*, every rhetorical situation contains a set of *constraints* made up of persons, events, objects, and relations. These are parts of the situation because they have the ability to constrain decisions and actions needed to modify the exigence. Ordinary sources of constraint comprise beliefs, attitudes, documents, facts, traditions, images, interests, motives and the like. The orator, when entering the situation, provides discourse that not only harnesses constraints given by the situation but provides additional constraints through, for example, his personal character, logical proofs, and style.

These three components--exigence, audience, and constraints—are the relevant aspects in a rhetorical situation and will help to structure the examination of James 2.1-13 to determine the social and cultural texture of the passage.

4.1.1 The rhetorical exigence

The rhetorical exigence in James 2.1-13 is evident in the first admonition seen in 2.1 regarding προσωπολημψίαι, 'acts of partiality.' This is the plural form of the abstract substantive προσωπολημψία, reflecting classical Greek usage and referring to the 'kinds, cases, occasions, [and] manifestations of the idea' that the substantive expresses (Smyth 1956). From the Hebraism λαμβάνειν πρόσωπον the noun προσωπολημψία was formed (Rom. 2.11; Eph. 6.9; Col. 3.25; Jm. 2.1). This is seen here for the first time in the NT but was likely already in use in Hellenistic Judaism.[70] Προσωπολημψία is often used concerning God's judgment of which there is no respect of persons. Hence Jews and Gentiles are judged in the same way, 'For God shows no partiality' (Rom. 2.11).[71] The exigence is demonstrated in the preferential manner with which the assembly treats the wealthy brother (2.2-3). Moreover, as was demonstrated earlier, 'to show partiality' is an act of injustice (Lev. 19.15).

'Acts of partiality' are characterized in this unit in several important and interconnected ways. It is significant to note that 'to show partiality' is viewed in James as a 'sin' (the word προσωπολημπτεῖτε only occurs here (2.9) in the NT), showing how the exigence of James 2.1-13 is related to what is most likely the principal rhetorical problem of the letter; these actions are incompatible with the faith of Jesus Christ (2.1). The analyses of the inner texture and intertexture of James 2.1-13 confirms this. Therefore, from James' perspective, to hold the faith of Jesus is synonymous with treating everyone impartially.

It should be noted that 'acts of partiality' are not simply sins of individuals but are considered by James as a social problem for the community of believers (2.2-4, 6a, 6b-7, 9) due to their detrimental impact on community life. 'In James 2.1-13 προσωπολημψίαι are a social-rhetorical problem. And the rhetoric of this unit is intended to modify this exigence' (Wachob 2000:160).

4.1.2 The rhetorical audience

The second constituent in the rhetorical situation of James 2.1-13 is the audience that is the focus of the rhetoric. This audience is composed of those able to impact the exigence through their thoughts and actions, thereby altering the situation. The audience here is those capable of changing their behaviour by not 'showing partiality' (2.1, 9; 2.8, 13) or, if they have previously done so, to refrain from acting with partiality in the future.

The letter of James indicates those who would be part of this audience through the language of the text. Hermogenes[72] suggests that examining the terms that an author or rhetor uses in referring to his audience indicates those that are most likely to develop rhetorically. He identifies seven groups into which references to persons in a rhetorical discourse may be divided, with four of these groups represented in the letter of James. Hermogenes recognised that any term might fit into more than one group or category. For the purposes of this discussion, 'the rich' are included in three categories and 'the poor' are included in two.[73]

There are no instances in the letter of James where persons in the audience are referred to specifically, which is Hermogenes' first category. This fact is consistent with the lack of specificity in the prescript (1.1) and with the overall structure of the letter, indicating that James' intended purpose is to deal with issues communally.

James' main communal emphasis is suggested by Hermogenes' second category, the relationship of one person to another. First in this category is 'brothers' (ἀδελφοί) which is seen in this unit twice (vv. 2.1, 5). The term occurs 19 times in various forms indicating a special closeness of the author to his audience (2.5 'beloved brothers'-ἀδελφοί μου ἀγαπητοί). The second category under communal relations is, 'the poor' (2.2, 3, 5, 6--πτωχός) and the third is 'the rich' (2.5, 6 —ὁ πλούσιος in various forms). Both of these categories under communal relations may be also considered as rhetorical constraints, the third category of the rhetorical situation.

Following Hermogenes' example for ranking and scrutinising persons,[74] James categorises 'the rich' in this unit in the following ways: the rich oppress [the beloved brothers] (2.6b) and drag them into court (2.7); the rich blaspheme the honourable name by which [the beloved brothers] were called (2.7). Other references to the rich throughout the letter indicate that the rich man will pass and fade away (1.10, 11), find that his riches have rotted, his garments are moth-eaten, and his gold and silver have corroded and will serve as a testimony against him (5.2, 3). The rich have gathered treasure for the last days, defrauded labourers and lived in luxury and self-indulgence (5.4, 5). They have fattened up their hearts in a day of slaughter and have condemned and murdered the righteous person (5.5b, 6).

Fourth under the category of communal relations are judges (2.4); then heirs (2.5), followed by the neighbour (2.8, 4.2), and the synagogue (συναγωγὴν) (2.2). Other categories elsewhere in the letter indicating relationship are the following terms: tribes (1.1), sister 2.14), widows (1.27), orphans (1.27), friend (2.23, 4.4), teachers (3.1), elders (5.14), and assembly (ἐκκλησίας) (5.14).

James assigns blame as he addresses the problems faced by his audience in their communal relationships. This coincides with Hermogenes' category of reference that carries connotations of blame, seen throughout the letter as judges with evil thoughts (2.4), the oppressive rich (2.6b, 7), those who dishonour the poor (2.6), those who show partiality (2.1, 9), those who commit sin (2.9, 4.8, 5.20), the transgressor (2.9, 11), those who fail the law in one point (2.10), those who commit adultery or murder (2.10, 4.4, 5.6), and those who show no mercy (2.13). Additional references throughout James that carry connotations of blame are as follows: the double-minded man (1.8, 4.8), the angry person (1.20), the foolish person (2.20), adulterous person (4.4), friend of the world (4.4), enemy of God (4.4), the proud person (4.6) and those who judge (4.12).

Other evidence throughout the letter that suggests character and values that are also important for defining the rhetorical audience in this unit are the following: the gold-fingered man dressed in fine clothes (2.2, 3); the poor man in shabby clothing (2.2, 3); the poor (2.5-6); the 'rich in faith' (2.5); those who inherit the kingdom (2.5); those who love God (2.5); those who fulfil the whole/royal law (2.8, 10); those who love their neighbour as themselves (2.8); those who are judged under the law (2.12); and one who shows mercy (2.13).

Other references in James that belong to this category are the blessed (μακάριος, 1.12, 25 and μακαρίζειν in 5.11). This would also include the humble person (1.9 and 4.6), field workers or harvesters (5.4), the rich (4.13-5.6), merchants (those who buy or sell (4.13-17), the farmer (5.7), the patient person (5.7, 8), the suffering person (5.1, 13), and those experiencing trials (1.2). By identifying this broad assortment of individuals more specifically he can then exhort them toward the character and behaviour he would like them to pursue.

They are presupposed to be the same audience included by the letter prescript in James 1.1—namely an unspecified community (or communities) of Christian Jews in the dispersion. The audience is identified as ταῖς δώδεκα φυλαῖς ταῖς ἐν τῇ διασπορᾷ--literally taken this phrase connotes Israel, the Jews. The Jews who returned after the exile (the northern kingdom in 722 B.C.E., the southern kingdom in 522 B.C.E.) were organised as clans (Ezra 2; Neh. 7). The 'twelve tribes of Israel' lived on in symbolic fashion and continued to function in representative structure for Israel's integrity and unity as God's chosen people.

The chief of the common problems that the author addresses is the conflict between the rich and the poor. For the most part, the audience appears to be the materially poor, although some members of the community are evidently wealthy (2.2-3; 6b-7). Moreover, both seem to be in this same community (2.4-'have you not discriminated among yourselves?'). This conflict becomes clearer when considered through the rhetorical 'constraints' associated with 'security' and 'well-being' (2.2, 3; 6b, 7) and the emotions traditionally aroused by these constraints, particularly 'desire' (2.4) as manifested in behaviour throughout this unit.

4.1.3 The rhetorical constraints

The third essential constituent of the rhetorical situation is the rhetorical constraints, called *extrinsic* and *intrinsic* proofs by Aristotle (Ar. *Rhet.* 1.2.2). Standard sources of constraints, as were previously mentioned, are 'beliefs, attitudes, documents, facts, traditions, images, interests, motives, and the like,' which the rhetor uses to persuade the audience (Bitzer 1968:8).

A fundamental constraint in this section of James is the *ethos* of the author that the letter evokes: James, the brother of Jesus. This *ethos* of the author constrains the entire discourse. Wachob (2000:170) explains:

> From a rhetorical perspective this embraces not only the reputation which the author brings to his or her discourse. It also involves the author's characterizations of himself or herself in the discourse and it includes the style and kinds of arguments employed in the discourse itself.

James, as the brother of Jesus, brings authority to his discourse which undergirds the entire letter.

Other key constraints which were mentioned earlier in the inner textual and intertextual analyses of this unit are as follows: the faith of the (glorious) Lord Jesus Christ (2.1); the *ethos* and *pathos* of the audience as God's 'chosen poor' (2.5); God (2.5, 11); the rich and their dishonouring behaviour (2.6-7); an allusion to a saying of Jesus (2.5); Scripture (2.7); the topics of honour/shame (2.1, 5, 6a) with subtopics such as justice (2.4), the law (2.8-11), love (2.8), and mercy (2.13); the topics related to security or fortune (2.2-3), promises, rewards, and warnings (2.5, 12-13), right behaviour (2.12); love (2.8) and mercy (2.13), mentioned a second time since they are viewed as 'complex' topics, being subtopics of both 'honour' and 'security'[75] (Wachob 2000:170-71). These constraints are all rhetorical in nature with the persuasive ability to compel the audience to believe the argument and adjust their behaviour to it.

Analysis of the pattern of argumentation of James 2.1-13 highlights the issues that reflect the socio-rhetorical problem of this unit; namely, 'acts of partiality' seen both inside (2.2-4) and outside (2.6b-7) of the Christian community. Dibelius (1976:48), identifies this as, '*the piety of the Poor*, and the accompanying opposition to the rich and to the world.' A helpful framework here is the research of social and cultural anthropologists regarding the type of culture that existed in the first-century Mediterranean world. This research suggests that there are cultural codes or scripts that informed the behaviour and self-understanding of James' initial audiences. These cultural codes and scripts are 'socially shared meanings by which people view and define themselves and their relationships with others' (Wachob 2000:178). They are significant markers for social formation and community structures, assisting the interpreter both for contextual understanding and for avoiding ethnocentric and anachronistic interpretation. They are particularly useful in the social formation, construction and ongoing maintenance of communities.

4.1.4 Identifying important social and cultural textures

For James 2.1-13, there are three main social and cultural textures at play that will be investigated. They are the cultural scripts of honour, limited good and patron-client relations.

i Honour and shame

First, *honour* stands for 'a person's rightful place in society, one's social standing' (Robbins 1996a:76). It indicates power boundaries, sexual status and standing on the social ladder. Honour serves as a social rating tool that, 'entitles a person to interact in specific ways with his or her equals, superiors, and subordinates, according to the prescribed cultural cues of the society... (that)... happens to a person passively through birth, family connections, or endowment by notable persons of power' (ascribed honour) or is 'actively sought and garnered most often at the expense of one's equals in the social contest of challenge and response' (acquired honour) (Robbins 1996a:76). Honour has a gender component. The male aspect is called honour, while the female counterpart is called shame. Shame implies the 'consciousness of some guilt or impropriety.'[76]

The dominance of the values of honour and shame as rhetorical constraints in James 2.1-13 is fairly clear. Bruce Malina (2001:27) writes that 'these two constraints were the prime focus and pivotal values in the social interaction of the patron-client culture.' For example, in James 2.1, honour is unequivocally connected to the faith of the Lord Jesus Christ, which is the overriding theme of the unit. In the *ratio* (2.2-4), James seeks to arouse shame in his audience by identifying the social behaviour of showing partiality as dishonourable (evil motives, thinking διαλογισμῶν πονηρῶν, 2.4). In verse 2.6a, the example here is the first proof of the *probatio*. God himself accords honour to the poor man (2.5). In contrast, the poor man is being dishonoured in the church while the rich man is accorded dishonour (implied) by the author through his bad behaviour (oppress, drag into court, blaspheme the honourable name, (2.6b,7)). The royal law of God—love your neighbour as yourself (2.8)—is honourable and such corresponding behaviour is considered honourable. However, 'acts of partiality' are violations of the royal law and are sin—dishonourable behaviour (2.9). This is further emphasised in 2.10, 11 by equating 'acting with partiality' as a violation of the whole law—equal in severity to the dishonourable and shameful status of adulterers and murderers. In the *conclusio* (2.12-13), the rhetor argues that honour belongs to those who speak and act without partiality as they operate under the 'law of liberty.' Those who dishonour the poor by acting with partiality toward the rich receive a merciless judgment, one without honour.

ii Appeal to mercy

There is an appeal to mercy in 2.13 that carries social implications. Aristotle (*Rhet.* 2.8.2)[77] defines ἔλεος (mercy, compassion) as, 'a feeling of pain caused by the sight of some evil, destructive or painful, which befalls one who does not deserve it, and which we might expect to befall ourselves or some friend of ours, and moreover to befall us soon.' Among the 'evils' that bring on this 'feeling of pain' are the misfortunes that happen to, 'those whom we know . . . as if we were in danger ourselves' (*Rhet.* 2.8.2). Fortune[78] could be the cause (2.8.9). Compassion (pity) can be aroused in people if suffering is close to them (2.8.13-14); for example, a πλησίος (neighbour) (2.8.2; cf. James 2.8) or others similar to us (2.8.13; James 2.2, 3, 5, 6a). Aristotle writes that ἔλεος is easily aroused among 'friends' with the broader topic of 'friendship' to include 'companionship, intimacy kinship, and similar relations' (*Rhet.* 2.4.28). This topic is 'treated as a subcategory of justice, honour, and advantage and it plays large in James, especially in the category of kinship' (Wachob 2000:179). Aristotle also holds that the rhetor can arouse mercy particularly in situations where there are 'signs', 'actions' and 'words' that are pitiable—'the garments and the like . . . ' (*Rhet* 2.8.16; James 2.2-3). This all contributes to 'unjust judgments' in the elect community (James 2.2-4), making the 'social texture of the appeal to mercy in the *adfectus* (2.13) . . . very appropriate for a rhetorical elaboration in which the "pitiable poor" are so prominent' (Wachob 2000:180).

iii Limited Good and patron-client social scripts

The idea of 'limited good' is apparently a common notion in a peasant economy like the one reflected by James. People living in the first-century world would 'see their existence as determined and limited by the natural and social resources of their village, their preindustrial city, their immediate area and the world, both vertically and horizontally' (Malina 2001:89). Their existence was governed by the dominance of a supreme and largely remote power, giving them little or no ability to control the conditions that dominated their lives.

Living in this socially prescribed and determined existence gave daily proof verifying that the goods available to a person are limited. Malina (2001:89) explains:

> (E)xtensive areas of behavior are patterned in such a way as to suggest to one and all that in society as well as in nature—the total environment—all the desired things in life, such as land, wealth, prestige, blood, health, semen, friendship and love, manliness, honor, respect and status, power and influence, security and safety—literally all goods in life —exist in finite, limited quantity and are always in short supply.

This thinking was the backdrop for all social experiences. Therefore, it follows that individuals, either alone or with their families, believed that improvement to one's social positions came only at the expense of others, making any attempt at improvement viewed as a direct threat to the entire community. One would seek merely to preserve his or her goods in a peasant community.

In ancient Mediterranean culture, the patron-client system was a way of dealing with limited goods. It was an interpersonal relationship between individuals or networks of individuals characterised by inequality and asymmetry in power and status. The most important characteristic governing these relationships was reciprocity. The favours of patrons to clients were extended in expectation of some sort of return.

> 'Social superiors gave food or money to their inferiors; municipal patrons gave buildings and endowments to cities; princes donated aqueducts and temples to client kingdoms. But they all did so in the expectation of loyalty, of honor, of military support, not of monetary return' (Stambaugh & Balch 1986:64).

Usually, in a peasant economy, the things exchanged were those things normally not available, even though badly needed, within the village or community. Acquiring these things often subverted traditional values and undermined the relationships or solidarity of a kinship group.

The backdrop underpinning the Epistle of James was what economists and anthropologists would call a 'zero- sum.' Wealth was considered in fixed supply so that the only way to have more than one could produce in a day was to take it from another through taxes, interest, or conquest. In modern society, it is taken for granted that it is possible to produce excess capacity or productivity, resulting in more output for the same *per capita* amount of labour. The 'pie' may always be expanded so the rich—and everyone with financial means— can have more without necessarily having to take it from the poor. A zero-sum society believes that the pie always remains the same size so that one wanting more means that others will have less. 'The daily challenge was not to climb another rung up the ladder of success but simply to find or earn enough to eat to survive. . . . life was unimaginably precarious and fragile' (Brosend 2004:66).

So how does the idea of 'limited good' within the 'patron-client system' work as a back-drop to help define the social scripts in James 2.2-4 and 6b-7? The underlying structure of the rhetoric in James 2.1-4 shows that 2.1 forms with 2.4 an enthymematic structure built around a social example (the *ratio*, 2.2-4, constitutes the basis for the proposition offered in 2.1) to define προσωπολημψίαι in terms of thinking and behaviour. The social example (2.2-4) which locates the theme (2.1) in the context of the meeting (συναγωγὴν, literally synagogue), applies to those gathering for Jewish and/ or Jewish-Christian worship whose behaviour has been observed by James. The example is suggested in two antithetical comparisons. The first compares the two social types, the first described as prosperous (gold ring, fine clothing), with the second described as poor (shabby clothing). The second comparison concerns the harsh treatment given to the poor by the rich in court (2.6-7b). While honour flows to the rich man who enters the gathering, the treatment shown to the poor is what Aristotle calls 'slight' (ἡ ὀλιγωπία): 'an actualisation of opinion in regard to something which appears valueless' (*Rhet.* 2.2.3). There are three kinds of 'slight,' according to Aristotle: 'disdain, spitefulness, and insult' (*Rhet.* 2.2.3). Based upon the statement in James 2.6a, the type of 'slight' seen here is 'insult' (ὕβρις), for 'dishonour is characteristic of insult; and one who dishonours another slights him' (*Rhet.* 2.2.6).

The assembly is making judgment upon the value of the person based upon the attire of the attendee. This display of προσωπολημψίαι brings about the descriptive invective from James who calls them 'judges with evil intent' (2.4). That remark, along with the further definition of προσωπολημψίαι as sin (2.9), is likely an intentional connection of this passage with the first mention of sin in 1.15, linking 'sin' with 'desire' which 'entices,' 'lures,' and 'tempts' a person with 'evil' (κακῶν, 1.13). This reference highlights the behaviour in 2.2-4, suggesting that the 'brothers' being addressed (2.1, etc.) are attempting to find favour with these wealthy attendees at great detriment to the community. In light of the patron-client system, these actions of favour toward the powerful can serve as a positive gesture toward someone who could become, or perhaps already was, a patron of the gathered community (Wachob 2000:182). Although favouritism runs against the biblical understanding of justice, such behaviour was not atypical within a patron-client system.

James is directly engaging the prevailing attitudes, values, and behaviour that characterises the social context embedded within the culture, especially when viewed according to the social scripts of a 'limited good' society and patron-client structure. The identified elect community 'replicates in its own fraternal relations the dominant mentality of the broader culture: acquisition' (Wachob 2000:185). For James, regardless of this social pressure or its motivation, such behaviour is inappropriate among God's people.

5 Inner Texture of James 2:14-26

5.1 Introduction

This section of the current chapter comprises an exegetical and rhetorical analysis of James 2.14-26 with the primary concern being an examination of the 'inner texture' of this unit by considering its form, structure, and argumentative pattern. As was discussed in the previous section, in the course of analysing the unfolding argumentation of this unit one will see that James 2.14-26 also approximates a complete argument based upon the structure as is found and displayed in the *progymnasmata* and rhetorical handbooks.

5.2 James 2.14-26 as a rhetorical unit

[14] What good is it, my brothers, if someone says he has faith but does not have works? Can that faith save him? [15] If a brother or sister is poorly clothed and lacking in daily food, [16] and one of you says to them, "Go in peace, be warmed and filled," without giving them the things needed for the body, what good is that? [17] So also faith by itself, if it does not have works, is dead. [18] But someone will say, "You have faith and I have works." Show me your faith apart from your works, and I will show you my faith by my works. [19] You believe that God is one; you do well. Even the demons believe—and shudder! [20] Do you want to be shown, you foolish person, that faith apart from works is useless? [21] Was not Abraham our father justified by works when he offered up his son Isaac on the altar? [22] You see that faith was active along with his works, and faith was completed by his works; [23] and the Scripture was fulfilled that says, "Abraham believed God, and it was counted to him as righteousness"—and he was called a friend of God. [24] You see that a person is justified by works and not by faith alone. [25] And in the same way was not also Rahab the prostitute justified by works when she received the messengers and sent them out by another way? [26] For as the body apart from the

spirit is dead, so also faith apart from works is dead (ESV).

Most scholars consider James 2.14-26 a self-contained unit with a discernible beginning and ending which are connected by an argument (van der Westhuizen 1991:90). As in 2.1-13, James 2.14-26 also functions as a treatise.[79] The rhetorical situation is similar to the previous section so that the issues of invention, arrangement, and style—those questions regarding how the author conceives, develops and verbalises his argument—can be discerned against this consistent backdrop. The strategies used by the rhetor in this passage to effect persuasion will be examined closely.

As this unit also begins with a theme rather than a chreia, there are a few patterns for elaborating a 'theme' and for developing the 'complete argument'[80] that will again be useful here. The following outline will guide the discussion.[81]

5.2.1 The theme (*propositio*) (2.14)

James continues his argument against showing partiality by expanding the topic to a broader discussion on faith and works. He presents the *propositio* in v. 14 as an elaboration of the theme from 1.22—'be doers of the word and not hearers only' by considering relationships to rich/poor (1.27-2.16) and obedience to 'the law of liberty' (2.12). The *propositio* is framed as two rhetorical questions that fully expect a negative answer (μή), especially considering the judgment mentioned in the *conplexio* of 2.12: 'So speak and so act as those who are to be judged under the law of liberty.' James' *propositio* for this sub-unit re-configures his theme in a way that sets up this new elaboration: 'What good is it, my brothers, if someone says he has faith but does not have works? Can that faith save him?' Stated simply, the *propositio* is 'Faith without works does not save.'

The content of the *propositio* is reiterated throughout the unit (2.17, 20, 24, 26). This is an illustration of the figure of thought known as ἐπιμονή or *commoratio* which 'occurs when one remains rather long upon, and often returns to, the strongest topic on which the whole cause rests' (*Her.* 4.45.58). The *topos* of gain or benefit (ὄφελος) is repeated in 2.16, forming an *inclusio*. For James, faith that is not visible through acts of mercy, especially towards the poor, does not save.

5.2.2 The causal basis (*ratio*) (2.15-16)

His argument is similar to that which is found in the first unit (2.1-13). The *propositio* is followed in 2.15-16 by its causal basis, the *ratio*. Here, as in 2.2-4, the *ratio* is an *exemplum*: 'If a brother or sister is poorly clothed and lacking in daily food, and one of you says to them, "Go in peace, be warmed and filled," without giving them the things needed for the body, what benefit is that?' This example is framed as a rhetorical question expecting a negative (μή) answer, which is different from that in 2.2-4, and intentionally incorporates the *topos* of 'benefit' as seen is the preceding *propositio*. A *propositio* supported by an example often uses the *topos* of 'benefit' (*Rhet. ad Alex.* 7.1428b.10ff.). Irony is at play here as well, for no one in the audience would think it normal to say such a calloused thing to one in need. The poor remain at the heart of James' argument (see 2.2-3) while illustrating the failure of faith without works.

5.2.3 The proof (*confirmatio*) (2.17-19)

James follows the *ratio* with the *confirmatio* in 2.17-19, beginning with a restatement of the *propositio*, amplified through repetition:[82] 'So also faith by itself, if it does not have works, is dead' (2.17). It is restated again at the close of this unit (2.26).

Verses 2.18-19 are what is referred to by Dibelius (1976:154) as 'one of the most difficult New Testament passages in general.'

> But someone will say, "You have faith and I have works." Show me your faith apart from your works,

and I will show you my faith by my works. [19] You believe that God is one; you do well. Even the demons believe—and shudder!

The questions posed are the following: 1). Who is the 'someone' introduced in 2.18 (ἀλλ ἐρεῖ τις)? and 2.) Where does the quotation in 2.18 end? The most plausible and simple explanation for this passage is found in consideration of the rhetorical perspective.[83]

The rhetorical response to these questions proposes an interlocutor as an imaginary opponent who only speaks in v. 18a. This opponent speaks in the continuation of the *confirmatio* from v. 17. 'But someone will say, "You have faith and I have works"' (2.18a).[84] The rhetor here anticipates and engages the objection of real or imagined opponents in this example of *anticipation*.[85] Anaximenes (*Rhet. ad Alex.* 36.1443a7ff.) states:

> After confirmation we shall put our case against our opponents, anticipating their probable arguments. If their line is to deny the acts, we must amplify the proofs that we have put forward and pull to pieces and minimize those that are going to be put forward by them.

Aristotle (*Rhet.* 3.17.1418b.14) also states, '(I)n both deliberative and forensic rhetoric he who speaks first should state his own proofs and afterwards meet the arguments of the opponent, refuting or pulling them to pieces beforehand.' Deliberative rhetoric includes *anticipation* as a central element of argumentation (*Rhet. ad Alex.* 34.1440a.24). Dibelius (1976:158) would concur, suggesting that James is anticipating this opponent, 'to provide a sharper statement of his thoughts' in further support of his *propositio*.

One method of rebuttal denies one's opponent's case in its entirety.[86] Having just affirmed three times that faith without works is dead faith (2.14, 15-16, 17), James uses an imaginary opponent to bring what could be considered a reasonable rebuttal: James has faith, but his opponent has works. The opponent is portrayed in a reactive stance here, being placed in 'the positive category of those having works and James in the negative category of those possessing only faith' (Watson 1993a:112).

These verses (2.18-20) have interpretive challenges. It is important to determine when the opponent's objection ends and where the author's words begin again to bring clarity to the scene, although there seems to be no acceptable solution to the interpretive problem.[87] Fortunately, the confusion does not obscure James' overall argument.

James appears to be posing a dilemma to the opposition in 2.18b: 'Show me your faith apart from your works, and I will show you my faith by my works.' This is the dilemma: by claiming to have works, the opposition must conclude that their works demonstrate their faith. It is impossible, according to the argument, to prove otherwise. Pseudo-Cicero validates the usefulness of a dilemma that is enlightening: 'Students in the rhetorical schools, therefore, in Proving the Reason, use a Dilemma . . .' (*Rhet. ad Her.* 2.24.28). James continues to build his case; even Abraham, considered the father of the faith, demonstrated faith by his works.

Verse 19 contains an intertextual reference to the *Shema* in Deuteronomy 6.4 and will be discussed more fully in the next section. But it also contains an interesting application of 'faith' to the point of *ad absurdum,* which further conveys James' point. 'If Christianity is to be nothing more than what the demons also have, this faith is in bad shape. . . it is an ironic demonstration of faith without works with the conclusion that this faith is worthless' (Dibelius 1976:154). James initially concedes here that this confession of faith is advantageous—'you do well'— likely causing the audience to assume that James is pleased by this response. However, what is seen as his initial approval quickly evaporates through his comparison of this confession of *Shema* with the same acknowledgment of faith by demons, which certainly has no benefit. 'Whoever acknowledges that the content of his faith is "that God is one" (ὅτι εἷς ἐστιν ὁ θεός) must also admit that he shares this faith with demons' (Dibelius 1976:160).

Irony is a powerful tool for the rhetor. Aristotle argues (*Rhet.* 3.18.1419b.7) that jest using irony was a useful way in debate 'to confound the opponents' earnest.' Quintilian argues that '(a)ll forms of argument afford equal opportunity for jests (Quint. 6.3.65), and all irony is a kind of jest (6.3.68). One such practise when using irony is to pretend to agree. Quintilian gives an example quite similar to James 2.19: 'Cicero, for example, when Fabia the wife of Dolabella asserted that her age was thirty, remarked, "That is true, for I have heard it for the last twenty years"' (6.3.73). It was advised to 'employ irony, and ridicule your opponent for the things on which he prides himself. . .' (*Rhet. ad Alex.* 35.1441b.20ff.), which appears to be the case here.

5.2.4 Amplification by repetition (*exornatio*) (2.20-25)

In James 2.20-25, the *confirmatio* is followed by the *exornatio*, as would be expected. With what appears to be a note of surprise, James asks his imaginary opposition, 'Do you want to be shown, you foolish person[88], that faith apart from works is useless?' The surprise noted in the text is the *amplificatio* (*Rhet. ad Her.* 2.29.46), 'a sort of weightier affirmation designed to win credence in the course of speaking by arousing emotion' (Cic. *Part. Or.* 15.53).[89] It also restates the *propositio* (2.14, 17) and intensifies it by repetition before providing additional evidence. James expresses surprise in this passage that his opponent requires further proof to validate his assertion that faith without works is dead, especially in light of the dilemma he used to buttress his argument. 'His surprise affirms for the audience that in his opinion, the proof already given is sufficient for his *propositio*' (Watson 1993a:114).

The surprise noted here is a rhetorically sophisticated tool, a combination of a type of rhetorical question which '. . . when the points against the adversaries' cause have been summed up, reinforces the argument that has just been delivered . . .' (*Her.* 4.15.22). It is a figure of speech called *exclamatio*, which '. . . expresses grief or indignation by means of an address to some man or city or place or object . . .' (*Her.* 4.15.22).[90] Moreover, he finishes 2.20 with an interesting play on words (*paronomasia*) for rhetorical effect: faith without works (ἔργα) does not work (ἀργός = α + ἔργον).[91]

5.2.5 The proofs (*exempla*) 2.21-25

James concludes his argument in this unit with two proofs from Scripture. The first proof is based on the historical *exemplum* of the '*Aqedah*, the binding of Isaac, traditionally seen as the most prominent example of faith demonstrated by works. The second proof, Rahab, the harlot, might serve as the most scandalous.[92] There is no break between 2.20 and 21, with verse 20 serving a rhetorical function that introduces the biblical proofs while summarising verses 18-19. As this passage also contains intertextual references, these verses will also be examined more carefully in the next section of this chapter.

James' choice of historical figures Abraham and Rahab is significant as a persuasive rhetorical tool. It is also important to note that Abraham and Rahab are both known for their hospitality and charity, key *exempla* in reference to the *ratio* with *exemplum* in 2.15-16.[93] The *exemplum* here in verse 21-22 is taken from Gen. 22:1-19, particularly the pronouncement of verse 12: '. . . for now I know that you fear God, seeing you have not withheld your son, your only son, from me.' God found Abraham righteous, which is the content of 2.21. The use of the plural 'by works' (ἐξ ἔργων) is mentioned by Dibelius (1976:162), notable since immediately after this phrase only one work is selected for reference:

Perhaps this is due to ἐξ ἔργων being used simply

> as a formula for 'by his conduct,' . . . but under no
> circumstance should one assume because of this
> enumeration . . . that the offering of Isaac is men-
> tioned here merely in order to fix the point in time
> when the justification of Abraham took place. . . .
> For then the author's thesis would be left without
> evidence . . . .

Instead, what James does here is to affirm what his opponent
has conceded to him: 'You see that faith was active along with
his works, and faith was completed by his works' (2.22). This
repeats the point of the exemplum in 2.21 and constitutes
amplification by repetition. It also incorporates another play
on words (*paronomasia*), for Abraham's 'faith worked together
with his works' (ἡ πίστις συνήργει τοῖς ἔργοις αὐτοῦ). The verse is
structured as a chiasm which, by function, amplifies through
repetition:

(a) ἡ πίστις συνήργει,   (b) τοῖς ἔργοις αὐτου,

(b) καὶ ἐκ τῶν ἔργων,   (b) ἡ πίστις ἐτελειώθη.[94]

This *exemplum* is followed with an *iudicatio* or judgment
(2.23).

> and the Scripture was fulfilled that says, "Abraham
> believed God, and it was counted to him as right-
> eousness"—and he was called the friend of God
> (2.23 ESV).

This is a supernatural oracle of a god, a type of judgment.[95]
Watson (1993b:115) writes,

> The judgment is the ultimate one of God himself
> through the Old Testament in Gen. 15.6. This is not
> a prophecy-fulfilment scheme, but the use of Gen.
> 15.6 for confirmation, one of the roles of a(n) *iudi-*
> *catio.*

James restates the *propositio* in 2.24 before giving one more
exemplum: 'You see that a man is judged by works and not by
faith alone.' This statement amplifies the *propositio* through
repetition in more general terms, thereby directing it to a

broader audience.[96] Abraham is no longer the subject, but 'a man' (ἄνθρωπος). The singular 'You see' (βλέπεις) in 2.22, which one could reasonably assume is still referring to 'you foolish person' (ὦ ἄνθρωπε κενέ) in 2.20, is now the plural 'You see' (ὁρᾶτε) in 2.24 to engage his more general audience.

The restatement of the *propositio* in 2.24 is followed in 2.25 by a second historical *exemplum,* the reference to Rahab (Josh. 2.1-21, 6.17, 22-5). This example is like the preceding one as is indicated by the introductory phrase, 'And in the same way' (ὁμοίως δὲ καί). This is expressed as a rhetorical question expecting an affirmative answer (οὐκ). Although Abraham seems a logical choice as an example of faith, Rahab (non-Israelite, female, sex worker, etc.) does not initially seem a worthy example. However, her use as an exemplum will be more closely examined in the intertextual examination in the next section. For the purposes of this discussion, Rahab is known in Jewish tradition as a proselyte and, in Christian tradition, as an example of faith and hospitality (Heb. 11.31).

5.2.6 Summary of the argument (*conplexio*) (2.26)

James concludes this unit with a *conplexio* or *conclusio* in 2.26. 'For as the body apart from the spirit is dead, so faith apart from works is dead.' The *conplexio* summarises the argument from 2.17 on, referring to the proclamation of faith being dead without works while presuming the subsequent argument, forming an *inclusio.* Watson (1993b:116) writes, '(t)his restatement of the *propositio* incorporates a similitude, a figure of thought,' which Pseudo-Cicero would describe as ". . . a manner of speech that carries over an element of likeness from one thing to a different thing"'[97] Similitudes provide vividness and clarity to style.[98] Verse 2.26 is an abridged similitude, meaning that there is not a one-to-one correspondence between the body/spirit and the faith/works. The relationship is broader so that the first element of the pair does not exist without the second. James hammers his point home, comparing faith without works to a body without a spirit—both are dead.

6 Intertexture of James 2.14-26

6.1 Introduction

There are numerous intertextual references located throughout this unit that provide unique insight into the interpretation of James 2.14-26. This investigation will be a limited one in that it is not possible to follow up every possible allusion to an earlier text in this unit. Therefore, this discussion will be confined to the rhetorical allusions that are relevant to the persuasive strategy of the author and key for the proper understanding of this unit. As in the earlier intertextual study, this unit will be examined from the perspective of the way that students were taught in the *progymnasmata* to apply antecedent texts for rhetorical purposes. This discussion shall also incorporate insights from modern literary and rhetorical studies to aid exegesis.

In James 2.14-26 there are three significant occurrences in which a citational formula signals an intertextual reference (James 2.19, 21, and 25). Within those texts are two additional references to be examined that will provide further insight into the texture of this unit.

6.2 The *Shema:* James 2.19

The first significant textual reference is found in 2.19, which serves as a theological confession. 'You believe that God is one; you do well. Even the demons believe---and shudder!' It appears that James is engaging his Jewish audience with this mention of the *Shema,* a confession at the heart of Jewish orthodoxy. James is likely referring to Deut. 6.4: 'Hear O Israel, the LORD our God, the LORD is one.' The focus of the *Shema* is the unity of God's being, his uniqueness and status as the one true God. For Jews, it was customary to recite the *Shema* in the morning and the evening, even in the First Century.[99]

For those priding themselves on right belief—in this example
merely believing that God exists—James sarcastically says,
So, you believe that God is one, relying on your Jewish heritage. Excellent! However, you are in the company of demons
who believe the same thing and are shuddering, fearing the
wrath of God to come. 'The demons are the ultimate example
of faith divorced from praxis, of right confession divorced
from right living' (Witherington 2007:476). It must also be
remembered that the affirmation in Deut. 6.4 is followed by
necessary behaviour (Deut. 6.5): 'and you shall love the LORD
your God,' is follow-up action that affirms belief.

This confession would also not be lost on a Greek audience,
as its formulation would also accommodate Greek understanding. '"There is one God" (εἷς θεός) is the confession of
enlightened, pious minds among the Greeks from Xenophanes
to Marcus Aurelius' (Dibelius 1976:159 ft.nt.). There is other
solid evidence to support this claim.[100] However, the formulation of this passage most certainly points to a Jewish
heritage, even though an enlightened Greek would have also
understood the idea and most likely agreed with it.

The whole point of the *Shema* is the proclamation of the
unity of God. James is inferring through this reference that
one ought also to believe the unity of faith and works. James
is carefully leading his opponent from one admission to another so that whoever acknowledges that the full content of
his faith is that 'God is one' falls short of what is necessary—
this belief is also shared with demons. Since the demons will
be destroyed at the End, this faith is not a faith that "can
save"' (Dibelius 1976:160).

6.3 Faith and action: James 2.21-25

James now continues his theme of faith in action with two
very different Old Testament illustrations. First, the nature
of faith is exemplified by righteous Abraham (2.21), "'our

father'—as he is called not only by Jews (*Pirkei Avot* 5.19),[101] and Jewish Christians such as Paul (Rom. 4.1, 12), . . . but also by Gentile-Christians' (Dibelius 1976:161).[102]

Abraham is known in Jewish tradition as the man who is proven by many trials, yet remains constant in his faith which is rewarded by God. James knows the extent to which Abraham is idolised in Jewish tradition, making Abraham an *exemplum* par excellence: 'Abraham was perfect in all his deeds with the Lord, and well-pleasing in righteousness all the days of his life' (Jubilees 23.10). 'Abraham was a great father of many people: in glory was there none like unto him; . . .' (Sirach 44.19), and 1 Maccabees 2.51-52: 'Was not Abraham found faithful when tested, and it was reckoned to him as righteousness?'

This Maccabean text, in addition to the specific similarities to Jas. 2.21—"our father" and the "was not ..." question form—suggests three key ideas in the Epistle of James: Abraham's "deeds"; "testing" (see 1.2–4, 12); and the "reckoned as righteousness" of Gen. 15.6 (quoted in v. 23). Furthermore, the 'test' in the Maccabees text is almost certainly a reference to the offering of Isaac. As was often seen in Midrashic exegesis, James combines two texts here in 2.21 to stress that it was on the basis of his obedient willingness to offer up Isaac that Abraham was ἐδικαιώθη ('justified or vindicated'). James' argument here, then, takes its origin from a widespread Jewish tradition.

But James 2.22–23 gives evidence that James qualifies the tradition in a critical manner: faith is introduced as the ultimate cause of the works through which Abraham was justified. Abraham's believing was evident by his obedience. He did what the Lord told him in going to Canaan, in bringing his son to offer as a sacrifice, and in many other ways. His faith was connected to works of obedience as an essential expression of faith. James has already said that faith without works is not able to save (2.14), is dead (2.17), and is barren (2.20). He now he adds that 'Scripture was fulfilled' (2.23) because 'faith was active along with his works, and faith was brought to completion by the works' (2.22). Adamson (1989:300) explains:

> The 'Aqedah, therefore may be said to "establish" and "interpret" Gen. 15.6, and this is a divine, "suprahistoric" verdict delivered on Abraham's whole life. As a co-partner with God, he (his faith) is reckoned "to be righteous." This righteousness is neither in the narrow classical nor in the purely Pauline sense, but in the sense of a right covenant relationship, expressed here in the highest terms of friendship.

The point, then, of James' argument is not a legal declaration of righteousness but that he had deeds that also flowed from that faith, thereby giving evidence to it. Witherington (2007:478) sums up this thinking:

> Thus, James is not dealing with works of the law as a means to become saved or as an entrance requirement (he never speaks of "works of the law"); rather, he is dealing with the conduct of those who already believe. He is talking about the perfection of faith in its working out through good works.

Paul refers to the same thing: '... work out your own salvation with fear and trembling' (Phil 2.12), '... only faith working through love' (counts for anything) (Gal. 5.6). For James, faith comes to mature expression—its perfect goal—in works. 'As the early church fathers noted, these two ideas are similar.[103] Of this relationship between faith and works, Melanchthon[104] summed it up in the following way: Faith alone justifies, but faith is never alone.

6.4 Friend of God: James 2.23b

One further intertextual part of the argument that remains significant in this examination is the recognition by James of Abraham as 'a friend of God' (2.23b). Abraham's 'faith was active along with his works, and was completed by his works;' (2.22). The result was that his belief was 'counted to him as righteousness'—earning him the title 'friend of God.' James cites Old Testament evidence for this title from 2 Chronicles 20.7 and Isaiah 41.8, a claim also acknowledged by other significant traditional sources,[105] including the Qur'an (4.124). 'The title 'friend of God' stands in a very close relationship to the merit of the righteous person,' thereby supporting James decision to use Abraham as the perfect choice for his *exemplum* (Dibelius 1976:173).

Verse 2.24 remains problematic in a straight comparison with the theology of Paul. However, in line with James' overall argument through the use of his *exempla*, he and Paul would find perfect agreement. One would not be considered 'righteous' for Paul, as mentioned earlier, without evidence of right behaviour ('works') after a personal acknowledgment of faith and one's death. Witherington (2007:469) sums up the argument rightly:

> Both James and Paul were concerned about what later came to be called 'dead orthodoxy'—faith without its living expression in good works. While it may be true that 'faith without works' spares individuals the embarrassment of radical disruptions in their lives or relationships, the truth is that both Paul and James were all about radical disruptions in the lifestyles that people had previously been accustomed to. James is busy deconstructing various prevailing social customs and habits and offering up in sacrifice various sacred cows, but Paul did the same thing in his own way.

6.5 Faith and hospitality: James 2.25

Ray Ward (1968) considers another important reason for Abraham being the perfect *exemplum* for James that also ties in with his use of Rahab as his second. Her status as a parallel to

Abraham might cause one to ask how she was to be considered such a 'glorious ancestress' (Dibelius 1976:166).

There is a list of pious persons in *1 Clement* 10-12 that may be helpful here to display the thread of mutual understanding. Following the brief mention of Enoch and Noah in *1 Clement* 9, there is mention of three Old Testament examples: Abraham, 'because of his faith and hospitality' (10.7), Lot, 'because of his hospitality and piety,' (11.1) and Rahab, 'because of her faith and hospitality' (12.1). All three are examples of hospitality while Abraham and Rahab also have faith.

It is worth examining the connection to hospitality for both Abraham and Rahab. Philo in *de Abr.* 167[106], proceeds directly from Abraham as the model of hospitality (Gen. 18) to the account of the testing of his faith through the near sacrifice of Isaac (Gen. 22). Jewish lore considers Abraham as the epitome of the hospitable man.

> Thus, in *Aboth de R. Nathan I*, ch. 7, Abraham surpassed even Job in showing hospitality to the poor. The same view of Abraham appears in the *Test. of Abr.* The title 'friend' appears to be given Abraham especially because of his hospitality (*Test. Abr.* I [long recens.]; 4 [short recens.]), and this hospitality deters the Angel of Death from touching Abraham (Test. Abr. 12 [long recens.]; 13 [short recens.]) (Ward 1968:286).[107]

In Genesis 18, Abraham sees the three travellers, receives them, washes their feet, provides rest and food (Gen. 18.4-8) and then sends them on their way (Gen. 18.16). The scene depicted in James 2.15-16 is that of an opportunity to care for someone in need, but then just sending them on their way. There is an interesting parallel to James 2.15-16 in *Yashar, wayera* 42b:

> If one was hungry, and he came to Abraham, he would give him what he needed, so that he might eat and drink and be satisfied; and if one was naked,

and he came to Abraham, he would clothe him with the garments of the poor man's choice, and give him silver and gold, and make known to him the Lord, who had created him and set him on earth.

This example, even if considered legendary, would be part of the cultural backdrop of the audience to which James was speaking. The offering of Isaac would be understood by this audience—as in Jewish tradition—as the testing of Abraham. He was a person who fulfilled in every way James' 'royal law of liberty.' Abraham's charitable acts had the practical effect of feeding, clothing, and housing the needy, thereby providing James with a good example of what it means to practice pure and undefiled religion.

Rahab is introduced in verse 25 by James with the purpose of using her as an additional example to prove his point—that there is no justification without works. The expression here 'was justified' ($\dot{\varepsilon}\delta\iota\kappa\alpha\iota\dot{\omega}\theta\eta$) has the same meaning as in 2.21. Her faith is evident through her 'having received' ($\dot{\upsilon}\pi o\delta\varepsilon\xi\alpha\mu\dot{\varepsilon}\nu\eta$) and 'having sent out' ($\dot{\varepsilon}\kappa\beta\alpha\lambda o\tilde{\upsilon}\sigma\alpha$) the spies, even though she was a pagan prostitute. These activities were events that testified to her faith. She states in Josh. 2.11b '. . . for the Lord your God, he is God in the heavens above and on the earth beneath,' thereby acknowledging her belief in God. Faith is attributed to her in Heb. 11.31 because, '. . . she had given a friendly welcome to the spies.' 'The mention of the faith of Rahab would have been quite appropriate in our context, since it involves precisely the cooperation of faith and works...' (Dibelius 1976:166). To James, Rahab, like Abraham, displayed her faith through her actions.

James closes out his argument by returning to a point he has made previously: 'faith apart from works is dead' (2.26b). He says the same thing in 2.17 and uses similar wording in 2.14 and 2.20. The 'figure of thought'[108] is this: in the same way that a body has no life without breath—it is dead—faith apart from works is dead. 'Faith is as dead without works as the "body" is without "soul"' (Dibelius 1976:167). James Adamson (1989:306) sums it up like this:

> Faith alone cannot save; nor can works alone save. It is vitally important to note that James does not present deeds at any time or in any way as a substitute for Christian faith; he holds that, if it is not maintained by Christian exercise in an active Christian life, faith, like many activities, perishes in a sort of parasitic paralysis.

7 The Social and Cultural Texture of James 2.14-26

The purpose of this section is to explore the social and cultural implications of the language in James 2.14-26, using the same methods of examination as were applied to the discussion around the social and cultural texture of James 2.1-13. Lloyd Bitzer's (1968) guideline for the rhetorical situation will again be used to guide the discussion.

7.1 Establishing the rhetorical situation of James 2.14-26

As was introduced earlier in this chapter, the rhetorical situation has three essential constituents. These constituents—rhetorical exigence, rhetorical audience, and rhetorical constraints—will be identified and discussed as follows.

7.1.1 The rhetorical exigence

The rhetorical exigence in James 2.14-26 appears as a series of rhetorical questions:

> 1. What good is it, my brothers, if someone says he has faith but does not have works?
> 2. Can that faith save him? (James 2.14)

The rhetorical exigence can be summed up as one question: Is faith without deeds sufficient (saving faith)? James understands what is at stake for the hearers of this message, and he takes great care to use this unit to continue the challenge that was announced in James 1.22 – 'But be doers of the word, and not hearers only . . . .' This exigence has culminated naturally from the argument against showing partiality from 2.1, which is the exigence of James 2.1-13.

James answers the question posed in the exigence six times throughout the unit in various forms using repetition for the sake of emphasis. They are listed as follows:

v. 15-16 Example from the life of the community using sarcasm.

v. 17   Answer to the question posed by the exigence as a declaration: faith by itself without works is dead.

v. 18   Objection by imagined interlocutor; Answer to the question raised by the exigence as an impossible hypothetical.

v. 19 Sarcastic acknowledgment of interlocutor's faith claim by comparison with demons.

v. 20   Restatement of the question posed by the exigence as a challenge by example.

v. 21-25 Two proofs from Scripture answering the question raised by the exigence.

v. 26   Concluding declaration in response to the exigence through analogy.

This is a masterful use of rhetorical tools to respond to the question posed by the exigence, 'Is faith without deeds sufficient (saving faith)?' James would unequivocally say no, using different methods to convince the various hearers/readers of the truth of his argument that faith without works is not sufficient. 'One is persuaded by analogy, another by reason, a third by humour and sarcasm, a fourth by compelling illustration from the life of the community' (Brosend 2004:85). No opportunity is lost by James in the effort to convince his audience.

7.1.2 The rhetorical audience

The second constituent in the rhetorical situation of James 2.14-26 is the rhetorical audience. The rhetorical audience is composed of 'those persons who, through their thought and action, can modify the exigence and thus alter the reality of their situation' (Wachob 2000:160). They are considered potential members of the community who will demonstrate the evidence of their faith through their actions. They are the same audience considered earlier—those members of an unspecified community or communities of Christian Jews in the Dispersion. Ben Witherington (2007:472) identifies several references in this unit that re-affirm the identity of the author as a Jewish Christian with a Jewish Christian audience. They are as follows:

1. Reference to Abraham as 'our father.' (2.21)
2. Midrashic treatment of the Old Testament stories of Abraham and Rahab.
3. Emphasis on works and the sort of righteousness that results from doing good deeds, especially deeds of charity.
4. Reference to Abraham as the friend of God—a popular Jewish designation of Abraham (2 Chron 20:7; Is 41:8; Philo *On Sobriety 56,* which renders Gen. 18:17 with the phrase 'Abraham my friend.)'
5. Anthropology: the human being is body and breath or body and Spirit—not soul (*psychē*) and body and not a trichotomy.

This all implies that James constructed his arguments under the assumption that at least some of his audience knew these references from the Hebrew Scriptures and understood their context, including the way they would be interpreted in Jewish culture. There is a rabbinic quotation recounted by Joseph Mayor (1910:96) that recounts the type of faith that James is fighting against: 'As soon as a man has mastered the thirteen heads of the faith, firmly believing therein . . . though he may have sinned in every possible way . . . still he inherits eternal life.'

In addition to the traits of the audience James describes in the first unit (2.1-13), the following characteristics are highlighted in this unit to help more clearly identify his audience: some are poorly clothed and hungry (2.15); calloused toward those in need (2.16); confident in their theology (2.18-19); mistaken in their theology (2.18b); foolish (2.20); children of Abraham (2.21). By so accurately identifying and understanding his audience he can exhort them to model the behaviour he would like them to pursue so that they will, hopefully, become the type of people he would like them to become. The diversity here is helpful in James' overall presentation: by acknowledging common traits throughout the community, mainly related to the 'Jewishness' of his audience, he can then engage the particular behaviour he is trying to change— mainly related to faith being claimed without corresponding works.

7.1.3 The rhetorical constraints

Rhetorical constraints represent the third essential constituent of the rhetorical situation and consist of 'beliefs, attitudes, documents, facts, traditions, images interests, motives and the like' employed by the author to persuade the audience' (Bitzer 1968:8). Many of these constraints were mentioned in the discussion of the previous unit and served to undergird this unit.

There appear to be three major constraints in this unit that are worth considering. First, James is arguing that faith alone is not enough to counteract the notion that faith alone is sufficient. This appears in 2.14 as a challenge through a rhetorical question engaging the belief. Is faith enough? It is a deliberative topic of 'what profits a person' that James is raising here.[109] At issue is salvation, 'Can that faith save him?' James' answer to this question is certainly 'no!'

To argue for his response to this issue, James focuses on the treatment of fellow Christians by Christians. He identifies the insufficiency of the engagement by using sarcasm: 'and one of you says to them, "Go in peace, be warmed and filled" without giving them the things needed for the body.' (2.16). This response would seem pleasant enough, even somewhat concerned in a superficial way, although it is truly unloving and anti-Christian. For James, deeds of mercy are not an option but an obligation for those claiming to have real faith. Luke Timothy Johnson (1995:239) writes, 'It is not the form of the statement that is reprehensible, but its functioning as a religious cover for the failure to act.' Accurate theology is only a foundation from which practice can unfold. It is the practice of the faith that is critical. Pheme Perkins (1995:113) writes, 'faith without works spares individuals the embarrassment of radical disruptions in their lives and relationships.' James is pushing for radical disruptions in the community with which he is engaging.

Proper engagement is critical to James' argument. James is insistent that this community reflects right practice over simply right thinking, with 'practice' acting as a contemporary meaning for the word normally translated 'works.' He uses, as an example, a brother or sister in the community in physical need. He is sensitive to the things 'needed for the body' (τὰ ἐπιτήδεια τοῦ σώματος—seen only here in the NT) as compared with the work of the spirit. The member from this early church community who offers a blessing to one who is hungry and naked without offering food or clothing has failed to act out of a living faith. James refers to the one in need as a 'brother or sister,' indicating that one certainly has responsibility for a member of the faith community, although as has been seen in the previous unit (2.8) one also has responsibility for one's neighbour.

The second major constraint in this passage is found in the examples of Abraham and Rahab as significant representative figures whose faith is made manifest by their works. Although many of the key insights around James' use of these two key *exempla* were covered in the previous discussion considering the intertextual references, it is worth noting the following.

Abraham is referred to as a 'friend of God,' as has been mentioned previously. Since this phrase is not part of the intertextual reference in Gen. 15.6, it must be assumed that James is referring to other sources, some of which have been mentioned. However, further insight can be gleaned from James' influence by both the worlds of the Torah and Greco-Roman moral discourse. Stanley Stowers (1986:29) writes 'friends were to be equals; equality was to characterize the relationship ... (with) friends sharing all things in common.' This view was born out in Hellenistic moral teaching concerning friendship that stressed the essential equality and unity of friends. They are 'Two friends, one soul,'[110] ... sharing. .. , 'all things in common'.[111] Friendship is a 'community of views on all matters human and divine together with good will and affection.[112] Such writing stressed the sharing of outlook between friends since friends, 'saw things the same way because friendship was equality.'[113] Moreover, as part of the same outlook, those who were sages could consider themselves as 'friends of God' (Johnson 1995:244).

The only individual in Torah directly referred to as a 'friend of God' is Moses, mentioning that God spoke with him face to face as to his friend (Ex. 33.11). However, Genesis 18.17 gives rise to the designation of Abraham as God's friend in the Hellenistic sense: 'Shall I hide from Abraham, my servant what I am about to do? Philo translated this text as "μὴ ἐπικαλύψω ἐγὼ ἀπὸ Ἀβραὰμ τοῦ φίλου μου;" (Shall I hide this from Abraham, my friend?')[114] Philo determined that God's resolve to share his decision making with Abraham is an example of how 'friends hold all things in common' (Johnson 1995:244). This is the background of the expression.

It is significant how James uses 'friendship' as a constraint in driving home his point. Abraham is seen as a 'friend of God' in that he did the things that friends would be understood to do in his relationship with God. Abraham 'believed God,' by living a life of active faith which was manifested by his works. Abraham accepted God's way of seeing the situation and acted upon it. According to 'the world's' standard, the sacrifice of his beloved son would have been senseless, especially since Isaac was a gift from God as had been promised. Johnson (2004: 2268) writes:

> If Abraham had seen things the way 'the world' did —a measure of reality which excludes God's claim —he would have rejected God's call to obedience. He would have striven 'according to the flesh' to create a blessing for himself with this possibility of biological descent. But he did not. He showed himself friend toward God. His faith made him act according to a measure that made the world not a closed system of meaning, but a system open to the meaning given by God's word.

Friendship with God is in direct conflict with friendship with the world, a point that James drives home in 4.4:

> You adulterous people! Do you not know that friendship with the world is enmity with God? Therefore whoever wishes to be a friend of the world makes himself an enemy of God.

James contrasts God (θεοῦ) and the world (κόσμου) as objects of human commitment and says that one must make a choice between them. For James, the world is not a place as much as it is a system of meaning or value by which people might choose to live (see 1.27, 2.5, 3.6). The choice is, for James, made in terms of friendship. This involved a 'serious commitment based on a complete sharing of outlook. To be "friends of the world," then, would mean to share completely its view of reality, its way of measuring value, to be of 'one mind" with it' (Johnson 2004: 452).

This is a powerful argument that would serve as a useful constraint. For a community of Jewish Christians, Abraham is the prime example: children of Abraham would be motivated to be like this man of faith. This is one's heritage. For James to follow the story of Abraham with reference to Rahab is a useful persuasive move that would be noticed by a Jew. Rahab, a pagan prostitute, is also assumed to be a 'friend of God' by her behaviour. She saw 'God's way of seeing the situation and acted on it,' as had Abraham (Johnson 2004:2268). If she had reacted to the situation from a worldly perspective, she would have turned in the spies and been considered a hero by her people. Rahab's deeds were an expression of faith. She recounts to the scouts all the works of God that she had heard and concludes by proclaiming: 'for the Lord your God, he is God in the heavens above and on the earth beneath' (Josh. 2.11b). She acts on this faith by hiding the scouts and sending them back to their people by another route. Rahab fits the paradigm of faith for James perfectly. Her faith is also singled out for mention in Heb. 11.31 and other references already referred to in a previous section of this chapter.

The third significant constraint used by the author is the analogy found in verse 26: 'For as the body apart from the spirit is dead, so also faith apart from works is dead.' The point, according to Johnson (1995:245), is 'not that deeds give life, but they express life, "demonstrate" that life is present. The obvious assumption is that whatever is living also acts.' This argument returns to the *propositio* of this unit in 2.14 as an answer to the question: Can this faith without works save anyone? The answer previously implied is now plainly stated: It cannot save. Faith without works is dead just as the body without a spirit is dead.

7.2 The cultural script of honour and shame

One may learn about the community under James' instruction from the hypothetical situation described in 2.15-16. Remembering what was discussed previously about honour and shame, one recalls that while physical needs were mentioned

—'poorly clothed and lacking in daily food'—there is much at stake here. Responding to these needs is important for the community, giving them the opportunity to restore a person or persons to honour. Brosend (2004:77) compares this passage with the one in 2.2-4: 'While the visitor in 2.2-4 was depicted as dressed in rags, the rags of the "brother or sister" in v. 15 had fallen to shreds, leaving them exposed, if not necessarily nude.' The fragile hold on life experienced by those at the bottom of the socioeconomic pyramid is represented here in this passage. Many lived a day to day experience so that one's failure to provide a need of this sort could be the difference between life and death. Certainly, one claiming to have faith would step in to meet the needs in this situation if he or she possibly could. This is James' argument. 'The point is never that the deeds substitute for the attitude, but the deeds reveal the attitude; and if there are no deeds, then the attitude is simply "empty" or "profitless" or "dead"' (Johnson 1995:247).

7.3 The social nature of the rhetoric in the unit

Chapter 2 of James reflects two distinct units that function as community-oriented rhetoric. In this unit, as with 2.1-13, James reveals an 'urgent concern that the members of the community look out for their fellows' . . . exhorting them to an 'ethical concern . . . positively centered on the intra-fraternal affairs of the elect community' (Ward in Wachob 2000:186). In this first unit, the theme is προσωπολημψία, defined by James as 'unjust judgments' (2.4) and 'sin' (2.9) to produce a community that does not show favouritism. For the unit now under consideration (2.14-26), James pushes to generate a community that has a living faith that works itself out in its concern for the needs of others. For both units, James desires to bring about a community conformed to a particular understanding of God and his truth.

The rhetoric does not appear to call for a systematic social reform of the community, but rather it presses for the solidarity of the entire community, 'including both its wealthy (powerful) members and its (powerless) poor members (2.2-4; 1.26-27; 2.15-17; 4.11-12; 5.12-20)' (Wachob 2000:188). James is calling for an immediate correction for the community in their interpersonal relations in thought, word and deed to mirror 'the faith in our Lord Jesus Christ, the Lord of glory.' (2.1) It is an enormous task since it engages the cultural scripts of limited good and the patron-client system, within which are the pivotal values of honour and shame. The careful structure of James' argument shows that he knows this is an uphill battle, so he deftly manoeuvres in ways that expose his audience. Aristotle accurately expresses the cultural under-pinnings:

> Now men think that they have a right to be highly esteemed by those who are inferior to them in birth, power, and virtue, and generally, in whatever similar respect a man is far superior to another; for example, the rich man to the poor man in the matter of money[115]

This is the type behaviour that James is engaging. It relates to the showing of partiality as well as the failure to care for the poor. Neither is an example of the behaviour found as an outflow of a living faith.

7.4 The cultural nature of the rhetoric of the unit

There are other elements of culture at play here worth a brief mention. Based on the analysis of James 2, there are two primary cultures represented: Hellenistic-Roman culture and Jewish culture. The rhetoric in this unit, as well as in the entire letter, is bi-cultural rhetoric, meaning that both of these cultures contribute to the rhetorical environment from which James emanates.

There is a thoroughly Jewish-Christian character of the Epistle of James that is recognised by the vast majority of New Testament scholars. There is nothing in the text that represents a hostile engagement with the Jewish tradition. The fact that James considers Jesus to be the Messiah and Lord (1.1; 2.1) can be regarded as an 'intramural disagreement within a Jewish subculture' (Wachob 2000:190). The Jewish-Christian rhetoric of James is considered subculture within traditional Jewish culture.

In a similar way, James shows himself quite comfortable with the traditional *topoi* of Hellenistic-Roman culture and arranges his arguments in a way that fits those structures. However, James offers his audience an alternative cultural script in conflict to that of the limited good and patron-client system, providing a rationale for the changed behaviour that he desires. These behaviours—acting without partiality and caring for those in need—challenge the usual scripts in the dominant culture. James is calling out a people that will be truly countercultural.

For Wachob (2000:191), James is practicing a cultural rhetoric that is subcultural and therefore different to the predominantly Jewish cultural rhetoric in that 'James is a Christian version of a Jewish value system.' In many ways this is true. The two units under consideration in this chapter both relate very clearly to 2.1 for those, 'holding the faith in our Lord Jesus Christ, the Lord of glory.' However, one could argue that although James' Christian reference is clear, his reliance upon Leviticus 19.18 as a summary of the whole law and reference to the faith of Abraham 'being active along with his works' (2.22) would likely have a similar impact for a non-Christian Jewish audience. There is a flawless implication: holding the faith of Jesus (active, living) (2.1), would look very similar to active faith in God throughout history. It would manifest in obedience to God's word.

8 Conclusion

This chapter has investigated some of the ways in which the rhetoric of James 2.1-26 captures the 'beliefs, assumptions and values of the author, the audience, and the broader culture' in an effort to persuade the audience that acts of partiality and failing to care for those in need are incompatible with active faith (Wachob 2000:194). James uses the strategies marked by his training in rhetorical discourse as a structure for his arguments. His audience is the broader community that apparently follows the general dynamics within this cultural context, defined as Jewish-Christians living within a Hellenistic-influenced society. The rhetoric is designed to establish boundaries for acceptable behaviour in those intending to live lives of active faith.

Chapter 2 of James has been considered historically as a rhetorical unit composed of two sub-units (vv. 1-13 and vv. 14-26). The inner texture of these units established them as progymnastic elaborations in the same method of those in the rhetorical handbooks and the *progymnasmata*, as has been previously mentioned. James' argument in each unit is established first thing in the *propositio* with the balance of the unit set to prove that case. Each unit is structured in a way that makes strong arguments according to his audience.

The probe of the intertextuality of these units shows that James applies other texts to these units in a progymnastic manner. The units are comprised of other antecedent texts from the LXX, common notions and themes in the broader culture, and sayings that can most likely be attributed to Jesus. These texts bring additional weight to bolster the arguments at hand. James shows a thorough understanding of his audience in the way that he positions these appeals to precedence.

And finally, the social and cultural texture of these units seeks to constrain the thoughts and actions of the recipients in such a way as to bring about a change in observed and potential behaviour. It confronts cultural scripts to impose living in a way that shows one to be a 'friend of God,' presupposing 'a radical willingness on the part of its audience to live in but not of the world' (Wachob 2000:200). This is a life of a living faith that shows no partiality and cares for the physical needs of those in one's midst.

There are insights from this investigation which are useful to the Church and particularly the Evangelical movement. Brosend (2004:82) writes that 'James challenges the reader with an understanding of faith intimately and intricately connected with the whole of human life. Faith is not so much "known" by its works, like the tree by its fruit, as it *is* its work, root, and branch as well as fruit.' James is seeking radical disruptions in the lives of his audience, presenting them with a stark choice—the choice between a living faith and dead faith. This is ultimately the choice between faith (and salvation) or death. Emil Brunner (1979:554) writes, 'If a Church produces no living acts of charity for the community as a whole it is impossible to avoid suspecting that she is sick unto death.' There is no such thing as faith without works, as works spring from a living faith.

James is engaging a type of dualism in this Early Church community that has become quite comfortable with faith being completely separated from works. James structures his arguments carefully throughout these two units, finally finishing with verse 26: 'For as the body apart from the spirit is dead, so also faith without works is dead.' This separation between the physical and spiritual manifested for the evangelical movement when the proclamation of the gospel was separated from deeds of mercy that served the poor as was discussed previously in Chapter Two. James 2 is a strong argument that any form of dualism that separates spiritual activities from physical deeds is not representative of living faith.

The hungry and naked before the Church need more than 'our lunch money and the extra coat in our closet, and more than our prayers,' even though those things are important (Brosend

2004:85). The challenge is two-fold: First, that human needs matter to God and must matter to those who would call themselves 'his friend.' Second, one's response is a critical representation of living faith. James is indicating through his arguments that if there is no engagement with the needs of those around one, faith does not exist since it is 'dead.' Johnson (2004:431) explains:

> the key verse for understanding the book of James is 2.22, whose significance can only be grasped if translated quite literally. Speaking of Abraham's offering of Isaac, James declares, "You see that faith was co-acting (or 'co-working') his deeds (ἔργοις), and faith was brought to completion out of his deeds (ἔργων)." Faith never becomes something else. It is perfected as faith by the deeds that it performs.

If there are no deeds, there is no faith.

Mother Teresa of Calcutta (1975:69) sums up what these living acts of faith could look like—must look like—for an evangelical community seeking to live by faith in a broken world:

> If sometimes our poor people have had to die of starvation, it is not because God did not care for them. But because you and I didn't give, were not instruments of love in the hands of God, to give them that bread, to give them that clothing; because we did not recognize him, when once more Christ came in distressing disguise—in the hungry man, in the lonely man, in the homeless child, and seeking for shelter.

> God has identified himself with the hungry, the sick, the naked, the homeless; hunger not only for bread but for love, for care, to be somebody to someone; nakedness, not of clothing only, but nakedness of that compassion that very few people give to the unknown; homelessness, not only just for a shelter made of stone, but that homelessness that comes from having no one to call your own.

To show great love for God and our neighbour we need not do great things. It is how much love we put in the doing that makes our offering something beautiful for God[116]

This social-rhetorical investigation of James 2 has provided a biblical foundation for the evangelical movement, showing that faith must be manifested by corresponding good works that will impact those in need if it is truly living faith. Chapter 5 will consider a theological model for the evangelical movement that will apply this truth to guide praxis.

CHAPTER FIVE

THEOLOGICAL METHODOLOGY FOR THE EVANGELICAL MOVEMENT

1 Introduction

There are two distinct paradigms of theology that co-exist today. One considers theology as a set of sub-disciplines, of which practical theology would be included. The other sees theology as 'essentially practical,' with the different sub-disciplines of theology considered 'interrelated in order to serve this practical end' (Hazle 2003:1). For many years the former paradigm was the dominant one, originating mainly from the Western theological academies. Practical theology, seen from this perspective, was the 'finishing school' of theological education, concerned with equipping theological students for the practical aspects of ministry, such as preaching and pastoral care.

However, the last three or four decades have been described by some as a 'rebirth' in this area of theology (Browning 1999:54). This rebirth has brought about a re-examination of the nature of theology as a whole and its relationship to practical theology as it exists within it. Additionally, it has nurtured the growth of socio-theological facets of theology and served as a challenge to traditional methodologies for theological reflection. The debates surrounding this renewal now view theology as having a more practical orientation. Those maintaining a notion of sub-disciplines in theology would consider practical theology as 'the branch of theology which is concerned to explore the relationship between, on the one hand, Scripture and the tradition of the Church and, on the other hand, the whole range of Christian praxis in the world' (Lyall 2001:54).

Although Lyall provides what is a general, working definition of practical theology, this chapter will study practical theology in more detail, identifying the methodologies of leading practical theologians to formulate a useful approach for the evangelical movement that is faithful to Scripture as it engages with local communities. Proper evaluation of these methodologies will determine an appropriate way forward.

This chapter will trace advances in practical theology through various leading practitioners. It will provide historical background, showing key influences that have shaped the movement and fostered growth. Moreover, it will motivate for a Christological focus that should serve to guide the evangelical movement, affirming perhaps forgotten practices that are crucial for moving the gospel forward in local South African communities.

2 Developments in Practical Theology and Missiology

According to Ray Anderson (2001:14), 'the core theology of the Bible, both Old and New Testament, is practical theology before it becomes systematic theology.' Practical theology, at its nature, centres around a discussion of the relation of theory to praxis. The discussion is important:

> If theory precedes and determines practice, then practice tends to be concerned primarily with methods, techniques and strategies for ministry, lacking theological substance. If practice takes priority over theory, ministry tends to be based on pragmatic results rather than prophetic revelation (Anderson 2001:14).

Karl Barth identifies the dynamic relationship between theory and praxis, seeing the task of theology as clarifying the presuppositions of church praxis in a way as to 'not allow so much as a knife blade between theory and praxis' (Gorringe 1999:9). Barth resisted all attempts to portray theory and praxis in opposition to each other and questioned those who tried to do so. 'Is there a Christian praxis which is not formed by Christian theory? Or conversely, is there a Christian theory which does not also have an element of Christian praxis?' The understanding of Christ as the light of life can be understood *only* as 'a theory which has its origin and goal in praxis' (Barth 1956:79). Barth's emphasis reflects the divisions that had emerged between theory and practice from historical processes around the view of reality.

This thinking emerged from Barth's earlier efforts to fill a suspected gap in the theology of the Reformers. They did not establish, according to Barth, what the "inner and vital connection is between service of God in Christian living . . . in the worship of the Church as such, and another form of service, which may be described as a 'political' service of God . . ." (Barth 1960:101-102). For Barth, this 'political' service refers to the affairs of human justice and life in general. Without this vital connection, it would be possible to build a highly spiritual message and a very spiritual church, a message that had 'ceased to seek or find any entrance into the sphere of these problems of human justice' (1960:104-105). Although the Reformers were involved in meeting the needs of the poor, as has been previously discussed in Chapter 2, Barth would argue that this behaviour was not wholly grounded theologically, thereby setting the stage for the 'Great Reversal' experienced in the early 20th century. This resulted in the dualism that has brought about the separation between living faith and corresponding works. Barth blamed this separation, at least partly, on the gap in the Reformers' teaching and set out to correct it in his context (1960:104-05). One could argue, based upon the rhetorical arguments of James, that dualism was at the foundation of the relational brokenness experienced in that Early Church and must continually be engaged to maintain vibrant, flourishing community, both then and now. Barth would likely agree with this assessment.

2.1 Philosophical foundations

However, societal constructs have a significant role to play. The medieval world had a metaphysical view of reality. From a human perspective, reality was only indirectly accessible through signs, symbols, and natural occurrences since it remained partially obscured. A theistic worldview helps 'hold things in place' when the physical world indicates there is the appearance of an ultimate reality. Religion, tradition, and tribal hierarchy tended to be social institutions vested with authority. Divine revelation as a historical event was accepted uncritically by medieval society simply because reality rested on a metaphysical belief in the existence of God, not on historical veracity. Modernity resulted with the ascendancy of abstract thought. Man, as a thinker, became autonomous.

Following the Enlightenment in Europe, the physical world came to be viewed as 'self-existent and self-explanatory' (Anderson 2001:16). Theory continued to dominate practice in this modern period, with epistemological and hermeneutical models setting the foundation for practical theology. While theory leads and determines practice, the way in which this happens is a matter of debate within theological circles.[117]

2.2 Praxis-focused orientation

Dietrich Bonhoeffer (1906-1945) gave credit to Dutch philosopher Hugo Grotius (1583-1645) for the modern concept of natural law as existing independently of divine existence— *etsi deus non daretur.* Bonhoeffer (1971:360) wrote that,

> '(w)e cannot be honest unless we recognise that we have to live in the world *etsi deus non daretur* [even if

there were no God]. And this is what we do recognise—
before God! God himself compels us to recognise it. . . .
God would have us know that we must live as men
who manage our lives without him. The God who lets
us live in the world without the working hypothesis of
God is the God before whom we stand continually. Before God and with God we live without God.'

For Bonhoeffer (1971:360), theology's sole object for reflection was the 'personal reality of God revealed through concrete human social relations—Jesus Christ existing as community (gemeinde).' He had no use for a theistic worldview
where God was merely a 'working hypothesis,' a *deus ex ma-
china* where people could turn as a justification for evil and as
a protector of the good.

This was the sense in which Bonhoeffer was a forerunner for
what was to become the general field of practical theology.
While attempting to overcome the individualism of Des-
cartes (1596-1650) through his social anthropology and concurrently accepting the Kantian analysis of pure metaphys-
ics, Bonhoeffer laid the groundwork for a 'praxis-oriented
theology through an ethic of discipleship and obedience,
where theory emerges only through engagement with truth as
an ethical demand in the form of the claim of Christ through
the other person' (Anderson 2001:17-18). Bonhoeffer's thinking, when seen in this sense, can be considered an early precur-
sor to what has come to be known as a form of postmodernism.

The metaphysical view of reality suffered a setback with the
rise of scientific empiricism. The reality of things could be determined through scientific enquiry by examining the behaviour of nature. Accordingly, reality was viewed as accessible
and provable through rigorous application of the scientific
method. However, theory continued to dominate with regard
to practice, even though reality was now well within the
reach of human self-understanding. 'Truth, mediated through

interpretive structures and paradigms, informed practice, which was largely relegated to the application of methods and skills based on theory' (Anderson 2001:18).

This focus led to a separation between the scientific study of biblical data (*Wissenschaft*) from its application in ministry through preaching, education, and pastoral care. This functional division between theory and practice appeared to reinstate previous epistemological dualism. Systematic and historical theology operated on its own in exploring divine revelation from a purely theoretical perspective, leaving practical theology to strategise ways to develop ministry principles focusing on efficiency and effectiveness. 'Truth' was theoretical and constituted objective reality over 'practice' which was purely instrumental and methodological.

2.3 Rise of existentialism

The metaphysical quest for reality was turned upside down with the rise of existentialism. Essence is *a priori* and determinative of existence in a metaphysical version of reality. It can be thought of as 'the objective and fluid flow of personal existence' as an object of philosophical thought (Anderson 2001:18). Søren Kierkegaard argued that the existing person defines and decides the essence of what is real. Theology was a 'work of love' grounded in 'edifying discourse' rather than philosophical fragments. By introducing anxiety (angst) as the deepest core of the human self, he undermined the self-reliance of modern humanity (Marino 1998:320). Faith can only be genuine when it 'leaps over' the chasm of irrational absurdity as it is suspicious of any rational certainty. Moreover, what was considered the moment of 'decision' for Kierkegaard became the small crack through which one could grasp the objective reality of God as the foundation of faith, even though this moment is still considered a subjective act.

This 'moment' for Kierkegaard made credible the dualistic thinking that weighted the 'decision' to follow Christ as primary at the expense of what would be necessary corresponding behaviour, although evangelicals would not likely agree to Kierkegaardian influence in this formulation. Walter Kaufmann (1956:17) notes Kierkegaard's importance for a major segment of modern thought: 'he attacks received conceptions of Christianity, suggests a radical revision of the popular idea of the self, and focusses attention on decision.' Kierkegaard played a pivotal role leading to the transition to postmodernism.

For Barth, theory and practice followed "the 'existentialist' formula, according to which 'being comes out of doing' (*esse sequitur agere, esse sequitur operari*), rather than the reverse followed by the 'essentialists' ('*agere sequitur esse, operari sequitur esse*'). This formula means, in effect, that one is what one does. This is true of man: 'Human being is a history.' This is even true of God, perhaps pre-eminently of God: '. . . the one free living God, who, in that he is such, has a history and indeed is a history.' Being and acting are not separable and successive; being is implicit acting, acting is implicit being" (Herberg 1960). This holistic approach confirms the model James the Apostle has put forward in 2.17: 'So also faith by itself, if it does not have works, is dead' (ESV).

The modern mindset was hopeful, always expecting progress as knowledge increased because knowledge in this model is inherently good. It valued objective certainty, basing the attainment of truth upon rational rather than supernatural means and believing that all rational minds operating independently would still come to similar conclusions about what is universally true and good. Modern knowers 'profess to be more than merely conditioned participants in the world they observe: they claim to be able to view the world as unconditioned observers—that is, to survey the world from a vantage point outside the flux of history' (Grenz 1996:4). This mindset has absolute faith in rational human capabilities.

2.4 Transition to postmodernism

The shift to postmodernism brought about the emergence of a pluralistic relativism that questions even the existence of an objective reality that can be known. It values diversity. The concept of truth is relative to each community's perspective and situation. Truth resides in the ground rules that facilitate the well-being of the community in which one participates. Postmodern thinkers label the modernist presumption of totality, universality, and objective truth a power play. Reality cannot be explained by overarching, grand stories called 'metanarratives.' These are considered modernist manoeuvres to legitimise the power of those holding authority, being nothing more than 'propaganda meant to impose particular preferences on others' (Anderson 2001:19). Both epistemologically (what we can know) and morally (what is right), reality is not what it once was.

With the death of objective truth, one cannot stand outside the continuous flow of experience as there is no transcendent point from which to view the world. All overarching statements of totality offered by reason are 'illusions, creations of our own language and a function of our own desire for power' (Anderson 2001:19). Truth is no longer discovered through rational investigation: it is created. Richard Middleton and Brian Walsh (1995:109-110) acknowledge this shift from a modern to a postmodern view of reality:

> If the modern autonomous self sought to dominate the world (and other human beings) in the name of what we now recognize to be a fictitious and ideological ideal (universal, rational human progress), the postmodern (or hypermodern) self fluctuates between the quest for a new form of autonomy and the experience of victimization. Compulsively seeking personal advancement, . . . the postmodern/hypermodern self is nevertheless overcome by a sense of meaninglessness, powerlessness, rootlessness, homelessness and fragmentation, where the self is incap-

acitated before its infinite possibilities, reduced to an effect of its plural contexts and consequently haunted by a deep-rooted sense of anomie. The 'I want it all' attitude is easily transmuted into 'I'm paralyzed in the face of it all.' The postmodern self exists in a perpetual state of dialectical self-contradiction.

Anderson (2001:20) lists significant implications for practical theology that arise from this view. First, diversity is celebrated in a postmodern context. In reaction to the 'totalising' of modernism, the celebration of diversity is reflected in moral relativism. 'What I feel comfortable with' or 'what is right for me' defines what is morally right. Consistent with this thinking, Nietzsche logically observed that 'if God is dead, anything is possible' (Kaufmann 1956:105). This concept naturally designates an important role to communities for the overall perception of reality since no one is an autonomous being removed from the influences of social traditions. The community to which one belongs shapes one's perception of reality. This means that the church, offered as a living community, demonstrates the truth of the gospel as it engages with postmodern society, thereby impacting its membership and inviting participation to those that don't yet 'belong.'

This celebration of diversity requires a demand for tolerance. If reality is nothing more than a collective 'hunch', then why exclude one group's collective hunch as invalid? There is significance in a postmodern narrative and story which acknowledges the importance of the meaning and purpose that such stories give. Though there is scepticism and even hostility toward metanarratives in the postmodern context, it seems unlikely that this condition could last. As the walls of modernism have crumbled, postmodernism has played a useful role by 'pulling the smiling mask of arrogance from the face of naturalism' although it has no answers for the future. (Anderson 2001:21).

Second, the social consequences of modernism included an

expanding secularism which would serve to free human reason from the constricting grip of religious authority. Increased social planning mirrored a confidence in human reason to correct social problems so that the 'need' for God was eliminated. From a theological perspective, to consider divine revelation under the banner of modern thought with its overarching claim to universal truth is arrogance. Similarly, to allow culture and community to define what is normative apart from the sheer reality of God's self-revelation is a veiled form of modernism. Helmut Thielicke (in Anderson 2001:21) would consider both activities forms of Cartesian thought that leaves one to serve as the standard for divine truth. The Holy Spirit instead appropriates the human subject to the truth of the revealed divine Word.

In the postmodern paradigm, the relation of theory to practice is interactive instead of linear. Theory is no longer a set of mental constructs that can exist independently of the physical, psychological and social structures of life. Theory and practice are interwoven in such a way that all practice includes theory and theory is only properly discerned through practice. This relationship is seen in 'contemporary physics as well as in attempts to understand the interactive relation between the human spirit and the Spirit of God as a social-psychological experience' (Loder and Neidhardt in Anderson 2001:21).

The older division between theory and practice that limited practical theology to reflection on practice should be reconfigured as the relation of vision and discernment. Robert Banks (1999:48) suggests

> unlike theory, vision is less likely to be regarded as 'irrelevant' or 'absolutist' in character. Unlike practice, discernment is less likely to appear 'pragmatic' and utilitarian.' Vision can incorporate the 'practical' contribution provided by the social sciences, and discernment the 'conceptual' clarification that comes

from philosophy. There is a dialectical relationship between vision and discernment, with each informing and correcting the other.

Although this seems like semantics, an interactive model demonstrates the relationship that exists between theory and practice. However, it does not appear to portray the connection between this dynamic and truth as an objective reality which validates both understanding and interpretation.

In summary, the transition from modernism to postmodernism has generally benefited the dynamic process of practical theology by bringing about reflective, critical investigation into the 'praxis of the church in the world and God's purposes for humanity, carried out in the light of Christian Scripture and tradition, and in critical dialogue with other sources of knowledge' (Anderson 2001:22). This transition has been difficult for the church to accept. Inherited concepts and entire ways of thinking are inadequate to describe the processes going on within and around one's cultural context. This crisis has forced practical theologians to grapple with the problems that have been raised which are not merely intellectual but instead amount to 'an intense spiritual, emotional and existential crisis' (Hirsch 2006:16). As a theological discipline, practical theology has as its primary purpose to faithfully reflect the nature and purpose of God's continuing mission to the world through the church's public dialogue and activity. If this is done in a genuinely representative fashion, the church will be authentic to the contemporary context in which it seeks to minister. The tools and techniques that fitted previous eras of Western history will need to be re-forged, requiring a new 'paradigm—a new vision of reality: a fundamental change in our thoughts, perceptions, and values, especially as they relate to our view of the church and mission' (Hirsch 2006:17). This new 'paradigm' will find its structure in the discipline of practical theology.

3 Practical theology as a discipline

Practical theology functions as a discipline to extend systematic theology into the life and praxis of the church and the world. It is the 'ministry of the Word to the world: the application of the Bible to all areas of life' (Vanhoozer 2007:15). While it includes cognitive reflection on truth as doctrine, it also considers truth as experience. John Swinton (2000:11) comments,

> Thus in contrast to models of theology which focus on the cognitive and rational aspects of theological knowledge, ... (there is an) understanding of theology that sees ... in terms of *whole person knowledge.* Human beings are lovers and worshipers as well as thinkers, and all of these aspects are potential sources of theological knowledge .... Critical, analytical thinking is important, but it is not the only source of truth.

Calvin echoes a similar theme at the beginning of *Institutes*:

> True and substantial wisdom principally consists of two parts, the knowledge of God and the knowledge of ourselves. But while these two branches of knowledge are so intimately connected, which of them precedes and produces the other, is not easy to discover.[118]

Practical theology plays a specific role in the discipline of theology. It requires that the theologian holds the practitioner accountable to the truth of God's historical revelation while requiring the practitioner to hold the theologian answerable to the truth of God's reconciliation in humanity. The reality and presence of Christ make theology a 'living theology.' This means that the task of practical theology ...

> is not simply to reiterate and apply dislocated theological truths, but rather to examine theological understandings in the light of contemporary experience, in order that their meaning within God's redemptive movement *in the present* can be developed

and assessed. Theological truth is thus seen to be emergent and dialectical, having to be carved out within the continuing dialogue between the Christian tradition and the historical existence of church and world (Swinton 2000:11).

This general definition helps provide the framework for a definition of practical theology found at the beginning of this chapter. Drawing on various emphases from the Protestant Reformation, the model of practical theology developed in the early part of the twentieth century focused on pastoral care. Edward Thurneysen (1962:11) produced the classic work *A Theology of Pastoral Care* which concentrated on the role of preaching as mediation of God's Word to humans. For Thurneysen, pastoral care is to be understood as 'a specific communication to the individual proclaimed in general in the sermon to the congregation' and must always be, and is nothing other than, the *word of forgiveness*. However, a significant shift from pastoral theology to practical theology took place under the leadership of Don S. Browning, who published a series of articles in 1983 that defined this change.[119]

3.1 Practical reasoning: Browning's model

Don Browning (1976:14) defined practical theology as, 'the reflective process which the church pursues in its efforts to articulate the theological grounds of practical living in a variety of areas such as work, sexuality, marriage, youth, aging and death.' He claims that Christian theology should be seen as entirely practical. Historical, systematic and practical theology should be considered subspecialties of the discipline called *fundamental practical theology*. He argues that 'theology as a whole is fundamental practical theology and that it has within it four sub-movements of *descriptive theology, historical theology, systematic theology*, and *strategic practical theology. . .* refer(ring) to what is commonly understood as the liturgy, social ministries, and so forth' (Browning 1991:8). He develops a model for practical theology from what he calls 'practical reason,' which contains an 'overall dynamic, an outer envelope, and an inner core' (Browning 1991:10). This model attempts to integrate theory and practice in a continual process of action and reflection that is worth exploring.

For Browning, the concept of practical reasoning places the theological task at the centre of the social context where the theologian and the church stand side-by-side mediating the gospel of Christ. This process begins with 'action-reflection prompted by critical incidents that ask how the gospel of Christ answers the questions "What then shall we do?" and "How then shall we live?" Practical theology thus moves out from this centre toward an "outer envelope" that includes interpretive paradigms, experimental probes, historical consciousness and communities of memory' (Anderson 2001:26).

Theological issues posit the relationship between the work of Christ in redemption and the word of Christ in Scripture. However, practical reason guides the process. Browning states it this way: 'When inherited interpretations and practices seem to be breaking down, practical reason tries to reconstruct both its picture of the world and its more concrete practices. The overall dynamic of practical reason is a broadscale interpretive and reinterpretive process' (Browning 1991:10-11).

For example, practical reason as defined by Browning may be what the Apostle Paul used when he made the decisions to circumcise Timothy and not to circumcise Titus: for Timothy, his Jewish heritage would have hindered his ministry to Jewish Christians while for Titus his circumcision would have compromised his freedom from the law (Acts 16.3, Gal. 2.3). There was a critical incident for each situation that demanded theological reflection preceding action. This can be viewed as the 'inner core' in Browning's model. By focusing on practical reason, Browning intends to point to the use of reason to answer the questions, What should we do? and How should we live?

The 'inner core' functions in this model, 'within a narrative about God's creation, governance, and redemption of the world. It also functions within a narrative that tells how the life and death of Jesus Christ further (displays) God's plans for the world. . . . This narrative is the outer envelope of practical reason. It constitutes the vision that animates, informs, and provides the ontological context for practical reason' (Browning 1991:11). For Browning, this model insists that practical theology always be in touch with the 'inner core' of human experience. Any theology that cannot respond to the questions 'What should we do?' and 'How should we live?' is confined to the outer envelope. However, practical theology becomes a living and vital theology of the church and its mission to the world when it engages the outer envelope in its action-reflection process.

Browning (1991:105-108) identifies five levels that he refers to as the '5 levels of moral thinking' where transformation can take place through strategic, practical theology. He lists these as follows:

(1) visional: a new or amended understanding of a person or community,
(2) obligational: a new integration of old traditions and practices,
(3) tendency-need: a more explicit way to allow people to deal with their needs in a conscious and intentional way,
(4) environmental-social: a transformation of the community or the environment to more intentionally reflect theological convictions,
(5) rules and roles: concrete patterns of living are changed.

Browning claims that these five dimensions are reconstructions of intuitive experience relating to the process of practical moral thinking, called so because they 'generally inter-penetrate so smoothly that we are unaware of the differenti-ated aspects of experience' (Browning 1991:108).

Objections and reservations have been voiced around Brown-ing's model in that it appears to lose theological focus. Brown-ing relies upon Hans-Georg Gadamer, a contemporary Ger-man philosopher, for application of a philosophical ground to academic disciplines such as history, philosophy, psych-ology, sociology and law. According to Gadamer, these are the disciplines that 'should study the meaning of the action of human beings considered as relatively free and intentional creatures' (Gadamer in Browning 1991:37). For Browning, this is significant. Understanding cannot be achieved through an objective act of description that involves isolating our personal prejudices and commitments. Instead, following Gadamer's lead, understanding was 'like a dialogue or con-versation where we actually use our prejudices and commit-ments in the understanding process' known as 'fore-under-standings or fore-concepts' (Browning 1991:38). The import-ant thing, then, 'is to be aware of one's own bias, so that the text may present itself in all its newness and thus be able to assert its own truth against one's own fore-meanings' (Brown-ing 1991:38). In his example from the ministry of the Apostle Paul, had the Apostle Paul rightly applied his 'fore-understandings and fore-concepts' to the issues around cir-cumcision, he would have missed an important movement of God's Spirit. This nuance is important. Practical reason could have dictated that Paul circumcises both Timothy and Titus to ensure their ability to minister unhindered in all contexts or circumcised neither man to display their freedom from the law. Either move would have been 'practical.' However, Paul separated himself from his own biases and made the right de-cision based upon the leading of God's Spirit, which seems to be a critical element missing from Browning's analysis.

This analysis also impacts hermeneutics. Browning leans

upon Gadamer's use of the Aristotelian concept of *phronēsis* (practical wisdom) to serve as a model for hermeneutics. This is an important part of his theological model. The hermeneutical process for understanding any human action, whether a text, work of art, sermon or political act

> is like a moral conversation, when the word *moral* is understood in the broadest sense . . . . In both hermeneutical conversation and moral judgement, concern with application is there from the beginning. . . . Understanding is a moral conversation shaped throughout by practical concerns about application that emerge from our current situation (Browning 1991:39).

Gadamer is more direct: 'Application is neither a subsequent nor a merely occasional part of the phenomenon of understanding, but co-determines it as a whole from the beginning' (Gadamer 1982:289). He sees hermeneutics as an enterprise that is broadly moral and practical, emerging out of the situations of our traditions of practice. When these situations become problematic, Christians would seek to re-orient around the Scriptures along with the major historical texts and traditions that have shaped present practices. This act brings understanding as interpretation and *phronēsis* as practical wisdom together in an interpenetrating relationship. Richard Bernstein (in Browning 1991:39) explains the way these processes relate:

> They are internally related; every act of understanding involves interpretation, and all interpretation involves application. It is Aristotle's analysis of *phronēsis* that, according to Gadamer, enables us to understand the distinctive way in which application is an essential moment of the hermeneutical experience.

According to Browning, this is the key explaining the relevance of Gadamer's philosophy to theology in general and for practical theology in particular. Application to practice does not follow understanding. It leads the interpretive process from its inception, often subtly, and breaks down the theory-to-practice (text to application) model of learning which, by analogy, also undercuts the model in theological practice as well. By implication, this defines practical theology as practice-theory-practice which, for Browning, gives the entire theological enterprise a more useful foundation.

3.2 'Christopraxis': Anderson's model

While affirming Browning's model as one that is contextual for theological reflection within a postmodern framework, Ray Anderson suggests that there is a lack of 'christological concentration at the core and a Trinitarian theology at the foundation' (Anderson 2001:29).

In revising Browning's model, he places Christopraxis, which he defines as the continuing ministry of Christ through the power and presence of the Holy Spirit, at the inner core. Browning would indicate that he does include Christology in his model, although it appears primarily as a component of systematic theology rather than at the inner core. Scripture plays a critical role as a 'normative, apostolic deposit of truth . . . critical for a hermeneutic of Christopraxis' (Anderson 2001:30). In this way, the ministry of Jesus as recorded in Scripture is as authoritative and revealing of God as is the teaching of Jesus. This is the 'Christological core' that Anderson believes is lacking in Browning's model.

For Browning, Christology belongs to the 'outer envelope' as part of the 'community of memory,' with its historical awareness expressed as creed and dogma. For the Apostle Paul, it was the presence of Christ through the power of the Holy Spirit that engaged his theological reflection. He saw the activity of the Holy Spirit as the ministry of the risen and reigning Christ, proclaimed God's son by his resurrection from the dead (Rom. 1.1-6). Furthermore, it was the Holy Spirit's presence in the lives of newly converted Gentiles that led Peter to baptise Cornelius and prompted Paul to proclaim that circumcision was no longer necessary for salvation through Jesus Christ (cf. Acts 10.47; Gal. 5.6).

This perspective changes the goal of practical theology from one of contextualization to one of transformation. Practical theology as a discipline has both a missional and ecclesial focus which must be considered in that order. Mission precedes and forms the church. 'Mission is the praxis of God through the power and presence of the Spirit of Christ. As a result of this mission, the church comes into being as the sign of the kingdom of God in the world' (Anderson 2001:31). This makes mission theology an integral part of practical theology and a necessary element in formulating a methodology for evangelical engagement. The mission of God through the incarnate Messiah flowing from Pentecost is the source for the mission and nature of the church, formed from a theology that views the nature and mission of the church as unified both in thought and experience.

Wolfhart Pannenberg (in Anderson 2001:31) details the mission focus of practical theology. He writes:

> As a theory of the churches' activity which includes the history of the church, practical theology will have to recognise the fundamental importance of missiology to its general theme. The mission directed to all mankind is not simply the practice which originally created the church, but also the ultimate horizon on which the whole life of the church must be understood. By its origin in mission the individual community is drawn into a history of divine election which looks towards a future in the kingdom of God —it is inserted into a Christian life-world which transcends its own particularity.

There is an ongoing ministry of Christ through the power and presence of the Holy Spirit that is the praxis of God's mission to the world through the church and its continuing ministry.

Moreover, as a church with a mission, practical theology is a function of those who are involved in that mission. Anderson (2001:31) explains:

> The nature of the church is determined in its existence as the mission of God to the world. For the church to exist as an end in itself, without a missionary praxis, is to sever its connection with the praxis of God's mission to the world.

The theology of the church as developed by the Apostle Paul found its source in the mission of Jesus as the praxis of God's Spirit. Paul became the theologian of Pentecost, transforming it from a Jewish festival into the foundation that defined the life and growth of the church. His primacy as **the** theologian of the church accurately defined the gospel of Christ as a missional imperative prior to it becoming a subject of proclamation in the church. This produced an authentic praxis theology, displaying the truth of the gospel in the framework of Christ's ministry in the world. Paul's theology was cosmic in its scope, able to see the entire cosmos as being under the incomprehensible love and grace of God made possible by the promise of redemption in Christ (Rom. 8). The church thrives in this environment as its mission theology flourishes unhindered. In reflection on its presence as a missionary community, it thereby defines its status as a base community for practical theology. This, according to Anderson (2001:32), provides the 'ecclesial focus for critical reflection on the church's nature with a view to its understanding of the nature of God and the triune life of the Father, Son and Holy Spirit.' As the church participates in mission defined as the continuing mission of Jesus through the praxis of the Spirit, its theological reflection gives evidence to a more comprehensive reflection upon exegetical and systematic theology. James Fowler (1985:49) suggests that practical theology

> is critical and constructive reflection on the praxis of the Christian community's life and work in its various

dimensions. As such, practical theology is not self-sufficient as a discipline. Though it has and must exercise direct access to the sources of faith and theology in Scripture and tradition, it does not do so in isolation. Practical theology is part of a larger theological enterprise that includes the specialties of exegetical, historical, systematic and fundamental theological inquiry and construction.

This means that the focal point of practical theology turns upon the critical interface between the church and the world which, as Fowler correctly argues, is where the praxis of the church's life and mission should be concentrated. This praxis is stationed between the normative texts and practice of Scripture and tradition on one side and the continuing experience of the church's mission to the world on the other. Practical theology is a form of *practical wisdom;* the church does what is informed by its understanding of God's activity through its life and mission.

Therefore, the practical theologian seeks to interpret Scripture, tradition, and praxis so that both the church and the world can be transformed. Thomas Torrance (1976:147) writes:

> In order to think out the relation of the Church in history to Christ we must put both (of) these together—*mediate horizontal relation* through history to the historical Jesus Christ, and *immediate vertical relation* through the Spirit to the risen and ascended Jesus Christ. It is the former that supplies the material content, while it is the latter that supplies the immediacy of the actual encounter.

Reflection on practice in practical theology must be founded upon the reality of Jesus Christ. It is his living presence that is part of every situation and practice and influences the reflection. This would suggest that a major focus of practical theology should be Christian reflection on practice, emerging in the wider context of the reality of the resurrected Christ.

Karl Barth (1956:212) describes it this way:

> As the history of salvation enacted in Jesus Christ imparts itself as such, and is thus the history of revelation, it reproduces itself. Invading the history of the world and men, it again creates salvation history in the form of Christian knowledge . . . the real presence of reconciliation, i.e. of the living Lord Jesus, is the theme and basis and content of Christian knowledge. This, then, is the supreme and distinctive way in which Jesus Christ is historical in his prophetic office and work. In his prophecy he creates history, namely, the history enacted in Christian knowledge.

Theory and practice are united in practical knowledge which works itself out within the praxis of the church.

This model of practical theology goes a long way towards healing the split between theory and practice in its emphasis on ecclesial praxis and the attainment of practical knowledge. Ecclesial context, according to Torrance and supported by Barth, fits well within the scope of practical theology where prayer, worship and obedient response to the Scriptures takes place. Practical theology, therefore, calls the church back to its origins as a missionary church with a specific vision and task to perform in the world. 'Christianity is missionary by its very nature, or it denies its *raison d' être*' (Bosch 2011:9). As a missionary church, it must remain faithful to its missiological vision and task, thereby requiring the practical theologian to minister in a way that ensures that the church is challenged and remains loyal to this charge.

Anderson follows this reasoning in a way that provides excellent insight into the ultimate focus of all theology and its intended recipient. In the survey of Jesus' life on display in Scripture, it is apparent that the needs of the world did not set the agenda for the ministry of Jesus. 'It is not the ministry of Jesus to the world on behalf of God that made him a servant, but his ministry to God on behalf of the world' (Anderson 2001:41). It is true that he reached out to heal the sick and feed the hungry when the needs of the world encroached upon him. But these needs—hunger, sickness or even death—did not set the agenda for Jesus' ministry. When Lazarus was sick and dying, Mary and Martha pleaded with Jesus to come (John 11) and were upset that Jesus came too late to do anything about their brother's illness. Jesus' response indicated the focus of his work: he waited two days longer, saying, 'Did I not tell you that if you believed you would see the glory of God?' (John 11.40 ESV). This need exhibited in the grief of his friends did not take precedence over his commitment to serve the Father.

It is the Father who loves the world and sends his Son (John 3.16). Jesus' ministry is defined by his obedience to the Father so that his first priority is to serve the Father who has sent him into the world. Mary and Martha had a concept of Jesus' ministry that was based upon his response to their human needs as they understood them. They knew that as long as Jesus arrived on time, Lazarus could be healed. Death is not a need that a healer can meet since it required, in their minds, a separate ministry: respect and care for the body, sealing the tomb, proper mourning. Death was a boundary, and this boundary limited their expectations of Jesus' ministry. Jesus crossed that boundary so that the glory of God might be displayed by Lazarus' walking from the tomb. Anderson (2001:42) offers helpful insight:

> The ministry of Jesus to the Father on behalf of the world is the inner logic of all ministry. Every aspect of the ministry of Jesus is grounded in the inner relation of mutual love and care between the Father and the Son. On behalf of the world, Jesus offers up to the Father a ministry of prayer, worship, obedience and service. His ministry is first of all directed to God and not to the world. The needs of the world are recognized and brought into this ministry but do not set the agenda.

As the incident unfolds around the illness and death of Lazarus, one can see this inner logic present in every act of Jesus' ministry. He clearly understood that he could only do what he saw the Father doing.

> 'Truly, truly I say to you, the Son can do nothing of his own accord, but only what he sees the Father doing. For whatever the Father does, that the Son does likewise. For the Father loves the Son and shows him all that he himself is doing' (John 5.19-20 ESV).

Jesus' ministry to the Father draws in human need as well. 'There is no ministry that belongs to the church or to members of the body of Christ that is not already grounded in the ministry of Jesus' (Anderson 2001:42).

Jesus did not minister in his own power. It is by the power of the Spirit that he heals the sick, proclaims the good news and casts out demons. 'But if it is by the Spirit of God that I cast out demons, then the kingdom of God has come upon you' (Mt. 12.28). Jesus, as the Messiah sent by God, was fulfilling the prophetic promise of the Spirit to come as the source of healing and hope (Is. 61.1; Lk. 4.16-19). Jesus came on behalf of the Father to display a true form of humanity in the midst of a broken world, living a fully human life as had never been lived before. Jesus took up both sides of the ministry of the Father, bringing the world the good news of the gospel of love while at the same time coming from the side of the rebellious and broken world to reconcile humanity to God. Thomas Torrance (1979:724) eloquently writes,

> The Church cannot be in Christ without being in Him as He is proclaimed to men in their need and without being in Him as He encounters us in and behind the existence of every man in his need. Nor can the Church be recognized as His except in that meeting of Christ with Himself in the depth of human misery, where Christ clothed with His Gospel meets with Christ clothed with the desperate need and plight of men.

Theology is interactive and intensely relational. Jesus stands with men offering up to God true ministry of service on their behalf while simultaneously standing among men as the very presence of God, providing the reality of divine mercy, grace, and love for those in need. The Spirit comes as a gift to the followers of Jesus as a continuation of his ministry on the earth. At Pentecost, the Spirit's presence established the believers as a gathered body and empowered them for ministry and service. In conforming to Christ, the early Church was sent into the world as ambassadors on his behalf, empowered by the Holy Spirit. This means that all ecclesiology is determined Christologically. 'The sending of God's Son into the world does not cease with the sending of the Church into the world. The Church is formed under the imperative of the incarnation —to know the world as it really is and to reveal the world to the world as it exists under judgment and as the object of reconciliation' (Anderson 1979:493).

This promise and anticipation of power leading to Pentecost were in the context of a community engaged in ministry, not personal edification as an end in itself. This is a critical distinction that helps to define the theological model needed by the evangelical movement. The promise of spiritual empowerment was given for the purpose of being witnesses of the power of the resurrection 'to the ends of the earth' (Acts 1.8). 'Empowerment for ministry is the express purpose for which one seeks the 'filling of the Holy Spirit'" (Anderson 2001:45). The evidences of the Spirit's presence are displayed in the manifestation of the Spirit's power, not always in obvious ways but often in the unswerving commitment and the inexplicable devotion to a task. One sees this is the life of Jesus as he moved relentlessly toward the cross. Although abandoned by everyone, the Spirit's power kept him on his journey. Moreover, his final words promised the power of the Holy Spirit for witness (Acts 1.8). Therefore, in a contemporary context, theology must continue to reflect on the work of the Spirit as the praxis of the risen Christ, needing a solid theological foundation so that the 'practical' does not overwhelm and determine the theological.

3.2.1 Defining Christological praxis

It is helpful to define Christological praxis for continued discussion. When we speak of praxis, according to Swinton (2000:11, 15) we are

> referring to a practical form of knowledge which generates actions through which the church community lives out its beliefs (holistic, theory-laden action). . . . In this sense, praxis finds its biblical foundation in the actualization of John 3:21: 'But whoever lives by the truth comes into the light, so that it may be plainly seen that what he has done has been done through God'. . . . Praxis then reveals theology in a very tangible form. In this sense, *actions are themselves theological* and as such are open to theological reflection and critique. Thus the praxis of the church is in fact the embodiment of its theology.

This is different from *practice* which ordinarily refers to the methods and means by which we apply theory or skill, often separating truth from action. In practice, one is left to assume that what is true can be inferred or discovered apart from the action or activity that applies it in practice. Graham (1996:7) explains:

> Christian praxis is understood as the medium through which the Christian community embodies and enacts its fundamental vision of the gospel. Theology is properly conceived as a performative discipline in which the criterion of authenticity is deemed to be orthopraxis, or authentic transformatory action, rather than (only?) orthodoxy (right belief).

The basis for this is Jesus Christ. One is given further insight by Dietrich Bonhoeffer as he helps to identify the Church as the 'space in the world' in which the reign of Jesus Christ over the world is displayed. The incarnation is the focal point and foundation from which the Church, 'bear(s) witness to Jesus Christ and to the reconciliation of the world with God through Him' (Bonhoeffer 1979:545). This insight is critical in defining theological praxis for the church. The 'space' of the church is something to be defended only by 'fighting not for it but for the salvation of the world' (Bonhoeffer 1979:545). Without this, the Church is turned into a 'religious society' fighting for its own interests whereby it immediately ceases to be the Church of God and of the world. For Bonhoeffer, the Church is only the Church if it witnesses to Jesus Christ before the world. This is the task for which the Holy Spirit equips those to whom He gives Himself. There is evidence of the inner corruption of the congregation if this witness to the world ceases, just as the absence of fruit signifies the decay of the tree.

It is at this juncture that the methodology for a movement of the gospel that engages the needs of society becomes evident. Bonhoeffer (1979:546) writes,

> The world is not divided between Christ and the devil, but, whether it recognizes it or not, it is solely and entirely the world of Christ....The dark and evil world must not be abandoned to the devil. It must be claimed for Him who has won it by His incarnation, His death, and His resurrection. Christ gives up nothing of what He has won. He holds it fast in His hands. It is Christ, therefore, who renders inadmissible the dichotomy of a bedevilled and a Christian world .... (This) is a denial of the reality of God's having reconciled the whole world to Himself in Christ....The world belongs to Christ....

The Christian mission does not bring Christ to the world. Rather, Christians testify by their presence in the world that Christ has come. He has taken up the cause of the poor, the estranged, the afflicted and the oppressed as his own cause. Solidarity between the Church and the world has already been established through the incarnation and this solidarity is the 'theological presupposition of all Christian mission in the world. . . . It is by the grace of God that the church exists in the world and for the sake of the world as those who bear witness to the transforming power and life of Christ' (Anderson 2001:118).

3.2.2 Praxis as embodiment of theology

The praxis of the Holy Spirit was interpreted by the Early Church as the continuing ministry of Christ, moving the church into the world as a missional community. With Scripture as its authority, the Word of Christ is interpreted in the context of the work of Christ as a hermeneutical task of the church. This grounds practical theology in Christopraxis as the inner core of its engagement with the Spirit's ministry in the world. The resulting theological activity will be both exegetical and experiential. 'Jesus has not simply left us a set of teachings. He has done that. But in addition, he continues to teach' (Anderson 2001:84). Discerning this teaching is not merely an exercise in historical memory, but it is a hermeneutical task. It must be clear that there should be no confusion between revelation that has been given through the inspired writings of Scripture and the interpretation that depends on that revelation for its authoritative source and standard. The focus is, instead, upon interpreting the Scriptures rightly, given the assumption that

> interpretation is a two-edged sword. One edge is the truth of *Gods holy Word*, which is 'living and active . . . piercing until it divides soul from spirit, joints from marrow; it is able to judge the thoughts and intentions of the heart' (Heb 4:12). The other edge is the truth of *Christ's holy work* by which he is active to do God's will in setting captives free and breaking down dividing barriers, preparing in his church, his body, a people who are and will be his brothers and sisters (Anderson 2001:87).

There is a tension here, but it is the creative and redemptive tension between what is 'now' and what 'will be.'

The living Christ is the Lord of Scripture and the church. The resurrected Jesus is not a criterion for new revelation that replaces or modifies Scripture; instead, he is the hermeneutical standard for interpreting Scripture in such a way that his present and continuing work of creating a new humanity fulfils the promises of Scripture. This activity is mediated by the church through the power of the Holy Spirit.

It is a critical responsibility. Can the church be trusted to mediate the resurrected, present and coming Christ as a 'hermeneutical community' of faith and practice, under the authority of Scripture? If not the church, how else will this happen? Every reading of Scripture is already an interpretation of that passage. The inability to interpret Scripture as the word of God that seeks to accomplish his purposes in and through mankind for his glory is a reading of Scripture that has failed. The church then, if it is rightly living out its mandate, is the community of the resurrected and returning Jesus Christ. It finds its true ministry in the, 'upholding, healing and transformation of the humanity of others as already grasped and reconciled to God through the incarnation, atoning life, death and resurrection of Jesus Christ' (Anderson 2001:180). This is Christopraxis, the authentic praxis of Christ's ministry through his humanity.

3.2.3 Christopraxis redefines humanity

Humanity is redefined through the incarnation as a new social paradigm in a way that impacts human social structures. Jesus, as he lived and ministered in Palestine, not only joined humanity as 'God with us', but re-created humanity as a community of shared life and common identity. Although he operated within a narrow circle defined by the calling of the twelve, he was also open to the unclean leper, the sick, the blind, the self-righteous, tax collectors and women with questionable character. In contact with Jesus, humanity was freed from the blind and unpredictable afflictions of nature and disease, as well as the cruel social and religious tyranny of the powerful over the weak. 'In the humanity of Jesus we see the humanization as well as the socialization of humanity' (Anderson 2001:253).

In Paul's letter to the Ephesians, the apostle highlights the implications of the gospel of Christ: the basic elements of society are to be humanised through the activation of the Spirit and the law of Christ. Paul was not interested in replacing the culture of Ephesus with a 'Christian' culture. Instead, he sought the release of authentic human life within the Ephesian culture, which emerged as freedom from what was inherently pagan.

For Paul, Christian community finds its foundation in Christ's identification with those in whom his Holy Spirit dwells. Both Jews and Greeks would need to shift their allegiance from the traditional authorities in which they were accustomed to the structure of social life in Christian community as the body of Christ (Eph. 2.11-22). Foundational social structures, economic structures, and existing political structures are wholly necessary, yet all of them only find their true value when qualified by the 'humanization of humanity' that comes through the incarnation of Jesus (Eph. 5-6). Christian anthropology does not begin with the

> humanity of humankind seeking relationship with God. Rather, a Christian anthropology begins with the humanity of God as observed in the historical person Jesus Christ and with the social structure of the new human community within which he is known' (Anderson 2001:253).

This community transcends all other communities, although it has no language or other custom than that of the particular people who become its expression. Existing cultural forms are not relativized to each other but are relativized instead to the real humanity of Jesus Christ, expressed through the embodiment of the gospel in the lives of Christians. In this way, the reality of the kingdom of God can be seen in the social structures of any culture through its own particular manifestations.

The effects brought about by sin and the Fall, recorded in Genesis 3, 'were the breakdown and confusion of the core social structure that bound the first humans to each other and, together, to God' (Anderson 2001:254). It is from that point that social and cultural patterns of human life reflected various degrees of brokenness. God's kingdom exposes this sin, seeking to overcome its effects by liberating humans from sinful structures that rule over them as well as the sinful inner motives related to pride and self-absorbed behaviour. A renewed social structure, not a more rigorous form of spirituality, helps to overcome the effects of sin. 'Love is defined as living peaceably in a domestic setting, as clothing the naked and feeding the hungry, and as loving the neighbour as oneself' (Anderson 2001:254).

This is the core of discipleship. Jesus defines true humanity. Justice and human rights issues are not ethical sensitivities subject to cultural adjustment but are instead grave violations against the core structure of humankind. Jesus broke through racial, sexual, social and other cultural barriers constructed against others when he healed on the Sabbath, ate with tax collectors and sinners and asked a Samaritan woman for water. His own nature would have been jeopardised had he drawn back from the humanity of others. He did not define a 'Christian ethic.' Instead, Jesus 'reinstated the criterion of goodness that belongs to true humanity as the biblical foundation for all the laws and commandments' (Anderson 2001:255). The prophet Micah saw this quite clearly: 'He has told you, O man, what is good; and what does the Lord require of you but to do justice, and to love kindness, and to walk humbly with your God?' (Micah 6.8).

3.2.4 Christopraxis is solidarity with the world

The failure to live in the light of this truth has serious consequences, both for the church and for society. The presence of a Christian witness tells the world that Christ has come to the world and taken up the cause of the afflicted, the estranged and the oppressed as his own cause. Solidarity between followers of Christ and the world has been established through the incarnation, which functions as the theological premise for all Christian mission in the world. Barth (1956:774-775) explains this relationship quite clearly:

> Solidarity with the world means that those who are genuinely pious approach the children of the world as such, that those who are genuinely righteous are not ashamed to sit down with the unrighteous as friends, that those who are genuinely wise do not hesitate to seem to be fools among fools, and that those who are genuinely holy are not too good or irreproachable to go down 'into hell' in a very secular fashion. . . . Hence it does not consist in a cunning masquerade, but rather in an unmasking in which it makes itself known to others as akin to them, rejoicing with them that do rejoice and weeping with them that weep (Rom 12.15), not forming and strengthening them in evil nor betraying and surrendering them for its own good, but confessing for its own good, and thereby contending against the evil of others, by accepting the fact that it must be honestly and unreservedly among them and with them, on the same level and footing, in the same boat and within the same limits as any or all of them.

The church, in its solidarity with the world, cannot abandon the world to itself, but has a responsibility to remain attached to the world in the same way that Christ has attached himself to the world. This is the obligation that Christ assumed in the incarnation. One cannot discharge this commitment to God through Christ by abandoning responsibility to the world.

This responsibility, according to Anderson, can be construed as *diakonia.* Jesus came to the world as 'one who serves' (Lk. 22.27), assuming the role of the servant as he washed the feet of the disciples (Jn. 13.5).

> He condescended to share and absorb human hurt, taking on himself the sickness and weakness of humanity. He allied himself with sinners against evil as their advocate. He hazarded his own existence, placing himself in the judgment that falls on the sinner, serving the creature from below. He places himself in concrete situations of human existence where he serves God by extending mercy and serves human beings by raising up a response of prayer and faith. He creates a healing reconciliation in his body, uniting both judgment and mercy, creating one person out of old estrangements. All of this is the incarnational nature of diaconal existence (Anderson 2001:119).

The church assumes this mantle of responsibility to the world which has implications on all of ministry. The church as a community is more than a social entity; it is the corporate body of Jesus Christ. Evangelism, as one aspect of the church's larger commitment, is carried out through an incarnational presence in the world where the kingdom of God intercepts the social structures of the community. The presentation of the incredible news that Jesus is the Saviour of humanity must also address core social structures native to the social and cultural context rather than merely attempting to alter the individual's self-perception through the mind only. One can listen to the Word of God preached and taught and mentally assent to its claims by saying, 'I understand that. I see what you mean, and I agree with you.' However, one can go away unchanged, continuing to live within the patterns of behaviour that contradict what has been heard. The Word must not be separated from the Spirit as though the Word is primarily mental and objective while the Spirit is primarily existential and subjective. God's Word brings change, not simply knowledge, through the movement of God's Spirit. Evangelism is not merely adding members to church congregations as an end in itself. Theological praxis defined along these lines is in contrast to the New Testament and leaves the church focused inwardly and doomed to fail. Instead, evangelism is a Pentecost event related to the mission of God in the world.

Implicit to the Christopraxis of the church must be a theology of evangelism that is;

- *numerically commissioned*—'make disciples of all nations' (Mt. 28.19)
- *geographically mandated*—'to the ends of the earth' (Acts 1.8)
- *Pentecostally empowered*—'you will receive power when the Holy Spirit has come upon you' (Acts 1.8), and
- *ecclesially multiplied*—'and day by day the Lord added to their number those who were being saved' (Acts 2.47) (Anderson 2001:130).

Church growth, with this focus, is a missional rather than a historical movement.

Jesus was an advocate—the first advocate—for those who were 'victims of social stigma, devastating disease, humiliating moral failure, and oppression, both demonic and economic' (Anderson 2001:199). This advocacy was observed when he accepted the hospitality of Zaccheus, a despised tax collector (Lk. 19), affirmed a woman of dubious reputation when she anointed him in front of those who deemed her unworthy to touch Jesus' feet (Lk. 7.37-50), and when he stayed on the side of a woman caught in adultery while the law called for her execution (Jn. 8). However, the Father sent another advocate, upon Jesus' request, to be with them. 'And I will ask the Father, and he will give you another Advocate, to be with you forever' (Jn. 14.16). The Holy Spirit is the second advocate, continuing the role that Jesus began so that those who receive the Spirit as their advocate then become an advocate for others (Jn. 14.26; 15.26; 16.7).

As a follower of Christ, one shares in the ministry of Jesus through the power of the Spirit. One is not merely given the demands of the Spirit; instead, one is grasped by the 'love of God as Father, upheld by the intercession of God as Son, and made to share in the inner life of Godself through the indwelling Holy Spirit' (Anderson 2001:199). One is no longer an individual but is incorporated into the fellowship of the body of Christ, the missionary people of God. As a member of this body and mission, one shares in the apostolic life of Jesus as a sent one to the world.

For the church as well as the evangelical community, this means that actions advocating for the full humanity of persons is grounded in the humanity and ministry of Christ and must have priority. It is a non-negotiable focus in terms of advocacy for persons suffering from any discrimination, oppression, and human suffering. This form of advocacy as a model of Christopraxis is 'God's own strategy, enacted in Jesus Christ and through Jesus Christ for the sake of the world' (Anderson 2001:203). A dualistic approach must be ruled out. To separate evangelism and social justice as two issues to be debated and then prioritised tears humanity apart. Theologically, it contradicts the incarnation. Jesus, in assuming the estrangement and brokenness of humanity, produced reconciliation 'in his own body' so that humanity can no longer be viewed apart from its unity in Christ. For Anderson (2001:203), to 'approach persons in the context of their social, physical and spiritual existence, and only offer healing and reconciliation for the spiritual is already a betrayal of the gospel as well as of humanity.'

Ministry of the church as Christopraxis expects the attendance of Christ through the presence of the Holy Spirit. The presence and ministry of the Holy Spirit are not merely deliverance from evil or emancipation from structures that are binding but are, instead, the empowerment to be truly human while living under circumstances and situations that are not yet redeemed.

> Pentecost occurs wherever and whenever the kingdom of God appears with the power of the Spirit manifesting the eschatological signs of healing, forgiveness of sins and restoration to emotional and spiritual wholeness in community. . . promis(ing) a paraclete to everyone who stumbles and falls, to everyone who is weak and powerless, to everyone who is tormented and torn by the demons of doubt, discouragement and despair (Anderson 2001:204).

The Holy Spirit is the Advocate sent by the Father to continue as the very presence of Jesus.

4 Practical Theology as an Emerging Methodology

The approach that emerges from this discussion is a theological model that is vital for the evangelical movement. Restoration of true humanity, both for the church and for the world, is at the heart of Christopraxis. The core social paradigm at the foundation of all human life regardless of cultural context proceeds from the creation story in Genesis 1-2. 'Humans are related to the concrete world (taken from the dust), to each other (bone of my bones, flesh of my flesh), and to a transcendent spiritual reality (made in the image of God)' (Anderson 2001:256). This three-fold attachment defines all people in all cultures. Jesus, in assuming human form, defines what it means to be truly human as he continues to live with us through the presence of the Holy Spirit. The gospel is the glorious news that we have an Advocate (1 Jn. 2.1) who truly understands us by joining with us—Immanuel (Mt. 1.23).

The moral foundation on which the commands of Scripture are given is not abstract principles of behaviour but is instead the core social bond of love. The two great commandments mentioned by Jesus—love God and love your neighbour as you love yourself—are both based upon love (Mt. 22.37-39; cf. Deut. 6.5; Lev. 19.18). The apostle Paul grounded his teaching in the same way:

> Owe no one anything, except to love one another; for the one who loves another has fulfilled the law. The commandments, 'You shall not commit adultery; You shall not murder; You shall not steal; You shall not covet'; and any other commandment, are summed up in this word, 'Love your neighbour as yourself.' Love does no wrong to a neighbour; therefore, love is the fulfilling of the law (Rom. 13.8-10).

Love is the core of discipleship and the essential aspect of what it means to live in community, whether in Christian community or in the world. Therefore, social justice is not an abstract principle, nor is it a noble ideal to pursue. Social justice is at the centre of what it means to be human. This is the theological basis for social justice, anchored in the incarnation of Christ. The apostle John tells us, 'We love because he first loved us' (1 Jn. 4.19). The structure of social justice is love, the empowering of co-humanity. It is not merely an ethical requirement added to being human. It is the very nature of humanity. The apostle John writes,

> By this we know love, that he laid down his life for us, and we ought to lay down our lives for the brothers. But if anyone has the world's goods and sees his brother in need, yet closes his heart against him, how does God's love abide in him? Little children, let us not love in word or talk but in deed and in truth. (1 Jn. 3.16-18).

According to John, if one closes one's heart toward those in need, an action which goes against the fundamental core of what it means to be human in community, the love of God is not present there. Although John's context in this passage is 'Christian brothers,' other passages allow this application to all those also considered outside the community of faith.

One can clearly see the composition of social justice. Injustice is not a violation of a principle or ideal but is a fundamental act against humanity. It is

> a human disorder; it is a breakdown of the essential structure of humanity. It is not totally an impersonal, inhuman, evil force . . . . It is our problem, because it is a human problem . . . . It is a problem of sin, not merely a problem of evil' (Anderson 2001:313).

This 'disorder' is the critical issue in the social and ethical problem of injustice. There is hope to be found. God is on the side of the oppressed—he hears their cries. Evil is not an impersonal force that marches on blindly as a result of fate. Injustice can be engaged and turned back. It is a problem that can be solved. The social order is a structure in which God himself participates since, as creatures created in his image, his own dignity is at stake. One finds the means for a solution at hand—through Jesus Christ. Therefore, social justice does not flow from the justice of God in an abstract sense, but from the humanity of Jesus as the continuing power of reconciliation. Our hope is not found in God's justice, significant as that is, but in his humanity through the incarnation. This is the theological basis for the retrieval of social justice—God's co-humanity. God bears the incongruity of sin in his body on the cross, thereby establishing a new humanity. The structure of sin and social injustice is taken within the humanity of God and overcome through Jesus' love and perfect obedience. The apostle Paul captures this clearly:

> For he himself is our peace, who has made us both one and has broken down in his flesh the dividing wall of hostility by abolishing the law of commandments expressed in ordinances, that he might create in himself one new man in place of the two, so making peace, and might reconcile us both to God in one body through the cross, thereby killing the hostility (Eph 2.14-16).

The hostility that was absorbed into humanity has been abolished, bringing peace. We live out that peace as a reconciled humanity called to wage war against all that would continue to separate us, including all forms of injustice. Anderson (2001:314) explains:

> Through the humanity of God, through the incarnation, this contradiction, this disorder that is against humanity, has been taken hold of at the extreme, at the borders where the pain is. The nameless ones have been named; the blind have been led to see; the oppressed have been given the kingdom of God—then and now.

This is the foundation from which injustice must be engaged and then reversed. We join with Jesus to bring about the reconciliation of humanity.

4.1 Methodology of active mission

The church, and particularly the evangelical community as the focus for this study, has a significant and considerable role to play. Although it is an agent of social justice, it is not the continuation of the incarnation nor is it another incarnation. Instead, the church is the place and the presence and the power of the incarnate Jesus who inhabits our humanity through his Spirit. In this the Church restores the new order of humanity in the midst of the old, taking risks for the sake of others, representing not only the power of the cross but of the crucified God. There is power in the cross as a symbol, but its greatest strength is in the power of the crucified One—the crucified humanity of God in solidarity with all mankind.

This is a theology of true liberation empowering ongoing mission. It may be helpful, for a full appreciation of the issues involved, to highlight an observation made by Reinhold Niebuhr (1960:57) regarding the tendency for dualism to take root in one's theology. A *rational ethic,* he suggests, focuses on *justice,* whereas a *religious ethic* makes *love* the ideal. This latter ideal is supported by viewing the soul of one's fellow human being from 'the absolute and transcendent perspective.' This leads to the presence—in every significant religion—of a millennial hope for a society in which the ideal of love and equity will be fully realised. However, this is complicated by the fact that, within the religious ideal, a 'mystical' emphasis exists side by side with a 'prophetic' emphasis. The mystical dimension tends to make an individual or group withdraw from the world, devalue history, claim that one's true home is not here but in heaven, and seek communion with God without attending to one's neighbour. The prophetic dimension prompts the believer to get involved in society for the sake of the neighbour.

There is danger with either of these tensions existing without the influence of the other. Bonhoeffer (in Bosch 2011:412) remarks on these extremes. He refers to the 'secularist temptation' in identifying the reign of God, either consciously or unconsciously, with an earthly goal that tries to craft not only our future but that of God's as well. He also identifies the other extreme—the things of earth pale in significance to the realities of all things spiritual. 'This is the danger in the evangelical position on the church's calling in respect to justice in society' (Bosch 2011:413). The problem, according to Niebuhr (1960:74), is that 'the religious ideal is often more interested in the perfect *motive* of the believer rather than fleshing out the consequences of love.' This preoccupation with motive, even though seen by many as virtuous, is perilous in its impact upon society. Slavery as an institution was left intact by many Christians motivated by love even though it was in conflict with their religious and moral values. 'The consistent God-world, spirit-body dualism, inherited from Augustine and the Greeks and reinforced by the Enlightenment mindset, defeats the ideal of love' (Bosch 2011:413). This dualistic thinking has continued to plague the evangelical movement, as has been mentioned previously.

A proper understanding of theology that places Christopraxis at the centre of its methodology is essential if one seeks to eliminate the dualism that exists within the evangelical movement. The uneasy dichotomy between evangelism and social responsibility is founded largely upon the formation of two mandates—one spiritual and the other social. The first refers to the commission to announce the good news of salvation through Jesus Christ; the second calls followers of Christ to responsible participation in human society, working for the holistic flourishing of individuals and for all-encompassing social justice.

4.1.1 Jesus is the model

Jesus is the model for this lifestyle. His Jewish contemporaries were familiar with the apocalyptic vision of Daniel, seeing the 'Son of man' receiving dominion and being served by all peoples (Daniel 7.14). However, Jesus came to serve before he would be served. He would have to endure suffering before receiving dominion. So, he merged two seemingly incompatible images from the Hebrew Scriptures: Daniel's Son of man and Isaiah's suffering servant, and said, 'the Son of man . . . came not to be served but to serve, and to give his life a ransom for many' (Mk. 10.45). This is the mission of the Son. After his resurrection, Jesus commissioned his disciples: 'As the Father has sent me, even so I send you (Jn. 20.21). Therefore, our understanding of the church's mission must be deduced from our knowledge of the mission of Jesus.

> He served in deed as well as in word, and it would be impossible in the ministry of Jesus to separate his works from his words. He fed hungry mouths and washed dirty feet, he healed the sick, comforted the sad and even restored the dead to life (Stott 1975:24).

Now he sends the church as the Father has sent him.

4.1.2 Christopraxis is missiological

In the incarnation, Jesus took humanity—flesh, blood, culture —upon himself. He experienced frailty, suffering, and temptations, bearing the sin of his creation and dying a horrible, vicious death. Now he sends his Church into the world to identify with others in the same way that he identified with us, becoming vulnerable in the same ways that he was. John Stott (1975:25) writes,

> It is surely one of the most characteristic failures of us Christians, not least of us who are called evangelical Christians, that we seldom seem to take seriously this principle of the Incarnation. 'As our Lord took on our flesh' runs the report from Mexico City in 1963, 'so he calls his Church to take on the secular world. This is easy to say and sacrificial to do'. It comes more natural to us to shout the gospel at people from a distance than to involve ourselves deeply in their lives, to think ourselves into their culture and their problems, and to feel with them in their pains. Yet this implication of our Lord's example is inescapable. As the Lausanne Covenant put it: 'We affirm that Christ sends his redeemed people into the world as the Father sent him, and that this calls for a similar deep and costly penetration of the world.'

This cements the relationship between evangelism and social action for followers of the Incarnate Christ. There is no option to exclude social action to concentrate upon evangelism or to make social action a substitute for evangelism. Christopraxis is missiological. For Jesus, the whole of Scripture finds its focus and fulfilment messianically in his life, death, and resurrection and in the mission to all nations which flows from this event. 'The proper way for disciples of the crucified and risen Jesus to read their Scriptures is *messianically* and *missiologically* .... The necessity of mission is as rooted in the Bible as the identity of the Messiah' (Wright 2012:38).

The need for mission is apparent. The challenges faced in South Africa and in a global context regarding poverty and injustice are so massive that only a missiological theology that has Christopraxis as its focus may be able to make a difference. It must be holistic in its scope. However, one must approach mission within a context that would build holistic, sustainable communities. 'Community is important from a Christian perspective ... (which) implies that the Christian should tend to build relations which would contribute to community building' (van Niekerk 2014b:53). Since the local context for the purposes of this research is South African, community building must be undertaken with this backdrop in mind.

What does Christopraxis look like in an impoverished South African community? African tradition has been understood to be communal in nature. Steve Biko, a martyr and significant player in the struggle against apartheid, maintained that African society had always been a "Man-centred society" (sic). People would converse, 'not for the sake of arriving at a particular conclusion but merely to enjoy the communication for its own sake.' There was no intimacy between friends because 'in the traditional African culture, there is no such thing as two friends.' For example, a group of people who find themselves together as residents in the same area would be considered friends. Biko continues: 'House visitation was always a feature of the elderly folk's way of life. No reason was needed for visits. It was all part of our deep concern for each other' (Biko 1978:41-42).

Others would agree with Biko's assessment of African culture. 'The community, in African literature, dominates all aspects of African thought. Dances are communal and worship is communal. Property was held communally before the colonial era and there are attempts today to reinstate that practice. This inbuilt bias toward the community means that individualism is always seen as a deviance . . . .' (Mutiso in van Niekerk 2014b:53). Jomo Kenyatta was a leader in the Kenyan struggle against British colonialism and became independent Kenya's first president. In his book *Facing Mount Kenya*, Kenyatta describes individualism as being associated with black magic. An individual is 'one who works only for himself and is likely to end up as a wizard... there is no really individual affair, for everything has a moral and social reference. .... (C)orporate effort is the other side of corporate ownership; and corporate responsibility is illustrated in corporate work no less than in corporate sacrifice and prayer' (Kenyatta in van Niekerk 2014b: 53).

Ikuenobe, in his discussion of African conception of personhood and community, acknowledges this same thinking: '... it is clear that there is a difference between the Western rational, liberal, and individualistic view of a person, and the African collective, communalistic, and normative view of the person.' For him, the group or community '... is not simply the aggregated sum of individuals comprising the community. Instead, the "we" as used here in African culture refers to 'a thoroughly fused collective "we."' One becomes a person by fulfilling one's duties to the community. This explains the 'relative absence of grief when a child dies. But when an old person dies, there is elaborate grief...' (Ikuenobe 2006:54, 56, 58). This sense of community is still widely held as part of contemporary African philosophy of life (Hallen in van Niekerk 2014b: 54).

However, there has been an erosion of traditional values that was already apparent in the 1960's as noted by Dutch sociologist Mia Brandel-Syier. Reflecting on her experiences, she argues that education and modernisation have weakened traditional communal awareness 'which had given sense and direction to man's life and which had determined man's values and patterned his behaviour. Nothing has come to replace it, and now there's just nothing' (Brandel-Syrier 1978: 182-184). Some fill this gap with an 'extreme individualism' which tends toward competition, strife and rivalry. This means they are available for any strong leader who tells them 'what to do, to think, to feel, to like .... they are in fact ready to do and think and feel *anything*.... Inwardly they are not committed to any particular place, job, or education, sentiment or attitude, opinion or preference, affection or conviction. There is no necessary connection between their words and their actions. There is no role consistency, no ego continuity.... they are an easy prey for anyone who wants to use them for his own ends' (Brandel-Syrier 1978: 182-184). Former South African president Thabo Mbeki came to conclusions similar to those of Brandel-Syier: 'the weakening of traditional culture left a gap, Christianity failed to fill the gap and it is now filled by nothing' (van Niekerk 2014b:54).

4.2 Strategy for contextual relevance

In light of the theological discussion from earlier in this chapter, what is the role of the Church in this context? The Church, with a theological foundation of Christopraxis undergirding its ministry, can be a key role player in society. H. Jurgens Hendriks (2007:1000) identifies reasons why the church has the means to realise this mandate:

> It reaches more people on a weekly basis than any other organisation. It has a stronger infrastructure than even the government in connecting, serving and influencing people ... (and) in Africa, the trust in spiritual leaders is 74%.... (T)heology is contextual and missional by its very nature and ... should address society's issues and problems in a holistic way.

Though failing to fill 'the gap,' at least according to Mbeki, the Church can still be pivotal in the fight against poverty as it maintains a level of significant influence within local South African society. This has been identified by Hendriks and also verified by community-based research to be discussed in Chapter 7. A look at what Christopraxis means from within a community influenced by Human Scale development principles will also be examined at that time. The goal is to describe a replicable, holistic approach that will assist the evangelical movement in the fulfillment of its mission mandate to fight poverty.

However, before doing anything, it is essential to understand the community, gleaning information from within. Insights

> must come from within the community itself, making use of strengthening what is there, even if somewhat damaged, such as: the contribution of that part of the community that has managed to overcome or escape the culture of poverty; the Christian faith of many; some elements of traditional culture; the relations between household members that are still providing inspiration; positive relations between some neighbours; the community activities that are going on and the general mood, not of despondence (sic) and bitterness, but of happiness and the feeling that life is, after all, good (van Niekerk 2014b:61).

This mandate is a missional theology, led by the presence of Jesus through his Spirit, that will focus on a contextual Christopraxis as it engages reflectively in communities. It is the methodology of practical theology. In this way, the practice of the church does not look the same in all communities. Instead, the missional Christopraxis of God is revealed contextually in communities as a movement of the Holy Spirit through followers of Jesus as they love God and love their neighbour. Discernment is key in this missional theology:

> And it is my prayer that your love may abound more and more, with knowledge and all discernment, so that you may approve what is excellent, and so be pure and blameless for the day of Christ, filled with the fruit of righteousness that comes through Jesus Christ, to the glory and praise of God (Phil 1.9-11).

True missional theology must be a theology that puts Christ at the centre. Everything related to life in a community hinges upon this. This is a shift away from a theology that empirically analysed the faith tradition towards an approach that obediently participates in God's missional Christopraxis.

The essence of theology in a missional paradigm is to know Christ and to discern his will and guidance through the Holy Spirit. A faith community cannot really understand Christ in a personal way without taking part in his missional praxis in the world. *Mission* is an activity initiated by the sending, missional God who, in his grace and mercy, enters into a covenant with the faith community in order for it to join with him as an instrument of his mission. 'Mission is no longer an activity *of* the church, but an expression of the *very being* of the church' (Bosch 2011:504). One must not think of the Church except as being both called out of the world and sent forth into the world.

Mission can never be peripheral to the life and being of the Church. It is for the 'sake of mission that the church has been elected, for the sake of its calling that it has been made "God's own people"' (1 Peter 2.9, Bosch 2011:505). However, mission is not defined only in terms of the church, even when the church is on mission by its nature. Mission goes beyond the church as the 'social continuation of the Incarnation, the social dawning of the mystery. . . into an ever changing present' (Illich in Bosch 2011:505). For the church to be essentially missionary does not mean that mission is church focused. It is *missio Dei,* mediating the love of God, the Father of all people in all places and all times. Therefore, mission concerns the world beyond the boundaries of the church which carries the church into communities of pain. God loves the world. It is for the sake of the world that the Christian community is called to be the salt and the light (John 3.16; Mt. 5.13). Mission means 'serving, healing, and reconciling a divided, wounded humanity' (Bosch 2011:505).

4.3 Practical theology requires mission focus

This posture has far-reaching consequences. Just as the church is no longer the church if it is not missionary, theology ceases to be theology without its mission-focused character. Theology, understood correctly, 'has no reason to exist other than critically to accompany the *missio Dei* .... For theology, it is a matter of life and death that it should be in direct contact with mission and the missionary enterprise' (Bosch 2011:506). For practical theology, without a mission focus it becomes

> myopic, occupying itself only with the study of the self-realization of the church in respect of its preaching, catechesis, liturgy, teaching ministry, pastorate, and diaconate, instead of having its eyes opened to ministry in the world outside the walls of the church, of developing a hermeneutic of missionary activity, of alerting a domesticated theology and church to the world out there which is aching and which God loves (Bosch 2011:507).

Christians are called to love their neighbour (Mt. 22.23) and that neighbour is defined as anyone in need (Lk. 4.10). The Son has set the model for the faith community, witnessing to the world in a particular time and place and context, answering questions such as 'What is happening here?' How must one respond to what one sees in light of the model of Christ through the power of his Spirit?

Hendriks (2007:1011) crystallizes the discussion:

> In Jesus Christ the Kingdom became flesh and blood. His life and death is intrinsically linked to the creation motive, because in his death and resurrection one finds re-creation, a new creation dawning upon us. Jesus' life and teaching teach us that the Kingdom of God is approaching and that it brings salvation. This is good news for all, especially the poor, the weak, outcasts, the unjust and sinners. It is a dream about the future that invites us to improve our present reality and, as such, is linked integrally to the process of doing theology.

This exegesis of the Word and the world must take place in a gathered faith community that actively relies on God's presence and leading. It fuses 'two horizons in which the interpreted social reality and the interpreted Christian normative sources meet in order to provide vision and guidance for an anticipated future' (Van der Ven in Hendriks 2007:1012). For followers of Jesus, this is to 'proclaim the incarnate, crucified, resurrected, ascended Christ, present among us in the Spirit and taking us into his future as "captives in his triumphal procession"' (Bosch 2011:530, 2 Cor. 5.14 NEB). Bonhoeffer (1971:300), reflecting from a Gestapo prison on the German church as he had experienced it, wrote:

> Our church, which has been fighting in these years only for its self-preservation, as though that were an end in itself, is incapable of taking the word of reconciliation and redemption to mankind and the world. Our earlier words are therefore bound to lose their force and cease, and our being Christians today will be limited to two things: prayer and righteous action among men.

The *missio Dei,* as the focus of the church as it follows the Incarnate Christ, purifies the church by placing it under the cross, the only place where it can truly exist. As a 'community of the cross', the church constitutes the 'fellowship of the kingdom, not just "church members"; as community of the exodus, not as a "religious institution." (I)t invites people to the feast without end' (Bosch 2011:532).

5 Conclusion

Theological reflection has influenced debates that consider theology as having a more practical orientation. This has focused the discussion on the relationship between theory and praxis. Bonhoeffer was a forerunner of the field of practical theology, laying the groundwork for a praxis-oriented theology through an ethic of discipleship. This was formed and defined in a postmodern context, impacted by the role of communities influenced by social traditions which tend to shape one's perceptions of reality. Truth, no longer considered objective by some, can be demonstrated by the church, offered to the world as a living community. It invites participation to those that don't yet belong.

As a theological discipline, practical theology has as its primary purpose to accurately reflect the nature and purpose of God's continuing mission to the world. It developed as a pastoral model with an emphasis upon administering appropriate pastoral care but shifted from pastoral theology to practical theology in 1983 led by a series of articles published by Don Browning. For Browning, Christian theology should be seen as entirely practical with descriptive, historical, systematic and strategic practical theology all functioning under the discipline called *fundamental practical theology*. This 'practical reason' model developed by Browning contains an 'overall dynamic, an outer envelope, and an inner core,' that attempts to integrate theory and practice in a continual process of action and reflection.

Browning's model has its objectors, with some stating that it appears to lose its theological focus. While affirming Browning's model as one that is contextual for theological reflection within a postmodern framework, Ray Anderson contends that there is a lack of core Christological focus without a foundational Trinitarian theology. Anderson, in revising Browning's model, places Christopraxis, defined as the continuing ministry of Christ through the power and presence of the Holy Spirit, at the inner core (diagram 5.2). Mission precedes and forms the church as the praxis of God through the power and presence of the Spirit of Christ, making it an integral part of theology and a necessary element in the formation of a methodology for evangelical engagement.

The promise of empowerment fulfilled at Pentecost became a witness to the power of the resurrection in the world. Christians testify through their presence that Christ has come and has taken up the cause of the poor, the estranged, the afflicted and the oppressed. This is the continuing ministry of Christ.

With Scripture as its authority, the Word of Christ is interpreted within the context of the work of Christ, forming the hermeneutical task of the church and grounding practical theology in Christopraxis. The theological task that results will be both exegetical and experiential. The Church, in solidarity with the world, cannot abandon the world to itself but has a responsibility to remain attached to the world in the same manner that Christ has attached the world to himself. The Church, in following Christ, comes to the world as 'one who serves.'

This has broad implications for ministry and brings great responsibility. As a member of the body of Christ, one shares in the apostolic life of Jesus as a 'sent one' to the world. This means that actions advocating for the full humanity of persons are grounded in the humanity and ministry of Christ. To separate evangelism and social justice as two issues to be debated and then prioritised tears apart humanity. This dualism is a theological contradiction to the incarnation. In assuming humanity in its condition of estrangement and brokenness, Jesus produced reconciliation 'in his own body,' meaning that humanity can no longer be viewed apart from its unity in Christ. If one only offers spiritual healing and reconciliation to individuals without addressing physical needs, one has betrayed both the gospel and humanity.

This is an important theological model for the evangelical movement. The full restoration of true humanity, both for the Church and the world, is the foundation of Christopraxis. Love is at the core of discipleship as an essential aspect of what it means to live in community, whether in Christian community or in the world. This means that social justice cannot be an abstract principle but is, instead, at the centre of what it means to be fully human. Injustice is not a violation of a principle or ideal but is an act against humanity.

The theological basis for the renewal of justice is God's co-humanity. This means that the Church has a considerable role to play as the place, the presence and the power of the incarnate Jesus who inhabits his people through his Spirit. The Church takes risks for others, representing not only the power of the cross but also of the crucified God. It is a theology of ongoing mission.

A proper understanding of theology that places Christopraxis at the centre of its methodology is critical if one hopes to eliminate the dualism that exists within the evangelical movement. Jesus is the model. One's understanding of the Church's mission must be informed by the mission of Jesus. He served in both word and deed as a holistic outpouring of love. The Church, including the evangelical movement, has been called to do the same if it takes the incarnation seriously. There is no option to exclude social action to concentrate upon evangelism or to make social action a substitute for evangelism. This is, quite simply, 'the participation of Christians in the liberating mission of Jesus, wagering on a future that verifiable experience seems to belie. It is the good news of God's love, incarnated in the witness of a community, for the sake of the world' (Bosch 2011:532).

CHAPTER SIX

ASSIMILATING METHODOLOGIES: PRAXIS DEFINED BY INTERPRETATION

[I]n our striving for political and economicdevelopment, the ANC recognises that social transformation cannot be separated from spiritual transformation (Nelson Mandela, ANC 1998:2).

1 Introduction

The Japanese character for 'crisis' is a combination of the characters for 'danger' and 'opportunity' (or promise); crisis is not the end of the opportunity but in reality only its beginning (Koyama 1980:4), that point where danger gives birth to opportunity, where the future is unclear and events can go either way. Danger provides opportunity, but crisis is the space that connects the two. And you cannot stay where you are because the danger is real, possibly affecting your ability to survive.

This is an appropriate illustration for the Church. David Bosch writes it is 'rather normal for Christians to live in a situation of crisis. It should never have been different' (Bosch 2011:2). Kraemer (1938:24) would agree, saying that '(s)trictly speaking, one ought to say that the Church is always in a state of crisis and ... its greatest shortcoming is that it is only occasionally aware of it.'

One would naturally ask why the Church is so seldom aware of the fact that it is in crisis? Kraemer (1938:25-26) would respond with two reasons that remain as true today as they were when written years ago:

In the first place, the Church too often has become reconciled to its being merely a religious and moral institution, whether a highly influential or a neglected one. In the second place, according to the testimony of history, it has always needed apparent failure and suffering in order to become fully alive to its real nature and mission.

For many years the Western church has suffered very little while believing that it is a great success. The correct perspective is incredibly important for properly understanding the present situation of the Church and the evangelical movement.

Due to the prevalence of technology, we are more aware than ever of the fact that the world is highly segregated between the rich and the poor. Anyone with internet access can see images from around the world vividly detailing the disparity between the rich and the poor with the rich, in many cases, considered by themselves and by the poor to be Christians. And according to most indicators, the rich are getting richer while the poor are getting poorer. In South Africa, inequality is greater today than at the end of Apartheid (OXFAM 2014:7). This circumstance creates a crisis: while there are feelings of anger and frustration among the poor, there is a reluctance among affluent Christians to share their wealth or their faith. Opportunity is before the Church, but it must recognise the crisis within which it finds itself.

Some see opportunity and rush into a hastily arranged response, oblivious to the pitfalls on all sides. Others see only the danger and become so paralysed that they retreat into ineffectiveness. The mission before the Church is a high calling which can only be accomplished in each generation by acknowledging the presence of both danger and opportunity while engaging those desperately needing the Gospel within their context. Clinging to previous mission paradigms will not be useful since it is not 'business as usual' in the proclamation of a gospel which often appears to have little connection to the conditions or context within which people find themselves. Jesus came to us incarnationally which, for most people living in Palestine in the first century, meant living life in the grips of extreme poverty.

The goal of this chapter is to bring together the investigations and findings thus far and construct a way forward for the evangelical community that applies these findings as a holistic application of the gospel. There is a strong historical argument from Chapter 2 that demonstrates a unique and important role for the evangelical movement to engage poverty. Examples from history can be useful tools to model a needed change in behaviour. James 2, as considered through a socio-rhetorical examination as discussed in Chapter 4, also motivates this right behaviour for people of faith. The presence of faith naturally determines praxis. And finally, taken as a whole the intended result is that these arguments from history and Scripture will guide theological methodology through informed developmental practices as discussed in Chapter 5 and Chapter 3 in a way that will encourage local evangelical churches to engage their local communities. The result will be, hopefully, useful motivation for encouraging the evangelical community to serve the world through a movement of the gospel that brings holistic transformation to those in poverty. Although the methodology that results should have universal applicability, it will be mainly focused on the South African context.

2 The Historical Precedent for Activism

2.1 Introduction

As previously mentioned in Chapter 2, David Bebbington (1989:2) identified four qualities that have been distinctive marks of Evangelical religion. They are listed as follows:

> *conversionism*, the belief that lives need to be changed; *activism*, the expression of the gospel in

effort; *Biblicism*, a particular regard for the Bible; and what may be called *crucicentrism*, a stress on the sacrifice of Christ on the cross. Together they form a quadrilateral of priorities that is the basis of Evangelicalism.

Bebbington sought to demonstrate that modern evangelicalism appeared as a new phenomenon in the eighteenth century, meaning that certain features of the movement were different or had not existed previously. Of the four trademarks that he settles upon, he acknowledges that three of these characteristics were not particularly new: 'conversionism, Biblicism and crucicentrism had been as much a part of Puritanism as they were of Methodism' (Bebbington 1989:35). What was the most distinguishing difference in the evangelical movement was 'its new dynamism or expansive energy for mission and service: its *activism*' (Hindmarsh 2008:328).

2.2 Early examples of 'activism'

But it seems as if 'activism,' as defined by Bebbington, did exist, although maybe without the same fervour and energy as witnessed during the Great Awakening. Bebbington (1989:10), as one may recall, defines 'activism' by referring to a remark by Jonathan Edwards: 'Persons after their own conversion have commonly expressed an exceeding great desire for the conversion of others (Edwards 1736:348). This passion of bringing the Gospel to others was a hallmark of 18th-century evangelicalism and fits the definition of 'activism.' Kraemer (1938: vii) describes the 'activism' of the church: 'All the ways in which the Church expresses and manifests itself in the non-Christian world, either in word or in deed, have to be impelled and inspired by its prime apostolic obligation of witness-bearing to the world.'

This more widely defined 'activism' also included a desire to serve others, something evident much earlier than Bebbington describes. Luther's emphasis on the Word relativised all human constructions by re-orienting them as service to your neighbour. John Calvin was also quick to identify injustice where it existed.[120] Clearly 'activism' was present as recorded in the ministry of these reformers, thereby pre-dating evangelicalism to an earlier time than Bebbington would acknowledge. As one would remember, the premise of this research is that modern evangelicalism has become dualistic in its approach to mission. Historical evidence shows that engaging with the needs of the poor was a foundational premise in an earlier dating of the evangelical movement and the structural dualism that emerged strongly during the late 19th and early 20th centuries was contrary to history and the clear teaching of Scripture.

2.3 Scriptural precedent

2.3.1 Example of Jesus

It is important to show that there is precedent in evangelical heritage that, through 'activism,' one would be passionate about sharing the gospel as well as serving one's neighbour. But it is a much weightier matter to consider the example of Jesus to determine right behaviour in regards to those around us. Jesus chose Isaiah 61 as the text for his inaugural sermon. In the account from Luke, he is given the scroll of Isaiah and locates the passage he wishes to read: Jesus states,

> 18"The Spirit of the Lord is upon me, because he has anointed me to proclaim good news to the poor. He has sent me to proclaim liberty to the captives and recovering of sight to the blind, to set at liberty those who are oppressed, 19 to proclaim the year of the Lord's favour" (Luke 4.18–19) (ESV).

When he finishes, he declares that he is the fulfilment of this Scripture. Jesus, in his incarnation, literally became poor (2 Cor. 8.9). He was born into a poor family—at his circumcision, they offered pigeons as was the prescribed offering for the poor (Lk. 2.24, Lev. 12.8) and throughout his life he lived with, ate with, and associated with the poor and undesirables in Jewish society. He taught that all humans are spiritually bankrupt (Mt. 5.3) and should do good to one's neighbours and enemies:

> [35] But love your enemies, and do good, and lend, expecting nothing in return, and your reward will be great, and you will be sons of the Most High, for he is kind to the ungrateful and the evil. [36] Be merciful, even as your Father is merciful (Lk. 6.35–36) (ESV).

2.3.2 Example of the early church

The Early Church reflects the teaching of the prophets and the words of Jesus in its teaching and practice. Christians are to be generous to brothers in need (1 Jn. 3.16-18 with Deut. 15.7-8 among others) so that in the church wealth would be shared so generously that much of the economic distance between the rich and poor would be reduced (2 Cor. 8.13-15 and Lev. 25). James 2, covered in greater detail in the next section, follows the prophets and the Lord in teaching that living faith will be evident in deeds of mercy (Is. 1.10-17).

Christ followers are also charged to remember the poor (Gal. 2.10) and widows and orphans (James 1.27), to practice hospitality to strangers (Heb. 13.2) and to avoid materialism (1 Tim. 6.17-19). Although one is to give first to those brothers and sisters in need within the church, one is required to show mercy to all people (Gal. 6.10). These teachings are all consistent with Old Testament revelation. The Bible calls on God's people to treat the poor in the same generous way that God has treated them (Ex. 22.21-24; 2 Cor. 8.9).

2.4 Warnings from Scripture

Scripture goes further. God insists that the failure to imitate his concern for the poor indicates that that individual is not part of his people—regardless of the frequency of one's worship or the orthodoxy of one's creeds. Israel failed to stop systemic oppression or to care properly for poor widows, so Isaiah referred to them as pagan Sodom and Gomorrah, telling Israel that, among other things, God will no longer listen to their prayers (Is. 1.10-17). God despised their fasting because they attempted to worship while simultaneously oppressing their workers (Is. 58.3-7). Jeremiah 22.13-19 teaches that knowing God is inseparable from caring for the poor. Through Amos, God states that he hates their feasts, refusing to look upon their sacrifices while there is no justice (Amos 5.21-24).

And Jesus was harsher. At the last judgment there are some expecting to be welcomed into heaven but, due to their refusal to feed the hungry, are instead condemned to hell (Mt. 25.31-46). Although this is only a brief survey of the passages dealing with the treatment for those in need, Scripture is quite clear: God has a great concern for the poor. He also expects that his people—if they really are his people—will share his concern and act with generosity.

2.5 Emphasis on justice

There is one other aspect of care and concern for those in poverty that will help guide the discussion around theology and its application further along in this chapter. The focus of Scripture is not solely on meeting needs, although this is important. There is also a desire for justice that includes restoration of the things needed for ones 'dignified participation in . . . community' (Sider 2007:72). Since man is created for community (Gen. 2.18) by God who dwells in community, there is great importance placed upon life in its social context. Biblical justice includes restored communal relationships. Safeguards were put in place to ensure this would be part of the community structure in Israel since justice was an important concept for God's people. [121] Leviticus 25.35-36 describes a mandate upon others to insure the poor remain in community by having them brought into one's house to live:

[35] "If your brother becomes poor and cannot main-

tain himself with you, you shall support him as though he were a stranger and a sojourner, and he shall live with you. [36] Take no interest from him or profit, but fear your God, that your brother may live beside you.

Those who can correct the situation must step in and do so to restore the poor back into communal relations. The reason? 'I am the LORD your God, who brought you out of the land of Egypt to give you the land of Canaan, and to be your God (Lev. 25.38). Because God has generously given and provided, he expects his people to act in the same way—to be holy as he is holy (Lev. 19.2).

2.6 Examples of generosity

Early Christians were remarkably generous in their care for those around them to the extent that Emperor Julian, intent on reviving the older pagan religions, found it difficult to do so because of the generosity of these Christians. In a letter to a pagan priest, he mentions the characteristics of Christianity that, in his mind, had made it so successful. 'It is disgraceful that ... while the impious Galileans (Christians) support both their own poor and ours as well, all men see that our people lack aid from us' (Lampe 1986:50). This was not a new development. In the century preceding this, the church provided financial assistance and help during the great plague to all members of the city. Many Christians gave their lives caring for the diseased out of faithfulness to the command to 'love your enemies.' This was in contrast with the conduct of many of the pagans so that Christians won great respect for their faith (Lampe 1986:52).

2.7 Evangelical dualism

Chapter 2 gives a detailed examination that follows the historical development of the evangelical movement as it continued the tradition of the early Christians. But a distinction began to develop that resulted in a dualism separating 'spiritual activities' from those that were considered 'physical.' 'Spiritual activities' would include the announcement of the good news of salvation through Jesus Christ; 'physical activities' call Christians to responsible participation in society which would include working for human flourishing and social justice. This shift toward the primacy of the 'evangelistic mandate,' 'coincided with the rise of premillennialism in what later became known as fundamentalism and the latter's growing protest against the this-worldliness of the Social Gospel' (Bosch 2011:413). There was broad involvement and interest in social reforms in the eighteenth and nineteenth century 'Awakenings' which included progressive social engagement. But by 1930, these activities had become suspect among evangelicals and had nearly disappeared completely (Marsden 1980:88). The 'Great Reversal' (as coined by Timothy Smith) had taken place with the evangelical movement retreating into a survivalist strategy that reflected this dualistic thinking. Choices were made that elevated the primacy of evangelism over issues around justice. In 1982, the 'Consultation on the Relationship between Evangelism and Social Responsibility' (CRESR) gathered in Grand Rapids, Michigan to attempt to bring clarity to the discussion around this issue. Dualism was upheld: The statement emanating from the CRESR was that 'the supreme and ultimate need of all humankind is the saving grace of Jesus Christ, and that therefore a person's eternal, spiritual salvation is of greater importance than his or her temporal and material well-being' (CRESR 1982:25). The official evangelical position remained that evangelism is primary. Success in evangelistic endeavours would hopefully yield 'fruits' in the form of social justice.

2.8 Shift in approach

Bosch (2011:416) rightly questioned whether this cause-effect thinking could be maintained as 'theologically tenable' based on the fact that 'converted individuals do not "inevitably" get involved in restructuring society.' Some progress was made in shifting the thinking of the evangelical community through follow-up consultations within the movement.[122] But the significant move in the argument over whether evangelism or social action was primary in the mission of God happened through a shift in the debate. The use of the term 'transformation' was defined as the process that would,

> enable God's vision of society to be actualised in all relationships, social, economic and spiritual, so that God's will may be reflected in human society and his love be experienced by all communities, especially the poor (Sugden 2003:72).

This is a holistic engagement intended to bring spiritual and physical change to the entire person. The shift was a significant breakthrough, although it has failed to be fully embraced by the evangelical movement.

Precedent from evangelical history would argue for a return to a vibrant faith that manifests itself in evangelism and ministry to the poor through transformational engagement. It is mission, defined by Vinay Samuel (2002:244), as bringing 'individuals . . . to Christ, challenging corrupt and sinful systems, structures and cultures and enabling individuals and communities to experience God's transforming power.' It is a return to what the people of God have historically understood through Scripture as their 'discipleship and mission in relation to the tasks and challenges of ministry with and for the poor' (Sugden 2003:72). One would affirm the need to invite people to accept Christ's Lordship over their lives while also underscoring the need for Christ followers to continue to be part of the world in which they live by engaging their faith within the context of culture.

2.9 Call to mission

Samuels and Sugden (in Sheffield 2007:7) encourage followers of Christ to return to a biblical focus to facilitate mission, which they outline as follows:

1.) There is an integral relationship between evangelism and social change; that is, the two cannot be separated or one given priority over the other. 2.) Mission is not an act of judgment but rather, a journey with people and communities toward God's intention: that is, "we are going in this direction, why don't you come with us?" 3.) Mission exists in a context—mission should demonstrate that the Christian faith is translatable; that is, mission will change the way we read the Bible. 4.) Mission requires praxis; that is, commitment to change the world in the direction of abundant life, equity and love. 5.) Mission engages with local context; that is, theology will engage with the issues of a community in particular, not in general. 6.) Mission enables freedom and empowerment; that is, mission will engage with the oppressed and the marginalized, those who need the gospel most. 7.) Mission facilitates reconciliation; that is, reconciliation between God and humans, as well as among humans themselves, is one of the most powerful demonstrations of the gospel. 8.) Mission is rooted in communities of change; that is, the primary agent of transformation is local Bodies of Christ.

In South Africa, a remarkable document was produced by a group of 'Concerned Evangelicals' in 1986 titled, *Evangelical Witness in South Africa.*[123] Evangelicals felt compelled to 'respond and articulate their views on evangelism, mission, structural evil, and the church's responsibility with respect to justice in society.' They were convinced of their calling to a ministry of proclaiming Christ as Saviour and inviting all to put their faith in him while being

equally convinced that sin was both personal and structural, ... that dualism was contrary to the gospel, and that their ministry had to be broadened as well as deepened. This represents an important shift in evangelicalism and not simply a return to a nineteenth-century position' (Bosch 2011: 417).

It seems that, more than ever before, evangelicals and ecumenicals more profoundly grasped 'the depth of evil in the world, the inability of human beings to usher in God's reign, and the need for both personal renewal by God's Spirit and resolute commitment to challenging and transforming the structures of society' (Bosch 2011:417).

2.10 Conclusion

The need for this approach seems clear. The result of modern capitalism has been the creation of a world very different from the past. Two hundred years after the Enlightenment, Newbigin (1986:110) writes that 'we live in a world in which millions of people enjoy a standard of material wealth that few kings and queens could match then.' For rich Christians, it was advantageous and acceptable to interpret the Scriptural passages on poverty metaphorically as their wealth grew. The poor were considered the 'poor in spirit,' those who, regardless of material wealth, recognised their complete dependence upon God. This interpretation has been useful to assuage guilt for those Christians with means in a world filled with poverty.

However, the global coverage that describes poverty before a media saturated world when viewed alongside a truly biblical, holistic interpretation of Scripture, no longer gives true Christ followers a place for cover. Conversionism, activism, Biblicism, and crucicentrism, defined rightly in today's context, provide a necessary return to the historical roots of the evangelical movement and correctly merge theology with praxis, creating a Church that is truly missional, defined as,

> a church that is shaped by participating in God's mission, which is to set things right in a broken, sinful world, to redeem it, and to restore it to what God has always intended for the world. Missional churches see themselves not so much sending, as being sent. A missional congregation lets God's

mission permeate everything that the congregation does—from worship to witness to training members for discipleship. It bridges the gap between outreach and congregational life, since in its life together the church is to embody God's mission (Barrett in Bosch 2011:548).

3 Socio-rhetorical Interpretive Results from James 2

3.1 Introduction

The historical precedent for 'activism' in the evangelical movement lays a foundation calling for a holistic presentation of the gospel that includes meeting both spiritual and physical needs. One cannot exist rightly without the other. Scriptural evidence supporting missions in this manner seems clear. Additional evidence is seen in the socio-rhetorical interpretation of James chapter 2, as was discussed in great detail in chapter 4 of this thesis. Some highlights and a summary of that discussion are as follows.

James 2 contains two rhetorical units structured in such a way as to help the author form specific arguments that bring shape to the entire book. The focus of the arguments rests on bringing about changed behaviour in the audience, helping these listeners more fully reflect the faith of Jesus. This reference is in James 2.1, translated by Luke Johnson (1995:217) as follows: 'My brothers, do not hold the faith of Jesus Christ our glorious Lord together with acts of favouritism.' This verse marks the beginning of the section containing these two rhetorical units that then closes in verse 26 with the conclusion that faith without corresponding action is dead.

3.2 Inner textual results of James 2.1-26

James chapter 2 clearly exhibits the characteristic features of the Greco-Roman diatribe: There is 'the direct address of the implied reader (2.1, 5, 14), the use of apostrophe[124] (2.20), of rhetorical questions (2.4, 5, 7, 14, 20), of hypothetical examples (2.2-3; 2.15-16), of *exempla* from Torah (2.8-11; 21-25), and of paronomasia (2.4, 13, 20)' (Johnson 1995:218). All of this functions in the service of an argument with instruments of persuasion applied through *exempla*, citations, questions and commands.

The dispute is singular, concerning faith and deeds. The faith is associated with Jesus the Messiah and given expression in fulfilment of the 'royal law' according to Scripture, calling one to 'love your neighbour as yourself' (2.8). The argument is in stages with each one carefully connected to the next. Johnson (1995:219) explains:

> The "royal law" in 2.8 picks up from the promise of "the kingdom" to the poor in 2.5; the "mercy that overcomes judgment" in 2.13 anticipates by way of pun the example of "merciless" behaviour toward the poor that begins the third part of the argument concerning the "uselessness" of faith without deeds; the sin of partiality, which is taken as the transgression of the law of love in 2.9, obviously corresponds to the prohibition of partiality in 2.1; the negative example of favouring the rich man over the poor man in 2.2-3, which is used to illustrate "partiality," matches perfectly the negative example of the rejection of the poor by members of the community in 2.15-16, and these refusals of hospitality are answered in turn by the positive examples of Abraham and Rahab in 2.21-25.

James crafts his argument in such a way as to lead his hearer or reader step by step to the point he wants to drive home: to 'hold the faith in our Lord Jesus Christ,' (2.1) one must demonstrate the appropriate deeds. The second unit in the chapter (2.14-26) provides general structure to the specifics argued in 2.1-13. This structure is helpful for understanding that James is not arguing to engage a Pauline position in 2.14-26, but is instead addressing specific points in 2.1-13 that will help to persuade his audience. The inner texture of the rhetorical structure is designed to enhance his argument.

3.3 Intertextual results of James 2.1-26

There are six intertextual references in James 2 along with a few general allusions to other texts. In the first unit (2.1-13) these references support the imperative to 'hold the faith of Jesus Christ without partiality' which forms the *propositio.* This behaviour is defined in this unit by the holiness code, which reaches so far as to define holiness concerning human relations as love—the love of neighbours without regard to kinship. One **must** love without prejudice according to Leviticus 19.18 and 19.33-34 to identify one as being in right relationship with God and to 'hold the faith of Jesus Christ without partiality.' And as was mentioned, there is sufficient evidence to suggest that the use of Leviticus 19.18 and 19.33-34 was meant to serve as a summary of the whole law. The failure to love in this way was consequential. Israel, in a relationship with a holy God, was expected to display behaviour that would reflect that special relationship. James' use of these references is calling for that same response in his Jewish-Christian audience.

3.3.1 Argument against partiality

At issue throughout James 2 is what appears to be a disdain for the poor that exists within this community. One seeks to justify this attitude by insisting that faith alone is all that counts (2.17, 24). Instead, James offers a picture demonstrating how faith should be understood, as attaining 'its true meaning ... when it is accompanied by – and expressed in - acts (of kindness and mercy), such as clothing and feeding the poor (2.15)' (van der Westhuizen 1991:91). The nature of genuine faith is at the heart of the matter. Is it merely 'right belief' expressed in an Orthodox confession (2.19), or is it instead practical, requiring deeds to confirm its authenticity?

James desires to hold this community to its professed standards. If they claim to hold the faith of Jesus, then they cannot follow the values of the world that treat the poor with contempt. If they claim to follow the 'law of love' as modelled by Jesus, then they must not practice discrimination against the poor that Jesus condemns. And if they claim to live in a community characterised by faith, then they cannot, in the face of human suffering, excuse their response by religious language. The important consideration is the authenticity of a faith that is professed but is not demonstrated by deeds, a classic issue for moralists in both Greco-Roman and Jewish cultures. There is a necessary unity between attitude and action that was a fundamental assumption for all ancient moral discourse. Johnson (1995:247) explains:

> It enabled polemicists to connect bad morals to bad convictions. It enabled parodists to mock the hypocrisy of those who said one thing and did another. Such an understanding is crystallized in the later scholastic dictum, *agens sequitur esse*: the way something acts follows on its being. The point is never that the deeds substitute for the attitude, but that the deeds *reveal* the attitude; and if there are no deeds, then the attitude is simply "empty" or "profitless" or "dead."

It is within this structure that this unit of James must be understood. His illustration in 2.15-16 provides a prime example: the brothers and sisters are in desperate need of food and clothing but are dismissed with good wishes and pious language. This illustration represents the false religion earlier mentioned by James (1.26-27) in its combination of callous speech that pretends to care while ignoring real need. This behaviour is not 'unstained from the world' nor is it 'pure and undefiled before God (1.27).

James uses parody in 2.19 to refute any attempt to separate the connection between faith and works. The faith declaration that 'God is One,' an intertextual reference to the Shema, is certainly not considered adequate faith for James. It is, instead, a mockery of true faith, 'a matter of cognition or confession but not genuine "love of God" (see 2.5), a fact obvious from the recognition given by demons to the true God even while they shudder in fear' (Johnson:1995:247).

3.3.2 Examples from Scripture

James reveals his models for genuine faith in the intertextual examples he cites from Torah. Abraham and Rahab both demonstrate faith by their actions. The reference to Abraham reference contains more detail, providing a closer look at the *'Akedah'* which James refers to as the 'testing of Abraham.' That act of trust by Abraham serves to make James' point: the *'Akedah'* did not replace Abraham's faith by this deed, but was instead a deed resulting from faith: 'You see that faith was active along with his works, and faith was completed by his works;' (2.22). The point of the example was that faith was represented through the works—Abraham's attempted sacrifice of his beloved son Isaac on the altar in obedience to God demonstrated the existence of his faith.

The references (2.21-25) that James uses from Genesis relating to Abraham serve to validate his argument. The issue is not the *claim* to faith as is mentioned in 2.18, but that faith is *expressed*. Abraham's faith in response to the call of God in Genesis 12 and 15 was carried to its fullest expression in the obedience he showed by the proffered sacrifice of his son. James' entire argument relies upon demonstration: 'Show me your faith apart from your works, and I will show you my faith by my works' (2.18).

As mentioned previously in Chapter 4, one unique element in James' treatment of Abraham is his designation of Abraham as 'a friend of God' (2.23b), something quite significant. James is taking issue with the systems and structures of the world in their relation to the measure of God, seen early in James 2 concerning the honour or shame given to someone depending upon whether he is rich or poor. This 'ethical dualism' or 'double-mindedness' becomes fully revealed in 4.4 when posed as a choice between 'friendship with the world' and 'friendship with God.' Abraham is not considered 'double-minded' since he is a person of faith who thinks and acts according to God's measure. 'Abraham's willingness to give back to God (Isaac) what God had given him demonstrated and perfected his faith and revealed what "friendship with God" might mean' (Johnson 1995:248).

The reference to Rahab is briefly sketched in one verse, but her appearance here leads one to question James' motive. He makes no mention of her faith in contrast to Hebrews 11.31, although it is evident from the intertextual reference to the Joshua narrative that she is a woman of faith. Instead, James singles out Rahab for her act of hospitality which, as was mentioned by Roy Ward (1968:289), causes one to ponder the Rabbinic traditions that relate Abraham and Rahab—along with Job—as figures highly praised for their hospitality. It also explains why the Greek plural ἔργα (works) is used regarding Abraham when only one ἔργον (work) is mentioned (the sacrifice of Isaac). It also presents a male/female model of hospitality to match the reference to a brother or sister in need (2.15). More generally, the mention of Abraham and Rahab fit the overall argument that James is making, namely that appropriate deeds accompany faith. The more specific argument relates this to the way that the poor are being treated in the community so that these references to Abraham and Rahab will discourage discrimination and model appropriate care for those in need.

James fittingly uses these intertextual references in support of his propositions: acting with partiality is unacceptable for those holding the faith of Jesus, and faith—to be living faith--must be represented by appropriate works. James' central focus in proving his propositions relates to the way in which the community of Christ followers cares for those in poverty.

3.4 The social and cultural texture of James 2.1-26

As mentioned previously in Chapter 4, rhetoric is social discourse with the intended desire of evoking a social response in the thinking and behaviour of the anticipated audience. The Epistle of James by this criterion was written within its culture as a social product functioning as a social tool, engaging interpersonal relations to influence them. James is designed to have a social function. It is always 'pragmatic discourse... not existing for itself.... To the contrary, rhetorical discourse is generated to change reality and is fundamentally a socially motivated mode of action' (Wachob 2000:154).

The language used in rhetorical discourse is a social possession inherently related to its rhetorical context. Since that context is a social context, the language spoken in the rhetorical discourse has a texture that provides evidence detailing the social setting around and within the dialogue. Thus, to probe the social effects of the situation within the discourse of this unit in James should, according to Wachob (2000:155), provide 'significant clues both to the social location of its thought and also to its intended social function within its argumentative situation.' Social context interprets language, while language illustrates social context.

Additionally, the analysis and interpretation of the common social and cultural themes in a text will likely take an interpreter beyond personal assumptions into the foreign social and cultural world of the text. The social and cultural understanding of the dialogue is enhanced when this happens. Meaning emerges through contextual comprehension. The rhetorical unit does not exist outside a contextual social and cultural framework, so by correctly understanding the socio-rhetorical function of a text one can create an interpretive structure to assist useful application into the modern contextual milieu in a way that reflects the author's rhetorical intention.

3.4.1 The rhetorical situation

To accurately probe the social and cultural implications of James 2.1-26, it is necessary to establish the rhetorical situation of these two units. The overall theme as previously mentioned relates primarily to the conflict between 'poor and rich' and whether saving faith can exist without any evidence of representative works. In both units, James is defining what Christian community must look like if it is following the pattern of the faith of Jesus.

There are three essential components in a rhetorical situation: an exigence, an audience and a set of constraints. James was aware of troubling communal relations in his audience of Jewish-Christians as evidenced by unjust preferential treatment of the rich and dishonouring treatment towards the poor. James defines this behaviour as sin. He uses inner textual structures in line with his Greco-Roman rhetorical training that provides a form for his arguments and intertextual references that engage historical precedence. He uses Scripture to afford context for his predominately Jewish audience in a way that draws them to inescapable conclusions: favouritism toward the rich versus the poor and refusing to care for the urgent needs of your poor brothers and sisters is sin. By doing so, one has violated the 'royal law' by failing to love your neighbour as you love yourself. The plain meaning of that passage would apply the command to those outside of the church as well, with the failure to act appropriately indicating that faith is 'dead.' This warning from James is as appropriate to 21st century Christ followers, including the evangelical community, as it was to the original audience of first century Jewish Christians. For James, deeds of mercy are not optional but are an obligation for those claiming to have faith.

3.4.2 Application to current context

As previously mentioned, although there are significant social and cultural differences separating contemporary society from the society that first experienced the discourse of James 2, there are insights from this investigation which are useful to the Church and the evangelical movement. Brosend (2004:82) writes that,

> James challenges the reader with an understanding of faith intimately and intricately connected with the whole of human life. Faith is not so much "known" by its works, like the tree by its fruit, as it *is* its work, root and branch as well as fruit.

James is seeking radical disruptions in the lives of his audience that brings them to a clear decision—the choice between a living faith and dead faith. This decision is ultimately the choice between faith (and salvation) or death. Emil Brunner (1979:554) writes, 'If a Church produces no living acts of charity for the community as a whole it is impossible to avoid suspecting that she is sick unto death.' There is no such thing as faith without works, as works spring from a living faith.

The hungry and naked before the Church need more than 'our lunch money and the extra coat in our closet, and more than our prayers,' even though those things are important (Brosend 2004:85). The challenge is two-fold: First, that human needs matter to God and must matter to those who would call themselves 'his friend.' Second, one's response is a critical demonstration of living faith. James indicates through his arguments that if one fails to engage with the needs in one's midst, faith does not exist--it is 'dead.' For the evangelical movement, this is a strong argument from Scripture identifying unacceptable behaviour for those considered Christ followers.

4 Definition of Poverty and Need

4.1 Introduction

All human beings have value and dignity based upon their unique status as beings created in God's image. This critical fact forms the basis that mandates concern for all people, including those considered by worldly status as being less valuable than others.

> Then God said, 'Let us make man in our image, after
> our likeness. And let them have dominion over the
> fish of the sea and over the birds of the heavens
> and over the livestock and over all the earth and
> over every creeping thing that creeps on the earth.'
> So God created man in his own image, in the image
> of God he created him; male and female he created
> them (Gen. 1.26-27).

God gives special value to the man and woman He made by implanting his image within them. All human beings, therefore, as the 'image bearers' of God deserve respect and dignity. All people are on equal footing regardless of financial standing, status or power. Those in poverty are no less the 'image bearers' of God than are those who are financially prosperous.

As God's image bearers, no one is insignificant, and no one is worthless. Life has meaning and importance because God's imprint is upon one's humanity. It is useful to recount Duane Elmer here (2006:63), who states, 'we must see others as God sees them, treat them as he would and name them as he names them.' Therefore, on the basis of this intrinsic value, all people should be handled with the respect and dignity bestowed upon them by God; one profanes God's image by mistreating people or valuing one over the other due to one's wealth or achievements. The distinctions in treatment witnessed in the Epistle of James between wealthy and poor members coming to worship find a basis in this status. 'One cannot honor God and at the same time treat another person in a manipulative, dehumanizing, disrespectful way' (Elmer 2006:63).

This belief underpins the Scriptural instructions requiring impartial treatment of all people with a special emphasis focused upon those in need. This acknowledges the image of God in all humanity and means that efforts aimed at restoring what has become the marred image of God in the poor should be critical undertakings for the church and the evangelical community.

4.2 Defining poverty

Poverty is essentially about relationships. Within these relationships the poor experience powerlessness, deprivation, physical isolation, financial need and all of the other characteristics that would define one's understanding of poverty. Relationships with those in poverty are often marred or broken, with those in poverty often held captive by 'the powerful'—those who stand to gain advantage through the continued poverty of the poor.

Broken relationships produce consequences. These consequences for those in poverty include exclusion from the mainstream of society and a distorted sense of community. Therefore, transformational initiatives must restore broken communities, moving beyond community organising to something more radical and foundational. This offers a significant opportunity for the evangelical movement as Christ followers unite in the formation of newly restored covenantal communities. They are communities of equals with, 'trust, celebration and redemption as its (their) chief characteristics' (Christian 2008:8). These initiatives model Jesus' activities of rebuilding a community by challenging the issues that brought division and were on God's heart. It requires investing in relationships, valuing individuals for who they are and celebrating the diversity that is sure to result. It is considering the end in mind—the coming Kingdom of God that looks to a promised future where all will 'behold a great multitude that no one could number, from every nation, from all tribes and peoples and languages standing before the throne and before the Lamb' (Rev. 7.9a).

4.3 Defining a process

But this requires a process. Developing a focused methodology that seeks to restore those in poverty is critical. By recognising the necessary role expected for those in the evangelical movement to play in alleviating poverty, one would look at how this could be done most effectively as a next step. A focused methodology must be developed that seeks to restore those in poverty as a missional gospel initiative.

The application of Human Scale Development methodology into situations of poverty appears to be a strategic tool for the evangelical community to consider in line with a Scriptural framework. Needs are met at the human scale level with self-reliance becoming the sustainable medium by which this process takes place. But instead of independence being the overall goal, it is rather about interdependence. The interdependence of micro-organisations in the invisible world is at the crux of Max-Neef's thesis around poverty alleviation. It is a conscious move towards maximising participation by encouraging networking at the human scale. It improves the quality of life by changing the way that people see themselves, thereby allowing the freedom for greater capacity and potential. New possibilities are created and expanded. For Max-Neef, as local becomes valuable then self-confidence increases. (Max-Neef 1991:65). This understanding could find a useful application in a local church community.

Human Scale Development 'offers suggestions, while remaining open to further elaboration' (1991: xii). Max-Neef states that,

> The proposal we have developed is not a model. It is an open option which is justified only to the extent that we understand it, internalize it and implement it through a praxis that is in itself a process in constant motion (1991:12).

The flexibility of this approach is of great benefit. It speaks to the concerns about its applicability outside of Max-Neef's South American context[125]. As a 'process in motion,' it can find application from the South American to the South African context and hypothetically to anywhere else. Anyone can apply and design this theory according to one's socio-economic environment. As a people-centred approach, it has strengths found in maximising inclusion through active participation, thereby allowing local ownership of the development processes. This focus on 'smallness' places development potential within the reach of any community in poverty. Community groups, and particularly churches, have a significant role to play as change agents within their local context.

5 Theological Model in Context

As previously mentioned, initiatives properly engaging poverty should have their basis in the understanding that God created people in his image. For the church as well as the evangelical community, actions advocating for the recognition or restoration of the full humanity of persons are grounded in the humanity and ministry of Christ and must have priority. Jesus was an advocate—the first advocate—for those who were 'victims of social stigma, devastating disease, humiliating moral failure, and oppression, both demonic and economic' (Anderson 2001:199). But the Father sent another advocate, upon Jesus' request, to be with them. 'And I will ask the Father, and he will give you another Advocate, to be with you forever' (Jn. 14.16). The Holy Spirit is the second advocate, continuing the role that Jesus began so that those who receive the Spirit as their advocate then become an advocate for others (Jn. 14.26; 15.26; 16.7).

5.1 Introduction

This section will include a summary of the theological model that developed from Chapter 5 and its application to a South African context. Max-Neef's Human Scale Development research from Chapter 3 will provide a useful framework to structure the intervention. It is likely that these principles could also find application in other global contexts where poverty is pervasive. The goal is to develop an approach that encourages the evangelical community to engage with poverty alleviation as a missional movement of the gospel.

5.2 Engagement as Christopraxis

As a follower of Christ, one participates in the ministry of Jesus through the power of the Spirit. One is not merely given the demands of the Spirit but is, instead, grasped by the 'love of God as Father, upheld by the intercession of God as Son, and made to share in the inner life of Godself through the indwelling Holy Spirit' (Anderson 2001:199). One is no longer an individual but is assimilated into the body of Christ, the missionary people of God. As a member of this body and mission, one shares in the apostolic life of Jesus as an incarnated 'sent one' to the world. It is a role of advocacy for persons suffering from any discrimination, oppression, and human suffering. This form of support as a model of Christopraxis is 'God's own strategy, enacted in Jesus Christ and through Jesus Christ for the sake of the world' (Anderson 2001:203). To separate evangelism and social justice as two issues to be debated and then prioritised contradicts the incarnation and tears humanity apart. Jesus assumed humanity in its condition of estrangement and brokenness, producing reconciliation 'in his own body' so that humanity can no longer be viewed apart from its unity in Christ. For Anderson (2001:203), to 'approach persons in the context of their social, physical and spiritual existence, and only offer healing and reconciliation for the spiritual is already a betrayal of the gospel as well as of humanity.'

Injustice, then, is not a violation of a principle or ideal but is a fundamental act against humanity. It is, 'a human disorder; it is a breakdown of the essential structure of humanity. It is not totally an impersonal, inhuman, evil force. . . . It is our problem because it is a human problem. . . . It is a problem of sin, not merely a problem of evil' (Anderson 2001:313). James would recognise this same argument. Failing to love one's neighbour by acting with partiality is a sin as it dishonours the poor man. (James 2.8-9).

God is on the side of the oppressed—he hears their cries and promises to act since his own dignity is at stake. Evil is not an impersonal force that marches on blindly as a result of fate. Injustice can be engaged and reversed. One finds the means for a solution at hand—through Jesus Christ. Social justice flows from the humanity of Jesus as the continuing power of reconciliation. The theological basis for the recovery of social justice is God's co-humanity. God establishes a new humanity in his body on the cross. Jesus' love and perfect obedience overcame the structure of sin and injustice. The apostle Paul clearly captures this:

> For he himself is our peace, who has made us both one and has broken down in his flesh the dividing wall of hostility by abolishing the law of commandments expressed in ordinances, that he might create in himself one new man in place of the two, so making peace, and might reconcile us both to God in one body through the cross, thereby killing the hostility (Eph. 2.14-16).

Hostility has been abolished, resulting in peace. As reconciled humanity, we secure that peace by waging war against all that would continue to separate us, including all forms of injustice. This reconciliation is the foundation from which injustice must be engaged and reversed. Scripture is quite clear in its mandate against injustice, which emanates from its source in the unsurpassed value and nature of God.

5.3 The South African context

Poverty exists on a massive scale in South Africa,[126] with many individuals struggling just to survive. Much of this poverty directly correlates to the national employment figures, which are labelled a 'crisis.'[127] Millions of South Africans face the prospect of never finding work in any sector of the economy, thereby creating a barrier to any of the financial and other benefits that employment provides. The correlative impact is that poverty will increase as will crime, cited as the leading cause of injury and death among poor people (Budlender 2000).

Many churches have found themselves unprepared to deal with the enormity of the challenges facing local communities and have, therefore, failed to properly engage. This is not an option. It is only possible for the church to give ground, according to Bonhoeffer (1995:207), 'provided they do so with the Word, provided their weakness is the weakness of the Word, and provided they do not leave the Word in the lurch in their flight.' Inhumanity in any form must not be abandoned without facing separation from the humanity of God.

5.4 Relational apartheid

Most South African Christians would feel scandalised to be told that forsaking the homeless, systematically excluding the socially unacceptable and overlooking the deep injustices that remain in society is the moral and spiritual equivalent of apartheid, but Johannes Verkuyl (in Anderson 2001:179-180) provides relevant insight:

> It is far easier to believe in a god who is less than love and who does not require a discipleship of love. But if God is love, separation is the ultimately opposite force to God. The will to be separate is the most complete refusal of the truth. Apartheid is a view of life and a view of man which insists that we find our identity in dissociation from each other. A policy of separate development which is based on this concept therefore involves a rejection of the central beliefs of the Christian Gospel. It reinforces divisions which the Holy Spirit is calling the people of God to overcome. This policy is, therefore, a form of resistance to the Holy Spirit.

The genuine humanity of the church lies in its relation between Jesus Christ and all people. Its ministry is found in the transformation of the humanity of others through the incarnation, death and resurrection of Jesus Christ as he reconciles humanity to God. The church is truly human when it affirms and upholds this truth, meaning that separation is anti-human and anti-Christ.

The Early Church experienced relational fractures when complaints arose based upon the failure to provide for the Greek-speaking Jewish widows in the community (Acts 6.1-7). Restoration happened quickly as the apostles assimilated these widows into the life of the community by establishing a structure that would ensure their provision. Where the Spirit moves, there is no room for discrimination based on race, gender or financial status, as there is no longer, 'Jew nor Greek, there is neither slave nor free, there is neither male nor female, for you are all one in Christ Jesus' (Gal. 3.28). There can be no 'acts of favouritism' as there is a 'royal law of liberty' that overcomes through Christ. To act with partiality is to commit sin (James 2.1-9) and to fail to care for a brother or sister in need runs counter to an active, living faith (James 2.14-26). Something must take place within the evangelical community to acknowledge what has been lost and restore what has been turned away.

The structures of human social and economic existence are available for redemption through the resurrection of Jesus Christ and the arrival of the Holy Spirit at Pentecost. The praxis of Christ in the church (Christopraxis) calls the church into radical submission to the Holy Spirit. This praxis is the formative reality of the transformed humanity. For Anderson (2001:182), 'Christopraxis becomes the hermeneutical criterion and spiritual conscience of the life and mission of the church.' It is an attitude of repentance.

> Theological repentance is demanded of the church when it offers flavoured water to those who come expecting the new wine and stale bread to those expecting a nourishing meal. The church repents through engaging in theological reflection on the

work of God's Spirit under the mandate of God's Word. Theological repentance begins with the confession that the church has exchanged its theological birthright for the fast food of cultural relevance. When the church confesses with the church at Laodicea that its theology is "wretched, pitiable, poor, blind, and naked," the Christ who stands at the door knocking will find a welcome. "Who do you say that I am," asks this Christ. When the church has answered that question fully and forthrightly, it will have rediscovered its theological heritage (Anderson 2001:182).

It seems clear that the movement of the Gospel has been hindered by the failure of the evangelical movement to reach out to those in need. It is in need of repentance from an attitude that demands privilege in the world without expressing concern for those without food or shelter or justice. It must recognise its failure and repent—turn from—its previous activities and move forward into realised truth formed from Scripture through the power of God's Spirit. It must recover a missional alignment that takes seriously the mandate to love God and love others as one loves oneself (Mt. 22.38-40).

5.5 Model of repentance

Nehemiah provides a model of repentance that can serve as a guide for the evangelical community. Upon hearing the news that things were not good in Jerusalem, that the 'wall of Jerusalem is broken down, and its gates are destroyed by fire' (Neh.1.3b), he 'sat down and wept and mourned for days, and . . . continued fasting and praying before the God of heaven' (Neh. 1.4). He confessed his sin and the sin of his fathers:

I now pray before you day and night for the people of Israel your servants, confessing the sins of the people of Israel, which we have sinned against you. Even I and my father's house have sinned. We have acted very corruptly against you and have not kept the commandments, the statutes, and the rules that you commanded...' (Neh. 1.6b-7).

Nehemiah recognises that it is his sin and the sin of his fathers that have brought about this devastating situation. His repentance, both personally and corporately, begins the realisation of his complicity in the current state of affairs.

In South Africa, this process may mean recognising and repenting from one's participation in a system that treated the majority of the population as less than human while benefitting from such an exchange. And it may mean recognising that the church has been far too slow to engage in the hard work of the gospel and acknowledging that this may bring incredible pain and loss. 'Once we recognise the identification of Jesus with the poor, we cannot any longer consider our own relation to the poor as a social ethics question; it is a gospel question' (Bosch 2011:447). It requires a 'different kind of conversion... which would include admitting complicity in the oppression of the poor and a turning from the idols of money, race, and self-interest' (cf. Kritzinger 1988:274-297 in Bosch 2011:448). The example of The Parable of the Good Samaritan (Lk. 10.25-37) was put forward in answer to the question 'And who is my neighbour?' (Lk. 10.29b). One would notice from the behaviour of the Samaritan that he willingly paid the innkeeper to care for the man who fell among the robbers, even though he was not responsible for the man's injuries and had already done more than would be reasonably expected. The promise from the Samaritan to the innkeeper was that if he spent more than had been given, the shortfall would be repaid. This parable serves as an excellent example for those in the evangelical movement who might claim that there is no need for repentance or restitution if one has no particular blame for the injury.

5.5.1 Transformation of the mind

Paul writes in Romans 12.2, 'Do not be conformed to this world, but be transformed by the renewal of your mind, that by testing you may discern what is the will of God, what is good and acceptable and perfect.' He also wrote to the Philippian church to describe what the renewed mind looks like:

> Let the same mind be in you that was in Christ Jesus, who, though he was in the form of God, did not regard equality with God as something to be exploited, but emptied himself, taking the form of a slave, being born in human likeness . . . . He humbled himself and became obedient to the point of death—even death on a cross (Phil. 2.5-8).

The mind of Christ runs contrary to the mind of the world, a mind in rebellion set on self-fulfilment and self-promotion.

> Christ assumed the form of humanity in its rebellion against God and bent that mind back into conformity and obedience to God through the empowerment of the love of the Son for the Father and the Father for the Son' (Anderson 2001:181).

One with the mind of Christ has a mind transformed from death to life and from self-serving to self-giving. The church is 'not of the world' just as Jesus is 'not of the world' (Jn. 17.14). But it is not to be taken 'out of the world'—separated out—because the church is 'sent into the world' as Jesus has been 'sent into the world' (Jn. 17.18). The church must be in the world, according to Karl Barth (1956: 773-74), 'on the same level and footing in the same boat and with the same limits as any or all of them' . . . (done) 'willingly and with a good conscience.' Without this context, separation in all of its manifestations continues to exist.

5.5.2 Dynamism of Christopraxis

Christopraxis finds its fullest meaning here. Jesus lives, 'as a dynamic event (as Christopraxis) not solely in memory or biblical text but as personal Spirit that can be experienced' (Root 2014b:92).

It is helpful again to define Christological praxis in continuation of this discussion. When speaking of praxis, as was mentioned previously in Chapter 5, Swinton (2000:11, 15) would claim that we are

> referring to a practical form of knowledge which generates actions through which the church community lives out its beliefs (holistic, theory-laden action). . . . In this sense, praxis finds its biblical foundation in the actualization of John 3:21: 'But whoever lives by the truth comes into the light, so that it may be plainly seen that what he has done has been done through God'. . . . Praxis then reveals theology in a very tangible form. In this sense, *actions are themselves theological* and as such are open to theological reflection and critique. Thus the praxis of the church is, in fact, the embodiment of its theology.

Paul tells followers of Jesus that 'we have the mind of Christ (1 Cor. 2.16), affirming this important way that one experiences the Spirit. Paul provides further insight when he calls the Church 'the body of Christ' (I Cor. 12.27), individual members acting as his hands and feet, under the influence of his mind. This insight describes one significant experience of true Christopraxis—the mind of Christ and the body of Christ engaged as his presence in the world. The presence and reality of Christ in the world must be known by the Christopraxis of the church through physical presence that builds a relationship with others. There are no other alternatives. 'If the church is to be the redemptive presence and power in the world that God intends, it will be where the Spirit of Christ crosses the boundary and breaks through the wall that separates us from each other, and where the world and the church live separate lives' (Anderson 2001:184-85). This is Christopraxis in its truest sense and involves a recalibrating back to Jesus as it is extending the movement that Jesus originated into community. It is incarnational, going 'deep into culture and speaking meaningfully from within it' (Hirsch 2010:11), as a 'contrast community and a catalyst for socio-economic transformation' (Osmer 2008:192).

5.5.3 Incarnational presence as Christopraxis

Incarnational presence as Christopraxis will open up opportunities for relational engagement. Christopraxis is participation in the being of God, for to do so is to join Him by entering into His ministry. For Anderson, God in Jesus Christ is

> a subject of action, not merely a source of knowledge. This action is the revealing of God's being in the action of ministry. Christopraxis is the assertion that God is first and foremost a minister, revealing God's self (revelation) for the sake of union with humanity (reconciliation) (Root 2014b: 89).

Missional theology and ecclesiology, led by the presence of Jesus through his Spirit, will focus on a developing contextual praxis, engaging carefully and reflectively. This contextual praxis is the methodology of practical theology. In this way, the practice of the church does not look the same in all communities. Instead, the missional praxis of God is revealed contextually in communities as a movement of the Holy Spirit through followers of Jesus as they love God and love their neighbour. Discernment is key to this missional theology and may manifest itself in various engagements according to context.

It is key in efforts to combat poverty and all other forms of injustice to change the way people see themselves. The message of the cross and the humanity of Jesus are crucial elements in this effort, meaning that the evangelical movement can play a significant role in bringing about this change. Independence for those in poverty or suffering from other forms of injustice is not the ultimate goal, but the goal is interdependence, a conscious movement towards maximising participation by encouraging networking at the human scale. Emphasis is on achieving this at the community level, meaning that the church as a community role player is strategically positioned for this local engagement. It is a 'process in constant motion' that should be applicable across all contexts as it maximises inclusion through active participation (Max-Neef 1991:12), allowing and requiring local ownership of the developmental processes.

5.6 Understanding context

It is important for the evangelical movement to understand the context within local communities, analyse the situation, gather facts and do necessary research that will guide engagement. This understanding is vital for mission. What is God specifically calling the church to do? The evangelical community has the same mandate as all Christ followers—look with a 'living hope' into local communities knowing that this hope is firmly established through the work of Jesus Christ:

> Blessed be the God and Father of our Lord Jesus Christ! According to his great mercy, he has caused us to be born again to a living hope through the resurrection of Jesus Christ from the dead, (1 Pt. 1.3) (ESV).

As ambassadors of hope the evangelical community needs,

> the wisdom to constantly evaluate, assess, analyse and read the signs of the times. (It) needs the courage to call the statements and actions of political leaders into question when they go astray and implement systems that favour just a few. (It) must serve as the moral conscience of society and ask the deeper justice questions and challenge structures that perpetuate inequalities in society (Pillay 2015:7).

The mission is God's mission. One must, 'become restless in the face of godlessness, injustices, immorality, violence and poverty' (Pillay 2015:7).

Multiple reasons indicate why the evangelical movement has

a mandate to engage in poverty alleviation efforts as a movement of the gospel. Arguments from James 2 identify as error the dualism suggested by a faith separated from accompanying works, meaning that the claim of faith without works is, according to James, the claim to no faith. As has been previously mentioned, this is a forceful argument against dualism. Additionally, historical precedent from early evangelicalism would also indicate that care for those in need was an essential part of evangelical mission. Although one could argue that more recent evidence from the evangelical movement would suggest that ministering to spiritual needs was primary, there is no indication from Scripture to support this while there is overwhelming evidence to refute such an understanding.

5.7 Understanding mission

But if one remains unconvinced by what has been a careful attempt to detail these arguments, other practical reasons identify the church and, by association the evangelical movement, the most likely candidate to bring about needed community transformation. In South Africa, the Church is the strongest and most influential non-governmental organisation (NGO), reaching, on average, 63% of the Christian population weekly with a growing consensus that the overwhelming endemic problems faced in South African society cannot be dealt with effectively without the assistance or even leadership of the church.[128] The crisis 'is economic—poverty and its gruesome consequences: hunger, sickness, landless, homeless. [T]he poor are trapped in a vicious circle, grappling with moral, social, physical crises...' (Coene in Dames 2010:4). This is a crisis ideally suited for the evangelical community in response to Scriptural mandate.

Sampson (2009:134) writes that the 'greatest challenge for all South Africans lies in the appropriate readdressing of poverty and the quality of transformation.' This readdressing would surely help to identify Christopraxis for the South African evangelical community. It would be a missional movement of the gospel that rightly engages society. It is 'not about bringing people into the church, it is about taking the church into the world—to transform the world to reflect the glory of God and God's kingdom or sovereign rule' (Pillay 2015:2).

> The church must be a sample of the kind of humanity within which, for example, economic and racial differences are surmounted. Only then will she have anything to say to the society that surrounds her about how those differences must be dealt with (Yoder 1972:154).

It is important to locate such activities as emanating from within the structures of a local church context. David Bosch (2011:389) is clear that 'the church is both a theological and a sociological entity, an inseparable union of the divine and the dusty.' For development work, the church comes with contradictory challenges that can be difficult to assimilate in one's mind. Bosch (2011:389) explains what this can feel like:

> We can be utterly disgusted, at times, with the earthliness of the church, yet we can also be transformed, at times, with the awareness of the divine in the church. It is *this* church, ambiguous in the extreme, which is "missionary by its very nature," the pilgrim people of God, "in the nature of" a sacrament, sign, and instrument, and "a most sure seed of unity, hope and salvation for the whole human race.'

The church, though representing a sign of the kingdom of God, is not itself that kingdom. The church is successful in being a sign only to the extent that the Holy Spirit enables this to happen. There is a transformational process that is already underway that points toward the kingdom, often evident in the form of a local church or churches. Development work does not begin when the development professional enters the community, but God has been at work in some form through this living sign of His kingdom. Even when considered a distraction or an obstruction to transformation, Newbigin (1954:20-21) reminds one to ponder the mission:

> It is surely a fact of inexhaustible significance that what our Lord left behind him was not a book or a creed, nor a system of thought, nor a rule of life, but a visible community. . . . He committed the entire work of salvation to that community. . . . The church does not depend for its existence upon our understanding it or faith in it.

The church must be what it is intended to be, playing the role in community that keeps it engaged, not relegated to the edge of community influence. Everyone is in need of transformation, everyone is on a journey, whether you are trapped in an impoverished community or a development practitioner. It is, therefore, necessary to work towards a relationship of mutual accountability with local churches as it takes both the gospel and the community context seriously. The church has a significant role to play. It can be,

> the servant of its community, harnessing the wind and wood and water into technologies that make the world a little more habitable, or singing with the rest of creation the wonder of existence, or working side by side with all people of good will toward a better social order. If the church is to lead at all, it is in serving; in applying the creative energies released in Christ towards the stewardship of creation and the bringing of fallen structures closer to God's original purposes (Maggay 1994:72).

This role is a high calling. When the church is at its best, it is a Godly source of value dissemination within the community. While it is not the only source, people who are reading and living the word and engaging in community under the power of the Holy Spirit are demonstrating Christopraxis as they work for its benefit. Newbigin (1989:139) again helps one here:

> The major role of the church in relationship to

the great issues of justice and peace will not be in its formal pronouncement, but in its continually nourishing and sustaining men and women who will act responsibly as believers in the course of their secular duties as citizens.

This role helps to ensure sustainability. Church partnerships either into community or within community serve to empower the overall engagement. Over twenty five years after the peaceful transition to democracy in South Africa, the challenges are clear with the understanding that it is an 'all hands on deck' moment. Working together across all types of boundaries has never been more important. Erasmus, Hendriks and Mans (2004:2) provide a workable framework for communities that is useful in assisting church collaborations, with slight modification to apply it fully into a local church context. The church should:

- Strive to develop sustainable communities
- To have sustainable communities, we have to network our resources and develop a holistic approach;
- Universities (Churches) should play an integral part in interdisciplinary co-operation in the process of developing theory and methodology that is applied in its teaching, research and service.

This framework requires expertise that may be outside of a local church's ordinary capabilities. But there are resources within communities, universities or other developmental agencies that can provide useful assistance. Whatever methodology is created, to deal effectively with poverty the approach must include local community involvement. Several questions must be considered:

1. What information is needed that will improve both the functioning of churches and the daily lives of people in the community?
2. How will information gathered be made accessible to people in the community?
3. How can community role players be engaged

both in the planning and execution of the initiative?
4. How can the methodology contribute to a process which forms part of the mobilising of the community for change?
5. How does the information acquired empower those involved to transform their community? (Adapted from Erasmus, Hendriks & Manns 2004:3-4).

5.8 Implementation

A research paradigm most suited for such engagement is *Participatory Action Research (PAR)*. It was developed during the 1970's and 1980's alongside the well-known paradigms of quantitative and qualitative research and was rooted epistemologically in critical theory. PAR will be explained in detail and modelled using a church-initiated project in Chapter 7. The strength of PAR rests in the shift in power from the researcher to a co-ownership between researcher and the subject of the study. The researcher and those being researched are partners in the study, making this tool the initial intervention in the process of transformation. The partnership is essential: 'The greater proportion of the target community claiming for itself ownership of a given project, the smaller likelihood of the project dying an early death or gradually sinking into the sand' (Schutte [s.a.]:7).

5.8.1 Human-Scale development

Key to the study is a needs analysis based on principles developed by Manfred Max-Neef in Human Scale Development (1991). For Max-Neef (1991:97), while our societies have become increasingly complex, our theories of society, whether social or economic, have become increasingly simplistic.' The approach is valuable in that it can be applied across all ranges of society irrespective of income, education or any other defining factor. It has shifted the discussion around poverty in a subtle way that has profound implications. For example, if a wealthy property owner is burgled, he is living with a poverty: his need for protection is not being satisfied. He has *a poverty* rather than he is living *in poverty*. Poverty is no longer a vague descriptor around one's sense of being: it is simply the lack of a satisfier for a specific need or a combination of needs, making it more contained and easier to address. One must then put *satisfiers* in place to ensure that the need is addressed, which is much different than an economistic view of poverty as insufficient income or utility.

One other dimension that Max-Neef (1991:19) adds to his interpretation of poverty is worth noting. He writes that 'poverties are not only poverties. Much more than that, each poverty generates pathologies. This is the crux of the discourse.' This central component of Human Scale Development is key to understanding the long-term impact of a poverty or poverties within a family or community. If fundamental needs remain unmet over an extended period, then poverty in one form or another will result, leading to a pathology which can only be addressed by radical engagement. Such poverty requires healing and may take extended intervention based upon a long term commitment. Sugden (1999:246) notes that:

> People cannot fulfil God's purpose for them if they have no sense of worth or of identity. Without identity or worth they will be prey to the idea (often fostered by others) that they deserve no more than the poverty and suffering that is their lot. They will have no hope for anything better.

It is important for churches to consider the nature of the role that is such a vital part of community transformation. Poverty profoundly alters one's sense of identity: what one is and what one is intended to be.

Additionally, what is important for Max-Neef is that development happens through important social actors that can be strengthened. The goal is to maximise widespread participation. These 'actors should organize horizontal networks, undertake mutually supportive action, articulate individual and group practices and this develops shared projects' (Max-Neef 1991:67). They can be mutually supportive and are therefore more likely to survive, ultimately serving each other to reach a higher quality of life. The model is one of the multiple micro-organisations that are decentralised. Max-Neef(1991:67) argues that it is necessary to, '(t)hink small and act small, but in as many places as possible. . . . Everything that can be done at local levels is what should be done at local levels.' For church partnerships, such essential collaboration serves greater kingdom purposes and appears to be a useful model for community engagement.

5.8.2 Applying social capital for impact

So what does this mean in relation to local church engagement in a South African context? Churches have social capital and are seen as a critical, even sought after role player in social development processes. The religious sector is seen 'as a 'special agent' and generator of social capital and, hence, the state (and other development role players) should capitalise on this opportunity' to collaborate in community developmental activities (Winkler 2008: 2104). The church, as this repository of social capital, has been promoted as a 'missing link' in development by the World Bank and the Development Bank of Southern Africa.

But the church has not used this available social capital to significantly impact the communities in need. Charles Elliot (1987) identified that 'a large gap exists between the theological principles and writings on development, on the one hand, and the actions of the churches, on the other.' For Elliot (1987), the Church's developmental model is stuck in relief mode. He argues that 'the churches' modern enthusiasm for development starts with the starving baby. . . . Christians are more easily persuaded that the gospel demands action in an emergency than that it demands a constant commitment to the poor and oppressed.'

5.9 Transformational mission

Effective community development led by the evangelical movement would seek to be transformative in focus with two goals: changed people and changed relationships. It would find its source in a local church that is missional and eager to see its community transformed. And it is the power of the Holy Spirit at the heart of this process that gives a restored sense of identity that brings lasting hope. This hope is Christo-praxis as Christ followers move into desperate communities to engage poverty as a movement of the gospel.

God places the church at the centre of his purposes for the world. And although God does surely work in redemptive ways outside of the church, this ought to happen to the fullest extent in and through the church. But what if the church is not interested in social action? For David Bosch (2011:381), 'since God is a missionary God, God's people are a missionary people.' God's intention and concern for the world stand central to the church's purpose in the world. For a church to see itself outside of caring about mission and engaging issues around social justice is to see itself out of God's mission.

The church is an agent of transformation infused with power. A dualistic stance that divides faith from works is not only contrary to Scripture but is powerless. This agency is a significant role, one that cannot be handled sufficiently by any other organisation. And one of the key functions of the church, as identified by Myers, is as a servant and source of encouragement of what God intends and what God offers, not as a condemner or judge. In this way the church may be regarded as the 'church with others—journeying with the poor, the marginalised, suffering and oppressed through and in their circumstances' (Bowers 2005:56).

There are elements underlying poverty that are fundamentally spiritual at their core. Broken relationships and damaged identities are challenges to God's intention for creation. Therefore, poverty by its very nature requires a spiritual response. And one cannot be an agent of transformation without 'a fundamental undergirding at the spiritual level' (Christian 2008:22). At its core, transformation is about defining the nature of the spiritual since it shapes and moulds all of life (attitudes, relationships, behaviour and worldview). Long term sustainability and empowerment will not exist without addressing the spiritual.

Transformation is more than evangelism plus social action. It is the analysis of poverty that recognises the all-pervading nature of spiritualities and a model of transformation that is fundamentally spiritual in nature. This is a critical understanding. For Myers (2008: xii), the dualism within the community development context was faulty. He writes,

> In the early days, we simplistically and incorrectly understood holism to mean that Christian witness was something to be added to the development mix to make it complete—just another sector, a wedge in the development pie. Over time we realized that this conceptualization was flawed. It implied that all the other development sectors had nothing to do with spiritual things. We were treating spiritual work as a separate sector of life.

This dichotomy has been deeply ingrained in Western culture and the church. On Sunday morning or during devotional readings or prayer one operates in the spiritual world: the rest of the week one operates in the physical world, 'unwittingly acting like functional atheists' (Myers 2008:xiii).

Lesslie Newbigin in his book '*The Gospel in a Pluralist Society*' has argued how this separation between the physical and spiritual realms describes the thinking and behaviour of modern society, which includes the church. There is a spiritual world covering an arena of sacred revelation which is known by believing. In the real world, we can know things with certainty proven by facts—we see, feel, and touch through scientific observation. Faith and religion are part of the spiritual world which is an interior, private place. In the real world, explanations are provided by reason and science which are dispersed in an exterior, public place. The result is that values are left to personal choice as they have no relevance in the public sphere. The facts are all on which one needs to agree. The church has bought into this system and has allowed itself to be relegated to the spiritual world while the state and other human institutions have taken control over what happens in 'real' life.

This sense of irrelevance explains how one has come to understand evangelism as being unrelated to community development.

> Loving God is spiritual work, and loving neighbors takes place in the material world. So evangelism (restoring people's relationship with God) is spiritual work, while social action (restoring just economic, social and political relationships among people) is not. This false dichotomy leads Christians to believe that God's redemptive work takes place only in the spiritual realm, while the world is left, seemingly, to the devil. . . . The fact that the Word became flesh explodes the claim that the spiritual and physical can be separated meaningfully (Myers 2008:xiii-xv).

Prayer and fasting are the tools for this social action, but presence is the means. The church can navigate this split by becoming the servant church, 'a community that does not live for itself but is deeply involved in the concerns of its neighbourhood' (Newbigin 1989:229).

6 Conclusion

There is historical precedence outlining the evangelical movement's active engagement with communities and households around them to meet their fundamental needs, including their physical needs. Evangelicals have been motivated by Scripture, a compassion for others in need, and the desire to spread the gospel to the world and it has been argued here that it must return to its historical roots to be truly evangelical and obedient to the claims of Jesus.

Additionally, the socio-rhetorical examination of James Chapter 2 painted a compelling argument that mandates care for those in need. James uses examples from Scripture and structures his arguments in such a way as to indicate that a claim to faith without corresponding acts of obedience is the claim to dead faith. James is fighting against this dualistic mindset arguing that to simply believe—spiritual assent—is enough. This belief is not only error but is dangerous for one who might rely on it for salvation (see James 2.14).

One participates in the ministry of Jesus through the power of the Spirit. This is Christopraxis, God's strategy 'for the sake of the world' (Anderson 2001:203). To separate evangelism and social justice as individual activities from which to select tears apart humanity and contradicts the incarnation, a serious charge which must not be taken lightly for one truly seeking to follow Jesus.

Overwhelming challenges are facing local communities in South Africa. The evangelical movement has largely ignored its mandate due to incorrect theological understanding or through disobedience. Additionally, many Christ followers feel overwhelmed and unprepared to engage properly. This feeling has hindered the movement of the gospel. Regardless, evangelicals—and all Christ followers—have a significant role to play in the transformation of society. Correctly defined missional theology, led by the Spirit, will seek to develop contextual praxis in a careful and reflective way.

Chapter 7 will outline a contextual model for community engagement based upon recognised developmental practices.

The purpose for discussing this model is to guide and empower the church as it enters South African communities in deep crisis, confronting poverty as a missional movement of the gospel.

CHAPTER SEVEN

THE ROLE OF THE EVANGELICAL MOVEMENT IN THE TRANSFORMATION OF SOCIETY

We seem to have retreated into religion as private practice rather than infusing political action with spiritual understanding (Ramphele 2008:20).

1 Introduction

The focus of this book has been to engage the modern evangelical movement around its existing missional focus in light of two basic themes: the claims of Scripture and historical precedent found within earlier examples of the evangelical movement. The second chapter of James has been examined using socio-rhetorical interpretive methods to guide future praxis, providing the Scriptural support necessary to urge the evangelical church toward mission within impoverished communities. The stakes are high in the South African context. Those with the opportunity and mandate to engage must do so with urgency.

This chapter will serve as a transition into a predominately South Africa context in two ways. First, to describe the historical context and the ways that the South African church has been involved in societal renewal. There have been pockets of mission engagement led by various communities from within the Church, although the extent of its overall undertaking has not gone nearly far enough. There are reasons for this shortfall that will be explored. Second, this chapter will describe a church-based model as an approach for the evangelical movement and the greater Church to consider in the current fight against poverty in South African communities. Human Scale Development principles have been applied into a theological framework of Christopraxis as the faith community engages with society. The research model, although discussed previously in other work,[129] represents an approach that may be helpful for the evangelical movement to contemplate and apply into one's local context. It appears here to illustrate how such an approach can be structured and implemented.

2 The Continuing Crisis

There have been various attempts by the modern Church to engage poverty, but they have often had limited or unexpected results. This section will consider briefly the findings of the first and second Carnegie Inquiries[130] in an effort to interrogate these findings and reflect upon how this played out in the South African Church context and in society. The Church realised that it had a role to play in the alleviation of poverty, although this was focused only upon impoverished white people.

It is also important to realise how the historical context of the South African church and its 'activist' activities, even though at times misguided, coupled with the fresh realisation of its role as a societal change agent, helped some structures within the Church unite to play a key role in engaging poverty and in the fight against apartheid. This is important to remember.

The following discussion will describe these inquiries and put forward an approach prescribing defining current praxis for transformational development to be directed by the Church. The role of the Church is understood in this discussion to include the evangelical community.

2.1 Carnegie 1 & 2

The president of the Carnegie Corporation of New York visited the Union of South Africa in 1927. This visit motivated a request initiated by the Dutch Reformed Church[131] to investigate the plight of poor, white South Africans. The church and rulers of the country were at that time quite concerned about the growing population of poor white people who lived predominately in rural areas.

> The Commission performed its task well and emerged at the end of several years with a number of reports that spelled out the dimensions of poverty amongst white (particularly Afrikaans-speaking) South Africans. . . . The failure of the Commission lay in the extent to which the limitation of its concern to whites only meant that its findings were used to promote strategies for improving the position of poor whites, often at the expense of poor blacks (Wilson and Ramphele: 1989: x).

Blacks and coloureds were seen as an 'economic hindrance' to the economic progression of the white population. The population growth of the black and coloured sections of the population was also viewed as alarming. These factors, combined with skill levels that were on par with those of many poor whites, were seen as both economically threatening and psychologically demoralising for the poor white. Job 'reservation' was proposed as a solution to the problem. 'The poor white problem receded as many of these findings were incorporated into National Party policies which formed, in part, the sociological and ideological motivation for apartheid and its subsequent policies' (Bowers 2012b:207). By the time of *Carnegie II* more than 50 years later, poverty was 'deep and widespread . . . (with) the degree of inequality as great as in any other country in the world'.... To uproot poverty would require 'radical action' (Wilson & Ramphele 1989:5).

2.1.1 Challenge to the Church in *Carnegie I*

The church[132] was challenged in 1923 by Dr. D.F. Malan regarding the condition of the poor whites within its communities: 'if the church wishes to say to the paralysed poor white: "your sins are forgiven," it must also be prepared to tell him "Rise up and walk"' (Boesak 1984:8). *Carnegie I* helped the church to redefine its thinking in regards to social justice, although its focus was on 'poor whites':

> There are many problems, but the point above all which should appeal to our Christian humanity and sense of justice is the fact that the poor white has no court of appeal . . . he is exploited, but has no refuge. . . he must put up with starvation wages. . . . he realizes that he is unwelcome in his own fatherland. This country is his only home. . . . Is it a wonder then that such people sink to despair? The wonder is that they do not resort to desperate deeds . . . .' (Boesak 1984:7).

The church took this challenge very seriously. Their many welfare institutions provided for the 'orphans, sick, widowed handicapped and aged. . . .' (Bowers 2012a:4). The general understanding was that, '(t)he working classes should be made to feel that in the church they have a champion for justice and mercy' (Boesak 1984:8). The church's involvement in poverty upliftment was viewed as having great value. However, its emphasis on activities to engage poverty, as was supported by the findings of *Carnegie I*, became focused almost exclusively upon benefitting the white population to the detriment of blacks. The justification for apartheid was promoted, at least in part, by the church.

Nevertheless, the church was not considered 'fully alive' to the vast social challenges highlighted in *Carnegie I*. One of the most prominent reasons given for the church's inadequate engagement with the poor—which still resonates as an accusation against the evangelical movement today—is that the Church has in the past aimed too exclusively at preparing its people for the hereafter, and has therefore bestowed too little attention on the amelioration of present conditions. It taught the poor to resign themselves to want and poverty, in the hope of better conditions hereafter, instead of actively assisting them to a better and higher life here (Albertyn & Rothman 1932:58).

Although Albertyn and Rothman acknowledge the dualism existing in the Church as considered incongruent with the message of Christ, they did not go far enough. It was only a partial solution as the focus of 'missionary' activity was almost exclusively on 'poor whites.' Although it was understood that if the church refused to engage with 'social conditions under which people were living,' it would lose 'influence and authority with regards to the great social questions of the country' (Albertyn & Rothman 1932:58), it failed to truly engage with society in regards to the deep racism that existed.

2.1.2 Challenge to the Church in *Carnegie II*

The *Carnegie II Inquiry* took place against the backdrop of what was considered a successful *Carnegie I*. For Boesak (1984:9), what was most needed was not 'more charity or emergency aid, but a qualitatively different society.' He weighed the enthusiastic engagement of the church in its response to the need for social upliftment for poor whites against the apathy present at the time of *Carnegie II* for a similar engagement on behalf of impoverished blacks:

One cannot help but notice the important role played by the white Dutch Reformed Church in the Carnegie Commission on Poverty. It was very much part of the initiative, it helped to define a new relationship with the state in coping with the problem of poverty, and in the process, it defined a new role for itself as agent for change in society' (Boesak 1984:6).

The churches were urged to take political action calling for 'the abolition of pass laws, influx control, land ownership laws[133] and therefore the improvement of family life' (Bowers 2012a:7). However, the role of the church during this time was often seen as quite ambiguous. Interestingly, the church (including those outside of the DRC community) was again accused of dualistic practices that spiritualised the gospel, characterised by Nash (in Bowers 2012a:8) as 'directing hope towards the life hereafter and (having) the same effects as Valium ... tend(ing) to buttress rather than challenge the status quo.'

2.2 The Kairos Document and Evangelical Witness in South Africa

Two significant documents emerged near the end of apartheid in South Africa. *The Kairos Document* and *Evangelical Witness in South Africa* both described the situation in the country as 'a crisis.' *The Kairos Document* (1988:7)[134] described in its first paragraph the extent of the crisis that was shaking the foundations of the Nation and looking to become even more threatening. This crisis brought about a time of reckoning for the country, signalling a moment of truth 'not only for apartheid but also for the church and all other faiths and religions' (The Kairos Document 1988:7). Similarly, under the heading 'Crisis' at the beginning of its first chapter, The *Evangelical Witness in South Africa* referred to a 'socio-political crisis.' It recounted that 'the death and injury toll in the townships has continued to escalate ... while state repression and harassment have continued unabated' (Concerned Evangelicals 1987:4). The document continued by stating on behalf of 'concerned evangelicals' in the country:

> Called as we are to minister good news, we find ourselves in the midst of bloodshed and death, of increasing bitterness and polarisation, and of rising anger in the townships. Our proclamation, there-

fore, has been swallowed up by the cries of the poor and oppressed that it is now even impossible to hold conventional evangelistic campaigns in this war situation. These voices have become so loud that it has become impossible to hear the church preach (Concerned Evangelicals 1987:4).

These documents described the profound social crisis that defined South African society prior to the end of apartheid. Almost 30 years after these documents were produced, the voices of those in intense poverty remain so loud that it may be still considered impossible to hear the church preach.

The Kairos Southern Africa document was written to the ANC by church leaders before the Centenary celebrations in 2012. There is a telling quote from the document that identifies the failure of the church to make any lasting progress in the fight against poverty after the demise of apartheid. There was a prophetic call to the church to fight against the evils of apartheid that seemingly ended at the birth of democracy in 1994.

Unfortunately, many Christians interpreted this call as a call to only become involved in the anti-apartheid cause, and when this cause came to an end, the involvement of many Christians in reversing social and economic injustice in South Africa also came to an end. Many Christians lapsed back into the default position of "Church theology" and thus the decline of progressive Christian involvement in the nurturing and formation of the new South Africa began (Kairos 2012:9).

The church has had an integral relationship with social delivery in South Africa going back to colonialism. Not only was the church instrumental in building the first infrastructure for schools and hospitals, but it also played a key role in the opposition to Apartheid and remains highly regarded by the state and civil society as a major player in welfare delivery. However, as has been previously discussed, the church has not always had a positive influence regarding social transformation, at times supporting and offering theological justification for Apartheid.

What has emerged from this discussion is the value placed upon the role of the church in addressing issues of poverty by 'the government (during the time of Carnegie I) and civil society (at the time of Carnegie II) . . . as the church's identity, loyalty, history, and people were a source of strength and initiative' (Bowers 2012a: 9). Recent studies confirm that the church can

> mobilise far more people than any other social movement and reach all sectors of society, is better positioned than the state to address issues of moral decay, has the greater level of trust than any other institution in society and contributes more than the state to social welfare (see Krige in Bowers-Du Toit 2012a:9).

As an institute considered trustworthy, it 'could be viewed by policymakers and other strategists as an important channel of opportunity to enter the respective communities and establish contact with the local people' (see Swart 2010 in Bowers-Du Toit 2012a:9).

However, when asked to comment on the role of the church since the advent of Democracy, many felt that the churches' role had lessened in comparison to 'the activist role of the churches before 1994 (which) helped to oppose and in the end, topple the Apartheid government' (see Erasmus in Bowers Du Toit 2012:209). Some felt that the church could play a more significant role in mobilising people as had been done in the past except now to address welfare problems faced by local communities. The church was becoming 'almost invisible, afraid to voice opinions on certain issues (which) makes them seem weak to the public' (see Erasmus in Bowers-Du Toit 2012b:209). Academics voice similar concerns, going as far as to state that the church seems to have 'moved to the margins' (see MacMaster in Bowers Du Toit 2012b:209). All of this presents a tremendous challenge to the church, which appears by all accounts to be able to play a significant role in addressing poverty but has thus far been unable or unwilling to do so.

2.3 Move to the margins

This 'move to the margins' may be the result of what has been suggested as a key challenge for the church: an inadequate theology that fails to engage its members. Poor theological underpinnings have contributed to the dualism that has plagued the church at various times in its history and retains sufficient strength in our current context. Other theological shortcomings are also apparent. In an interview with clergy and other church leaders in the Paarl WRIGP project,[135] Nadine Bowers-Du Toit (2012b:214) acknowledges that theology

> has a significant impact on the way the church engages with poverty and vulnerable groups both for "better" and for "worse". As "friends," praxis has the potentiality to be more effective as it engages with theologies that challenge the church to be more incarnational and address issues of self-worth and vocation. As "foes" biblical motivation that is valid, yet remains unexamined, may hinder the church in exercising the kind of praxis that moves beyond charity or the boundaries of their own community or congregation.

For Bowers-Du Toit (2012b:214), there remains a gap that exists in the discourse that fails to move beyond the 'liberation paradigm or the current pragmatic debates in South Africa.' Theological training is key. Some of this training deficit is the result of the absence of formal instruction for clergy on theology and development. It is also the result of a failure to provide grass-roots level workshops or conferences that explore a biblical basis for development with the real-world application into current local contexts. Engaging texts that consider God's desire for justice and concern for the poor and marginalised could become a framework for sermons, Bible studies, and other useful resources.

This process is a function of discipleship. By claiming to be a Christ follower, it is assumed that one will make decisions to follow clear Scriptural teaching. It is also important to set about community engagement in a useful way. Undergirding the discussion in this chapter is a look at Christopraxis from a structured theology that leans heavily upon a mission framework. Andrew Root (2014a:102) helps guide one here:

> The Spirit unveils God's ministry as God's being in Jesus Christ (revelation) to and through human experience (encounter), calling the human agent into ontological union with God, through Christ, connecting the human spirit with God's own Spirit (reconciliation). Yet, this connection comes not through a magical transcendental state but by a calling of the human agent into ministry (as mission)—to swing open the doors and preach (Acts 2), to feed the widows (Acts 6) and orphans, to go to a friend with a word of comfort, to feed the homeless, to listen and not talk, to leave the kitchens of the powerful and cook comfort food for campers. Union with God comes to us through the act of ministry itself that takes us into divine encounter.

This is quite different from giving bread to the hungry so that they can hear and quickly respond to the proclamation of the gospel, although giving bread to those in need is certainly necessary according to Scripture. But by only giving one bread to stop hunger means that the one hungry will be hungry again tomorrow. The intention here is to encourage the evangelical movement toward focused behaviour that brings change to the lives of people trapped in poverty that is sustainable and empowering. This is a mission agenda with a development focus that recognises that it is insufficient to 'give fish to the hungry . . . . It is also necessary to teach the hungry how to fish, to help them acquire a fishing rod, to ensure equal access to the fishing waters and to address the problem of overfishing' (Conradie 2005:6). Although the New Testament gives little explicit teaching on evangelistic or developmental *methods*, it has, instead, called 'the church to be a caring, inclusive and distinctive community of reconciliation reaching out in love to the world' (Hughes 2009:184). To accomplish this calling requires that the evangelical movement, as a subset of the church, steps into activities of poverty alleviation, acknowledging that it must have a long range view if it is to bring about true transformation. 'Our response to this Christopraxis is not to harvest spiritual experiences like a religious consumer, but rather to be led by the Spirit to participate in Jesus' own praxis, to act in ministry ourselves' (Root 2014a:93). Ministry is not meant as taking on

> clerical or institutional functions, but a relational, personal, and embodied (even emotive) encounter of love and care, a willingness to share in the other, to join in the concrete experiences of homelessness, imprisonment, and hunger, to enter the experiences of suffering for the sake of participating in the transformation toward new life (Root 2014a: Preface).

This is the role for the Church as the mission of Jesus in communities in need.

3 Discipleship for Social Responsibility

The people of God are called to give expression to his redemptive work throughout their lives, which impacts everything. The challenges that this brings are formidable, but it is from within this framework that the evangelical movement must engage with poverty. How does one call the Church and the evangelical movement to engage? Leadership must comprehend 'the nature of these challenges and offer a vision of formation adequate to the task of discipling the church and its members for a time such as ours' (Hunter 2010:226). This vision is nothing more or less than the dogged pursuit of the

'Great Commission.' It is the task of making disciples, seeking to be conformed to the image of Christ, having the 'mind of Christ,' serving as the 'body of Christ.' But how does one understand this task of formation?

3.1 Spiritual formation

It is sometimes assumed that spiritual formation will occur as an outgrowth of conversion functioning as a natural process that is guided by the Holy Spirit. However, Jesus stated that making disciples involves, 'teaching them (converts) to observe all that that I (Jesus) commanded you' (Mt. 28.20a). In a similar way, the Apostle Paul describes mature believers as those who would be 'filled with the knowledge of his will in all spiritual wisdom and understanding, so as to walk in a manner worthy of the Lord, fully pleasing to him, bearing fruit in every good work and increasing in the knowledge of God' (Col. 1.9-10). This formation as mature disciples is concerned about developing faithfulness in all of life. Paul also 'proclaimed [Christ], warning everyone and teaching everyone with all wisdom, that we may present everyone mature in Christ' (Col. 1.28). He 'toil(ed), struggling with all (the) energy that he powerfully works within me' (Col 1.29). This process of 'making disciples' requires the difficult work of training and teaching and warning Christ followers with wisdom to journey with Christ in a way that makes them prepared for any calling or service requested by him.

The problem in this process, and where it breaks down, could be that one's faith is weak or inadequate. There are certainly instances where this may be true. However, what is more likely is that one has been formed by the *'larger post-Christian culture*, a culture whose habits of life less and less resemble anything like the vision of human flourishing provided by the life of Christ and witness of scripture' (Hunter 2010:227). Christians have not been formed 'in all wisdom' in a way that would help them 'rise to the demands of faithfulness in a time such as ours, "bearing fruit in every good work"' (Hunter 2010:227).

To achieve formation—a holistic formation that seeks the renewal of all aspects of life—requires a culture that does, in fact, embody these things. If the evangelical movement does not have a culture that expresses this vision for renewal that impacts everything, then it will not be possible to 'make disciples' capable of facilitating this work. 'In formation, it is the culture and community that gives shape to it that is the key' (Hunter 2010:227). Healthy formation is not possible unless there is a healthy culture embedded within the community.

It starts with what one would consider conversion to truly be. A genuine conversion to Christ can be understood as hearing the call of Christ to find reconciliation between both God and man through him. This reconciliation brings transformation. In the context of South African community, conversion is lived out in a passionate concern 'about the deepest problems of this context, which include the search for identity and dignity in our multi-cultural context and the search for sustainable lifestyles in which such an identity exists' (van Niekerk 2014c:419). These deep problems engage all aspects of humanity—physical, spiritual, and emotional. Conversion yields fruit which desires true reconciliation in all of these areas for others.

3.1.1 Bringing *shalom*

What makes formation for the evangelical community the primary focus leading missional engagement into impoverished communities? Impoverished communities suffer from a series of broken relationships. Although this intentional focus on formation may seem uncomfortable and unnecessary to most Christians and most churches, there must be a vision for this task that has a clear goal that leads this undertaking. The vision for the evangelical community and for all communities within which one undertakes mission is the vision for *shalom*, a vision that brings 'order and harmony, fruitfulness and abundance, wholeness, beauty, joy and well-being' (Hunter 2010:228). Before relationship between God and man was broken in the garden, this was God's intention in creation and God's promise for the end of time.

The entire narrative of Scripture centres around how God's intended *shalom* was broken and the great lengths that have been undertaken to bring about restoration. The details of this narrative—the Fall, its consequences and God's response —give the backdrop to the narrative. It also helps one understand why God acts on behalf of the poor, the orphan, the widow and the stranger. These groups lack a protector who can stand up for them against the powerful, so he calls his people to co-labour with him to establish this *shalom*. This co-labouring is mission by its very nature, bringing healing to the evangelical community and then to other broken communities throughout South Africa. Hunter (2010:229) helps one here:

> In the most momentous event in history, God became incarnate in Christ, not only to model shalom (by forgiving the sinner, feeding the hungry, healing the sick and infirm, raising the dead, loving the outsider, and caring for all in need) but, as St. Paul writes, to be "our shalom" (Eph. 2:14). The kingdom of God—the shalom of God—was at hand.

Until God inaugurates the new heaven and the new earth, his call is to all Christ followers, as individuals and communities, to conform to Christ and express with every facet of their lives the *shalom* of God.

So what does this look like individually for Christ followers and then congregationally for the evangelical movement as a whole? Lesslie Newbigin would argue for a concept of conversion that cannot be separated from its sociological context, illustrating it with reference to the message of Moses and Aaron to the people of Israel in the house of bondage. They told the elders of Israel that God had seen their plight and was ready to lead them out of the house of slavery '. . . and the people believed . . . and bowed their heads and worshipped' (Ex 4.30-31). From that time onwards the people were facing the other way, comments Newbigin. Turning towards God is in itself turning away from slavery and undertaking the journey towards life (Newbigin 1969:94-95).

As Christians acknowledge the rule of God in all aspects their lives, their engagement with the world is a proclamation of the *shalom* that is still to come. When this rule is established in the hearts and souls and minds of believers in a way that reflects through their daily lives and into their spheres of influence, Christ is present, and he is glorified. His presence is Christopraxis as Jesus lives in community through his followers. Although this Christ-centred living may not fully bring about the kingdom of God, it is a benefit not only to the Christian community but also works towards the flourishing of all. However, the critical understanding here is that the focus is not on the transformation of the community, but is instead the result of caring for Someone more than the benefit that has been created.

> If there are benevolent consequences of our engagement with the world, in other words, it is precisely because it is **not** rooted in a desire to change the world for the better but rather because it is an expression of a desire to honor the creator of all goodness, beauty, and truth, a manifestation of our loving obedience to God, and a fulfilment of God's command to love our neighbor (Hunter 2010:234).

Evangelicals can comprehend all of the many reasons, some of which have been stated in this research, whether Scriptural, historical or even practical, for the certain responsibility to love one's neighbour. However, the more pertinent question for those in the evangelical community is, does one truly love

God?

> As a natural expression of its passion to honor God in all things and to love our neighbour as ourselves, the church and its people will challenge all structures that dishonour God, dehumanize people, and neglect or do harm to the creation (Hunter 2010:235).

For the evangelical community, the war against poverty in our local communities is a fight against all that mars and disfigures God's vision for the people he loves and has created in his image. It engages with him in the struggle against all that dishonours him. Redemption through Christ is a reaffirmation of the creation mandate that was declared by God as 'very good.' When God saves people through faith in Jesus Christ, they

> are not only being saved from their sins, they are saved in order to resume the tasks mandated at creation, the task of caring for and cultivating a world that honors God and reflects his character and glory. God indeed forgives people of their sin. As they are formed into disciples, more and more conforming to the image of Christ, they are liberated from the corrupting and oppressive power of sin, healed and renewed to the end that they might love God and enjoy him forever (Hunter 2010:236).

This process has massive implications for every aspect of life for Christ followers, impacting one's work, leisure, family life, and community engagement. Moreover, this is the motivation for daring mission activities to alleviate and seek to eliminate poverty in one's closest area of need. It is about learning to faithfully live the alternative reality of the kingdom of God within one's sphere of influence. Such intentional, motivated living will bring about transformed communities of transformers fit for any calling and any service.

3.1.2 Faithful presence within communities

What is hopefully clear by now is that good intentions are not sufficient to motivate action for the massive challenges entrenched within local South African communities. To bring about transformed communities ignited by a redemptive mission mandate, those within the evangelical community must practice Christopraxis, 'faithful presence within' communities of engagement. 'To participate in Christopraxis is to take on the form of and join Jesus' own action, which is to join the praxis of ministry itself' (Root 2014a:93). We take the 'divine being's form not in the way of ontological essence (this is not possible) but through action, by ourselves becoming ministers, joining God's being (ontology) not through shared essence but through concrete shared action of ministering' (Root 2014a:96).

Having set the motivational framework drawing together the 'why' of missional community involvement, the balance of this chapter will describe the 'how' in a way that guides praxis for the evangelical movement.

4 Developing an Approach for Mission

The previous section provided the necessary groundwork to form the motivational influence to engage the evangelical movement. God's honour is at stake and one engages in a way that struggles against all that brings dishonour to God and those that he loves. This section will concentrate on developing an approach for doing theology that seeks, ultimately, to engage the evangelical community in strategic, mission-focused activities in the fight against poverty in South African communities.

4.1 Defining the framework of the engagement

It is important to shape the process with the end in mind for one to construct a framework that will be useful for mission engagement in poverty-afflicted communities. For this research, the model will be based on a transformational development approach that is understood to be a method that facilitates

> God's vision of society to be actualized in all relationships, social, economic and spiritual, so that God's will may be reflected in human society and his love be experienced by all communities, especially the poor (Samuel in Sugden 2003:72).

This is God's better future in which everyone is invited to participate. God's kingdom is the future that has already invaded the past and present and is growing 'like leaven hidden in flour' (Mt. 13.33). Transformation broadly points to 'a number of changes that have to take place in many societies if poor people are to enjoy their rightful heritage in creation' (Samuel 1999:265). Basic development principles found in the broader debates have been retained in transformational development—values such as participation, self-reliance, and a people-centred influence. However, they are placed here within a different framework.[136]

4.1.1 Need for a transforming community

What does this mean for a church seeking to do mission in areas of extreme poverty? Any vision with a kingdom focus must include,

> a vibrant, growing living Christian community. . . . Such a church is in love with God and with all its neighbours, celebrating everything that is for life and being a prophetic voice, telling the truth about everything that is against or that undermines life (Myers 1999:115).

It is hard to imagine a transforming community without the benefit of a transforming church within its midst.[137] Newbigin (1995:91) helps one here. He writes

> God's will is to be done on earth. The call of Jesus to believe the good news of the impending kingdom leads at once to the call "Follow me." There can be no separation between believing and following, be-

tween faith and obedience. The prayer "Thy will be done" is in vain if it is not made visible in action for the doing of that will. Consequently, missions have never been able to separate the preaching of the gospel from action for God's justice.

Transformation from a Christian perspective is unique. As previously mentioned, sin has distorted and marred the genuine nature of all relationships so that poverty manifests in a number of spiritual and material forms. Therefore, the goal of human transformation is the 'discovery of true identity and vocation' (Myers 1999:122). It seeks to

> repel the evil structures that exist in the present cosmos and to institute through the mission of the church the values of the Kingdom over and against the values of the principalities and power of this world (Bragg 1987:39).

The evangelical movement must see itself as a 'transforming community' that witnesses against the evil and challenges it.

> Jesus challenged the power of evil consistently right to the end. At the very end, when the limit was reached, he surrendered, not to the power of evil, but into the hands of the Father. The final surrender is not defeat, but victory (Newbigin 1995:107-08).

Through Jesus, the coming of a new world order heralding the Kingdom of God breaks through. This event changes relationships on all levels: 'through him to reconcile to himself all things, whether on earth or in heaven, making peace by the blood of his cross' (Col. 1.20). Transformational development points to the supremacy of Christ over all things by recognising that through this reconciliation is the only hope for true *shalom*. Sugden (2005:5) states this in the following way:

> The calling of the church in the present age is to live by the life that is the resurrection life, to live the life of the Kingdom of God. The church lives this

life in forming communities of faith. Such communities proclaim Jesus and the resurrection in the face of death especially for those to who death is untimely; they proclaim Jesus and the resurrection in the face of the oppression of those who think that they are the lords of this world; they proclaim Jesus and the resurrection to those who are without hope in this world, not by promising escape to another world, but by the assurance of the recreation of this world by the just and loving creator in which they are invited by faith to be inheritors.

The evangelical movement, as a subset of the church, should be the bearer of reconciliation to communities in need. Transformational development seeks the restoration of these relationships with others and with God.

4.1.2 Process is important

Starting with the vision for engagement is not enough, however. The process by which one arrives is essential. There is a myriad of choices that can be taken, but not all of them are useful, and many of them can be destructive. A Christian process of change must begin with the acknowledgement that, at the most basic level, transformation takes place because God wants it and is enabling it to happen. Newbigin (1989:135) writes,

(I)t is the action of God, the triune God---of God the Father who is ceaselessly at work in all creation and in the hearts and minds of all human beings whether they acknowledge him or not, graciously guiding history toward its true end; of God the Son who has become part of this created history in the incarnation; and of God the Holy Spirit who is given as a foretaste of the end to empower and teach the church and to convict the world of sin and righteousness and judgment.

We are not the authors of change nor even the primary actors.

However, one must be clear that change takes place because

humans partner with God in the process and invest whatever gifts and resources he has given to further his kingdom and bring him glory. We receive everything from his hand.

i Role of a servant

Myers (2003:127) reiterates this by identifying three key roles of the church in the process of development. First, the church plays a role as that of 'servant and source of encouragement of what God intends and what God offers . . .' It is finding its meaning in its service to the world. Bonhoeffer (1971:382f) wrote from a Nazi prison camp that 'the church is the church only when it exists for others . . . . The church must share in the secular problems of ordinary human life, not dominating, but helping and serving.'[138] It is a living sign of God's kingdom in the community to which it is called. 'If the church is to lead at all, it is in serving; in applying the creative energies released in Christ towards the stewardship of creation and the bringing of fallen structures closer to God's original purposes (Maggay 1994:72).

ii Source of values formation

Second, the church can and must be a leading source of values formation within the community. Other sources also have influence, but people who are reading Scripture and living as disciples of Jesus should be a significant source of inspiration and hope. 'When the church is its best, it is a sign of the values of the kingdom and is contributing holistic disciples to the community for its well-being' (Myers 1999:127).

iii Hermeneutical community

Finally, the church is the hermeneutical community that understands the biblical story as its own story as it applies it to the context and circumstances of the community. The church is the community that, because it knows the true story, can and must challenge the delusional assumptions and the web of lies (Myers 1999:128). It is the community within the community from which Christopraxis is revealed. In Christ, the church finds the foundation and source of its service to the world as 'the one who prompts us to go beyond ourselves—even up until the point of death' (Bowers 2005:57).

As members of the church, evangelicals are called to facilitate the re-formation of broken and needy people and communities. One serves with an attitude of dignity and respect, reaching out to every form of need in the world while journeying in relationship, becoming slaves as representatives of our King to 'embody God's great love and compassion for His world' (Bowers 2005:57).

iv Praying community

It also means that the church, relying on God as the change agent, must put prayer at the core of any intervention. The challenges are enormous even on the surface:

> Unemployment, hunger, malnutrition, famine, the widening gap between the affluent and the poor and economic injustices.... Furthermore, one may mention the many contemporary manifestations of violent conflict: domestic violence, rape, patriarchal oppression, the abuse of children, racial conflict, incidences of ethnic and tribal violence. . . various forms of violent crime including murder, hijacking and armed robbery (Conradie 2005:5).

Local communities are in pain. As the church journeys with those in pain, it may cry with them as an expression of suffering, compassion, empathy and perhaps a sense of guilt. Crying may be an expression of righteous indignation or anger over the injustices experienced by those in the community. Crying may also be expressed to God in the context of prayer. This is a critical activity. Transformation requires pushing against the 'evil structures that exist in the present cosmos and institut(ing) through the mission of the church the values of the

Kingdom over and against the values of the principalities and powers of this world' (Bragg 1987:39).

This relationship between crying and prayer is necessary. One cannot engage the destruction that is happening in local communities without engaging with the pain that manifests from the brokenness. Jesus was not aloof to the pain of the world, but he engaged in a way that was true to his mission, ministering to marginalised people of every description. This was true incarnation.[139] It is also a model for the evangelical movement as a witness bearing society defined by the biblical injunction to be salt and light:

> As 'salt' we penetrate society and act as a preservative against social putrefaction, restoring and affirming whatever is good and just and lovely in the things around us (Philippians 4.8). As 'light,' we stand before forces of darkness, a sign of the truth about the human condition and the meaning of history and human existence (Maggay 1994:48).

By having the understanding of its role in these specific ways, the evangelical movement can help to restore the communities that it serves. It is this closely defined sense of crucial relationship and God's grace that empowers those in the community to discover its sense of God-given destiny.

Feeling the pain by engaging it from within helps one pray with understanding. This creates a significant role for the evangelical movement to play. Walter Wink (1992:306) comments extensively on the necessity of prayer in his book, 'Engaging the Powers,' but notes early on the reluctance of many to pray;

> by now I can sense certain social activists bristling with impatience. I am in complete sympathy. We have all known Christians for whom prayer is a substitute for action, who dump on God the responsibility for doing what God's groaning in us is seeking to impel us to do.

This reluctance is a misunderstanding of the role of prayer and one's role in the community to simply serve God's vision for the poor. A disconnect takes place separating what would normally be understood as 'spiritual practices' such as prayer/reflection from what is considered the 'real work' of community engagement. However, the need for prayer is critical in the process. Prayer 'defies the cosmic powers that keep the poor powerless. Prayer is an act against the powers who through their rebelliousness, resistance, and self-interest, hinder the redemptive intentions of God' (Wink 1992:311). Wink understands that prayer speaks hope into a hopeless situation and remains subject to God as the ultimate intercessor. Prayer that 'acknowledges the powers becomes a form of social action' (Wink 1992:317).

Failure to recognise this can bring about a faith-motivated praxis instead of a faith-based praxis, returning one to a dualism that subscribes to the modernistic view that human nature is compartmentalised into physical and spiritual. As has been previously mentioned as a core theme in this study, such a mindset lacks theological basis and has resulted in the failure of the evangelical movement to remain engaged in fighting poverty as gospel motivated mission. Gutiérrez (2003:16) acknowledges this dualism among those working with the poor and highlights that the brutal realities of poverty can assault the spiritual foundations of those unprepared for these circumstances. He states

> an important and painful example of the lack of vital unity (which every spirituality demands) is the separation that takes place, beneath all the resplendent phrases, between prayer and action. Both are accepted as necessary, and in fact, they are. The problem is to establish a connection between them.

As is hopefully evident, this dualism not only determines to a large extent whether or not churches engage in activities to fight poverty, but it also figures into the character of their engagement and what are seen as the critical activities that shape their engagement. Myers (1999:158) continues to highlight the nature of this process:

> Care must be taken to avoid the temptation to think of spiritual formation and professional training as two unrelated activities. Both are inseparable parts of developing the holistic practitioner. This means that spiritual formation, learning the spiritual disciplines, becoming competent in popular education . . . are all part of the (process needed for) formation. We need to integrate being Christian with being professional.

Holistic engagement is different from secular poverty alleviation models and must look that way.

4.2 Defining the character of the engagement

It is the nature of the engagement that must now important be considered. Many churches currently engage in what is called 'social outreach,' which normally includes soup kitchens, food parcels for the poor and visits to old age homes or other community institutions. This is a 'First generation' approach in line with David Korten's (1991) generational framework to trace the progress of developmental work. This model has been interpreted by Swart and Venter for a South African context.[140] First generation strategies are identified as relief or welfare involving the direct delivery of basic services (such as food, shelter, and health care) by an organisation for the benefit of the community. This provision may be necessary as 'disaster relief,' but it should be seen as a short-term response to satisfy basic needs. For Swart (2004:1), churches

> are locked within a charity mode of thinking and practice and they do not know how to go beyond such mode. This is what the churches have always done best and what they continue to do best. But

this is not responsible community renewal. Our attempts to reach out to our fellow human beings in need, to relieve social need, are not changing this world for the better. They cannot, because they are only works of relief, works of charity.

This approach lacks a developmental focus and is unsustainable since the recipients of the services are passive receivers. A church in this role functions as the 'doer' of development, thereby creating dependency, not holistic empowerment. Instead, a mission-led engagement looks for ways to 'make a difference (be a change agent) within the changing society within which it carries out its task' as a movement of the gospel (Swart & Orsmond 2011:1).

The church must be understood as a missionary body. The members of the church should be identified as being sent by God into the world. It is

not a closed circle, but rather an inviting community. The missionary church has an outgoing orientation, both in witness and service and in word and deed. The concept "missionary church' does not in the first place describe (extra or additional) activities, but rather a fundamental attitude (way of life) (see Dijkstra-Algra in Swart & Orsmond 2011:2).

Mission, in a South African context, is engaged from within a racially fragmented society, separated socio-economically and geographically in ways that make the restoration of human dignity incredibly difficult to realise. Even though inequality has continued to grow, there is the potential for the church to bridge the gaps in society by seeking to facilitate a movement to bring about justice. The church should play this role. What may not seem as clear to a church considering such engagement is what form this should take and what will constitute healing and rebuilding within a context of poverty and inequality.

A Collective case study[141] undertaken by Nadine Bowers-Du Toit and Grace Nkomo (2014), gathered 'perceptions of ministers and congregational social ministry leaders. . . with regard to their understanding of reconciliation, restitution and reparations' as related to poverty and inequality within a post-apartheid context. The study used qualitative methodology. Unstructured interviews were given by four clergy and one ministry leader representing what would be considered 'wealthy'[142] churches from within the Western Cape. The focus of the questioning was around issues of reconciliation, reparations and restitution. Churches engaged in these activities are also likely contributing to a developmental process, meaning that the findings from this study should be applicable to the creation of a church-based approach for the evangelical movement to fight poverty in a holistic way.

The research revealed that every church leader interviewed felt that the church had a role to play in reaching the poor and marginalised and to fight injustice. Although there was quite a bit of variance in the ways that the churches were involved in the lives of the poor, most of the leaders acknowledged that more could be done. The following section specifies what may be necessary to help local congregations be more effective in ministering to the poor.

4.2.1 Key elements for engaged congregations

Four key results emerged from the case study of Bowers-Du Toit & Nkomo (2014: 7) that were present in congregations engaged in activities to relieve poverty. These findings are listed and described as follows:

i Clear theology

First, there is a clear theology regarding the poor and social justice. The churches in the sample were all convinced of the importance of reconciliation and involvement in the lives of those in poverty and considered it the role of the church to bring hope and demonstrate God's love to them. 'The churches that were most assimilated and had the most church-led initiatives had a very clearly articulated theology of the poor.' What was evident, in varying degrees, was that 'a clear doctrine had led to clear teaching and strong implementation by the leadership and the congregation' (Bowers-Du Toit & Nkomo 2014:7).

ii Hands on leadership involvement

Second, there was direct involvement by top levels of leadership in the lives of the poor. The leaders were modelling the importance of active participation in the lives of those in poverty which had impacted the congregation to the extent that they were also reaching out to the poor. In addition to hands-on involvement, church leaders were also 'consistently teaching and motivating the congregation towards a biblical response to the poor....l' (Bowers-Du Toit & Nkomo 2014:7).

iii Long term relationships

Third, long-term relationships had been developed. Genuine relationships had been formed, often with a cost. 'This long-term investment of time into relationships demonstrated a consistency that, along with visible, practical and sacrificial involvement, earned the trust of those from poor communities . . . .' Relationship building allowed for a more developmental approach instead of the easier and more common charity model 'as churches engaged with the poor, learnt what their needs were and worked together to find solutions,' . . . allowing 'reconciliation, restitution and reparations to occur in a relationally based context' (Bowers-Du Toit & Nkomo 2014:7). These more integrated congregations had the strong belief that the poor needed to be part of the church community for it to be authentic and a true reflection of the community, which then impacted their mission and community life.

iv Sacrificial and practical involvement

Fourth, there was sacrificial and practical involvement with these communities. The more racially assimilated church congregations have a great deal more practical engagement with the poor. They have given sacrificially of their finances, volunteer resources, time and mobilising opportunities to assist their target communities. This has given them credibility in these communities while empowering the people upon whom they are focused. What is noticeable is that the very practical and highly intentional engagement with communities by church leadership and congregations has brought significant relational dividends that are yielding fruit.

Bowers-Du Toit and Nkomo provide helpful insight through their study that has application for the evangelical movement in practical ways. First, this must be something that church leadership sees as important—so important that they willingly invest the significant effort to clearly articulate their theology of the poor and social justice. Without this, it would be highly unlikely that the congregation would make any real investment in efforts to fight poverty. Second, strong, consistent leadership that recognises the necessity for a long-haul type of engagement is also critical in the process to mobilise a congregation or a movement. It will take prayer, financial investment, relational equity, significant time and perseverance to manage the challenges that are sure to come. Third, leaders must personally lead this movement in their teaching, preaching, and stewardship of both time and money for this to have the chance to succeed, thereby modelling the process for their congregation.

4.2 Orientation to community

However, the decision to adapt to a changing environment as is found in a local South African context is ultimately the decision of the congregation as it discerns the way forward, even when encouraged by its leadership. Each congregation has a distinctive culture and identity that symbolises its understanding of what it means to live the Gospel in its context—if it is truly trying to do so. Nancy Ammerman (1997:338-342) writes in her book, '*Congregation and Community*,' that there are four ways in which congregations orientate themselves toward their communities as a reflection of that culture. Although she is writing from an American context, her insights seem applicable to South African congregations as they adapt in various ways to the changes happening around them. Her perceptions are listed as follows:

- Congregations with a civic orientation. These congregations motivate their members to be upstanding and co-operative citizens of the community, helping out where they can. They will not significantly challenge the *status quo*.
- Activist congregations. Members also want to be upstanding citizens, but they see the goal as requiring advocacy and change. They are more involved and want change in the community.
- Sanctuary congregations. These seek to shield their members from this world's temptations and prepare them for the world to come. They try to be isolated from the community and its problems.
- The evangelistic congregations. The church is seen as an agent for changing individual lives. Evangelistic orientations are not guarantees of success. They think of evangelism primarily in terms of recruiting people like themselves.

Activist congregations are more likely to be engaged in mission, seeking to be a catalyst for change. Managing a process of change is difficult at best, but it is important not to ignore the opportunity. Ammerman (1997:345) describes the relationship between conflict and change; 'Congregations that systematically avoid conflict are also very likely to avoid changing.' This is why a maintenance mindset is often the *status quo* for mainline, older congregations. It is a choice not to adapt to a new or changing situation. Moreover, by making that choice, there are real consequences.

> After a period of slow decline, these congregations are likely to disappear from the scene, perhaps making way for utterly different congregations to sprout up in their stead. As with any other ecology, death is an inevitable part of the life cycle (Ammerman 1997:345).

This is the reality for many congregations struggling for survival. By failing to engage with the significant challenges within the South African community landscape, there is a likelihood that these congregations will fail, an unfortunate prospect when there is so much opportunity. Congregations, as a part of the community's institutional infrastructure, are a part of the 'structures and connections that make social life possible' (Ammerman 1997:346).

Interdependence exists between a congregation and its community. A community provides social resources from within which people find support for their basic needs to create meaning with their lives and find enjoyment. This social capital is the 'essential stuff of our lives, the network of skill and trust that makes possible civic life. . . the raw material out of which new organisational species can be created, the residue left when old organisations die' (Ammerman 1997:347). For those without other assets, these relationships, associations and networks are critical for survival, helping to keep individuals from becoming marginalised or vulnerable. Congregations are critical generators of social capital, giving them a comparative advantage over other institutions since they have considerable levels of trust invested in them and they can mobilise volunteers for activities that help to build the community.

The church has a natural role and significant opportunity for partnership in community building work. The legacy of Apartheid effectively undermined levels of trust within communities, which thereby eroded social capital. 'Participation, co-operation, sharing and community development through networks, then, become a key challenge for the true community church' (Swart 2004:6). However, it may be that this might happen most effectively through partnerships *between* churches, providing opportunities for collaboration to achieve goals within a community that neither congregation could reach on its own. These partnerships are made for the mutual benefit of congregations and their community, meaning that no church community could claim that there were not sufficient resources to move beyond the relief paradigm. 'True partnership building implies a new way of structuring relationships, of going beyond mere co-operation between stakeholders in ways to avoid co-option and domination' (Botes & Abrahams in Schoeman 2012:15). Partnering creates mutually beneficial relationships by building networks of trust that benefit the collaboration and each other. Although this method of community engagement could add complexity to what is already a complicated process, for an under-resourced church this could be a useful paradigm for holistic community development.

5 Proposing a Model for Mission

The following section will describe a community research project undertaken by a local church in Cape Town based upon Human Scale Development principles promoted by Manfred Max-Neef and discussed in detail in Chapter 3. Although this community was able to facilitate the research without an additional church partner, it is anticipated that this could be a process undertaken by multiple churches partnering together in an impoverished local community. Additionally, although the overall process looks somewhat complicated, it is anticipated that the core structure of the research will provide a framework that will be useful for a congregation or group of partnering congregations to define their engagement in a way that is holistic and sustainable.

The Church has significant social capital resources that can be employed to make a difference in the endemic poverty that exists within our local communities and this church was able to employ that capital in a way that provided one sustainable solution in the fight against unemployment.

A methodology was constructed in 2007 to assist Pinelands Methodist Church, a Southern Suburbs church community in Cape Town, in its desire to make a difference in the intense poverty of its neighbouring township community of Joe Slovo in Langa. Disaster relief was the initial contact with the community when a series of shack fires destroyed hundreds of homes in 2000. Responding to this crisis provided the church a first-hand look at the significant challenges that existed. The Pinelands church began to engage in many ways to bring improvement to the community with seemingly limited success. This engagement continued for many years. In 2007 the church community began a research project to move from relief-focused interventions to a structure that would be its ongoing intervention to help unemployed people find work.[143] The information is presented here to demonstrate a developmental model that would assist the evangelical movement or other church communities desiring to engage holistically in mission. Although the intervention described here is specific to unemployment, the core elements of this approach could be used to guide other initiatives endemic to impoverished communities. And while this method is not the only way to engage in poverty alleviation, it is hopefully a useful start.

5.1 Constructing the model

Members of the church leadership team[144] approached Learn to Earn, a local Cape Town based NGO with holistic developmental expertise to assist in building a development model that could be used to specifically address the intense poverty and affiliated unemployment that exist in the Langa community. The research had six specific aims:

- Mapping of the institutional landscape of the geographical areas specified.

- Identification of employment, market and product opportunities and the presence of business in and surrounding the target community area.

- Verification of the desired qualities sought by business for prospective employees.

- Evaluation of the availability and strengths of resources within the target community.

- Determination of the major challenges, constraints and needs facing the target community, as indicated by community members participating in the Focus Groups.

- Quantification and qualification of each of these aims. (Delport & van Wyk 2008:3)

This research process is interactive and cyclical with each phase being under continuous evaluation and revision should that become necessary. The research methodology was structured to engage the residents of the Langa target community in all levels of the research process, seeking to foster community ownership of the project from its inception. The goal is for the initiative to be completed **with** the community, not done **to** the community. Thus, the research itself served as the beginning of a community intervention process by introducing the church as a capacity-building agent to the target community. The research programme is also useful as a marketing tool to promote the church-based project[145] as an employee resource for the local business community. This is a multi-disciplinary research approach, combining quantitative and qualitative data collection with the social science tools and techniques to provide accurate results in line with the research objectives. The research was intended to be comprehensive so that the target community could be more fully understood, enabling the research to be useful for other interventions in addition to this one directed at unemployment.

5.2 Mapping the process

The research process was divided into four phases that are summarised as follows:

- The first phase of the research looked at the institutional landscape of the research area, including places of social influence. Research teams systematically gathered data from the identified business areas and plotted business location coordinates with a hand-held GPS device.

- The second phase involved taking the processed data from phase one and selecting some these businesses for an in-depth interview using random proportionate sampling. The aim of the interviews was to gain further insight into what the businesses require for their entrance-level staffing needs and then ascertain possible employment opportunities.

- The third phase identified three focus groups in a needs assessment of the target residential community using a technique called the Priority Index (P-Index) research technique. By using a measuring scale (Schutte Scale) that is a reliable measurement for both literate and non-literate persons, this technique distinguished between the **actual** needs of the community over their **perceived** needs or wants.

- The fourth phase analysed the research to determine appropriate interventions that reflect the actual needs of both the target residential community and the local business communities.

Phases one and two could be modified depending on the intended research outcomes. The planning phase of the research began a month before the launch with a meeting between members of the church and Learn to Earn staff to discuss the vision, scope, time schedules and objectives of the research project and the basic format of the questionnaires and presentation techniques. These meetings continued on an ongoing basis. A pamphlet for distribution was developed introducing the church and the local NGO as partners in the initiative. The pamphlet would also be used to explain to the business communities the purpose of the research.

At the same time, a team of fieldworkers was enlisted to conduct the institutional mapping phase of the research. This team consisted of students from local colleges, a local university, and church members from the target community. A training day was held to teach these fieldworkers how to work with a basic hand-held GPS device and how to record the captured data. The training also included basic interpersonal skills and interviewing techniques.

5.3 The literature search

The background literature search for the target community found reports of similar research conducted in 2004 by the Unit for Religion and Development Research [URDR] at the University of Stellenbosch (2004) in partnership with Transformation Africa for the target area. While the URDR research had used a similar process, the ultimate aims of that investigation were to:

- Establish the major challenges facing society (such as HIV/AIDS, crime, violence, poverty, and unemployment, racism, sexism and family crises)
- Quantify these factors—in location and extent
- Assess the potential impact of the Church on the community

(URDR 2004:5).

This most recent community analysis includes places of social and economic significance along with the nature of their activities and the overall availability of employment opportunities. This information would be used to assist in the identification and evaluation of job vacancies and the necessary skills or training needed to fill any available positions. 'The goal, therefore, is to establish interventions that are contextual, market-related, and product-related so that unemployed people may obtain positions in the nearby business sectors' (Black 2010:149). The Chamber of Commerce also provided information relating to companies within the research area employing more than thirty people, thereby charting the primary market and industry trends to note during the research.

5.4 Institutional mapping

The four phases of the research were conducted over a period of 2 months. The process is as follows:

The first step of the research mapped the institutional business landscape of the research area, including places of social influence. It was not limited to only those activities occurring inside buildings. The teams worked systematically, capturing GPS coordinates for all of the formal and informal business locations as well as manually recording any additional information that was observed.

The data points gathered were then plotted onto corresponding maps to identify the location of each business in the community and its physical relation to other businesses. The fieldworkers also collected literature from the businesses that provided them access and handed out flyers explaining the purpose of the research project. This engagement was an important first interface between the business community and the church.

5.5 Sample business interviews

The second phase of research involved assembling the raw data collected in the GPS phase of the research and selecting a sample of businesses to be interviewed. The interviews were used to establish desired employee characteristics put forward by employers, basic entry level requirements, and potential new business opportunities. This phase of the research has the added benefit of being a marketing and public relations campaign for the church initiative, resulting in opportunities to potentially raise funding and develop networks within the local business community. It also indicated the general attitude of the businesses in the local area towards new initiatives designed to combat poverty and provide development opportunities.

The methodology for the selection of businesses was *proportionate random sampling*, a variation of *stratified random sampling* and the technique most often used when subgroups in the sample population vary dramatically in size. In this instance, businesses were divided into sectors, namely manufacture, wholesale, retail, service, petrol, and import-export. These groupings were then further divided into sub-categories with closer attention paid to categories where the church initiative would be most able to provide training resources that would impact the greatest number of people.

5.6 Community needs assessment

The third phase of the intervention is a community needs assessment. It is important to determine what the actual needs are from the perspective of the community members. De Wet Schutte explains that a need 'can only be actual if it is what the community regards as important for its development at a given time ... (so) it follows that if we can succeed in identifying the actual needs of a given community, the timing will be automatically right' (2000:7).

It is important to understand the significance of this phase of the research. Although other elements described in this process of assessing a community are helpful for obtaining a full picture of the target community, this phase helps to ensure target community buy-in at the beginning of the intervention process. Buy in is critical as without it the initiative, regardless of how well intentioned, could have the appearance of being imposed upon the community from the outside.

Three focus groups were facilitated comprised of members

from the target community, one group per week respectively. These groups consisted mainly of unemployed individuals and/or those working part-time or irregularly. One might consider changing the composition of these groups depending upon the research aim. The composition of the groups was random, based upon those able to attend at the specified time on a weekday. For Schutte (2000), the probability of success in any social development intervention depends on three core issues:

- the degree of bonding by residents within a community,
- the satisfaction of basic human needs, and
- the satisfaction of individuals' social needs.

The satisfaction of such needs can be met negatively or positively.

The purpose of the needs assessment was to determine the social development needs of the members of the community. The evaluation technique used was the Priority Index (P-Index) research technique as modelled by De Wet Schutte (Schutte 2000). There is a threefold advantage of using this particular technique:

- simplicity in usage,
- a prioritisation of actual needs as opposed to perceived needs or wants,
- the use of a non-verbal measurement instrument (the Schutte Scale) that proves accurate for the broad spectrum of literacy levels.

This technique differentiates between the importance and the priority of a need within the community. The needs arising from group discussions are brought forward by the group members (community members) themselves, thereby ruling out 'steering' by the facilitator. In prioritising needs, the scale is used to first measure an individual's perception of the importance of the need, followed by his or her satisfaction with how it is currently being met. Needs are then rated on a scale from 1 to 11, where 1 is the lowest and 11 is the highest. For example, an item may rate as a need of high importance, but the group members may indicate that it is sufficiently addressed, thus giving it a low priority. An item indicated as both important and unsatisfactorily met would be registered as a high priority.

The second phase of the needs assessment involved creating a community profile based on the data collected during the group facilitations. This report defines overall community satisfaction in relation to thirteen basic human needs listed by Schutte, modified from Max-Neef's Human Scale Development as detailed in Chapter three. The first six needs refer to the needs necessary for survival, while the remaining seven social needs relate to essential interaction needs between humans. The needs are listed as follows:

1. Shelter	7. Safety
2. Health care	8. Income
3. Sanitation	9. Education
4. Water	10. Recreation
5. Food	11. Religion
6. Energy	12. Welfare
	13. Transport
(Schutte 2000:23)	

The third phase of the needs assessment involves determining the level of social bonding within the community. Bonding looks at social relationships between community members and focuses on three critical areas:

- A sense of belonging to the community
- Friendship circles and social relations

- The social support system perceived by community members in times of need or crisis.

5.7 Analysing the results

Phase 4 involves analysing the collected data. The results of the community analysis are divided into two sections:

- The first section discusses the needs indicated by the *sample businesses* relating to desirable employee qualities and training requirements. It also highlights employment opportunities and potential opportunities for entrepreneurship within the business areas.

- The second section focuses on the *residential community needs assessment* and discusses the results and possible intervention strategies.

5.7.1 Business analysis

i Desirable employee qualities and values

This section concentrates on the qualities and values that **businesses** desire in their employees and is divided into three categories.

- The first category is **personal** values. The majority of the business respondents (73.5%) indicated that a high ethical standard (including, for example, integrity, honesty, trustworthiness, etc.) was the most desirable quality in an employee, much more important than vision, drive or ambition (17.6%).

- The second category illustrates **organisational qualities**, sometimes referred to as 'Business IQ.' These qualities are generic in nature, depicted by a graph ranking importance as indicated by the business respondent (see Figure 7.1 below).

Respondents rated each category from their perspective as a quality they would desire in an ideal employee. It does not mean that other qualities are unimportant, but only that the

ranking has been established by what each employer believed
to be most important.

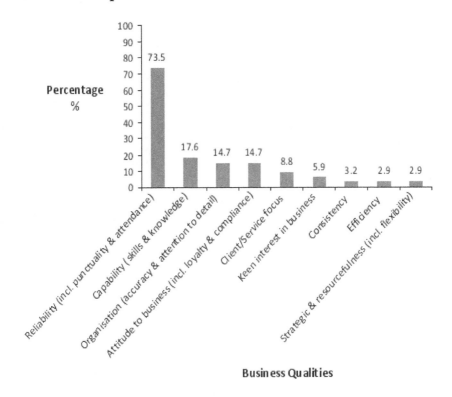

Figure 7.1 Business organisational qualities – Business IQ (Delport
& van Wyk 2008:10)

- The third category is **'Social IQ and EQ'** and depicts
  qualities that are more general in focus but quite
  essential in a work environment. Social intelligence
  [IQ] and emotional quotients [EQ] are often reflective of personality traits in an individual. Another
  graph indicates the results of this survey. (see Figure
  7.2 below).

341

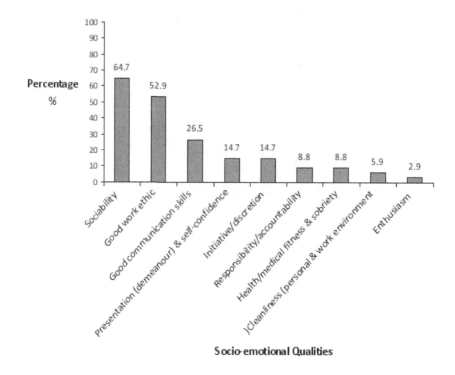

The chart shows percentages for various socio-emotional qualities:
- Sociability: 64.7
- Good work ethic: 52.9
- Good communication skills: 26.5
- Presentation (demeanour) & self-confidence: 14.7
- Initiative/discretion: 14.7
- Responsibility/accountability: 8.8
- Health/medical fitness & sobriety: 8.8
-)Cleanliness (personal & work environment: 5.9
- Enthusiasm: 2.9

Y-axis: Percentage %

X-axis: Socio-emotional Qualities

Figure 7.2: Social IQ and EQ – 2008 (Delport & van Wyk 2008:11)

These three categories are quite useful for designing training to help unemployed people become more employable. In
combining the categories, employers assign a high value to
employees that have clear ethical standards, are reliable, and
get along well with colleagues. Employees should also have a
good work ethic. Other qualities may also be relevant to certain employers, but they were not rated highly among these
business respondents during personal interviews. Although
these findings are specific to this research, it is assumed that
they could be transferable to other business communities.

Training specifically structured to enable prospective employees to develop or hone these desired characteristics has
great benefit, as has been identified by the assessments. Upon

completion of a training session, successful participants can be put forward to employers as prospective job candidates specifically trained to the business respondent's specifications. The community intervention now has a specific focus to become part of a training methodology.

ii Job market opportunities

The questionnaire results also revealed what entry-level work opportunities were available within the respective businesses surveyed. General conversation with these respondents indicated that hundreds of jobs were available, but remained unfilled due to a lack of qualified applicants. Businesses were generally unwilling to take a risk in hiring potentially unqualified candidates. The research revealed that many of the baseline jobs that were available were focused upon skills useful in a warehousing environment. These results indicated a clear opportunity for a warehousing course to facilitate the general skills desired to fill open positions. A course of this nature would focus on aspects of warehousing, such as:

- Packers course, including lifting and handling goods
- Stock rotation and stock control
- Order-making
- Dispatching procedure
- Goods-receiving procedure
- Forklift/Hyster operation
- Health and safety
- Warehouse maintenance and cleaning

Courses may also be targeted to the specific skills needed by businesses if a demand becomes evident. These skills courses should also include those qualities previously mentioned as the desired character traits of prospective employees, possibly as the first general training initiative before any further specialised training.

iii Staff training opportunities

The following list indicates training needs requested by businesses relating to their current employees:

- Literacy and numeracy
  - Life skills—includes nutrition, drug awareness, attitude, personal responsibility, accountability and problem-solving

- Computer skills

- Basic business skills (including basic finance)

- Management and leadership skills

- Technical skills—machine operation

- Carpentry skills

- Geography (map reading)

- Sales

Facilitating these training needs could serve as additional income stream opportunities for the church and value–added service to the local business community.

iv Entrepreneurial opportunities

Business respondents indicated additional possibilities for employment as indirect needs that could be filled to provide a service for the existing businesses and their employees. Meeting these specific needs presents other training opportunities. Opportunities mentioned are as follows:

- Opening a cafeteria to provide a place for employees to eat, reasoning that an eating establishment in closer proximity to businesses would minimise or eliminate the time and travel required for workers to obtain meals.

- Opening a day-care facility for employees' children would be seen as a convenient and secure employee benefit.
- One business indicated that it has a lunch venue available on premises that it would be willing to outsource. (Whether that would be useful for job creation would need to be determined.)

Additionally, many businesses lack promotional material or other work-related literature, suggesting an opportunity to train people in computer graphics and design skills to be used as 'for fee' services offered to the local business community. Other needs mentioned were: delivery personnel, staff transport, security services, typing, sewing, and handymen. Although further research would be necessary, it seems likely that other employment-generating opportunities could also exist.

5.7.2 Residential analysis

An adequate needs assessment must include a survey of the residential target community. The *Nominal Group Technique* (NGT)[146] was used with target community residents. Focused discussions were conducted with three groups totalling 36 people. The focus of the discussion centred upon available resources within the community, needs of the community, and community bonding.

Focusing on resources within the community encourages individual empowerment and helps to restore dignity and self-respect. It brings to light the existing strengths of the community and identifies areas where individuals can help themselves as opposed to highlighting only their needs and weaknesses.

Community bonding involves three elements: social services available to assist those needing help within the community, socialisation within the community (i.e. friendship circles) and a sense of belonging to the community. Bonding increases the likelihood of the community members seeking to transform their environment through personal involvement.

The results of the nominal group discussions are illustrated below in a chart followed by a brief explanation of each point. Please note the following when reading the graphs: the P-Index is a measuring technique which establishes the priority of the items in question by subtracting the mean scores indicating the overall satisfaction with the current state of affairs from the mean scores of the overall importance attached to the items in question. For the Community Resources chart (see Figure 7.3 on the following page), the lower the P-Index score, the better the resource (for example, St Francis with a P-Index of -0.62 is perceived as a better resource by the survey participants than the local old age home, which has a P-Index of 6.69). The particular comments regarding the resource are formed by the responses from the community. It is obvious to see the needs in communities, but it is important to recognize strengths that exist prior to the initial community engagement.

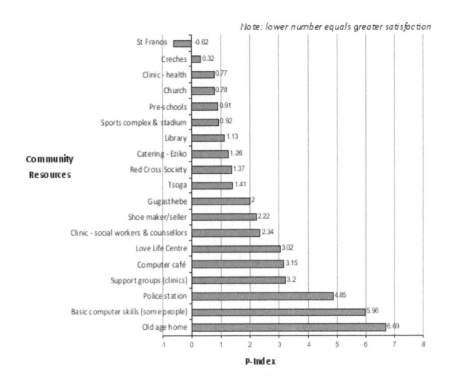

Community
Resources

Resource	P-Index
St Francis	-0.62
Creches	0.32
Clinic - health	0.77
Church	0.78
Pre-schools	0.91
Sports complex & stadium	0.92
Library	1.13
Catering - Eziko	1.26
Red Cross Society	1.37
Tsoga	1.41
Gugasthebe	2
Shoe maker/seller	2.22
Clinic - social workers & counsellors	2.34
Love Life Centre	3.02
Computer café	3.15
Support groups (clinics)	3.2
Police station	4.85
Basic computer skills (some people)	5.96
Old age home	6.69

P-Index

Figure 7.3: Community resources chart indicating/showing satis-faction levels with existing community resources – 2008 (Delport & van Wyk 2008:18)

i Top community resources in the target community as measured by the P-Index

Community Resource	P-Index	Resource
St Francis	**P= - 0.62**	Adult education centre run by the Catholic Church. It has been running for about 20 years and is well known within the community. It offers courses that enable adults to finish school (obtain Matric), and to obtain basic skills, for example,

		sewing.
Crèches	**P= 0.32**	The crèches in the area allow parents to put their children in a safe place while they work or seek employment. The parents feel secure knowing that their children receive good care.
Clinic	**P= 0.77**	The clinic is free which is important for those in the target community who are sick (especially those with TB or HIV/Aids) seeking medical help.
Church	**P= 0.78**	The churches provide a place for positive moral influence, especially for the children, and spiritual training.
Community Resource	**P-Index**	**Resource**
Pre-schools	**P= 0.91**	The pre-schools are considered safe places for parents to leave their children while they are seeking employment. Under the right guidance, pre-schools also provide a positive start to the education and socialisation of children.
Sports stadium/ complex	**P= 0.92**	It is a venue where people can come together to play various sports or to observe and support sports. Hosting sporting events here would also bring others into the community.
Library	**P= 1.13**	The library keeps literacy alive by allowing community members access to resources. Knowledge brings people closer to empowerment,

		and the library is seen as a vehicle for this process.
Catering – Iziko	P= 1.26	A coffee shop/restaurant that doubles up as a training centre to teach people how to cook.
Red Cross Soc.	P= 1.37	The Red Cross Society has been very active in crisis intervention, especially providing aid during the shack fires. They are also active in helping the homeless with basic resources.
Tsoga	P= 1.41	Tsoga is a recycling depot that is a resource in two ways. First, by providing materials and resources that can be re-used, thereby saving money and second, as a tourist attraction to the area, thus improving the community's economy.
Gugasthebe	P= 2.00	It is a venue for arts and culture, bringing the community together for events/functions. Crafts and traditional wear are sold there, making it an attractive venue for tourists. The constraint of this resource, however, is the fact that an entrance fee is charged which excludes those who are unable to afford it.
Shoe-maker	P= 2.22	This individual teaches others in the community the skills needed to make and sell shoes. A constraint, however, is that there is a lack of materials and funding for these "learners" to be able to practice and put these skills to use.
Clinic – social workers	P= 2.34	Counseling services and

and counselors		family help are available at the clinic for those needing access.
Community Resource	**P-Index**	**Resource**
Love Life Centre	**P= 3.02**	This centre houses computer training facilities and runs courses for life skills, family planning, and HIV/Aids awareness, etc. However, it is not open to everyone and so is not considered to be used to its full potential. Also, the programmes appear to be inadequate, according to the group members, because no visible change has been observed since its establishment (for example, teenage pregnancy is still rife in the area).
Computer café	**P= 3.15**	Access to computers opens doors for people in the community by providing access to wider networks of information and resources (for example, via the internet) and, with the necessary training, creates business opportunities.

Support groups (Clinics)	**P= 3.20**	These support groups tend to focus around HIV/Aids and TB, making it easier for people with these illnesses to cope.
Police Stations	**P= 4.85**	While the police station provides a place of safety, as well as a place to go to for trauma counseling (there is one volunteer counselor on duty), if

		victimised by crime, the community members in the group unanimously felt that the police are far too lax in their duties. Respondents said police do only the bare minimum of what is required and refuse to go beyond their job description. They gave the example of a stabbing victim who ended up dying in the street next to the police station because the police refused to take him to the hospital, claiming instead that it was not their duty, but rather was the responsibility of the ambulance.
Basic computer skills (only some people)	P= 5.96	These skills allow people access to wider networks of information if, for example, they also have access to the computer café. Having these skills also opens up doors for employment opportunities.
Old-age home	P= 6.69	The home is a place for the elderly to go to be cared for when their families are no longer able to support them; however, the homes in the target community are considered 'stagnant.'

The following were mentioned by the groups, but were not given a P-Index value:

Individual Skills/Resources Available in the Target Community	
Tourism	The fact that tour groups pass through the area is considered positive as it makes the target community known and more visible, thereby increasing the chances or potential for community upliftment. Tourists spend money in the area, which aids local businesses and creates more job opportunities.

Individual Skills/Resources Available in the Target Community		
	Woodwork skills & experience	These skills have been passed down from elders within

	the community and are improved through experience. It is important to note that the skill is learned from others in a mentorship role. The constraint now, however, is that community members are no longer passing on these skills to one another. Furthermore, there is a lack of sufficient resources to enable one to put these skills effectively to use, as in, for example, starting one's own business.
People & Communication skills/ Sales & Marketing skills	These are important personal resources regarding tourism and effective marketing of the area, or to market oneself to prospective employers.
Private security companies	The visibility of security personnel and vehicles acts as a deterrent for opportunistic criminals, thus improving safety in the area. These companies tend to be used more as the police are trusted less.
Leadership abilities	Could mentor and guide, or facilitate groups.
Compassion for children	Could help at the crèche, or start another care centre for the children, but lack the necessary skills.
Catering skills	Having these skills creates the potential for a business opportunity, but the individual noted the constraints as being a lack of funding for capital to start a catering business, or to study further in this regard. Also, the individual lacks the knowledge related to business manage-

	ment.
Gardening skills	Allows for the possibility of finding employment opportunities in surrounding residential areas.
Basic business skills	Important in starting one's own business, but it is currently limited.
Skills to offer home-based care	Could start a program to care for elderly who are not in old-age homes; however, most would not be able to afford this service. More advanced training is required.
Sewing skills	Creates business potential as well as the potential to teach sewing skills. However, a lack of funding and resources has stopped this from going forward.

Knowledge & skill in arts & culture	Could teach or promote as a business opportunity. Knowledge must come from experience, as opposed to studying.
Office administration, organisation & planning	Essential tools in the establishment and running of a business.
Individual Skills/Resources Available in the Target Community	
Instructor	Able to facilitate and run training groups.
Beadwork/ Crafts	Could create and sell goods.

(Delport & van Wyk 2008:19-22)

For the community needs chart (see Figure 7.4 below), the interpretation of P-Index is reversed. In other words, the higher the P-Index, the greater the need (for example, safe houses for children with a P-Index of 10 are perceived as being a higher priority than signs and speed bumps for roads with a P-Index of 6.23). This information is important as it informs the researchers of potential opportunities to serve the community by providing other services, e.g. offering a drug rehab centre in the community could give addicted young people a place for recovery that may not currently exist.

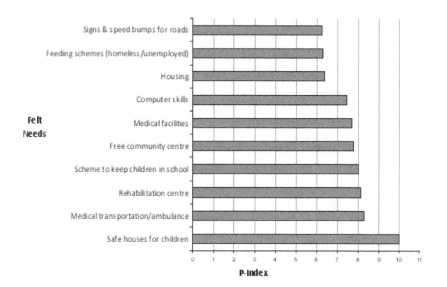

Figure 7.4: Felt needs of the target community – 2008 (Delport & van Wyk 2008:23)

ii Top ten felt community needs

Felt Community Needs	P-Index	Resource
1. Safe houses for children and relevant training to run them	P= 10.00	Children are often made to remain in homes where there is ongoing abuse. If they run away from home, they often end up living on the streets where they may become targets for predators or become involved in crime. People need to be

			trained to run these centres adequately. *(Note: While a registered social worker is imperative for this kind of organisation, there may be employment opportunities for general staff as well (e.g. cleaners, cooks, etc.)*
2.	**Medical transport**	**P= 8.29**	There are no ambulances or medical transport vehicles in the area. So, for example, pregnant women have to use unreliable public transport to get to the hospital.
3.	**Rehabilitation centre**	**P= 8.09**	Drugs are prevalent among the youth, and there is no support for those trying to break free from addictions. The high drug prevalence plays a role in the high crime rate in the target community.
4.	**Scheme to keep youth in school (to give hope)**	**P= 8.00**	There is a serious problem involving many young people dropping out and leaving school early because they fail to see the point of finishing with no foreseeable future ahead of them due to a lack of employment opportunities.
5.	**Free Community Centre**	**P= 7.77**	A Community Centre is especially important for young people. Group members indicated that there needs to be a place where young people can keep themselves off the streets and occupied. A place is also needed where the community can come together for activities. While there is a place where this currently happens (Gugusthebe), one has to pay to enter which, in effect, excludes those members of the community who cannot afford it.

	P-Index	Resource
6. Medical facilities	P= 7.69	There is currently one clinic in the area, but it is only available to young people up to age 17, or those members of the community who have either HIV/Aids or TB. For general illnesses, people must visit Vanguard Clinic and may then need to wait more than a day to be seen.
7. Computer skills	P= 7.43	Having computer skills would improve one's chances in the employment market, and opens chances for self-employment. Many marketplace jobs require some basic computer knowledge.
Felt Community Needs	P-Index	Resource
8. Housing	P= 6.36	Many people are still living in shacks and are unable to afford houses due to unemployment. While housing is important, as indicated by the P-Index, it is still lower on the priority scale than "job opportunities," as the latter would be one of the core issues to tackle, with the result that, as personal income increased, housing would improve.
9. Feeding schemes for homeless and unemployed	P= 6.29	People need food to live. While there are feeding schemes in the schools for the children, homeless and unemployed people do not have money to buy food. Since the majority of the community is living is either relative or extreme poverty, food donations from within the community

		are rare.
10. Signs and speed bumps for roads	**P= 6.23**	Drivers tend to speed or drive recklessly down the roads used by school children and other pedestrians.

(Delport & van Wyk 2008:24-25)

iii Constraints

The constraints listed by the group were not unique to any particular resource but rather refer to the situation as a whole. The main obstacle, as would be expected, is a lack of *sufficient funding*. While people may have some basic personal skills, for example, they are unable to afford the necessary materials needed for their trade. Furthermore, skills are rudimentary, with most having been passed down from previous generations. To adequately prepare people for employment requires a more formalised approach to skills training that is cognizant of local market conditions and product requirements.

Within the target community, there is a sense that people lack *networks or established connections* from within which to operate. They also believe that there is a breakdown in communication among community members. It is important to note that the most common problem mentioned by individuals that hinders them in using their skills and resources is that they do not know how to access employment for which they are qualified as they lack the *channels* to source available opportunities. Additionally, there no longer seems to be a transferring of essential skills among community members, especially the younger generations. Thus, only a select few have these personal resources.

A lack of *entrepreneurial facilities and venues* for micro-business was also mentioned to be a hindrance. For example, people who were making goods to sell had nowhere to market and sell their products. Additionally, two of the group members said that *age* was a problem in their search for work. They felt that people would not hire them because they are too old.

It is useful to note that target community churches in general and St. Francis, a Catholic Church more specifically, are esteemed very highly as trustworthy resources that add value to the community. This understanding corroborates other findings noting the high regard that communities have for churches, meaning that interventions related to or associated with local churches will receive more positive community support simply because a church's overall standing in the community is very high.

iv Comparison to previous needs assessments in the target community conducted by Stellenbosch University (2005).

It is useful to compare the results of the research undertaken in the target community to a similar study conducted by the University of Stellenbosch for Transformation Africa in 2004 (URDR 2004). There are interesting similarities to note between the studies regarding the needs that were considered to be of high priority. (See Figure 7.5 on the following page)

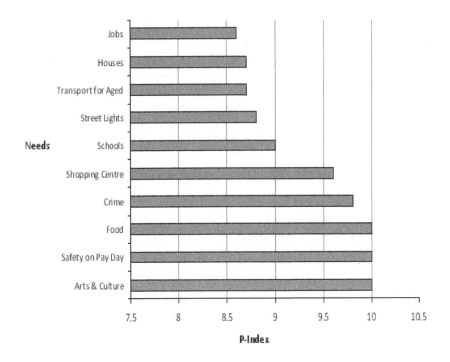

*Figure 7.5: The P-Index of the felt needs of the target community –
2004 (URDR 2004:26)*

It is evident that the target community continues to deal with
major issues. The two studies identify very similar needs that
portray a community struggling corporately and individually. The studies place housing, hunger and elements associated with crime in the 'top ten.' Transport issues, particularly
for the elderly, sick or injured were also indicated as being
quite essential. In addition, the needs of children rank highly:
Safe houses for children were listed as the greatest need in the
2007 research and schools were listed as the 6th highest need
in 2004.

However, one of the differences is worth noting. Although the
P-Index difference is only 3.1, jobs were listed as the 10th
highest need in 2004 and ranked 19th in 2007. It was some-

what surprising that jobs did not rank higher in 2007. It is likely that this difference can be attributed to the composition of the focus groups rather than to any other statistical significance since many of the other indicated needs are income-related.

v Bonding within the community

Understanding the bonding pattern of a community unlocks access to the community. By noting the community pride *(bonding of 7.94 out of 10) and* socialisation *(indicated by friendship circles bonding of 9.5 out of 10)*, it seems clear that the marketing approach most likely to be successful in the target group would be word-of-mouth (Delport & van Wyk 2008:28). The same method would apply to any fundraising strategy. The target community appears very relational in line with Xhosa culture. Therefore, any intervention would need to focus on building a reputation within the community through traditional oral means of communication; the use of print media should be a last resort since it would likely be the least effective marketing tool in this context. The intervention would need to identify the *gatekeepers, gossipers, movers and shakers, and flack catchers* of the community—essentially those community members who seem to have a powerful influence. The pride in the community represents a good foundation for an approach that would facilitate the restoration of personal dignity and self-respect, a feeling of ownership visible through community participation. It also indicates why the target community has a reputation for being highly political (Delport & van Wyk 2008:28).

An essential element of socialisation is that momentum will play a significant role in any course offered, meaning that few people on a course at the beginning of the initiative could eventually lead to full classes later with minimal advertising and effort. Since there is a high regard for friendship circles, word-of-mouth advertisement is extremely effective. In the same way, a poorly run course or initiative will suffer.

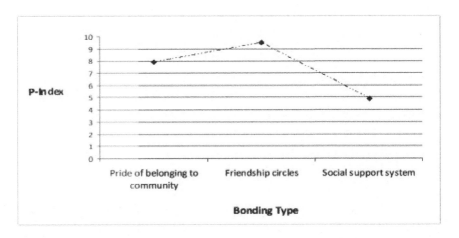

Figure 7.6: Types of social bonding in the Langa community – 2008 (Delport & van Wyk 2008:28).

This finding has bee validated over the years as multiple training events have been filled mainly through word of mouth acvertising. Significantly, bonding can also create some negative indicators. Companies are reluctant to employ too many people from the same family or clan because any significant event in the family, such as a death or serious illness, could impact a large percentage of the workforce, thereby hindering production. Furthermore, the dismissal of a member of the family can lead to a larger-than-normal adverse reaction which can negatively impact a company.

Low bonding (4.89 out of 10) regarding social support indicates that there is a perception among members that the community itself will provide little or no support during a personal crisis. Community communication channels, outside of friendship circles, appear to be quite poor (Delport & van Wyk 2008:29). It is important to consider the positive impact that a healthy church community can play in reversing this perception.

5.7 Application

The research findings were reported to the Church leadership team in February 2008, and it was determined to begin the process of implementing a training strategy for the target community in line with the indicated results. A part-time Training Coordinator was appointed to help develop a suitable curriculum, incorporating the following essentials gleaned from the research: Character and integrity training, identity and individual value, HIV/Aids awareness, health and hygiene, literacy/numeracy testing, employee rights, constructing CVs, conducting an interview, and performing a job search. These elements made up the core of an initial two-week curriculum. Each day began with a devotion focused on a Scripture passage relevant to the topics of the day, and the gospel was at the core of the curriculum. The project was named *Zanokhanyo* (Xhosa for 'bringing light'), and the first training course began at a sister church in the Langa community in July 2008. Utilising the results from the research helped structure the community initiative along three areas: training, business partnering, and resourcing the training graduates.

5.7.1 Training

The two-week course required payment of a fee of R150.00 per participant. Although this amount does not cover costs incurred by the project for the training, it gives perceived value to the course without placing an excessive financial burden on the participant. This vested financial interest also provides an incentive for successful completion of the training.

The course simulates a workplace environment where participants are expected to arrive promptly every day if they wish to graduate and have access to any job information available through the business partnership network. There is an opportunity to make up a missed day during the next scheduled training course; graduation, in this case, would happen with the next group. Enforcement of this strict attendance policy by carefully monitoring punctuality and attendance facilitates the 'vetting' of the training graduates for future employers. The participants are also observed throughout the course to see how well they participate in a classroom environment and relate with others.

One of the main goals of the training is to address some of the debilitating effects of apartheid by helping course participants realise that they are valued, not because of the colour of their skin nor their cultural heritage, but because they have been created in the image of God. By definition, all men and women are created as equal and should be treated as such regardless of previous practices or experiences. This course addresses the spiritual and psychological issues critical for charting the way forward for impoverished and traumatised local communities. The course programme is outlined on the next page as an example of the soft skills and hard skills considered as a necessary part of the training:

Training Outline

Day	Theme		Content
1	Introduction, "Who am I?" & family		• Introduction of *Training Initiative* • Participant Introductions

		• My family • Who am I? • Types of relationships
2	Emotional healing	• How did I get where I am now? • Feelings and responsibilities • Anger & guilt • Forgiveness
3	Character	• Integrity • The Golden Rule • Rationalisations • Types of communication • Conflict styles • 'I' messages
4	Problem-solving & Customer service	• Introduction to Interviews • Exercises in problem-solving • Steps to problem-solving • Customer service • Literacy testing
5	Human rights, Domestic violence, HIV/AIDS	• Human Rights • Domestic violence • Nutrition and hygiene • Drugs • Alcohol • Facts about HIV/AIDS • Living with HIV/AIDS
6	Personal finance	• Attitudes to money • Budgeting • Debt • Numeracy test
7	You in the workplace	• In-depth Interviews • The working environment • Basic Conditions of Employment Act
8	CV's & cover letters	• Your skills and abilities • Looking for the right fit (matching the person and the job)

			• Putting together a CV • Personal timelines • Cover letter • Exercise on cover letters
9	Phone calls &	interviews	• Individual interview practical • Newspapers & phone calls • Introduction to the Resource Centre
10	Goals &	graduation	• Goal setting • Share goals and dreams • Reflect on two weeks: feedback of course • Mentoring questions • Celebration and Graduation

Table 7.1 Training Course Outline (Black 2010:179-180)

The course was adjusted in the third year to include a mandated computer training module.

The training is intended to achieve at least five overall goals:

- Bring healing and self-discovery
- Provide spiritual transformation/emotional development
- Provide positive character development
- Assess numeracy/literacy
- Enable participants to find and remain in an economically viable situation.

The training is designed to be instructional in two ways. First, it aims to prepare unemployed people to navigate the job-search process successfully so that they can find available work opportunities for which they may be qualified. The training encourages good character traits along with the skills to prepare an excellent CV and instruction for conducting oneself during a job interview. However, secondly, and equally as important, the training assists people in the process of psychological and emotional healing. The damage inflicted upon the majority of South Africans through the machinations of apartheid has inflicted pain and brokenness upon most individuals. These individuals need restoration to go forward, helping them to realise that they are valuable both to God and to society and that they have a unique role to play in their community. Such a process is not quick, nor is it easy. However, it is essential if South Africans are to claim the heritage that was birthed in 1994.

5.7.2 Business partnership

'Business Partners' are businesses that agree to hire training graduates and give feedback on the employee's job performance. The first Business Partners were respondents to the questionnaires in the research phase and were initially approached as a follow-up and given the first opportunity to hire the people that had been trained according to their business specifications. Many of these 'partners' indicated surprise that there had been a follow-up to the questionnaire and that their preferred qualities had been incorporated into a training curriculum. Consequently, they were often quite eager to fill vacancies with trained programme graduates.

5.7.3 Resourcing

The *Zanokhanyo Training and Resource Centre,* a project established from the research, was envisioned to become a place that would help graduates take ultimate responsibility for their personal development and employment situation. Graduates are given access to computers and available information and for nominal fees are permitted to make employment-related document copies and send faxes. Training personnel are also available to help update CVs and provide additional mentoring or counselling.

In August 2009, the *Zanokhanyo Training and Resource Centre* opened in one of the business communities 'mapped' during the research project on the outskirts of the Langa community approximately 300 meters from the train station. It initially contained a Resource Centre with five computers and a copy/scan/fax/print machine for use by graduates at nominal rates. Job adverts from local newspapers and postings by Business Partners are readily accessible at the Centre. Graduates are encouraged to use the computers to set up a personal e-mail account, search/browse the Internet for job openings, learn basic computer skills and update CVs. Hundreds of training graduates have found or been placed in jobs or have returned to finish schooling. Transformational shifts happen during the training enabling trainees to find hope and opportunity. Moreover, through the training process, many graduates become followers of Christ or renew their faith.

Additionally, follow up research undertaken by the UCT Sociology Department[147] has indicated that the training is having a positive benefit on the businesses in which *Zanokhanyo* graduates are working. Employers indicated they preferred hiring Zanokhanyo graduates because they have 'better CVs, they are better prepared for the interview process and tend to be more honest, dedicated and willing to learn . . . than other workers without similar training' (Hangala and Mutesha 2013:23). This has been an opportunity perfectly crafted for the church as a transformational development mission strategy to fight poverty as a movement of the gospel in local communities.

One could rightly question whether this type of initiative could be properly initiated by an organisation outside of a faith-based paradigm with similar effect. In the case of unemployment intermediation efforts, certainly there are organisations effective at placing people operating from a secular framework.[148] However, poverty is a result of relationships that are broken, 'the absence of shalom in all its meanings' (Myers 1999:86). Providing an opportunity to provide for one's physical needs through employment is important and satisfies a number of the axiological needs mentioned by Max-Neef and detailed in chapter three (page 67). However, there are needs relating to identity and transcendence that remain unsatisfied.

Myers remarks that the core of the understanding of poverty is 'the idea of the poor not knowing who they are or the reason for which they were created' (Myers 1999:87). Without the knowledge that one is created in the image of God with purpose and value, one's understanding of personal identity is deeply marred. The biblical story identifies sin as being at the heart of the broken relationships that have marred creation, severing relationships between God and man and man with man. 'Sin is what distorts these relationships. Sin is the root cause of deception, distortion and domination. When God is at the sidelines or written out of our story, we do not treat each other well' (Myers 1999:88).

Transformational development that is Christian must address what is at the heart of poverty to bring about its elimination. 'There can be no practice of transformational development that is Christian unless somewhere, in some form, people are hearing the good news of the gospel and being given a chance to respond (Myers 1999:88). At the heart of all broken relationships is the broken relationship between God and man that can only be answered through Jesus Christ.

Chapter three contained stories of hopelessness portrayed through the lens of the World Bank Report (1999) that described the lives of people trapped within a cycle of poverty from within which they felt unable to escape. The crucial call to the Church, and by definition the evangelical movement, to fight poverty as a faith-demonstrating act of mission is displayed poignantly through the stories of people impacted by the Zanokhanyo training model. These stories from Zanokhanyo training course graduates present a picture of the impact of mission that goes beyond economic transformation to holistic development.

- 'When I came to Zanokhanyo I had lost hope and faith. I have opened up since taking the training and have been helped a lot. I have grown spiritually and learned to forgive. My relationship with my mom has been restored. Thanks to all at Zanokhanyo. You have a gift from God and have helped a lot' (female graduate from December).

- 'I was looking for work and met Sis Pam, the Face of Zanokhanyo. She said, "We can't give you a job, but we can give you hope." I was angry and hopeless and without forgiveness. I have learnt to control my anger. Thanks to all the team, till we meet again' (female graduate from December).

- 'I didn't know there was a place like Zanokhanyo, such a magnificent place. Thanks to all for adding value to our lives. You all play a huge role in our lives. You taught us emotionally, spiritually, academically. I feel like staying forever. I have never been in a place that puts God first. We need more places like this in our communities. You re-instilled hope and taught me about the Bible as well. I learned how important God is in every area of life, each and every step. I want to go add value to other people's lives. I was reminded I still have a chance to succeed. I'm so grateful God brought me here. I love you guys' (male graduate from February).

- 'Whoever's idea this was, it was a good one. I was very skeptical about all the biblical stuff, but I came to realize they know what they're doing. God has been here for me. I started praying and immediately things started happening. I have a job that starts 1 March! The environment in our society is bringing us down. We need to stop listening to the voices that are trying to bring us down. You are more! Thanks to all' (male graduate from February).

- 'Zanokhanyo brings light to everyone. I used to think my problems were bigger than anyone's, but not now. Thanks to the whole team. Phil. 4.9 – Whatever we have seen and heard, that we will put into practice. Commit yourself to the Lord and your plans will succeed. I'm now cleansed inside and out, born again. Keep on doing your hard work, Zanokhanyo' (female graduate from December).[149]

The Church on mission offers hope and a way forward through the message of the gospel. If it is true that sin is the fundamental cause of one's lack of *shalom*, the consequences of failing to deal with this are massive. 'The good news is that through Jesus Christ there is a way out of sin toward transformation. The bad news is that if this news is not accepted, there is a sense in which those who refuse sit wrapped in chains of self-imposed limitations' (Myers 1999:88). Although a secular NGO can participate in activities related to poverty alleviation, the gospel is the necessary ingredient for bringing holistic transformation. This confrontation with extreme 'poverties' falls within the realm of the mission of the Church.

5.8 Summary

It is important to summarise this process in light of some of the earlier findings from this chapter. What one hopes will emerge from this study is the motivation to construct a holistic church-based model for engaging poverty in local South African communities from a gospel mandate. The model envisioned is led by Christopraxis as the church engages, bringing light and healing to communities in pain. Ammerman (1997:370) describes this well: 'Congregations are both sacred places, making claims for the power of a transcendent Other in the midst of this world, and civic places, mobilizing all sorts of resources for the sake of the community.' These churches are led by leaders modelling engagement in the lives of the poor for their congregations with a clear theology, well articulated for the church community. They have a strong relational focus that builds bridges into areas of pain. They are developmental in nature. Bowers-Du Toit & Nkomo (2014:8) write:

> The charity and 'ad hoc' approaches employed by congregations in addressing poverty within South Africa, whilst well-meaning, do not acknowledge the structural nature of the system of poverty and inequality engendered by apartheid. To repair the past demands more than this. . . .

A church congregation looking for ways to engage in a way that moves beyond a 'charity only' model is heading in the right direction.

> 'Majority white' congregations, who not only acknowledged the injustice of apartheid, but have sacrificially reached out in intentional ways to build relationships across the divide as part of their attempt to restore the socio-economic injustices of the past, have made the most progress... although there is still a long way to go before we can say we have seen true reconciliation and transformation in this country (Bowers-DuToit & Nkomo 2014:8).

The church-based initiative detailed in this study contained the elements necessary for a sustainable engagement at the inception of the initiative and throughout its early years. The church community was called to action by engaged leaders who shaped a theological understanding regarding the poor and injustice that was clear and compelling. The engagement was modelled by these leaders as a response to the Gospel. A strong partnership was established with a congregation within the same denomination located in the target community that was highly relational. The NGO that was created as a structure for the initiative had Board members from both churches that played an equal role in decision-making.

The training model was launched from within this partnering church in the target community.

As the years progressed, the training programme for unemployed people was successful as many hundreds of graduates found employment and hope. Additional computer training helped many graduates to source their own employment in addition to the placement opportunities available through business partners. However, the partnership between the two congregations diminished, although they remain within the same denominational structure. The leadership of the implementing congregation changed and there was no longer a clear theology formulated to articulate the need for continued relationship and engagement. There was a lack of clarity around the ongoing role of the church in this mission and the church retreated into programmes mainly focused upon welfare and charity, activities more easily managed. Recently, the project was merged into another organisation backed by a large non-denominational church with a clearly articulated theology regarding justice and poverty, modelled by leaders teaching this as a lifestyle. Their approach is developmental and oriented toward partnering with community churches seeking to empower their congregations and communities. The merger, although difficult, has benefitted both organisations as the model has been re-examined and strengthened.

This backdrop highlights the importance of leadership for the sustainability of these initiatives, leadership that maintains a clear theology that motivates active mission towards the poor. This is key for the evangelical movement—or any church—if one is to make a sustainable difference in South African society.

6 Conclusion

The church enjoys significant credibility around South Africa, ranking at 74 percent as a social institution with the highest level of trust in South African society (URDR 2004:5), underscoring the fact that interventions connected to churches have credibility that can serve to open doors in the community. Whether they remain open will probably be determined by the quality and usefulness of the projects undertaken.

One hopes that at this point in the study some clear concepts have emerged. First, for those within the evangelical movement and all Christ followers, there is an unavoidable responsibility for the care and provision of the poor. This responsibility has been argued from a coherence with the historical evangelical movement, seen as a core part of 'activism.' The evangelical movement was actively engaged in care for the poor until the 'Great Reversal' of the early 20th century. Reasons were given in Chapter two for this almost wholesale abandonment of the poor by evangelicals, chief of these being the dualism that had developed emphasising spiritually focused activities over those that are physical. Evangelical 'activism' was steeped in care for the poor in a passion that emanated from adherence to the clear teaching of Scripture. This activism fell away so that it has been considered more important to focus one's energies on the rescue of souls to the exclusion of meeting physical needs, a division of labour that is unbiblical at its core.

Old Testament prescriptions for the poor mandated care for those in need through specific provision so that no one would be able to remain in poverty as a permanent state. Although God's mandated provision was followed inconsistently by his people, at the heart of the law was the understanding that God was the rightful owner of everything and that humans were exercising stewardship on God's behalf. Failure to recognise this brought God's judgment.

The New Testament is also clear regarding responsibility for the poor. Jesus was born into poverty and ministered in a way that met both the spiritual and physical needs of those around him, encouraging his followers to 'love your neighbour as you love yourself,' a modifier that requires care in provision for one's neighbour to the extent that one cares for oneself. Each human carrying the image of God has value and should be honoured. Andrew Root (2014a:116) is helpful here:

> The neighbour is not first of all an ethical construct based on some general ethical principle of duty or even love. The neighbour is both God and the other. To deny the other as neighbour is to deny God. To recognize the other a neighbour is to recognize the good and the right as the demand of God on me through the neighbour.

James 2 is clear that there is to be no preferential treatment for the rich by engaging in behaviour that dishonours the poor. Faith that is living faith is manifested by corresponding works. James makes no allowance in his teaching for those who would practice dualism: 'For as the body apart from the spirit is dead, so also faith apart from works is dead' (James 2.26). His arguments are well articulated to bring about change to his original church community as well as to the Church throughout the ages.

Second, there is an unimaginable opportunity for mission. At its core, the post-apartheid church appears to struggle to define its role in the new South Africa. So

> ... there is evidence which suggests that churches are trusted institutions, much involved with serving the poor and hence perceived positively by the population. On the other hand, similarly pervasive evidence suggests that churches inhibit change, are reluctantly involved with poor and vulnerable people, and that they supported Apartheid (See Erasmus in Bowers-Du Toit 2012a:11).

However, the evangelical movement has a significant role to play in the continuing process of transformation so necessary for the rebuilding of society. Much of what is required is, in fact, spiritual, far more than just rearranging the economy. Mamphela Ramphele defines this work as 'transcendence ... which is usually associated with the spiritual realm ... [requiring] openness to a radically different frame of reference; it takes one beyond the known to the unknown, demanding courage and a willingness to take risks' (Ramphele 2008:17). She further observes that humanity is 'framed in significant ways by spiritual and psychological impulses that go beyond material needs' (Ramphele 2008:17). This means much more than just financial prosperity. Ramphele warns, '(m)aterial freedom disengaged from inner spiritual freedom puts us at risk of losing the focus on the larger purpose of freedom—freedom to be fully who we can be in our democracy' (2008:18). It is much more than just engaging with the economic effects of poverty.

But to avoid falling into dualism, one must be aware that much of what is required is physical, a physical presence in community that walks with one's neighbour. This is a function of Christopraxis. Andrew Root (2014a:114) would remind one that

> a practical theology of Christopraxis seeks to examine human relationships of shared humanity as places where the ministry of God as event is occurring, using the very epistemological criterion of sharing in death for the sake of life as its hermeneutic that allows for both discernment and re-envisioned practice.

One operates as the hands and feet of Jesus, sharing in pain and brokenness as the presence of Jesus in communities.

> We join God's ministry by going to Egypt, by walking with the heartbroken woman into the morgue, by entering the impossibility of death, but in so doing we are drawn into God's act of giving God's eternal being through Jesus so those ministered to might live and experience God's presence as com-

ing to them (Root 2014a:113).

The evangelical movement has the opportunity to do this as an act of mission through a process that meets needs by building relationships in communities. Poverty is a result of 'relationships that do not work, that are not just, that are not for life, that are not harmonious or enjoyable. Poverty is the absence of shalom in all its meanings' (Myers 1999:86). This refrain, though often repeated during the course of this thesis, should be at the heart of evangelical mission into communities of need. The evangelical community can engage with an approach that identifies areas of need and works in a holistic manner built upon relationships, seeking sustainability. Human Scale Development is a tool to facilitate the process. The approach modelled for unemployed people may function as a guideline to serve praxis.

The way forward is challenging. The factors that create persistent poverty are often intractable, without an easily defined solution. However, the church, above any institution, should be involved in making a difference. The paradigms of church leaders and congregations must be challenged, examined in light of the clear directives of Scripture. Theology defining God's care and concern for the poor should be clearly articulated. Activities should be focused on specific ways that the gospel can engage with community in light of the needs of society. There are research models that can assist in this endeavour. Jesus had a specific mission and purpose, which he clearly identified:

> The Spirit of the Lord is upon me, because He has anointed me to bring good news to the poor. He has sent me to proclaim release to the captives and recovery of sight to the blind, to let the oppressed go free, to proclaim the year of the Lord's favour (Lk. 4:18-19).

He inaugurated a movement that has shared the 'good news'

with those in need by speaking words of life and living in total obedience to the will of his Father. Each gathering of believers has a role to play in developing sustainable interventions that address poverty and other poverty-related issues. No church, if it seeks to live in obedience to Scripture, is exempt from this task.

Strategies must be developed that will begin to implement community transformation. Developmental initiatives can be designed that will enable those in poverty to become equipped to succeed, although the church will likely need to prepare for the long-term commitment necessary to bring about needed change. Strategic partnerships can be developed among churches to combine resources toward a common purpose, thereby strengthening community and focusing larger groups for greater impact.

The evangelical community has a rich heritage of social engagement. Early Evangelicals were successful in transforming society in tangible ways, motivated largely by the desire to see the gospel presented to the world. The evangelical community, though still largely dormant, can usher in a movement that could fundamentally transform local South Africa communities. The proclamation of the gospel must arise from the church within a context of authenticity.

It is important for the evangelical movement to understand the context, gather facts, analyse the situation and do its research. It must understand its mission and be willing to partner with others in this endeavour. By knowing its mandate, according to the history of its movement and Scriptural guidance, it can function as a significant role player in the fight against the massive challenges that confront not only South African communities, but communities across the world.

REFERENCE LIST

1. Adamson J 1989. *James: The man and his message.* Grand Rapids, MI: Wm. B. Eerdmans.

2. Albertyn J and Rothman M 1932. *Die Armblank-Vraagstuk in Suid Afrika: Verslag van di Carnegie Kommisie—Deel V: Sosiologiese Verslag.* Stellenbosch: Pro Ecclesia

3. Alter R 1989. *The pleasures of reading in an ideological age.* New York: Simon & Schuster.

4. Ammerman N 1997. *Congregation and community.* New Brunswick, NJ: Rutgers University Press.

5. Anderson R 1979. Editor's introduction. In: Anderson R (ed), *Theological foundations for ministry.* Grand Rapids, MI: Eerdmans.

6. _____ 2001. *The shape of practical theology: Empowering ministry with theological praxis.* Downers Grove, IL: InterVarsity Press.

7. Aune D E 1987. *The New Testament in its literary environment.* Library of Early Christianity, vol VIII. Meeks W A (ed). Philadelphia, PA: Westminster Press.

8. Banks R 1999. *Reenvisioning theological education: Exploring a missional alternative to current models.* Grand Rapids, MI: Eerdmans.

9. Barth K 1956. *Church dogmatics, vol IV, 3.1.* Trans. Bromiley G. London: T & T Clark.

10. _____1960. *Community, state and church. Three essays by Karl Barth.* New York: Anchor Books.

11. Bebbington D 1989. *Evangelicalism in modern Britain: A history from the 1730s to the 1980s.* New York: Routledge.

12. Betz H D 1985a. *Essays on the Sermon on the Mount.* Philadelphia: Fortress Press.

13. _____ 1985b. *A commentary on the Sermon on the*

Mount, including the Sermon on the Plain (Matthew 5:3-7:27 and Luke 6:20-49). Minneapolis: Fortress Press.

14. Biko S 1978. *I write what I like.* San Francisco: Harper & Row.

15. Bitzer L 1968. The rhetorical situation. [Online] Accessed from: <http://www.comphacker.org/comp/engl335fosen/files/2012/08/Bitzer.pdf> 2016-03-05.

16. Black T 2010. A biblical approach to poverty alleviation: A case study of Pinelands Methodist Church, Phambili ngeThemba's community building efforts through job creation in Langa Township. [MA Thesis]. University of Pretoria.

17. Blomberg C 1999. *Neither poverty nor riches: A biblical theology of possessions.* Downers Grove, IL: InterVarsity Press.

18. Boesak A 1984. Poverty: The moral challenge. 'Get up and walk.' Paper no. 308. In: *Second Carnegie Inquiry in poverty & development.* Southern Africa Labour and Development Research Unit. [Online] Accessed from: <http://opensaldru.uct.ac.za/bitstream/handle/11090/20 1/1984_boesak_ccp308.pdf >2016-07-28.

19. Bonhoeffer D 1971. *Letters and papers from prison.* New York: Macmillan.

20. Bonhoeffer D 1979. Christ, the church, and the world. In: Anderson R (ed) *Theological foundations for ministry,* 534-566. Edinburgh: T & T Clark.

21. _____1995. *The cost of discipleship.* New York: Simon and Schuster.

22. Booth W 1890. *In darkest England and the way out.* London: Salvation Army.

23. Bosch D 2011. *Transforming mission: Paradigm shifts in theology of mission.* Maryknoll, NY: Orbis Books.

24. Bowers N 2005. Development as transformation: The local church in Lavender Hill as agent of change in a post-Carnegie II context. [Phd Dissertation]: University of Stellenbosch.

25. Bowers-Du Toit N 2012a. The church as an agent of change: Reflections of the role of the church in Carnegie 1, II and now III? Conference: Strategies to overcome poverty and inequality, 'Towards Carnegie III?' 3-7 September 2012, University of Cape Town. [Online] Accessed from:<http://carnegie 3.org.za/ docs/papers/34_Bowers_The church as an agent of change-reflections on the role of the church in Carnegie I, II and now III.pdf. > 2016-06-13.

26. _____ 2012b. Remembrance and renewal: Exploring the role of the church as an agent of welfare after 15 years of democracy. *The Eradication of Poverty*, Volume 53, (2). [Online] Accessed from: <http://ngtt.journals.ac.za/ pub/article/ viewFile/ 207/pdf> 2016-07-19.

27. _____ 2015. "Rise up and Walk": Tracing the trajectory of the Carnegie discourse and plotting a way forward. [Online] Accessed from: <https:// www.researchgate.net/ publication/273389345_'Rise_up_and_Walk_Tracing_the_trajectory_of_the_Carnegie_discourse_and_plotting_a_way_ forward >2016-07-15.

28. Bowers Du Toit N and Nkomo G 2014. The ongoing challenge of restorative justice in South Africa: How and why wealthy suburban congregations are responding to poverty and inequality. In: *HTS Teologiese Studies/Theological Studies,* 70 (2), Art.

#2022, 8 pages. [Online] Accessed from: <http://dx-doi.org/10.4102/hts.v70i2.2022 >2016-07-18.

29. Bragg W 1987. From development to transformation. In: Samuel V and Sugden C (eds), *The church in response to human need*, 25-61. Grand Rapids, MI: Wm B Eerdmans.

30. Brandel-Syrier M 1978. *Coming through. The search for a new cultural identity*. Johannesburg: McGraw-Hill.

31. Brosend W 2004. James and Jude. In: Witherington B (ed), *The new Cambridge Bible commentary*, 1-206. Cambridge: Cambridge University Press.

32. Browning D 1976. *The moral context of pastoral care*. Philadelphia: Westminster Press.

33. _____ 1991. *A fundamental practical theology: Descriptive and strategic proposals*. Minneapolis, MN: Augsburg Fortress.

34. _____ 1999. Towards a Fundamental and Strategic Practical Theology. In: Schweitzer E and van der Ven J (eds), *Practical Theology: International Perspectives*. New York: Peter Lang.

35. Brueggemann W 1980. Covenant as a subversive paradigm. In: *Christian Century*, 1094-1099, 12 November. [Online] Accessed from: <http://www.religion-online.org/showarticle.asp?title=1727> 2016 07-31.

36. Brunner E 1979. *The divine imperative*. Louisville, KY: John Knox Press.

37. Bryant D 1973. *Rhetorical Dimensions in Criticism*. Baton Rouge, LA: Louisiana State University Press.

38. Budlender D 2000. Human development. In: May J (ed), *Poverty and inequality in South Africa: Meeting the challenge*, 97-140. Cape Town: David Philip.

39. Calvin J 1997. *Institutes of the Christian religion*. Bellingham, WA: Logos Bible Software.

40. Calvin J & Anderson J 2010. *Commentary on the book of Psalms*. Bellingham, WA: Logos Bible Software.

41. Chester T 2009. Eschatology and the transformation of the world: Contradictions, continuity, conflation and the endurance of hope. In: Grant J and Hughes D (eds), *Transforming the world? The gospel and social responsibility*, 224-245. Nottingham, England: Apollos.

42. Christian J 2008. An alternate reading of poverty. In: Myers B (ed), *Working with the poor: New insights and learnings from development practitioners*, 3-27. Colorado Springs, CO: Authentic Publishing.

43. Clarke J 1993. Human scale development: A South African perspective. *EFSA Institute for Theological and Transdisciplinary Research*, Studies and Reports. University of the Western Cape:EFSA.

44. Clawson M 2012. Misión integral and progressive evangelicalism: The Latin American influence on the North American emerging church. *Religions* 2012, 3, 790-807. [Online] Accessed from: <http://www.mdpi.com/journal/religions-03-00790.pdf> 2013-12-24.

45. Coffey J 2008. Puritanism, evangelicalism and the evangelical protestant tradition. In: Haykin M and Stewart K (eds), *The advent of evangelicalism*, 252-277. Nashville, TN: B & H Publishing Group.

46. Concerned Evangelicals 1987. Evangelicals Critique their own Theology and Practice. *Transformation*, 4(1), 17-30. [Online] Accessed from: <http://www.jstor.org/stable/43052184> 2016-07-08.

47. Conradie E 2005. Mission as evangelism and as development? Some perspectives from the Lord's

Prayer. *International Review of Mission*, 94(375). [Online] Accessed from: <http://repository.uwc.ac.za /xmlui/ bitstream/handle/10566/385/ ConradieLordsPrayer2005.pdf>2016-07-08.

48. Corbett E P J 1969. *Rhetorical analysis of literary works*. New York: Oxford University Press.

49. Corbett S and Fikkert B 2009. *When helping hurts: How to alleviate poverty without hurting the poor and yourself*. Chicago: Moody Publishers.

50. Cosby B [s.a.]. Toward a definition of 'puritan' and 'puritanism': A study in puritan historiography. [Online] Accessed from: <http://www.biblicalstudies.org.uk/pdf/churchman/122-04_297.pdf> 2013-12-21.

51. Cowper W 1835. *The works of William Cowper: poems*. Grimshaw T S (ed). Vol 6. London: Saunders & Otley.

52. CRESR 1982. *Evangelism and social responsibility: an evangelical commitment*. Exeter: Paternoster.

53. Dames G 2008. Missional encounter of the gospel engaging cultural edges as agents of adaptive change. *Practical Theology in South Africa*, Vol 23(1). [Online] Accessed from: <http://uir.unisa.ac.za/ bitstream/ handle /10500/10526/Missional %20Encounter%20of%20the%20Gospel%20Engaging%20Cultural%20Edges%20as%20Agents %20of%20Adaptive%20Change.pdf?sequence=1> >2014-03-20.

54. _____2010. The dilemma of traditional and 21st-century pastoral ministry: Ministering to families and communities faced with socio-economic pathologies. In: *HTS Teologiese Studies/Theological Studies*, 66(2). [Online] Accessed from: <http:// www.hts.org.za > 2014-06-23.

55. Davies-Kildea J 2011. 'Soul salvation whole sal-

vation': Towards a theology of social justice. Thought Matters Conference, 2-4 September 2011 [Online] Accessed from: <http://www.sarmy.org.au/en/Social/JustSalvos/About-Us/Theology/Unwrapping-our-Bounded-Salvation/>2013-12-22.

56. Dayton D 1976. *Discovering an evangelical heritage.* Grand Rapids, MI: Baker Academic.

57. Delport K and van Wyk R 2008. *Community analysis of Langa, Western Cape.* Unpublished research material compiled for Pinelands Methodist Church, Phambili ngeThemba. Cape Town.

58. Deppe D 1990. *The sayings of Jesus in the paranaesis of James: A pdf revision of the doctoral thesis of the sayings of Jesus in the Epistle of James.* [Online] Accessed from:<http://www.oldinthenew.org/pdf/deppe _the.sayings.of.jesus.in.the.paranaesis.of.james.pdf>. 2016-02-06.

59. Dibelius M 1976. *James: A commentary on the Epistle of James.* Koester H (ed), Williams M (trans.). Philadelphia: Fortress Press.

60. Dunn J D G 2003. *Christianity in the making, vol. 1: Jesus remembered.* Grand Rapids, MI: Eerdmans.

61. Edwards J 1736. A narrative of surprising conversions. In: *The works of Jonathan Edwards, Vol 1.* Peabody, MA: Hendrickson Publishers.

62. Elliot C 1987. *Comfortable compassion? Poverty and power and the church.* London: Hodder and Stoughton.

63. Elmer D 2006. *Cross-cultural servanthood: Serving the world in Christ-like humility.* Downers Grove, IL: InterVarsity Press.

64. Erasmus J, Hendriks H J and Mans G 2004. Religious research as kingpin in the fight against poverty and

AIDS in the Western Cape, South Africa. [Online] Accessed from: <http://www.a-dademia.edu/4442022/ Religious_ Research_as_Kingpin_in_the_fight_against_Poverty_and_AIDS_in_the_Western_Cape_South_Africa1> 2014-01-11.

65. Fowler J 1985. 'Practical theology and Theological Education: Some models and Questions,' *Theology Today* 42, 43-58. [Online] Accessed from: <doi:10.1177/004057368504200106>2016-06-23
.

66. Gadamer H 1982. *Truth and method.* New York: Crossroads.

67. George T 1999. If I am and evangelical, what am I? In: *Christianity Today*, 43(9) 62. [Online] Accessed from: <http://christianitytoday.com/ct/1999/august9/9t9062.html> 2013-12-31.

68. Goheen M 1992. Mission in the evangelical and ecumenical traditions. In *Pro Rege, Dec-1992.* [Online] Accessed from: <http://www.dordt.edu/publications/pro-rege/crcpi/64314.pdf> 2013-12-20.

69. Goldingay J [s.a]. Is election fair? [Online]. Accessed from: <http://infoguides.fuller.edu/content.php?pid=190354&sid=3819594> 2014-12-25.

70. Gorringe T 1999. *Karl Barth: Against hegemony.* Oxford: Oxford University. [Online]. Accessed from: < http://www.questia.com/read/62970 102> 2014-07-24.

71. Gossai H 1993. Justice, righteousness, and the social critique of the eighth-century prophets. *American University Studies, Series 7: Theology and Religion, vol. 141.* New York: Peter Lang.

72. Gowler D 2010. Socio-rhetorical interpretation: Textures of a text and its reception. In: *Journal for the Study of the New Testament*, 33(2), 191-206. [Online] Accessed from:<http://jnt. sagepub.com/content/ 33/2/191.refs. html> 2011-02-14.

73. Graham E 1996. *Transforming practice: Pastoral theology in an age of uncertainty.* New York: Mowbray.

74. Greer P and Smith P 2009. *The poor will be glad: Joining the revolution to lift the world out of poverty.* Grand Rapids, MI: Zondervan.

75. Grenz S 1996. *A Primer on postmodernism.* Grand Rapids, MI: Wm. B. Eerdmans.

76. Gutiérrez G 2003. *We drink from our own wells: The spiritual journey of people.* Maryknoll, NY: Orbis.

77. Halliday M A K 1979. *Language as social semiotic. The social interpretation of language and meaning.* London: Arnold.

78. Hazle D 2003. Practical theology today and the implications for mission. In: *International Review of Mission* 92, no. 366. [Online] Accessed from: <http:// www.questia.com/ read/1G1-107761086.>2014-07-24.

79. Helm P 2008. Calvin, A.M. Toplady and the Bebbington thesis. In: Haykin M and Stewart K (eds), *The advent of evangelicalism,* 199-220. Nashville, TN: B & H Publishing Group.

80. Hendriks H J 2007. Missional theology and social development. In: *HTS Teologiese Studies/Theological Studies,* 63(3), 999-1016. DOI: 10.4102/hts.v63i3.244 [Online] Accessed from: <http:// www.hts.org.za/index.php/HTS/article/ view/244>2014-03-24.

81. Henry C F H 1947. *The uneasy conscience of funda-*

mentalism. Grand Rapids, MI: Wm. B. Eerdmans.

82. Herberg W 1960. The social philosophy of Karl Barth (Introduction). In: *Community, state and church. Three essays by Karl Barth*. New York: Anchor Books.

83. Hindmarsh D 2008. The antecedents of evangelical conversion narrative: spiritual autobiography and the Christian tradition. In: Haykin M and Stewart K (eds), *The advent of evangelicalism*, 327-344. Nashville, TN: B & H Publishing Group.

84. Hirsch A 2006. *The forgotten ways: Reactivating the missional church*. Grand Rapids, MI: Brazos Press.

85. _____2010. Reawakening a potent missional ethos in the twenty-first century church. In: *Missiology: An International Review*, Vol XXXVIII, no. 1, January 2010.

86. Holy Bible: English Standard Version [ESV] 2001. Wheaton, IL: Crossway.

87. Howitt Q and Morphew D [s.a.]. The Kingdom, human dignity and the poor. [NBI/VBI Online Course] Accessed from: <http://www.vineyardbi.org> 2008-06-05.

88. Hughes D 2009. Understanding and overcoming poverty. In: Grant J and Hughes D (eds), *Transforming the world: The gospel and social responsibility*, 168-186. Nottingham: Apollos.

89. Hunter J 2010. *To change the world: The irony, tragedy and possibility of Christianity in the late modern world*. New York, NY: Oxford University Press.

90. Ikuenobe P 2006. *Philosophical perspectives on communalism and morality in African traditions*. Lanham: Lexington Books.

91. James S [s.a.]. Continuity or discontinuity in evangelical history? [Online] Ac-

cessed from:<http://www.reformation-today.org/issues/articles/Continuity orDiscontinuity.pdf> 2013-07-24.

92. Johnson L 1995. *The letter of James.* Anchor Bible 37A. New York: Doubleday.

93. _____ 2004. *Brother of Jesus, friend of God: Studies in the letter of James.* Grand Rapids: Wm. B. Eerdmans. Kindle edition.

94. Kairos Southern Africa 2012. *Kairos Southern Africa: Theological and ethical reflections on the 2012 centenary celebrations of the African National Congress, 28 December 2011.* [Online] Accessed from: <http://us-cdn.creamermedia.co.za/assets/articles/attachments/ 37301_ kairos-2012.pdf >2016-07-08.

95. Kaufmann W 1956. *Existentialism from Dostoevsky to Sarte.* New York: Meridian Books.

96. Kennedy G A 1984. *New Testament interpretation through rhetorical criticism.* Chapel Hill, NC. University of North Carolina Press.

97. Kirk J A 1985. *Good News of the Kingdom coming.* Downers Grove, IL: InterVarsity Press.

98. Kloppenborg Verbin J S 1999. Patronage avoidance in James. In: *HTS Teologiese Studies/Theological Studies, 55(4), 755-794.* [Online] Accessed from: <http://www.repository.up.ac.za/bitstream/ handle/ 2263/ 15461/ Klop penborgVerbin_Patronage(1999).pdf?sequence=1>2015-06-23.

99. Knierim R 1995. *The task of Old Testament theology: Substance, method, and cases.* Grand Rapids: Eerdmans.

100. Koester H 1990. *Ancient Christian Gospels: Their history and development.* Philadelphia: Trinity Press.

101. Korten D 1991. *Getting to the 21ˢᵗ century; Voluntary action and the global agenda.* West Hartford, CT: Kumarian Press.

102. Koyama K 1980. *Three mile an hour God.* Maryknoll, NY: Orbis Books.

103. Kraemer H 1938. *The christian message in a non-christian world.* London: Harper & Brothers.

104. Kritzinger J, Meiring P, and Saayman W 1994. *On being witnesses.* Halfway House: Orion.

105. Lampe G W H 1986. Diakonia in the early church. In: McCord J I and Parker T H L (eds), *Service in Christ: Essays presented to Karl Barth on his 80ᵗʰ birthday.* Grand Rapids, MI: Eerdmans Publishing.

106. Larsen T 2008. The reception given *Evangelicalism in modern Britain* since its publication in 1989. In: Haykin M and Stewart K (eds), *The advent of evangelicalism,* 21-36. Nashville, TN: B & H Publishing Group.

107. Laws S 1980. *The epistle of James.* London: Continuum.

108. Le Bruyns C 2006. Can any public good come from evangelicals? Theological paradigms and possibilities toward a transforming South Africa. In: van den Heever G A (ed), *Religion and Theology,* 13:3-4, 341-358. Unisa Press.

109. Leibbrandt M, Woolard I, and Bhorat H 2001. Understanding contemporary household inequality in South Africa, In: Bhorat H et. al. (eds), *Fighting poverty: labour markets and inequality in South Africa.* Cape Town: UCT Press.

110. Lightstone J 2002. *Mishnah and the social Formation of the early rabbinic guild: a socio-rhetorical approach.* Waterloo: Wilfrid Laurier University Press.

[Online] Accessed from: <https://muse.jhu.edu/>
2016-01-25.

111. Lindberg C 1981. Through a glass darkly: a history
of the Church's vision of the poor and poverty.
In: *The ecumenical review,* 33 (1), 37-52. New York:
WCC.

112. Loder J and Neidhardt 1992. *The knights move: The
relational logic of Spirit in theology and science.* Colorado Springs, CO: Helmers & Howard.

113. Lovelace R 1981. Completing an awakening. In: *Christian Century,* Mar 18,
296-300. [Online] Accessed from: <http://
www.religion-online.org/show article.asp?
title=1743> 2013-12-24.

114. Lyall D 2001. Integrity of pastoral care. In: *New Library of Pastoral Care.* London: SPCK.

115. Mack B 1990. *Rhetoric in the New Testament: Guides
to biblical scholarship.* New Testament Series. Minneapolis: Fortress Press.

116. Mack B & Robbins V 1989. *Patterns of persuasion in
the Gospels.* Sonoma, CA: Polebridge Press.

117. MacKenzie C 2008. The evangelical character of
Martin Luther's faith. In: Haykin M and Stewart K
(eds), *The advent of evangelicalism,* 171-198. Nashville, TN: B & H Publishing Group.

118. Maggay M 1994. *Transforming society.* London: Regnum.

119. Malina B 2001. *The New Testament world: insights
from cultural anthropology.* Louisville, KY: Westminster John Knox Press.

120. Marino G 1998. Anxiety in the concept of anxiety.
In: Hannay and Marino C (eds), *The Cambridge com-
panion to Kierkegaard,* 308-328. Cambridge: Cam-

bridge University Press.

121. Marsden G 1980. *Fundamentalism and American culture. The shaping of twentieth-century evangelicalism: 1870-1925.* New York: Oxford University Press.

122. Mayor J B 1910. *The epistle of St. James.* London: Macmillan.

123. Max-Neef M 1982. *From the outside looking in: Experiences in barefoot economics.* London: Zed Books.

124. _____1991. *Human scale development: Conception, application and further reflections.* New York: Apex Press.

125. _____2005. Foundations of transdisciplinarity. In: *Ecological economics,* 53, 5-16. [Online] Accessed from: <http://artsci.unsw. wikispaces.net/file/view/Max_Neef_Foundations_of_transdisciplinarity.pdf > 2015-03-17.

126. Middleton J and Walsh B 1995. *Truth is stranger than it used to be: Biblical faith in a postmodern age.* Downers Grove, IL: InterVarsity Press.

127. Moo D 2000. *The letter of James.* Grand Rapids, MI: Wm B. Eerdmans

128. Moorhead J 1984. The erosion of postmillennialism in American religious thought, 1865-1925. In: *Church History,* 53(1) Mar., 1984, 61-77.

129. Mott S 1982. *Biblical ethics and social change.* New York, NY: Oxford University Press.

130. _____ 1993. *A Christian perspective on political thought.* Oxford: Oxford University Press.

131. Myers B 1999. *Walking with the poor: Principles and practices of transformational development.* Maryknoll, NY: Orbis.

132. _____2008. Preface: Setting the table. In Myers

B (ed), *Working with the poor: New insights from development practitioners.* Colorado Springs, CO: Authentic Books.

133. Narayanan Y 2013. Religion and sustainable development: Analysing the connections. In: *Sustainable Development,* 21, 131-139. [Online]. Accessed from: <http://www.academia.edu/ 5497953 /Religion_ and_ Sustainable_ Development_Analysing_ the_ Connections>2014-03-18.

134. Newbigin L 1954. *The household of God: Lessons on the nature of the church.* New York: Friendship Press.

135. _____ 1969. *The finality of Christ.* London: SCM.

136. _____1986. *Foolishness to the Greeks: The gospel and western culture.* Geneva: World Council of Churches.

137. _____ 1989. *The gospel in a pluralist society.* Geneva: World Council of Churches.

138. _____ 1995. *The open secret: An introduction to the theology of mission.* London: SPCK.

139. Niebuhr H R 1959. *The kingdom of God in America.* New York: Harper & Brothers.

140. Noll M 1994. *The scandal of the evangelical mind.* Grand Rapids, MI: Wm B Eerdmans.

141. _____2001a. *Turning points: Decisive moments in the history of Christianity. 2nd ed.* Nottingham, England: InterVarsity Press.

142. _____ 2001b. *American evangelical Christianity: An introduction.* Oxford: Blackwell.

143. _____2003. *The rise of evangelicalism: The age of Edwards, Whitefield and the Wesleys.* Downers Grove, IL: InterVarsity Press.

144. Osmer R 2008. *Practical theology: An introduction.* Grand Rapids, MI: Eerdmans.

145. OXFAM International 2014. Even it up: time to end extreme inequality. [Online] Accessed from: <https://www.oxfam.org/ sites/www.oxfam.org/ files/file_attachments/cr-even-it-up-extreme-inequality-291014-en.pdf> 2016 -05-22.

146. Packer J 1978. The uniqueness of Jesus Christ: Some evangelical reflections. In: *Churchman*, 92(2) 102. [Online] Accessed from:<http://church society.org/churchman/documents/Cman_092_2_Packer.pdf> 2013-09-21.

147. _____ 1990. *A quest for godliness.* Wheaton: Crossway Books.

148. Padilla C 2009. The biblical basis for social ethics. In: Grant J and Hughes D (eds), *Transforming the world? The gospel and social responsibility,* 187-204. Nottingham, England: Apollos.

149. _____ 2011. The future of the Lausanne movement. In: *International Bulletin of Missionary Research,* vol. 35(2). [Online] Accessed from: <http://www.internationalbulletin.org/system/files/2011-02-086-padilla.pdf> 2013-11-09.

150. Pauw K and Mncube L 2007. The impact of growth and redistribution on poverty and inequality in South Africa. *International Poverty Centre,* Country Study (7). [Online]. Accessed from: <http://www.sarpn.org.za/ documents /d0002634/ SA_poverty_IPC_CountryStudy7_June2007.pdf> 2008-06-17.

151. Perkins P 1995. *First and second Peter, James and Jude.* Louisville, KY: John Knox Press.

152. Pillay J 2015. The missional renaissance: Its impact on churches in South Africa, ecumenical organisations, and the development of local congregations. In: *HTS Teologiese Studies/Theological*

Studies, 71(3). [Online] Accessed from: <http// dx.doi.org/10.4102/hts.v71i3.3065> 2016-06-18.

153. Piper J 1996. *Desiring God.* Sisters, OR: Multnomah Books.

154. Ramphele M 2008. *Laying ghosts to rest: Dilemmas of the transformation in South Africa.* Cape Town: Tafelberg.

155. Robbins V 1988. The chreia. In: Aune D (ed), *Greco-Roman literature and the New Testament: Selected forms and genres,* 1-23. Atlanta: Scholars Press.

156. _____ 1991. Writing as a rhetorical act in Plutarch and the gospels. In: Watson D (ed), *Persuasive artistry: Studies in New Testament artistry in honor of George A. Kennedy,* 157-86. Sheffield: JSOT Press. [Online] Accessed from:<http:// www.religion.emory.edu/ faculty/robbins/ Pdfs/ PlutarchGospels.pdf>2016-02-13

157. _____ 1996a. *Exploring the texture of texts: A guide to socio-rhetorical interpretation.* Harrisburg, PA: Trinity International Press.

158. _____ 1996b. *The tapestry of early Christian discourse: Rhetoric, society and ideology.* London: Routledge.

159. _____ 1999. *Socio-rhetorical interpretation from its beginnings to the present.* [Online] Accessed from: <http://www. religion.emory.edu/ faculty/ robbins/Pdfs/ SNTSPretSocRhetfromBeginning.pdf >2012-10-27.

160. Root A 2014a. *Christopraxis: A practical theology of the cross.* Minneapolis, MN: Fortress Press.

161. _____ 2014b. Evangelical practical theology. In: Calahan K and Mikosi G (eds), *Opening the field of practical theology: An introduction,* 79-96. Lanham,

MD: Rowman & Littlefield.

162. Ropes J H 1926. *A critical and exegetical commentary on the epistle of St. James.* ICC 40. Edinburgh: T & T Clark.

163. Sampson C 2009. Ethical leadership and the challenges of moral transformation. In: Dames G (ed), *Ethical leadership in and through politics,* 131-144. Stellenbosch: SUN MeDIA.

164. Samuel V 1999. Mission as Transformation. In: Samuel V and Sugden C (eds), *Mission as transformation: a theology of the whole gospel,* 227-235. Oxford: Regnum.

165. _____ 2002. Mission as Transformation. In: *Transformation: An International Journal of Holistic Mission Studies,* vol. 19, (4), 243-247.

166. Schaff P 1878. *The creeds of Christendom, with a history and critical notes: the history of creeds.* New York: Harper & Brothers.

167. Schoeman W 2012. The involvement of a South African church in a changing society. In: *Verbum et Ecclesia,* 33(1), Art. #727. [Online] Accessed from: <http://dxdoi.org/10.4102/ ve.v33i172720>16-04-26.

168. Schutte D 2000. *People first: Determining priorities for community development.* Parow East: Ebony Books.

169. _____ [s.a.]. Identifying community needs: Laying the foundation for success or failure in planning community development projects. UniSearch Draft 3.

170. Sheffield D 2007. Encountering the other: Mission and transformation. [Online] Accessed from: <http://www.sheffield.typepad.com/dan-

sheffield/ files/encountering_the_othermission_
transformation.pdf> 2016-05-26.

171. Shelley B 2008. *Church history in plain language.* 3rd
ed. Nashville, TN: Thomas Nelson.

172. Sider R 1997. *Rich Christians in an age of hunger:
Moving from affluence to generosity.* 5th ed. Nashville, TN: W Publishing Group.

173. _____ 2007. *Just generosity: A new vision for overcoming poverty in America.* Grand Rapids, MI: Baker
Books.

174. Sine T and Sine C 2003. The state of God's world:
Globalization and the future of integral mission.
In: Chester T (ed), *Justice, mercy, and humility,*
65-77. [Online] Accessed from: <http://www.m-
icahnetwork.org/sites/default/files/doc/library/
integral_mission_in_context_sine_0.pdf>
2013-12-30.

175. Smith D 1998. *Transforming the world? The social
impact of British evangelicalism.* Carlisle: Paternoster Press.

176. _____ 2009. Evangelicals and society: The story
of an on-off relationship. In: Grant J and Hughes
D (eds), *Transforming the world? The gospel and social responsibility,* 246-267. Nottingham, England:
Apollos.

177. Smyth H W 1956. *Greek grammar.* Cambridge: Harvard University Press.

178. Stambaugh J & Balch D 1986. *The New Testament in
its social environment.* The Library of Early Christianity, Vol II. Meeks W (ed). Philadelphia: Westminster Press.

179. Statistics South Africa 2000. Measuring poverty in
South Africa. [Online] Accessed from: <http://

www.statssa.gov.za/publications/statsdownload.
asp?PPN=PovertyReport&SCH=2349>
2009-05-31.

180. Stewart K 2001. Did evangelicalism predate the eighteenth century? An examination of the David Bebbington thesis. [Online] Accessed from: <http://reclaimingthe mind.org/papers/ets/2001/Stewart/Steward.pdf> 2013-09-25.

181. Stott J 1975. *Christian mission in the modern world.* Downers Grove, IL: InterVarsity Press.

182. _____ 1984. *Issues facing Christians today.* 4th ed. Grand Rapids, MI: Zondervan.

183. _____ 1985. *Involvement: Being a responsible Christian in a non-Christian society.* Old Tappan, NJ: Fleming H. Revell.

184. _____ 1992. *The contemporary Christian: Applying God's word to today's world.* Downers Grove, IL: InterVarsity Press.

185. Stowers S K 1986. *Letter writing in Greco-Roman antiquity.* The Library of Early Christianity, Vol V. Meeks W (ed). Philadelphia: Westminster Press.

186. Studies in Poverty and Inequality 2007. The measurement of poverty in South Africa: Key Issues. [Online] Accessed from: <http://www.sarpn.org.za/documents/d0002801/index.php> 2008-06-03.

187. Sugden C 1999. What is good about good news to the poor? In: Samuel V and Sugden C (eds), *Mission as transformation: a theology of the whole gospel.* Oxford: Regnum.

188. _____ 2003. *Transformational development: Current state of understanding and practice.* [Online] Accessed from: <http://

www.ocrpl.org/ wp-content/uploads/2015/08/
Transformational-Development.pdf>2016-05-26.

189. _____2005. Death, injustice, resurrection and
transformation. In: *Transformation,* 22(2), 67-71.
[Online] Accessed from: http://www.jstor.org/
stable/43052901> 2016-06-28.

190. Swart I 2004. Community-centred congregational
ministry in South Africa: A plea for renewal. [On-
line] Accessed from:< http://ojs. Reformed journal-
s.co.za/index.php/ngtt/article/
view/319/612>2016-07-23.

191. Swart I and Orsmond E 2011. Making a difference? Societal entrepreneurship and its significance for a practical theological ecclesiology in a
local Western Cape context. In: *HTS Teologiese Stud-
ies/Theological Studies,* 67(2), Art. #1045. [Online]
Accessed from: <http:// dx. doi.org/ 10.4102/ht-
s.v67i2.1045>2016-07-10.

192. Sweeney D and Withrow B 2008. Jonathan Edwards: Continuator or pioneer of evangelical history? In: Haykin M and Stewart K (eds), *The advent
of evangelicalism,* 278-301. Nashville, TN: B & H
Publishing Group.

193. Swinton J 2000. *From bedlam to shalom: Towards a
practical theology of human nature, interpersonal relationships and mental health care.* New York: Peter
Lang.

194. Thurneysen E 1962. *A theology of pastoral care.* Rich-
mond, VA: John Knox Press.

195. Torrance T 1976. *Space, time and resurrection.* Grand
Rapids, MI: Eerdmans.

196. Unit for Religion and Development Research
[URDR], 2004. *Athlone/Langa Area, Transformation
Research Project.* Stellenbosch: Stellenbosch Uni-

versity. [Online] Accessed from: <http://www. sun.za/theology/urdr.htm> 2006-11-30.

197. van der Westhuizen J D N 1991. Stylistic techniques and their functions in James 2:14-26. *Neotestamentica,* 25 (1), 89-107. [Online] Accessed from: <http://www.jstor.org/stable/43070321> 2016-03-22.

198. Vanhoozer K 2007. What is everyday theology? How and why Christians should read culture. In: Anderson C, Sleasman M and Vanhoozer K (eds), *Everyday theology: How to read cultural texts and interpret trends,* 15-60. Grand Rapids, MI: Baker Academic.

199. van Niekerk A 2014a. The missional congregation in the South African context. In: *HTS Teologiese Studies/TheologicalStudies,* 70 (1). [Online] Accessed from: <http://dx.doi.org/10.4102/hts.v70i1.2648> 2016-07-12.

200. _____ 2014b. The cultural basis for a sustainable community in a South African township. In: Rathbone M, von Schéele F and Strijbos S (eds), *Social change in our technology-based world. Proceedings of the 19th annual working conference of the IIDE,* 6-9 May 2014, 50-63. Lindengracht, Amsterdam: Rozenburg.

201. _____ 2014c. The need for ethical quality of life practices. In: *NGGT DEEL,* 55, (1), 407-424. Stellenbosch: University of Stellenbosch. [Online] Accessed from: <http://ngtt.co.za> 2016-08-22.

202. _____ 2015. A centre for community life in its fullness. In: *Verbum et Ecclesia,* 36(3). [Online] Accessed from: <http://dx.doi.org/ 10.4102/ ve. v36i3.1448> 2016-07-16.

203. Wachob W 2000. *The voice of Jesus in the social*

rhetoric of James. Cambridge: Cambridge University Press.

204. Ward R 1968. The works of Abraham: James 2:14-26. *Harvard Theological Review,* Vol 61, No. 2 (April 1968), 283-290. Cambridge: Cambridge University Press. [Online] Accessed from: <http://www.jstor. org/ stable/ 1509 280> 2016-03-26.

205. Watson D 1988. *Invention, arrangement and style: Rhetorical criticism of Jude and 2 Peter.* SBLDS 104. Atlanta: Scholars Press.

206. _____1993a. James 2 in light of Greco-Roman schemes of argumentation. In: *New Testament Studies,* 39, 94-121. [Online] Accessed from: <http://journals.cambridge.org/ab-stract_S0028688500020312> 23-03-2016.

207. _____1993b. The rhetoric of James 3:1-12 and a classical pattern of argumentation. *Novum Testamentum,* 35, (1), 48-64. [Online] Accessed from:<http://www.jstor.org/stable/1561425?seq=1&cid=pdf-reference#references_ tab_contents> 22-03-2016.

208. Wesley J 1903. *John Wesley's Journal.* London: Charles H. Kelly.

209. Widmer C 2003. Be my witnesses: A vision for evangelism. [Online]. Accessed from: <http://www.esa-online.org/Images /mmDocument/Holistic MinistryMaterials/HolisticReferences/evang-vision.pdf> 2010-11-15.

210. Wilson F and Ramphele M 1989. *Uprooting Poverty: The South African challenge.* Cape Town: David Philip.

211. Wink W 1992. *Engaging the powers: Discernment and Resistance in a world of domination.* Minneapolis: Fortress Press.

212. Winkler T 2008. When God and Poverty Collide: Exploring the Myths of Faith-sponsored Community Development. In: *Urban Studies Journal*, 2008, (45), 2099-2116. [Online] Accessed from: < http://usj.sagepub.com/ content/ 45/ 10/2099> 2011-10-29.

213. Witherington B III 2007. *Letters and homilies for Jewish Christians: A socio-rhetorical commentary on Hebrews, James and Jude.* Nottingham, England: Apollos.

214. _____ 2009a. *The Living Word of God: Rethinking the theology of the Bible.* Waco, TX: Baylor University Press.

215. _____ 2009b. *What's in the word: Rethinking the socio-rhetorical character of the New Testament.* Waco, TX: Baylor University Press.

216. Wolterstorff N 1983. *Until justice and peace embrace.* Grand Rapids, MI: Wm. B. Eerdmans.

217. Woolard I and Leibbrandt M 2001. Measuring poverty in South Africa.
In: Bhorat H et al. (eds). *Fighting poverty: Labour markets and inequality in South Africa.* Cape Town: UCT Press.

218. World Bank Report 1999. Can anyone hear us? Voices from 47 Countries. [Online] Accessed from: <http://siteresources.worldbank.org/INTPOVERTY/ Resources/335642-1124115102975/1555199-1124 1151 877 05/ vol. 1.pdf > 2016-07-31.

219. Wright C J H 2004. *Old Testament ethics for the people of God.* Leicester, England: InterVarsity Press.

220. _____ 2006. *The mission of God: Unlocking the Bible's grand narrative.* Downers Grove, IL: InterVarsity Press.

221._____ 2010. *The mission of God's people: A biblical theology of the church's mission*. Grand Rapids, MI: Zondervan.

222._____ 2012. Word of God and mission of God: Reading the whole Bible for missions. In: Barnett M and Martin R (eds), *Discovering the mission of God*, 33-45. Downers Grove, IL: InterVarsity Press.

223. Yoder J 1975. *The politics of Jesus*. Grand Rapids, MI: Wm. B. Eerdmans Publishing.

----

[1] Statistics SA recorded this as the official unemployment rate 1st quarter 2020. With the Covid-19 pandemic, it is estimated that the official rate will sour to over 50%.

[2] Although there are variations within evangelicalism that will be described in greater detail in Chapter 2 of this thesis, historians of evangelicalism often refer to David Bebbington's classic definition which highlights four specific hallmarks of evangelical Christianity(1) 'biblicism (a reliance on the Bible as the ultimate religious authority), (2) conversionism (a stress on the New Birth [conversion]), (3) activism (an energetic, individualistic approach to religious duties and social involvement), and (4) crucicentrism (a focus on Christ's redeeming work as the heart of essential Christianity) (LeBruyns 2006:343 footnote).

[3] John Oliver, 'A Failure of Evangelical Conscience,' *The Post-American, May 1975, pp 26-30* from Dayton, D 1976. Discovering an evangelical heritage. Grand Rapids, MI: Baker Academic. (Prologue p. 3).

[4] '*Christianity Today*, after all, was already considered by many to be *the* authority on evangelicalism back before Bebbington had even been baptised as a believer' (Larsen 2008:27).

[5] Philip Melanchthon, 'Funeral Oration Over Luther' (1546) reprinted in Lewis W. Spitz, The Protestant Reformation: Major Documents. (St. Louis, Concordia Publishing House), 1997:70.

[6] His work Evangelicalism in Modern Britain: A history from the 1730s to

the 1980s (London: Unwin Hyman, 1989) has been universally highly acclaimed (Larsen 2008:23).

[7] As early as the Leipzig Debate (1519), Luther remarked that among the articles of John Hus and the Bohemians, 'many were plainly most Christian and evangelical [evangelicus]' (MacKenzie 2008:171 ftnt).

[8] John and Charles Wesley were both 'converted' in part by Luther's writings (Noll 2003:97).

[9] 'Christians are taught that he who gives to the poor or lends to the needy does a better deed than he who buys indulgences' 'Ninety-Five Theses' (1517), number 43 in *Luther's Works*, Philadelphia & St. Louis, 1955, Volume 31, p. 29. (in Lindberg 1981:45 ftnt.)

[10] The German Mass, (1526), number 53 in *Luther's Works*, Philadelphia & St Louis, 1955, Volume 53, p. 64.

[11] *Luther's Works*, Philadelphia & St. Louis, 1955, Volume 35, p. 69.

[12] Calvin J & Pringle W 2010. *Commentary on the book of the prophet Isaiah.* Bellingham, WA: Logos Bible Software.

[13] For an example of Finney's passion on the relationship of the church to reform, see 'The Pernicious Attitude of the Church on the Reforms of the Age' quoted in its entirety in Dayton (1976:19-20).

[14] Smith coined the term 'great reversal' in 1957 to describe the evangelical movement's change in mission focus. See Smith T 1957. *Revivalism and social reform: American Protestantism on the eve of the civil war.* New York: Harper and Row.

[15] *History of Opinions Respecting the Millennium*, American Theological Review 1 (1859:655).

[16] Smith A 1776. *An inquiry into the nature and causes of the wealth of nations.* Edinburgh.

[17] For a detailed discussion containing the key Hebrew and Greek words referencing the poor and groups of people normally considered poor, please see Black (2010:89-106).

[18] 'This is consistent with the Hebraic worldview, in which relationship are the highest good, while alienation is the lowest' (Myers 1999:254).

[19] Harris R, Archer G, and Waltke B (eds) 1980. Theological wordbook of the Old Testament (TWOT). I-II. Chicago, IL: Moody Press.

[20] The following section was discussed previously in Black (2010:107-129). It is referenced here to underscore the level of care required to be given to the poor by those within the community of faith as a model for the evangelical movement.

[21] God also acted because of His covenant with Abraham, Isaac and Jacob. (Ex. 6.2-5, 8).

[22] By the time that Jesus finished in the synagogue, this audience had

turned into an angry mob that tried to throw him off a cliff (Luke 4.29).

[23] 'A very similar case scenario resides in Africa today' (Howitt & Morphew [sa]:51).

[24] The offering that was presented for purification after the birth of Jesus showed that his parents were a poor couple. They could not afford a lamb, so they brought a pair of doves or pigeons (Lk. 2.22-24). This sacrifice was according to the Law of Moses found in Lev. 12.8.

[25] Now when they had departed, behold, an angel of the Lord appeared to Joseph in a dream and said, 'Rise, take the child and his mother, and flee to Egypt, and remain there until I tell you, for Herod is about to search for the child, to destroy him.' And he rose and took the child and his mother by night and departed to Egypt and remained there until the death of Herod. This was to fulfil what the Lord had spoken by the prophet, 'Out of Egypt I called my son.' (Mt. 2.13-15).

[26] But when Herod died, behold, an angel of the Lord appeared in a dream to Joseph in Egypt, saying, 'Rise, take the child and his mother and go to the land of Israel, for those who sought the child's life are dead.' And he rose and took the child and his mother and went to the land of Israel. But when he heard that Archelaus was reigning over Judea in place of his father Herod, he was afraid to go there, and being warned in a dream he withdrew to the district of Galilee. And he went and lived in a city called Nazareth, that what was spoken by the prophets might be fulfilled: 'He shall be called a Nazarene' (Mt 2.19-23).

[27] Then Jesus came from Galilee to the Jordan to John, to be baptized by him. John would have prevented him, saying, 'I need to be baptized by you, and do you come to me?' But Jesus answered him, 'Let it be so now, for thus it is fitting for us to fulfil all righteousness.' Then he consented' (Mt. 3.13-15).
John was a prophet who challenged the rich to show sincere repentance by sharing what they had with the poor.
And the crowds asked him (John), 'What then shall we do?' And he answered them, 'Whoever has two tunics is to share with him who has none, and whoever has food is to do likewise' (Lk. 3.10-11).

[28] And a scribe came up and said to him, 'Teacher, I will follow you wherever you go.' And Jesus said to him, 'Foxes have holes, and birds of the air have nests, but the Son of Man has nowhere to lay his head' (Mt. 8.19-20).

[29] See Mt. 5.25-26; 18.30; Lk. 12.57-59.

[30] See Lk. 4.18; 7.21-22; 14.13, 21; 18.35. Also see the year of jubilee provision (Lev. 25.35; Is. 58.7) for providing shelter for the poor and homeless mentioned in Lk. 14.13,21 (Hanks in Howitt & Morphew [sa]:53 note).

[31] Poverty relief refers to interventions that seek to give short-term assistance to people living in poverty, usually in response to an external emergency situation that pushes people into a state of increased vulnerability (Studies in Poverty and Inequality 2007).

[32] For a discussion by other noted 'experts' in the field of poverty alleviation that would share this basic thinking, please see Myers (1999:57-86).

[33] The central examples are Ecuador and Brazil with Max-Neef being from Chile.

[34] Contemporary scholarship increasingly emphasises the fact that, 'while epistolary theory and rhetoric were not integrated in antiquity, letter writing, at least by the first century BCE, was nonetheless significantly influenced by classical rhetoric' (Wachob 2000:8).

[35] Vernon K. Robbins, "The We-Passages in Acts and Ancient Sea Voyages," in Perspectives on Luke-Acts, ed. C.H. Talbert (Edinburgh: T & T Clark, 1978), 215-42.

[36] Please see Chapter 1 for a detailed description of these textures.

[37] David Gowler is not a fan of Witherington's socio-rhetorical analysis. He writes that Witherington 'hijacked the term for a series of commentaries that Witherington misleadingly labelled as "Socio-Rhetorical Commentary."' Gowler calls this a classic "bait-and-switch" tactic, replacing Robbin's sophisticated multi-dimensional socio-rhetorical approach with a "method" that 'utilises some rhetorical and social-science insights to argue for his rather conservative historical agenda' (Gowler 2010:193-94). Since the epistemology of this research is located within the evangelical tradition, Witherington's insights are considered useful and will be used to engage the interpretive processes along with other sources.

[38] *Rhetorica ad Herennium* 4.43-44.58; 2.18.28-29.46; 3.9.16; *Rhetorica ad Alexandrum* 1.1422a25-27; Hermogenes, 'Elaboration of Arguments' and *Progymnasmata* [discussion of the elaboration exercise for the chreia] (Witherington 2007:449).

[39] Early rhetorical exercises, literally 'first exercises.'

[40] The judicial speech 'provides the fullest conventional structure' (Kennedy 1984:23) and could consist of as many as six parts: (1) introduction, (2) statement of facts, (3) proposition, (4) partition, (5) refutation, and (6) conclusion (Watson 1988:20-21).

[41] [Cicero] *ad Herennium* 2.18.282.31.50: "The most complete and perfect argument, then, is that which is comprised of five parts: the proposition (*propositio*), the reason (*ratio*), the proof of the reason (*confirmatio*), the embellishment (*exornatio*), and the résumé (*conplexio*). Through the proposition we set forth summarily what we intend to prove. The reason, by means of a brief example subjoined, sets forth the causal basis for the proposition, establishing the truth of what we are urging. The proof of the reason corroborates, by means of additional· arguments, the briefly presented reason. Embellishment we use in order to adorn and enrich the argument, after the proof has been established. The résumé is a brief conclusion, drawing together the parts of the argument" (2.18.28). See also *ad Herennium* 4.43.56-44.56 and the discussion by Mack & Robbins (1989, 53-57).

[42] E.g. the occurrence of καταδυναστεύω and its cognates at Jer. 7.6; 13.18; 22.3; Ezek. 18.7, 12, 16; 22.7,29; Amos 4.1; 8:4; Micah 2.2; Zech. 7.10; Mal. 3.5; Wis. 2.10.

[43] *Rhetorica ad Alexandrum* 1.1421b.26.

[44] The phrase connotes the act of being given a surname, occurring several times in the LXX in reference to God adopting or taking possession of persons (or Israel): Gen. 48.16; Deut. 28.10; Is. 63.19; Amos 9.12; Bar. 2.15; 5.4.; Dan. 5.12; 10.1.

[45] For Watson (1993a:105), verses 8-11 function as embellishment (*exornatio*), based on the strength of [Cicero] *Rhetorica ad Herennium* 2.29.46, which refers to embellishment as 'consist(ing) of similes, examples, amplifications, previous judgments (*rebus judicatus*) and other means which serve to expand and enrich the argument...' Wachob (1993:144, 197-223) claims it to be a second part of the proof, divided into four parts (v 8: a Proposition based on written law; verse 9: Argument from the contrary; verse 10: Rationale for Judgment based on the Law; verse 11: Confirmation of the Rationale, using written testimony) (Kloppenborg 1999:761 ft.nt).

[46] See Boyle M O 1985. "The Stoic Paradox of James 2: 10." *NTS* 31 :611-17, which cites Augustine, *Epistulae* 167 (MPL 33:733-42); Seneca, *De beneficiis* 5.15.1 (*qui unum autem habet vitium, omnia habet*); cf 4.27.1 to identify this as a stoic maxim.

[47] Dibelius (1976:144-6), 'Whoever is Guilty of One is Guilty of All.'

[48] [Cicero], *Rhetorica ad Herennium* 2.30.47; *Rhetorica ad Alexandrum* 36.1443b-1445a.

[49] For further discussion, see Mack and Robbins (1989: 31-67), and Halliday (1979:27, 36, 101, 114).

[50] This phrase has its origins in Vorster W S 1989. *Intertexuality and redaktionsgeschichte in Draisma*.

[51] Jms. 2.8 refers to Lev. 19.18; Jms. 2.9 refers to Lev. 19.15, Jms. 2.11 refers to Ex. 20.14 and 13; Jms. 2.23 to Gen. 15.6 (cf. Rom. 4.3; Gal. 3.6), and Jms. 2.25 refers to Josh. 2.1 and following).

[52] This expression is found frequently in the LXX (Deut. 10.4; 1Chr. 15.15; 2 Chr. 30.5; 35.4; 1 Esdr, 1.4, 2 Esdr. 6.18). It is similar to κατὰ τάς γραφάς in 1 Cor. 15.3-5. (see Wachob 2000:117).

[53] Wachob (2000:119) details the enthymematic reasoning as something like this: (Major premise): You loved yourself when you sojourned in Egypt. (Minor premise): The stranger who sojourns with you in your land is as you were when you sojourned in Egypt. (Conclusion): The stranger who sojourns with you in your land you shall love as yourself.

[54] '... early Christianity was historically united on the fact that Jesus taught the fulfilment of the Torah in the love-commandment' (Betz 1985a:37). See also Rom. 13:9, Gal. 5:14.

[55] See Theon, III, 139-42 in Butts 1987:204-05 (Wachob 2000:120).

[56] Global allusions are 'invocations of a whole corpus, and a world' (Alter 1989:124). According to Wachob (2000:122), from an intertextual perspective, we may say that James 2.1 appears to set 'acts of partiality' over against what the Lord Jesus Christ believed, taught and did.'

[57] Brown, F., Driver, S.R. & Briggs, C.A., 1977. *Enhanced Brown-Driver-Briggs Hebrew and English Lexicon.*

[58] For further discussion see Robbins (1991:155).

[59] For further discussion see Dibelius (1976:144-146).

[60] 'And of them [i.e., the Graces] it may justly be said, what is often said of the virtues, that the possessor of one is the possessor of all' (Philo, *Vit. Mos.* 2.7). 'Hence Philo knows this doctrine in the form of a well-known axiom' (Dibelius 1976:145 ft.nt 114).

[61] For further discussion, see Dibelius (1976:147 note 122).

[62] See James 2.8

[63] See Deut. 28.1, 15; Ps. 1.1-2, 19.7-11; 119.32,45,97.

[64] See Mt. 5.7,6.14, 7.1

[65] See Lk. 6.20.

[66] See the discussions in Wachob (2000:136-140) and Deppe (1990:17-18).

[67] See Mt. 5.3, Lk. 6.20b, Gos.Thom. 54, and Pol. Phil. 2.3

[68] See Theon (III, 1-138) in Wachob (2000:149).

[69] The social and rhetorical significance of the word 'slave' carried rich meaning. A slave was not only under ownership but was also considered a spokesperson and representative of his master. A slave represents more firmly the 'unquestioned authority of the founder whom they represent' (Wachob 2000:136).

[70] In the post-apostolic fathers there is reference to regard for persons in the following places: λαμβάνειν πρόσωπον, Barn. 19, 4; Did., 4, 3; προσωπολημψία, Pol. Phil., 6, 1; ἀπροσωπολήμπτως, 1 Cl., 1, 3; Barn., 4, 12.

[71] Kittel, G., Bromiley, G. W., & Friedrich, G. (Eds.). (1964–). *Theological Dictionary of the New Testament* (electronic ed., Vol. 6, p. 780). Grand Rapids, MI: Eerdmans.

[72] *On Stases*, Rabe, vol. vi, p. 30.

[73] For a more detailed discussion on the rhetorical audience see Wachob (2000:160-163).

[74] See categories 5 and 6 in *On Stases*, Rabe, vol. vi, p. 30.

[75] Cicero *Inv.* 2.53.159, Cicero *Rhet. ad Her.* 56.169.

[76] Aristotle *Rhet.* 2.6.2.

[77] http://rhetoric.eserver.org/aristotle/rhet2-8.html.

[78] 'The topic 'fortune' includes noble birth, wealth, power, and their opposites (*Rhet.* 2.12.2).

[79] Dibelius (1976:125).

[80] *Rhetorica ad Herennium* (4.43.56-44.56).

[81] For a helpful description of the elaboration patterns in their many forms, see Watson D (1993b:51).

[82] Cic., *Part. Or.* 15.54

[83] For a detailed analysis exploring these questions see Watson (1993a:109-111).

[84] This is the same phrase used in 1 Cor. 15.35 by Paul to introduce an imaginary interlocutor (ἀλλὰ ἐρεῖ τις).

[85] See *Rhet. ad Alex.* 18; 33; 36.1443a.7-1443b.14 for a full discussion of anticipation.

[86] Cic. *Part. Or.* 12.44.

[87] Dibelius (1976:149-151) offers excellent analysis of the discussion.

[88] Dibelius (1976:161 ftnt. 62) translates κενός as 'he who boasts foolishly' in accordance with Epict. *Diss.* 2.19.8 and in Justin, *Dial.* 64.2., basically, You braggart!, which corresponds to the invective which is customary in diatribe.

[89] A full discussion of *amplicatio* can be found in *Rhet.* 1.9.1368a.38-40.

[90] Cic., *Part. Or.* 3.54.207.

[91] Moo (2000:107). See also Dibelius (1976:161).

[92] Witherington (2007:477).

[93] This will be explored more fully in the intertextual analysis of this unit.

[94] Watson (1993b:115).

[95] See *Rhet. ad. Alex.* 1.1422a.25ff.; Quint. 5.11.42-4.

[96] Cic., *Part. Or.* 15.54.

[97] *Rhet. ad Her.* 4.45.59.

[98] *Rhet. ad Her.* 4.47.60.

[99] Dibelius (1976:159).

[100] See Dibelius (1976:159) for further discussion.

[101] 'The disciples of our father Abraham have a good eye, a meek spirit and a humble soul.'

[102] See 1 Clem. 31.2, 'For what reason was our father Abraham blessed? Was it not because he did righteousness and truth through faith?'

[103] See Johnson (1995:243).

[104] Melanchthon, *Apology of the Augsburg Confession*, 126.

[105] See Dibelius (1976:172-174) for detailed discussion of this.

[106] Philo in *de Abrahamo*. Translated by Colson, F H 1935. Cambridge: Harvard University Press

[107] There is a Christian exhortation added at the close of the *Test. of Abr.*: 'Let us too, my beloved brethren, imitate the hospitality of the patriarch Abraham and let us gain his virtuous behaviour that we may be counted worthy of eternal life.'

[108] This is what it would be called rhetorically: see *Rhet. ad Her.* 4.45.59.

[109] *Rhet. ad Alex.* 7.1428b10.

[110] Euripides, *Orestes* 1046.

[111] Aristotle, *Nichomachean Ethics* 9,8,2.

[112] Cicero, *Laelius de Amicitia,* ¶ 20.

[113] Plato, *Laws* 757A; 744B.

[114] Philo, *On Sobriety*, 56.

[115] *Rhet.* 2.5.7.

[116] Mother Teresa of Calcutta 1975. *A gift for God. Prayers and meditations.* New York: Harper Collins.

[117] There are four different models cited by Paul Ballard and John Pritchard: (1) the applied theory model, (2) the critical correlation model, (3) the praxis model and (4) the habitus/virtue model (Ballard P and Pritchard J 1996. *Practical theology in action: Christian thinking in the service of church and society.* London: SPCK). Ballard and Pritchard prefer the *habitus/virtue model* suggested by Stanley Hauerwas, which emphasises that truth is found in the community of shared meaning and is appropriated by a process of growth into wisdom (Anderson 2001:16).

[118] Calvin J and Allen J 1816. *Institutes of the Christian religion* (Vol. 1:45). New-Haven, Philadelphia: Hezekiah Howe; Philip H. Nicklin.

[119] See Don S.Browning, ed., *Practical theology: the emerging field in theology, church and world* (San Francisco: Harper & Row, 1983).

[120] See Chapter 2, pp 24-29 for further discussion.

[121] For discussion on Scriptural provision for the poor that included year of Jubilee, year of sabbatical and other protective laws, please see Black (2010:109-115).

[122] The *Wheaton 1983 Statement*, paragraph 26 declared, 'Evil is not only in the human heart but also in social structures.... The mission of the church includes both the proclamation of the Gospel and its demonstration. We must therefore evangelize, respond to immediate human needs, and press for social transformation.' Bosch (2011:417) remarked that for the first

time in an official statement emanating from an international evangelical conference the perennial dichotomy was overcome.'

[123] This document was reprinted in *Transformation 4* (1987), pp. 17-30.

[124] Apostrophe is a sudden turn from the general audience to address a specific group or person or personified abstraction whether absent or present. (Glossary of Rhetorical Terms)

[125] The central examples are Ecuador and Brazil with Max-Neef being from Chile.

[126] 56.8% of the total population were living in poverty in 2009. (http://www.statssa.gov.za/). Accessed 15 June 2016.

[127] The unemployment rate for the third quarter of 2019 is 29.1% of the total work force (http://www.statssa.gov.za/?p=12689/). Accessed 31 January 2019.

[128] Erasmus, Hendriks and Mans (2004:1).

[129] See Black (2010:142-184).

[130] 'Carnegie Commission on the Poor White Problem' and 'Second Carnegie Inquiry into Poverty and Development in Southern Africa'

[131] The Dutch Reformed Church of South Africa is also known by its Afrikaans name *Die Nederduits Gereformeerde Kerk* (NG Kerk) and was instrumental in helping to propagate the concept of separate development upon which Apartheid was based.

[132] The 'church' here refers to the Afrikaans family of Reformed churches (see note 131, p. 312).

[133] The Native Land Act (1913) and Native Laws Amendment (1937) limited black ownership and settlement to existing tribal 'reserves.' Africans could not own land in urban areas and their movement was limited—they could only reside in an urban area if they were employed and carried a pass (van Donk in Bowers 2012a:7 ftnt.).

[134] For a compilation of all kairos documents to date, see Gary S D Leonard (2010): [Online] Accessed from:< http://ujamaa.ukzn.ac.za/Libraries/manuals/The_Kairos_Documents. sflb.ashx> [2016-08-22], 1-378.

[135] The WGRIP study was an interdisciplinary study led by The Unit for Religion and Development Research (URDR) who, with Swedish partner the Centre for the Study of Religion and Society (CSRS) at the University of Uppsala, received a three-year grant (2006-2008) for a research project called "Welfare and Religion in a Global Perspective: theoretical and methodological exchange across the North-South divide" (WGRIGP) (Bowers-Du Toit 2012b:206 ftnt.).

[136] Bragg (1987:40) proposes transformation, 'as a Christian framework for looking at human and social change,' not as an alternative development theory.

[137] Many churches are 'predominantly maintenance institutions con-

cerned with the maintenance of the church structures, ministries and ideals' (Dames 2008:10).

[138] Sundermeier found this statement part of the 'typical liberal-humanist bourgeois climate,' preferring instead 'the church with others' (Bosch 2011:384).

[139] For discussion regarding Jesus' ministry to the poor as a man living in poverty, please see Black (2010:118-123).

[140] See Swart I and Venter D 2001. NGOs and churches: Civil society actors and the promise of fourth generation development in South Africa. In: Coetzee J, Graaf J, Hendriks F, and Wood G (eds), 483-496, *Development: Theory, policy and practice.* Cape Town: Oxford.

[141] A Collective case study selects cases 'so that comparisons can be made between cases and concepts and so that theories can be extended or validated' (Fouche in Bowers and Nkomo 2014:5 ftnt.)

[142] As classified at the time of the dismantling of apartheid in 1994.

[143] A detailed description of the research initiative can be found in Black (2010:142-184). It will be referenced in this chapter to highlight the elements of the initiative that could provide a useful blueprint for a church considering a developmental approach to fight unemployment. One trusts that this approach could be used as a framework for other poverty alleviation initiatives with a different focus.

[144] The author was a member of the church leadership team and oversaw the research process on behalf of the church, becoming the project leader of the newly formed initiative that resulted.

[145] An NGO was established by the church leaders to provide governance for the project called Pinelands Methodist Church, Phambili ngeThemba (Xhosa for 'going forward with hope') (NPO 055-644).

[146] The **Nominal Group Technique** (NGT) is a group process involving problem identification, solution generation, and decision making. It can be used in groups of various sizes wanting to make quick decisions with everyone in the groups opinions taken into account (as opposed to traditional voting, where only the largest group is considered).

[147] Hangala S and Mutesha T 2013. Evaluation of competency in soft skills of the graduates of Zanokhanyo's job readiness course. Research Report. Cape Town: University of Cape Town Sociology Department.

[148] Harambee (http://harambee.co.za/) and Dreamworker (http://dreamworker.org.za/) are two excellent examples of organisations that are tackling unemployment from outside of a faith-based paradigm in the South African context.

[149] Sample training course graduate stories from the Zanokhanyo Job Readiness Course, 2014.

ABOUT THE AUTHOR

Tim Black

Tim and his wife, Leslie, moved with
their family from Blacksburg, VA USA to
Cape Town, South Africa in 2003 and
quickly fell in love with the incredible
beauty and significant challenges of this
amazing country. This publication
formed the basis of a PhD dissertation
that was the culmination of more than 10
years thinking and dreaming around the
role of the church in transforming society. That dreaming continues to this day.

Youth ministry is his second vocational passion and he currently serves as General Director of Scripture Union South Africa.

Printed in Great Britain
by Amazon

23463673R10235